Patrick Pearse

M000312377

Also by Joost Augusteijn:

FROM PUBLIC DEFIANCE TO GUERRILLA WARFARE.
THE EXPERIENCE OF ORDINARY VOLUNTEERS IN
THE IRISH WAR OF INDEPENDENCE

Edited, IRELAND IN THE 1930s: NEW PERSPECTIVES

Edited, THE IRISH REVOLUTION, 1913–1923

Edited, THE MEMOIRS OF JOHN M. REGAN,
A CATHOLIC OFFICER IN THE RIC AND RUC, 1909–1948

Edited with Mary-Ann Lyons, IRISH HISTORY: A RESEARCH
YEARBOOK (number 1)

Edited with Mary-Ann Lyons and Deirdre MacMahon,
IRISH HISTORY: A RESEARCH YEARBOOK (number 2)

Patrick Pearse

The Making of a Revolutionary

Joost Augusteijn

Lecturer in European History,
Leiden University, The Netherlands

© Joost Augusteijn 2010

All rights reserved. No reproduction, copy or transmission of this publication may be made without written permission.

No portion of this publication may be reproduced, copied or transmitted save with written permission or in accordance with the provisions of the Copyright, Designs and Patents Act 1988, or under the terms of any licence permitting limited copying issued by the Copyright Licensing Agency, Saffron House, 6–10 Kirby Street, London EC1N 8TS.

Any person who does any unauthorized act in relation to this publication may be liable to criminal prosecution and civil claims for damages.

The author has asserted his right to be identified as the author of this work in accordance with the Copyright, Designs and Patents Act 1988.

First published 2010 by
PALGRAVE MACMILLAN

Palgrave Macmillan in the UK is an imprint of Macmillan Publishers Limited, registered in England, company number 785998, of Houndmills, Basingstoke, Hampshire RG21 6XS.

Palgrave Macmillan in the US is a division of St Martin's Press LLC, 175 Fifth Avenue, New York, NY 10010.

Palgrave Macmillan is the global academic imprint of the above companies and has companies and representatives throughout the world.

Palgrave® and Macmillan® are registered trademarks in the United States, the United Kingdom, Europe and other countries

ISBN 978–0–230–24871–7 hardback
ISBN 978–0–230–27765–6 paperback

This book is printed on paper suitable for recycling and made from fully managed and sustained forest sources. Logging, pulping and manufacturing processes are expected to conform to the environmental regulations of the country of origin.

A catalogue record for this book is available from the British Library.

Library of Congress Cataloging-in-Publication Data
Augusteijn, Joost.
  Patrick Pearse : the making of a revolutionary / Joost Augusteijn.
    p. cm.
  Includes bibliographical references and index.
  ISBN 978–0–230–24871–7 — ISBN 978–0–230–27765–6 (pbk.) 1. Pearse, Padraic, 1879–1916. 2. Ireland—History—Easter Rising, 1916—Biography. 3. Revolutionaries—Ireland—Biography. 4. Ireland—Politics and government—1910–1921. I. Title.
  DA965.P4A94 2010
  941.5082'1—dc22
  [B]

2010027479

10 9 8 7 6 5 4 3 2 1
19 18 17 16 15 14 13 12 11 10

Printed and bound in Great Britain by
CPI Antony Rowe, Chippenham and Eastbourne

To the memory of
Marcus Bourke

Contents

List of illustrations

All photographs courtesy of the Pearse Museum unless otherwise indicated.

Preface

In the 2006 reprint of her seminal biography *Patrick Pearse: The Triumph of Failure* Ruth Dudley Edwards argues that there is no need for any revision of her book because 'little new material has appeared since 1977 and subsequent books and articles on Pearse have been tangential'.[1] It is hard to uphold this position now. Many important works have appeared analysing various aspects of Pearse's life and activities, including works by eminent academics such as Sean Farrell Moran, Charles Townshend and many others. Since the 1970s a range of archive collections has also become available which sheds new light on Pearse's life. The release of the archives of the Bureau of Military History in particular has provided material which certainly adjusts our view of the 1916 Easter Rising and its preparations.

Furthermore, through the curators of the Pearse Museum a new line of inquiry has been developed into Pearse's family background, which so far had been largely confined to the information we had from a small autobiographical piece by Patrick himself. Through the kind intervention by the late Marcus Bourke I have also come in possession of the private collection of the late judge Michael Lennon, a family friend of the Pearses, who during the 1940s collected material and information on Patrick from his relatives and family friends. This has enabled the development of a much fuller picture of Patrick Pearse as a person, particularly by providing new information on his early years.

John Tosh, who has written widely on historical methodology, has argued that 'biography is indispensable to the understanding of motives and intention' and that 'the motives of individuals have *some* part to play in explaining historical events'.[2] In light of the above and the now ever more pressing question of how ordinary people become involved in the use of physical force for a political ideal, combined with the virtual end of violence in Northern Ireland, I feel it is possible and necessary to try to understand Patrick Pearse and his thinking even better. Hence this new biography.

Finding the time to research and write a monograph in between a busy family life and full-time work as a lecturer is difficult. This book would not have come to fruition without the support of various individuals and institutions. I have to thank the Netherlands Organisation for Scientific Research which has provided me with a year long fellowship, and the Institute for History at Leiden University which has supported me financially as well as academically in this endeavour. My colleagues have provided me with a stimulating environment and facilitated me in various ways, for which I am grateful. This also applies to those who I have encountered in various academic venues at which I have vented my ideas on Pearse. Furthermore, a number of people have to be singled out for appreciation by making this book possible through large or small contributions. First, my family, Maureen, Freya and Shiel, for their usual indulgence. Second, Tessa van Keeken, Regina Uí Chollatáin, Arnout Augusteijn, Brian Crowley, Pat Cooke, Margaret Ó hÓgartaigh, Joep Leerssen, Ruth Ireland and all those friends, neighbours and others who have shamed me into activity by their occasional gentle enquiries about the progress of this book.

Lastly, Marcus Bourke has to be singled out. He not only provided me with the initial incentive to write this book by, out of the blue, handing me the collection of Michael Lennon with the gentle suggestion I might do something with it as he would not get around to it, but mainly he provided inspiration through his eternal enthusiasm for pursuing historical research on Ireland. Unfortunately he did not live long enough to see the book being published but he wholeheartedly deserves to have it dedicated to him. Hereby!

Joost Augusteijn
Leiden, 2010

Introduction

I was in school with Pearse. He was gentle and quiet and always went home by the rere way from Westland Row thru the lane. The boys would go under the railway arch noisily but he seemed to like to be alone. He wore a big round collar, type now no longer seen. This riled the boys. I remember a rough boy once holding him up – they all mocked his collar – and began to bully him. I intervened. 'Let the chap alone', said I. The tough lad turned on me and in the end I got a black eye. Pearse walking away quietly whilst I was being beaten.[1]

Less than twenty-five years after the above incident this out-of-place and frightened son of an English sculptor and an Irish post office worker was executed as the leader of the most famous uprising in Irish history. The central question this book deals with is how this came about. What kind of man was Patrick Henry Pearse and how did he come to his revolutionary ideas?

It is argued here that the development of Patrick Pearse's thought can only be understood against the background of the growth of nationalist feelings throughout Europe and his personal experiences in the late nineteenth and early twentieth century. Pearse was born in 1879, a crucial year in the establishment of broad-based nationalism in Ireland. The international agricultural crisis of the late 1870s had generated mass support for the home rule movement and propelled the radical politician Charles Stewart Parnell to the leadership of the Irish Party. The establishment of widespread support for a party striving for Irish autonomy was, however, primarily dependent on Parnell's charisma and on the economic deprivation associated with the agricultural crisis. Although a sense of Ireland's distinctness was certainly already widely accepted, cultural nationalism was still largely an elite consideration as it had been from the late eighteenth century. In itself this was not unusual in a European context where nationalism only became a mass phenomenon towards the end of the nineteenth century.[2]

1

The merging of political and cultural nationalism had two distinct trajectories. First, a top-down approach in which those in power used it in a nation-building effort to tie their citizens to the state. This state-based nationalism, in which governments narrowed the political nation down to a specific group of people with a specific culture, first came to the fore in the second phase of the French Revolution but became ever more dominant in the nineteenth century. Second, often in reaction to this a bottom-up form of mass nationalism developed in which peripheral elites used a growing sense of identity among groups who did not feel represented by the new dominant national cultures to generate support for a separatist movement.[3]

Both of these forms can be identified in Ireland. State involvement in the lives of the people and particularly in education was much stronger in Ireland than in other parts of the United Kingdom. National schools intended to instil the English language and culture were introduced in Ireland in 1831 long before state-funded education was established in England in 1870. In a linguistic sense this was very successful. By the late nineteenth century Irish had become the language of the illiterate and poor farmers, and was largely considered a sign of backwardness even by those who spoke it. Nevertheless, the attempts by the government to create a UK-wide form of nationalism accepted by all citizens of the state increasingly failed in Ireland in this period.

The Irish reaction to the homogenising efforts of the state was typical for a peripheral area which did not benefit fully from the modernisation which took place elsewhere in the country. On the one hand, growing attention was paid by the mainly Protestant Irish elite to what distinguished the area culturally from the centre by salvaging the Irish language and local culture. On the other hand, resistance grew, particularly among the middle classes, against the economic and social policies of the government. This began with the successful struggle for legal equality for Catholics under Daniel O'Connell in the first decades of the century, which made clear that Irish grievances would not be settled voluntarily by the parliament in Westminster, and found an extreme form in the uprisings of the Young Irelanders in 1848 and the Fenians in 1867.

Although the Young Irelanders contained an element of often Protestant intellectuals which propagated the resurrection of a lost Irish culture, political and cultural nationalism did not come together in Ireland among the masses until the 1880s. The advent of modern urban industrial society, with its ever deeper state penetration in the lives of the population, and the development of mass transport and communication, facilitated a growing involvement of the people in politics. At the same time it created a need for defining what brought and held people together. Such could be found in various new ideologies ranging from socialism and anarchism to nationalism. The concept of a united nation in particular began to capture the imagination of the wider public and thus became a key mobilising force in the political arena for the state as well as for separatist movements.[4]

Even in the strong centralised states of western Europe there were many who lost out in the modernising tendencies, including artisans who struggled against the impact of industrialisation, and young members of the lower classes who had availed of the new educational opportunities but were frustrated in their careers. These groups populated the separatist movements which burgeoned towards the end of the nineteenth century. In the absence of real political power these groups concentrated primarily on the regeneration of cultures from Catalan, Basque and Breton to Welsh and Irish. Materially inferior to their 'oppressor' they tended to stress the spiritual, moral and cultural superiority of their nation as found in an idealisation of a Golden Age, and they often identified a history of resistance. Most lay particular emphasis on the benefits of their traditional rural society versus the corrupting influence of modern urban life.[5] This linked into a widespread concern associated with the disappearance of rural communities in reaction to the advent of industrialisation and modernisation. These separatists generally expressed a longing for the small integrated communities where everyone had face-to-face contact and which they perceived to be under threat from a modern large-scale impersonal society. In many of these movements the Catholic clergy played a central role from Poland, Slovakia, Croatia, Ukraine, Brittany and Basque to Ireland.[6]

These new mass movements were strongest in the cities where a dedicated hardcore of mostly young men steeped in the new values and tastes had taken the lead. Separatists were often members of the local intelligentsia who had been excluded from power or influence. Their movement attracted other strata with specific material interests and often conflicting aims. Most of these were also townsmen and socially mobile youngsters from the non-dominant group seeking to make a mark, often socially rising in comparison to their parents' generation. These movements were most successful if these upwardly mobile and well-educated groups failed to assimilate in the new state nationalism, had access to modern forms of communication and were engaged in a conflict of interest with the centre.[7] This was certainly the case in Ireland.

In the final two decades of the nineteenth century the connection between nationalism and real economic grievances facilitated the development of cultural nationalism into a mass phenomenon. The wide acceptance of Ireland's right to autonomy in the 1880s and the inability of the Irish Party to extract any effective form of autonomy gave rise to increasing attention to what made Ireland different. The founding of a whole array of cultural movements and organisations from the Gaelic Athletic Association stemming from 1884 to the Irish Literary Theatre founded in 1899 (renamed the Abbey in 1901) popularised this idea to every layer of society. In particular the Gaelic League established in 1893 used growing literacy rates and the introduction of the mass media to reach out to all sections of the population with their exclusively cultural message. To these nationalists, which came to include Patrick Pearse, gaining political independence was secondary to saving and regenerating the Irish language and culture against the undermining influence of English culture, with its modern, vulgar, industrial and urbanised base. This was most clearly articulated in Douglas Hyde's 1892 lecture *The Necessity to De-Anglicising Ireland* which initiated the founding of the League.[8]

The publication of Standish O'Grady's *History of Ireland: Heroic period* in 1878 had provided a first popular interpretation of Ireland's mythical past. Knowledge of old sagas and mythology was by then largely confined to a small section of the rural population, but even they were unaware of many ancient stories and heroes. Intended as a role model for aristocratic virtue, O'Grady's Cúchulainn became a national hero in the 1890s.[9] W.B. Yeats' *The Wanderings of Oisin* published in 1889 was instrumental in the idealisation of Ireland's rural society where the peasant preserved a world view which combined the mystical and national with the pastoral. A kind of cultural pilgrimage to the west of Ireland where the Irish language was still spoken became popular among urbanised nationalists in the

1890s. The celebration of folklore appealed to the intelligentsia while the moralistic rejection of civilisation, decadence and empire attracted the lower-middle class.[10] The tensions this dichotomy caused would plague the League right up to the First World War.

The British Government responded fairly liberally to the demands of the movement. Under influence of the elitist Society for the Preservation of the Irish Language founded in 1876 more and more space was provided in the school curriculum for the teaching of the Irish language from the late 1870s. The government also sponsored the establishment of a national museum and library just as it did in Scotland and Wales where similar movements had taken root and cultural heritage was popularised much earlier.[11] The Irish movements were, however, never truly satisfied with the actions of the government. They moved on quickly from the stage of salvaging the national culture to stimulating fresh productivity, some in English and others in Irish, which emphasised the separateness of Ireland. The efforts of popular national and regional movements throughout Europe were broadly similar. Partly dependent on the attitude of the local government all managed to ensure that the national language, literature and history were somehow taught in schools. Festivals, pageants, ceremonies, historical monuments and pantheons which proclaimed the nation's rootedness and presence were instituted everywhere. Newly built streets were given dedicatory names taken from the nation's past and the architecture developed vernacular features. Discussion about the correct dialect and whether traditional forms should be cultivated or modernised were also common to all.[12]

In this exciting atmosphere, in which constitutional nationalism was dominant and cultural nationalism was reaching out to the masses, Patrick Pearse grew up and formed his ideas. His teenage years coincided with the European-wide rise of popular forms of cultural nationalism in which he was fully caught up. He was well aware of these developments and positioned himself always in a European context. He read international newspapers and literature and from an early age placed Irish literature and developments in a European perspective. Initially he believed a resurrection of the ancient tradition of Irish writing could benefit the world, but later he became more realistic about the supposed inherent superiority of Irish writing and believed it should connect with the developments in literature worldwide. He also mirrored cultural and political developments in

Ireland on events in other countries. The move from resurrecting the language to political emancipation in Hungary and Flanders became important examples guiding his own policies. In many ways, therefore, Pearse personifies the development among cultural nationalists from collecting and resurrecting the old language and literature to proclaiming the need for a modern interpretation of it, and then to the propagandist use of it in political terms. Politically it could be argued he travelled the same route as many Irish nationalists from constitutional to revolutionary means.

Patrick Pearse's thought thus closely connects with the mainstream in European thinking. A study of his life and the developments in his thinking can therefore illuminate this phenomenon through the spectrum of one of its main characters in Ireland. This investigation is divided here into six separate themes. It starts off with the establishment of his personality in his early years as part of a family of mixed Irish-English parentage and through his time at the Christian Brothers School. Then it traces his evolution towards a cultural nationalism as a young man who through the restoration of the Irish language tries to resurrect an Irish nation. In the process he becomes convinced that such a regeneration could only be achieved through education. The development of his educational thought is followed into the founding and running of his own bilingual secondary school. The fight for control over education policy also brought him into the arena of politics. At first hesitantly but with the abolition of the Lord's veto in 1911 and the introduction of a home rule bill in 1912 he became increasingly politically active. The perceived impossibility of achieving home rule and the outbreak of the First World War brought him to a militarisation of his ideas and eventually to rebellion. In the final chapter the influence of Patrick Pearse's thinking after his execution is traced through an examination of historical and political debate. All these developments are here traced and positioned through an intimate assessment of his thought and actions in a thematic and generally chronological manner, based primarily on an analysis of his own writings in the context of his personal experiences and influences.

1 Person

When my father and mother married there came together two very widely remote traditions – English and Puritan and mechanic on the one hand, Gaelic and Catholic and peasant on the other; freedom loving both, and neither without its strain of poetry and its experience of spiritual and other adventure. And these two traditions worked in me and fused together by a certain fire proper to myself, but nursed by that fostering of which I have spoken made me the strange thing I am.[1]

In this way Patrick Pearse describes the formative influences on his persona. He had indeed a fairly unusual family background, and it is clear from all available evidence that most of his early experiences were centred on this family. Whether a consequence of his mixed background or not, Patrick certainly was not an ordinary man and had a multifaceted personality. To appreciate the impact of the two disparate traditions, his upbringing and the development of his personality will be explored in this chapter.

Father's background

Although like most Victorians Patrick's father James may not have played a very prominent part in his son's upbringing, his background and attitude did have a distinct influence on young Patrick. James Pearse, a stonemason, later master sculptor, was born in a working class family in Bloomsbury, London, on 8 December 1839 as the second son of a local frame maker. Much to Patrick's disappointment, who later tried to identify an Irish background, the family was distinctly English. The family bible showed four previous generations of Englishmen, and the research Patrick did in the registry office in Somerset House around 1900 apparently showed this English ancestry went back 400 years to an army colonel.[2]

James frequently recalled to his children the poverty he experienced as a youngster: 'Often the father and mother and their three boys would dine on a single rasher – "but then", my father would add in telling us the story, "we had dipped bread for second course".'[3] However, he emphasised his was also a happy home.[4] Patrick's grandfather the frame maker, also named James, was forced to leave London around 1847 probably due to an economic crisis and moved to rapidly industrialising Birmingham with his wife Mary, who was six years his senior, and his three sons, William (1838), James and Henry (1840). In Birmingham, life was a bit better but the family always lived in small houses in a relatively poor part of town. In 1851 they occupied half a cottage at 6 Ellis Street before moving down the road to 12½ Gough Street where the father stayed until the 1870s. Around the time of the death of his first wife James moved to Bell Barn Road 3, Court 7, where he lived with his second wife until his death at the end of 1890 aged 73.[5]

The younger James had a strong artistic streak which he seemed to have inherited from his father, and which continued to run through this branch of the family. Patrick remembers his grandfather as someone who fashioned beautiful things from wood which no one would buy. He recalls his grandfather's single but fairly prolonged visit to Dublin probably around April 1884: 'a little old white bearded man, quizzical and original, who spent all his time making bird-cages of rare woods, and carving them exquisitely; he left us about twenty of them when he went back again to England'.[6]

Patrick's father had a long struggle with an urge to pursue an artistic career. To a young family friend he later explained: 'Laddie I have done many things, but I always wanted to be a sculptor. I would visit churches, see figures, you call them saints. I was about 16. ... I was struck by it.'[7] Family lore has it that 'Jim taught himself drawing with a board by copying from shop windows.' His younger brother Henry was supposed to have been holding up the board for him even on dark winter nights.[8] In the 1851 census the eleven-year-old James was registered as attending school but soon after was sent out to work. There was apparently no desire or financial capability to let him pursue his artistic interest and he was initially sent to a chain factory. His older brother William became a gun maker while his younger brother Henry became an apprentice in his father's frame making business. However, unlike his brothers James refused to settle in the chosen career and held various other jobs as a teenager, allowing him to attend night classes in drawing at the local art school and eventually starting an apprenticeship with a local sculptor. He was also an avid reader at this time, insistent on improving himself.[9]

After his apprenticeship Patrick claimed that his father had tried to become an artist in his own right. 'For a moment in his lusty young manhood, he had the ambition to bequeath memorable gifts to the world and to win long fame as a great sculptor.' Apparently James travelled the country for a while pursuing this ambition. From the friends he made it is clear he moved in arty circles. Patrick recalls his father's friends from England visiting them in Dublin: 'Those who came to see him were mostly artists and bohemians whom he had known in other places, and who looked in upon him when passing through Dublin. I liked them for their quaint costumes, and their humour and their gentleness ... Most of those that came to see us seemed poor, and many of them seemed sad.'[10]

However, the attempt to become an artist did not bring James much more than the aforementioned unusual circle of friends. Economic necessity forced him to work on the sculptures for various church and public buildings throughout England, where he apparently made something of a name for himself among fellow stone masons and artists.[11] He later emphasised that his lack of official training may have been accountable for his inability to establish himself as an artist proper.[12] His supposed habit to work straight from the block of stone, which was seen as unusual for a sculptor, betrayed this lack of formal training.[13] The son of his first employer also claimed that after James came to Dublin he needed some extra training: 'They all said he was a 1st rate sculptor but had to be sent to the Maison de Dante.'[14] His exceptional craftsmanship was nevertheless soon recognised. In 1867 his Dublin employer sent him to London to help carve the twenty-six princesses for the Queen's robing room in the House of Lords.[15] His work was widely celebrated not least when his own business won a first class award at the Dublin Exhibition of 1882.[16]

Some of the contacts James had made in the trade invited him to come to Dublin in the late 1850s. He may have been there as early as 1857 when he was just eighteen, but the most reliable sources indicate he was asked to come over around 1860 to work as a foreman on the Kildare Street Club by a fellow carver named Charles Harrison who worked for the O'Shea brothers and whom James had met while working on Lincoln Cathedral.[17] He himself described this opportunity later as a chance of a lifetime.[18] According to *The Dublin Builder* the carvings of the billiard playing monkeys on the Kildare Street Club, whom James claimed responsibility for, were executed by the O'Shea brothers under an architect called Woodward, and were placed between 1859 and 1861.[19] It seems likely that the job on the Kildare Street Club was simply part of the movement of tradesmen from one building site to another within the United Kingdom, as the census records indicate James was at home in Birmingham in April 1861.[20]

His first steady employment in Dublin seems to have been with John Hardman & Co., a Birmingham company specialised in furnishing churches. In response to the boom in church building in Ireland after the Famine, they had opened a showroom at 48 Grafton Street in 1855. Business was apparently sufficiently profitable to allow them to open up a stone carving section in 1860. The workshop initially opened at 1 Upper Camden Street, and in 1862 the entire business moved to these somewhat less fashionable but probably more affordable premises. Over the years Hardman & Co. brought a number of tradesmen over from Birmingham. These included John and Tom Early, Edward and Henry Powell, Edward Sharp, John and Charles M'Gloughlin, and some others. John Early, a forge man of Irish ancestry, was set up as manager in Dublin and was probably responsible, with his brother Thomas, for appointing their friend James Pearse as principal sculptor.[21]

The exact date James moved to Dublin permanently is difficult to establish. Contemporaries place this in 1862, about two years after the branch in Camden Street was started. However, it is certain that James was in Birmingham on 28 April 1863 when he got married to an eighteen-year-old girl named Susan Emily Fox.[22] It is also clear that he lived in Dublin in 1864. He was then recorded as working for the firm of Early and Powells and his first child was born in Dublin on New Year's Eve 1864. What is not clear is whether he lived in Birmingham until his marriage or whether he went back to get married there. The origins of his wife could shed some light on this, but unfortunately little is known about her apart from the fact that her father William Fox was a chandelier maker, that she was born around 1845 and was considered attractive.[23] The marriage certificate indicates that Emily was residing in another parish in Birmingham at the time of the wedding, but this may well have been a temporary address as no William Fox with a daughter called Emily is named in the 1851, 1861 or 1871 census in Birmingham. James's nieces in Birmingham also claimed to know nothing of Emily or her family.[24] The fact that no William Fox with a daughter called Susan Emily, or alternatively Susan, Emily, or Emily Susanna as she is respectively called on the birth certificates of her children, can be found in the birth and census records in the whole of England and Wales opens the possibility that she was in fact Irish and James may indeed have established himself in Dublin shortly after the 1861 census.[25]

Eventually many of the craftsmen brought over to Dublin started out for themselves, forming various partnerships and running several companies sometimes side by side. They often shared the same buildings and eventually congregated around Great Brunswick Street, which is now Pearse Street. James worked for Hardman & Co., which was taken over by John Early and Edward Powell in 1864, until 1873 when he joined P.J. O'Neill in a partnership under the name O'Neill and Pearse specialising in monumental works at 182 Great Brunswick Street. O'Neill was an Irish-American who had worked for the Early's for a while but had apparently enough money to venture out for himself. Shortly before starting the partnership he had opened a marble works company, which he continued to operate. In 1875, James also began his own business as a stone mason which he ran from his family home around the corner at 31 South Great Clarence Street. In 1878 when James was remarried to Patrick's mother the partnership with O'Neill was dissolved and Pearse set himself up as an independent architectural sculptor at 27 Great Brunswick Street.[26]

In his first years in Dublin directly after his first marriage, James moved house frequently but always remained in the area close to his existing work in Camden Street. All his homes were around what is now Robert Emmet Bridge linking Clanbrassil Street with Harold's Cross where his fellow masons and friends the M'Gloughlins lived. The birth records of his children indicate that in December 1864 the Pearses were based at 3 Pleasant View, two years later they had moved to 3 Bloomfield Place, and another two years later they live in 1 Wharton Terrace, Harold's Cross. In 1871 they had moved around the corner to 1 Harold's Cross before moving into town to 31 South Great Clarence Street over James's business which opened in 1875. Initially James did not do as well financially as could be expected from a skilful tradesman. Contemporaries put this down to his lack of social graces and his wayward estimates which meant he did not make a lot of money on his commissions.[27]

With the aid of his second wife, Margaret Brady, who was a much more agreeable attendant in business, the financial side seemed to have improved in the 1880s.[28] Initially only occupying the cellar and one bedroom of the premises at Great Brunswick Street and letting the rest out, the family gradually took over the whole building while Patrick was still very young. They were then also able to take in a nanny.[29] In 1880 James invited his foreman Edward Sharp, also hailing from Birmingham, to become a partner. The business was renamed Pearse and Sharp and continued to trade from the same premises. As part of the deal James assigned to himself an annual income of £250, indicating business was good. Records show the company had extended to include the ground floor of two and later three houses at 156, 160 and 162 Townshend Street adjoining the yard of Great Brunswick Street at the back. In the 1880s they employed an average of thirty workmen, paying out about £1700 in wages each year and making a 5 per cent profit on a turnover of about £12,000.[30] Sharp may also have been brought in as a partner to strengthen the commercial side. James did introduce some business novelties in this period such as having photographs taken of all his work, to function as a kind of catalogue which he used 'to induce the next Canon or PP who called to order from him'.[31]

The partnership with Sharp eventually broke up in 1891. Relatives and former employees mention a row over a bill with those who had employed them to do the high altar in Michael and John's Church, and a conflict over how to deal with a dishonest clerk. One of these cases threatened to go to court but against Sharp's wishes James settled beforehand. Sharp then decided to start his own business further down the street at number 180. The conflict turned ugly when Sharp systematically tried to undercut Pearse in an attempt to damage him.[32]

Over time all the Birmingham expatriates firmly established themselves in Dublin. By 1916 they or their offspring were still active in usually expanded businesses in the same streets as in the 1860s.[33] Apart from Sharp and Pearse they all seemed to have remained friends, in particular the Pearses and the M'Gloughlins had close ties. Edward Sharp was apparently the odd man out. His less than serious attitude to work and indiscretions with young women in particular seem to have clouded his relationship with the others.[34] James Pearse was apparently among the better sculptors and a hard worker who had plenty of commissions. In the *Freeman's Journal* he was described as 'the pioneer of modern Gothic Art, as applied to church work, in this country'.[35] Although he struggled for a while after his rupture with Sharp, he eventually became the owner of the largest stone mason business in Ireland and left a very substantial estate of over £1400 when he died in 1900. His co-workers felt that he should have done even better.[36]

By all accounts James did not have a particularly pleasant personality and treated neither his customers nor his employees very well. '"What brings you in here", he would say to anyone who came into his workshop. "I'm busy."'[37] He also had a habit of picking a fight with new employees: 'When new workmen joined the firm he usually caused a quarrel which ended in a fight held in the lane at the back of the works during dinner hour and if the worker proved his match his job was secure.'[38] Apparently this celebration of physical prowess was common in his family as two of his nephews became professional wrestlers and prize-winning weightlifters.[39] However, his bark was usually worse than his bite as a tendency to fire his workmen on the spot was rarely followed through if they simply refused to leave. On one occasion these two elements came together when James threatened to sack the father of one of Patrick's class mates for failing to physically challenge their teacher who had hit the workman's son.[40]

Apart from his immediate family, all agree that James Pearse was not an easy man to get on with.[41] Generally referred to at the time as 'the Governor', which implied a certain respect for him, the terms used to describe him were not generous: rough, dour, aggressive, choleric, dogged and impulsive were most frequent among them.[42] His social skills also left something to be desired: 'He was gruff and unpleasant and one day would salute you and the next would pass you by. ... About a month after my marriage he talked about a baby to me. I didn't like it.'[43] His drinking sessions with his compatriots from Birmingham and later also with the son from his first marriage are frequently remarked upon. Particularly after finishing a project he tended to go on a binge.[44]

James's interests did not confine themselves to the artistic field. Although having limited education, he developed a strong passion for reading. He bought a lot of books mostly on English literature, art, architecture, history and religion, including a Koran. This seemingly unusual desire for knowledge for someone from a working-class background was probably a result of his close association with what has been termed the 'earnest minority'. This movement of working-class men and women was particularly strong in Birmingham. They 'sought to challenge the middle- and upper-class monopoly on learning and knowledge' by self-study. They read a lot, joined so-called Mutual Improvement Societies or Mechanical Institutes and attended evening classes or lectures, inspiring a questioning attitude to social, political and religious orthodoxies.[45]

Politically James, like his father and brother in Birmingham, was an ardent follower of Charles Bradlaugh, the radical MP for Northampton, and even knew him personally. Bradlaugh was a strong advocate of the movement of self-reliance, much supported by members of the artisan class.[46] Like James he had a self-educated working-class background and had made it to MP as a champion of workers' and women's rights, birth control, Irish Home Rule, and the rights of subject people in the empire. He was an avowed republican, opposing inherited privilege including the monarchy, aristocracy and the House of Lords, advocating the break-up of landed estates and universal suffrage. Although a radical he was no supporter of force in Britain or Ireland but nevertheless helped draft the 1867 manifesto of the Fenians, the Irish secret republican brotherhood, and was linked to one of its main activists Jeremiah O'Donovan Rossa. Bradlaugh is best known for his exclusion from parliament in 1880 after he refused on principle to take the oath of allegiance to the Crown and God.[47]

Although not taking an active part in the volatile politics of Ireland at that time, James was particularly shocked by the Phoenix Park murders of 6 May 1882 in which the newly appointed Irish chief secretary, Lord Cavendish, and one of his undersecretaries were killed by the Invincibles, a radical section of the Fenians. A close friend remembers him pacing up and down Great Brunswick Street in a state of fury, denouncing the Park Murders.[48] Possibly influenced by the fact that one of the culprits lived not far away in Denzill Street, he believed all English people in Ireland to be under threat, and even bought two revolvers for protection. With his business partner Edward Sharp he practised shooting using a flat piece of iron as target.[49] He even told his family when visiting them in Birmingham that he had nearly been killed when Fenians called for him, only to be saved when his wife pulled him away from the door.[50]

This experience apparently changed his outlook. He increasingly involved himself in politics and became convinced of the need to give Ireland home rule. He supported Charles Parnell, the leader of the constitutional nationalists, and admired the more radical self-made activist Michael Davitt.[51] His marriage to Margaret Brady, who came from a nationalist family, probably influenced him in this move. He also sympathised with the self-reliance idea behind home rule, which was part of the motto of the Pearse and Sharp business: 'Self Reliance: Labor omnia vincit' (Labour conquers all).[52] A pamphlet written by Thomas Maguire, professor of moral philosophy at Trinity College, in 1886 in which home rule was rejected as dangerous and Parnellites as 'the most degraded section of the inhabitants of the British Isles',[53] so infuriated James that he felt compelled to write a 20,000 word answer to 'this most extra-ordinary ebullition of quasi religious political fireworks', and publish it entirely at his own cost.[54]

In a fair and humorous if slightly pompous manner he tried to refute all of Maguire's arguments concerning the disastrous effects of home rule. 'I have not presumed to place as relatively high a price upon this reply, as the Doctor has done upon his attack, for two reasons; the first being, that I want the people to read it, and the second, that I have not so high an opinion of my powers of abuse as he has of his; and which indeed in his case is well founded.'[55] James basically asserted that a country could not be ruled in direct opposition to the wishes of its inhabitants and that England should give effect to the democratically expressed will of the people of Ireland and introduce home rule. 'Let this be done and we may reasonably expect, that bitterness and strife may depart from the land in spite of all the professors and owls who hoot and screech from the walls of old Trinity.'[56] Following this he became for a short while involved in harnessing support among Protestants for home rule. He appears to have spoken at a meeting and it is claimed that he collected as many as 7000 signatures from protestants for a petition in support of home rule.[57]

The pamphlet clearly positions James as a self-educated man from the working classes. The published answer to Professor Maguire was, however, probably not James's only foray into the world of public discussion. Brian Crowley has convincingly argued that James Pearse is the man behind a series of pamphlets published by the Freethought Publishing Company written under the pseudonym Humanitas. The Freethought Publishing committee was headed by Charles Bradlaugh and aimed at furthering the causes of atheism and agnosticism. The first two pamphlets Humanitas published, *Is God the First Cause?* and *The Follies of the Lord's Prayer*, were both published in 1883 and indeed ridiculed many of the central tenets of Christianity. The other works were more political. In 1885 he published a pamphlet on *Charles Bradlaugh and the Irish Nation* followed by two arguments against socialism published in 1884 and 1889.[58] Although Crowley refutes it, James probably published another pamphlet which contained a discussion between Charles Bradlaugh and Henry Hyndman, leader of the Marxist Social Democratic Federation, in 1885.[59] James's papers also contain an unpublished tract on why the moon causes the tides, which he clearly did not fully understand.[60]

Further support for Crowley's argument comes from a number of comments from family friends and acquaintances. A colleague and later employee of James recalls there was some concern that James had published a pamphlet in which the existence of God was denied.[61] He was strongly advised by his clerk, the ex-RIC man Mr Free, not to publish this considering his dependency on orders from the Catholic Church: 'Do you want never to get another order for an altar or a statue of St Joseph?'[62] The books in his library also represent the interests of Victorian agnostics and sceptics.[63] All this apparently seriously worried the young Patrick who is stated to have asked his father whether he thought he was going out of business over the furore around a pamphlet.[64] None of these concerns could reasonably be referring to the pamphlet in favour of home rule which James had published under his own name and with which the greater majority of Catholics and clergy agreed. In the last ten years of his life, James seems to have lost his interest in active participation in public debates, as no evidence of any publications after 1889 have been found. According to Patrick's early biographer Le Roux, James 'reached more settled convictions towards the end of his life and immersed himself in the ordered life and vision of mysticism where he found again all the serenity and spiritual peace which intellectual scepticism had never given him'.[65] This may well account for his retreat from public life.

James Pearse's religion had always been a contentious issue. He came from a Unitarian background with a particularly devout mother. His inquisitive nature, however, had a detrimental effect on his religious education from an early age. 'Of schooling in the ordinary sense he had got none except in the reading class of a Sunday School; and this he had had to leave while still a lad, inasmuch as his questions had caused the divine who presided there to regard him as an atheist; which in due time he became.'[66] His first marriage in April 1863 was nevertheless solemnised 'according to the rites and ceremonies of the Established Church'. He also displayed a great interest in religious sculptures. Patrick compared his father to the nameless artists who lovingly decorated medieval churches and monasteries.[67] In Dublin his knowledge of saints impressed some around him, although he himself described them as figures and explicitly not as saints.[68]

His publication record indicates he remained an atheist most if not all of his life.[69] In 1870 he and his first family had nevertheless officially converted to Catholicism apparently influenced by his friend John Early. In a letter Fr Pius Devine of Mount Argus Church testifies to the fact that James and his first wife and children were received into the Catholic Church around 1870.[70] Fr Devine vividly recalls James's continued questioning attitude when he was preparing for his conversion:

> I recollect well your sensible objections and difficulties, whilst you were under instructions and the clearheaded manner in which you saw the answers as soon as they were proposed to you by me. Indeed I don't think I ever received a convert – and I received a good many – with whose disposition before and after reception I was so pleased with as I was with yours.[71]

Although Fr Devine was convinced of James's sincerity, the depth of the family's conversion remains questionable. Being a Protestant let alone an atheist would of course be very problematic for a stone carver largely dependent on commissions from the Catholic Church. The conversion did take place a few years before James actually branched out on his own, but business concerns were probably at the heart of it. From Devine's letter it is clear that James had done work for the local Catholic church before and James was promised that if more work came up he would be preferred again. The letter was actually explicitly written on James's request to protect his business interests after some Irish stone carvers led by the son of James's former business partner P.J. O'Neill, probably jealous of James's business success, had objected on religious and racial grounds to work on churches going to Pearse. Their attempt to exclude James would of course only be effective if there were grounds for doubting the depth of his beliefs.

Although Patrick liked to think his father's conversion was a deeply felt one,[72] the evidence indicates that at least up to 1890 this was mainly a front put up for business purposes. For a recent convert James showed an unusual lack of religious fervour. James's observation of religious duties was questioned by some at the time of the challenge by O'Neill in 1877. 'He used to act the atheist here for years and had to give this up when he married.'[73] In his letters to Margaret Brady during their courtship James teased her occasionally with her simple Catholicism. When she told him she had prayed to God to make him better when he was suffering from a long-lasting throat infection he asserted it seemed to be God's wish to keep him ill and away from her. 'It is no use saying please God this nor please God that it never will be well and there is no end of it. It appears to me if he is pleased in the matter at all it is to keep it bad.'[74] Even after their marriage, which was indeed solemnised according to the rites of the Catholic Church, it was said that 'Old P did not believe in anything or go anywhere',[75] and his habit to work on Sundays was remarked on.[76]

The pamphlets published in the 1880s under the pseudonym Humanitas are strong evidence but it cannot conclusively be proven they were written by James. What is certain, however, is that James took out a debenture worth £50 in the Freethought Publishing committee in 1889. He also advertised for a pamphlet in *The Freethinker* and in the *Agnostic Journal*, journals an active Catholic at that time would not dream of reading let alone advertising and investing in.[77] Bradlaugh was at that time known as one of the most prominent agnostics in Great Britain, so support for his work constitutes clear evidence for a double life. The less than total sincerity concerning his conversion is also revealed by events surrounding his death. James collapsed due to a brain haemorrhage while having dinner in his older brother's house during a visit with his wife and son Patrick to Birmingham in 1900. When a priest was sent for, his brother asked him: 'Are you a Catholic, Jim?' to which he is supposed to have replied: 'If it makes them happy, let them do it their way.'[78] In the death notice the family stressed that James had died 'fortified by the rites of the Roman Catholic Faith', possibly indicating this might be doubted.[79]

James's political and religious development was also influenced by his Dublin surroundings, and his marriage to Margaret Brady in 1877. Patrick claims that James's marriage to Emily had been marred in the end by the fact that James blamed her for the death of one of their children by neglect.[80] Although Patrick and his sister Margaret are only aware of three children having been born during his father's first marriage there were in fact four.[81] Apart from Mary Emily and James Vincent there was a third child Agnes Maud born on 30 November 1869 and a fourth child Amy Kathleen born on 18 June 1871. Whether either or both of the latter indeed died is unclear, as there are no entries in the Irish death register for them. There are some references to the possibility that Patrick had a sibling who was mentally retarded and institutionalised. The unsympathetic Bulmer Hobson, who had reasons to malign Patrick, was most outspoken about this: 'It was said by his friends that he had a sister in a mental home. I heard this more than once and accepted it as being true because it was said by people who knew him better than I did and were friendly with him. ... I had no reason to doubt its truth. The abnormality of the two brothers made it seem the more probable.'[82]

The death or otherwise of one or both of their last children by neglect may have been influenced by Emily's poor health. She died on 26 July 1876, aged just thirty, of what was recorded on her death certificate as an inflammation of the spinal marrow. This probably brought her a lot of discomfort and may have led to a certain amount of drinking, revealed in James's niece's assertion that she drank herself to death.[83] James may have resented this but Emily and James were not estranged, they continued to live together and according to the death certificate James was present at her deathbed.[84]

A certain measure of estrangement in the final stages of the marriage could nevertheless be inferred from a letter James wrote to Patrick's future mother Margaret Brady, who was then nineteen years old, less than five months after Emily's death. In it James expressed his love for her in no uncertain terms, and betrayed a familiarity indicating an already well-established relationship. This may mean they already knew each other intimately before Emily's death. This might be explained by the possibility that one of Margaret's uncles was married to a Fox which may indicate a longer-standing acquaintance between the two families than has so far been assumed.[85] This would also strengthen the case that Emily was Irish. However, other references point to James getting to know Margaret in John Weldon's newsagent and post office at 167 Great Brunswick Street where she worked and where James bought his daily newspaper during 1876. In December Margaret indicated in a letter to James that she was not yet acquainted with his children. 'I am glad to hear the children are well. If I was acquainted with them I would send them some Christmas Cards but as I am not I suppose I must wait for some future time.'[86]

Whatever had happened in their relationship, the death of Emily posed serious problems to James. He was left with his two surviving children Mary Emily and James Vincent who were then nine and eleven years old. Running a growing business required his full attention, and there was little time to attend to his children's needs. During his wife's illness the family had moved in with his friend John M'Cloughlin at 5 Parnell Place, Harold's Cross, and that is where he remained for the time being. The exact arrangements are unclear but in a letter James described having a landlady who was 'one of the kindest creatures alive'.[87] The two families were already very close, and John M'Cloughlin's English wife had cared for Emily while she was ill.[88] However, this situation could not last. James would marry Margaret just fifteen months after Emily's death on 24 October 1877 in St Agatha's Catholic Church. After the wedding the couple moved into 27 Great Brunswick Street where James operated his business.

In a number of ways Patrick was influenced by his father's Victorian background and personality. The strict work ethic, the love of learning and desire to improve oneself and get involved in public discourse as well as a questioning attitude are traits shared by both men.[89] A strong orientation on the family and a certain lack of social graces can also be observed in them. Although Patrick supported home rule in his young days like his father and later became a revolutionary nationalist, he never rejected his English background. He also had a warm admiration for his father's liberal views on political freedom.[90] Only in his attitude to religion did Patrick deviate. Although also questioning the authority of the clergy, he never doubted his Catholicism.

Mother's background

The latter was largely due to Patrick's mother who had a fairly conventional Irish background. Margaret was just twenty years old at the time of her marriage, while James was already thirty-seven – a large age difference frowned upon by some.[91] Although possibly due to the dark winter nights, Margaret's parents had their doubts as they prevented her from seeing James in the evening during their courtship and James clearly felt uneasy about meeting them for the first time. 'Depend upon it they will not think as much of me at your house as you do. You know you are apt to see with your heart whilst they see with their eyes.' Margaret's background was also distinctly different from that of James. Her traditional Catholic farmers family originated in Co. Meath with a line back to Co. Cavan. According to Patrick his great-grandfather Walter Brady was forced off his land in Meath by the famine and had moved to Dublin with his family of five sons and two daughters. There the sons originally worked as hackney drivers and the girls went into service. Two of the sons, Larry and John, died before reaching middle age but the others Phil, Patrick and Christy did well, all three settling down as farmers on the outskirts of Dublin providing dairy products for the city. Walter Brady eventually died while living with his childless son Christy who was considered the most capable and genial and also had done best for himself. Margaret Brady remembers her grandfather Walter as 'a tall old man who wore knee-breeches and a silk hat and who spoke Irish'.[92]

Margaret's father Patrick lived long in enmity with his more successful brother Christy. Not uncommon in rural Ireland they apparently had fallen out over a piece of land. Patrick was supposed to have been much gentler and less vivacious than his brother. He married a Brigid Savage from Fingal who was remembered as a great step dancer. Two of their children Walter and Brigid died young, and only Catherine and Patrick's mother Margaret, born 2 February 1857, survived. At the time of Margaret's wedding to James Pearse in 1877 her father had left farming and was registered as a coal factor living at 7 Aldborough Avenue in the North Strand area. He did quite well leaving an estate at his death in 1894 which included three cottages in Aldborough Avenue, a house in North Clarence Street, various cattle, horses, cars and carts, with a total value of £216.14.6d.[93]

The Brady family claimed strong republican roots. Patrick Brady's father, Walter, was supposed to have fought in the 1798 Rising while his brother was hanged by the Yeomen and buried in croppies field in Tara. In an open letter to the nationalist leader William O'Brien in 1912 Patrick claimed his grandfather Patrick had supported the Young Irelanders and had joined the Fenians in the rebellion of 1867.[94]

Nevertheless, Margaret Brady was not known for her nationalist sympathies. The rejection of British rule was not one that had been passed down the generations with a strong passion.[95] Patrick recalls that the most outspoken aspect of his mother's family was their knowledge of Irish. According to Patrick his great-grandfather only spoke Irish and he recalls learning his first words of Irish from his grandfather's brother Christy and sister.[96]

Margaret's letters to James during their courtship show her as a quite emotional and not very intellectual person who was truly in love with James.[97] Apparently the romance between them started after James had left his passbook on the counter of the post office where she worked.[98] James clearly revelled in Margaret's attention following the death of his first wife. 'Your affection seems to fill up a great void in my existence.' He had more problems expressing his own feelings. He apologised repeatedly to Margaret for not showing his affection in his letters as much as she did. 'Don't mind dear if I have not said so many kind things in this as you have in yours, stop till you have me upon your own doorstep then give it to me hot.' In contrast James indeed seems to have been quite forward with his physical affections, much to her discomfort. 'I mean when I am in your company and trying all my might to be circumspect. I trust you will help me in that most difficult task for solemnly I do not mean to embrace you more that ninety times and kiss you a trifle over twice as many times during the whole afternoon.' This even caused Margaret some friction with her confessor. 'I promise you his reverence shall have no cause to chide you when next you seek his ghostly presence.' At other times he was nevertheless quite romantic and gentle: 'indeed Maggie – I cannot tell you how sincerely I love you, be sure all your kind thoughts and wishes for me are reciprocated'.[99]

His verbal reticence nevertheless made Margaret wonder whether he really loved her. She expressed particular concern in the spring of 1877 when James rarely saw her because he was suffering from a throat infection. James was clearly frustrated but nevertheless tried to reassure her. 'I am completely miserable and out of patience. I cannot feel let alone act as I ought to do. I am not surprised at your having uneasy thoughts. I believe the more care I take the worse I get. I am sick of myself, and I think other people must be sick of me.' When James subsequently stood her up one night Margaret expressed her worry that he was losing his interest in her. 'I hope it was a statue that kept you in last night.' In response James assured her he had not been well and that it was just business that was going before pleasure. 'You say you hope I was engaged upon a statue. I suppose you mean to hope it was a stone one. Shurely Maggie you don't think I was engaged upon any other sort of one, a live one for instance.' And he quickly bounced the ball back. 'I say I am wondering if you need any consolation all this time, and if so are you seeking it in the bosom of the church or upon the breast of that same stalwart countryman of yours which you mentioned.'[100]

When feeling well James displayed a strong desire to get married and create a happy home. 'I think it must be a great blessing and consolation to be permitted to pass through the world of change with one who will be all to you at all times. One whom you can turn to when the world frowns. A home in which you can find peace and rest. I believe I could make great efforts to render such a home happy.' In his anxiety he sometimes became quite blunt: 'It is a pity there are not a few good large babies for you to practise upon.'[101] This emphasis on family life is also a strong current in Patrick's life who always functioned in the context of his (extended) family.

When Margaret married James some months later she was not much older than her two stepchildren, who were then twelve and ten. She nevertheless seemed to have got on well with them, particularly with Emily. In one of James's letters during their courtship he wrote: 'The little girl tells me to be sure and give her kind love to you, she knows who I am writing to.' With some interruptions Emily remained a frequent visitor to the house as an adult and even moved back in for a while after her marriage ran into difficulties.[102] Margaret's relationship with James junior seems to have been somewhat more fraught. When he became older he worked in his father's workshop for a good while. He accompanied him on his drinking sessions, apparently often outdoing him in that department.[103] James junior married the daughter of Dan Byrne, a carter in the gas company, and had a son. Later he looked after the loans business Byrne ran on the side. However, he eventually died a pauper in the South Dublin Union aged forty-three in 1912 apparently without contact with the rest of the Pearse family.[104] It is said that Margaret never fully trusted her stepson, but the reasons for that are unclear.[105]

Family life

With Margaret, James had four more children in fairly rapid succession. Margaret Mary, named after her maternal grandaunt and paternal grandmother, was born a good ten months after their marriage on 4 September 1878. Patrick Henry, named after his mother's father and his father's younger brother, followed fourteen months later on 10 November 1879. Aunt Margaret, who was present at the birth of all the children of her favourite niece, was responsible for his christening and registration. Much to his father's annoyance she misspelled their family name as 'Pierce' and forgot to mention Patrick's second name, so Patrick Henry Pearse was recorded as Patrick Pierce. This only came out in 1891 when a birth certificate was required for Patrick's school and a special declaration from his father was needed to have the mistake corrected.[106] Two years after Patrick's birth on 15 November 1881 William James arrived after what was apparently a very difficult birth. There were fears that Margaret would die and Willie was sent to his uncle Christy to be nursed on cow's milk. He was named after his father's elder brother and father. Mary Bridget, later gaelicised to Brighid, was born on 24 April 1884 and named after her two grandmothers.

There is not a lot known about Patrick's early relationship with his vivacious mother. She loved her children and was caring towards Patrick. In later life it was even said that she idolised him, something not uncommon to Irish mothers.[107] However, when he was young she seemed to be fairly occupied with running the business and the household, both of which she seemed to control.[108] In his autobiographical piece, probably written at the end of 1915, Patrick rarely mentions her, referring to her simply as 'all sweetness and strength'. He does, however, recall receiving 'many a good and well-deserved smacking' from his mother 'for going into some forbidden place or breaking some precious thing'.[109] Patrick apparently received little affirmation from her and always maintained a certain emotional distance to his mother. Although in private he called her first mama and later mother, he usually signed his letters to her with 'P.H. Pearse'.[110] His attitude to her in later life was certainly affectionate but from a distance. In a letter to a friend who had lost her mother he states that the greatest sorrow in his life would be to lose his mother, but the relationship never seemed very physical.[111]

Throughout Patrick's life one of the motivating forces was a desire to please and impress her. Some argue he never really gained a psychological independence from her and that he was suffering from what they called a mother complex.[112] When he was appointed editor of the Irish language newspaper *An Claidheamh Soluis* the first thing he did was rush home to tell his mother.[113] Even at the end of his life he still was somewhat submissive to her. When he went out on Easter 1916 his mother is supposed to have said: 'Now, Pat, above all, do nothing rash!' Apparently he dutifully replied 'No, mother' after which he went into Dublin and started a rebellion.[114] After his imprisonment and shortly before his execution he found time to write a poem for his mother on her request. 'A Mother Speaks' was written from the point of view of a mother who was losing her son. This perspective was inspired by poems Patrick's father had written for her when her father and her sister died.[115] In his final letter to his mother accompanying this poem Patrick was very affectionate: 'I have not words to tell my love of you and how my heart yearns to you all. I will call to you in my heart at the last moment.'[116]

In his early days he seems to have had a closer emotional bond with his grandaunt Margaret of which he speaks most fondly. His grandaunt was a spinster who frequently visited their house, sometimes just dropping in, other times staying for a couple of days. She identified closely with Margaret Pearse's family. Patrick's grandfather was her favourite brother and Margaret Pearse her favourite niece, and she felt a special bond with Patrick the first born son: 'she has told me how her heart leaped when it was found that I was a boy'. She sometimes prevented Patrick being punished and he was told that she and his mother argued about who was entitled to care for him when he was very ill during the first year of his life. She also nursed him through his scarletina when he was seven and held vigils next to his bed when he was plagued with nightmares. As a young boy Patrick reciprocated this special attention:

> When she came I used to bring a little square stool that was recognised as mine and sit beside her. I would show her any new toys or picture books that I had got. She would tell me where she had been, and of the white chickens that she was rearing for me, and of the foal that my grandfather's

black mare had, which I must ride when it was a little bigger. She would put back my hair on my forehead, and pull up my red socks and sew in tightly any button that was loose on my jacket. Often she brought me something, and she used to make me guess what it was she brought. When I was in bed she would steal up to me to share her supper of bread and cheese with me … and whisper some story or some old song into my ear. She had many endearing names for me, and I for her, but those names are too sacred to be written here.[117]

These stories often seemed to contain a strong Irish and nationalist element. Patrick remembers how Aunt Margaret sang old ballads and snatches of songs in Irish and in English. Napoleon and men 'dead or in exile for love of Ireland', like Wolfe Tone, Robert Emmet and Jeremiah O'Donovan Rossa, were her favourite topics. The same songs Patrick's mother had sung to the children as lullabies.[118]

Much of the life of the Pearse children was spent indoors. Their mother had aspirations for her children which apparently did not allow mixing with the working class youths in the neighbourhood, while their father's anxiety concerning their health following the death of one or two of the children from his previous marriage may well have contributed to this. Together with their grandaunt the children learned to observe but rarely to participate in the outside world: 'Often she would draw us all to the window and we would watch the pageant of the street. We got to know everyone that came and went, and the time of every coming and going.'[119] Even during their school days the children's social life did not extend much beyond their own home.

Patrick had vivid memories of his early childhood, some apparently dating back to before he was two. Most of these memories concerned fantasy games, initially engaged in with his older sister Margaret but later mostly with his brother Willie. Possibly due to the isolated upbringing and lack of interaction with other children, Patrick's imagination was unusually well developed. His autobiography is full of the tales he invented. He imagined the downstairs kitchen to be a mountainside, inspired by the sounds from his father's workshop in the next room. The living room on the ground floor, which the family moved into when Patrick was almost two, soon became his private theatre. To him this room seemed so big he imagined himself travelling through it with sailing ships, sleighs, Roman chariots and on the back of elephants. He pretended the room contained jungles with wild beasts, sandy deserts with caravans in it, and oceans on which many adventures were played out often riding his wooden horse called Dobbin. Patrick preferred to re-enact epics on a grand scale like the quest for the Holy Grail or the relief of Ascalon or Trebizond.

This fantasy life was developed into a penchant for plays and other theatrical expressions which contained many elements of Patrick's future activities. From a very young age a lot of time was spent acting. This involved parts of Shakespeare but from the age of ten Patrick also wrote and directed his own plays with his siblings and cousins as actors. His first play was called 'The Rival Lovers' for which they built their own theatre using their mother's clothes as a backdrop, and which ended with a duel between Patrick and Willie with pea-shooting pistols. None of these plays contained Irish heroes. They were obviously inspired by the romantic swashbuckling stories he read in the English books and magazines his father bought for him. Another theatrical form was found in acting out the serving of mass, which was a fairly common form of entertainment for children in Ireland who had few acting models at that time.[120]

At around nine years of age he also started his own weekly magazine which contained all the attributes of a children's magazine, including articles, jokes, puzzles, sketches and a serial called 'Pat Murphy's Pig'. When the boys attended the Christian Brothers School they built their own theatre from cardboard, acting out *Uncle Tom's Cabin*, a love story, a battle between Christian and Pagans and another romantic play about the legendary Irish High King Brian Boru. When Patrick was about twelve he became greatly interested in the magic lantern. He saved his pocket money and bought a small toy one. When it turned out not to work his father got him a real one. This started Patrick off lecturing with the aid of slides. Twice a year his father proudly organised a special evening at which Patrick spoke for a gathering of his father's friends and acquaintances. All these creative activities dominated his home life until Patrick started to work seriously for his Intermediate Exams.[121]

Although his lively imagination meant that Patrick was very good at entertaining himself and his siblings in the daytime, it also gave him quite an anxious childhood. Particularly at night he was plagued by nightmares, which were peopled by fantasy creatures. There were what he termed the Brooms, 'large headed squat creatures with saucer-like eyes', who were terrifying but not unfriendly. More malign was what he termed the Little Man, a creature the size of a boy but with a bearded face and an idiot laugh, who haunted his dreams. Pursued by the Little Man he would often awake sobbing, after which his mother or grandaunt would sit by his side until he fell asleep again. Other times he would be too scared to go to sleep and too afraid to call out: 'how often have I lain bathed in sweat, tossing from one side to the other, trying to call their names yet fearing to raise my voice lest it might attract the notice of some grisly thing outside the door!' He would then only go to sleep when his parents, who slept in the same room, came up to go to bed. Occasionally even that was not enough to settle him and he lay awake imagining fantastic horrors peering at him. Even the prayers his mother taught him to drive these away failed to aid.

He acted out many of his daytime fantasies with his sister Margaret, but they did not truly get on: 'One of the chief grounds of quarrel was her frequent insisting on my putting Dobbin to what I considered base uses. She was perpetually killing people in the most terrifying and unheard of ways, and calling upon me to bury them.' For a while he played along with her: 'In those days she was both bigger and of a more domineering character than I, and she generally had her way.' Eventually, however, he lost the respect she had instilled in him for her when she convinced him that if he cut the tail of the toy horse his father had brought home for him from London it would grow back again more luxurious. When it failed to do so Patrick lost his faith in her and became more interested in his younger brother Willie with whom he formed an extremely close relationship.

Patrick later recalled Willie's birth in glowing terms: 'What greater thing has ever happened to me than the coming of that good comrade? Willie and I have been true brothers. As a boy he was my only playmate, as a man he has been my only intimate friend.' As the younger and somewhat more timid brother of a forceful personality such as that of Patrick's, Willie looked up to Patrick all his life, and was even described as his hero-worshipper.[122] In return Patrick looked out for him: 'I was always wounded when Willie was slighted or ill-used.' At various times Patrick stood up for his brother against their teachers. At the same time their closeness also allowed Willie to really get through to Patrick unlike most other people.[123] The relationship between the brothers grew ever stronger. Even as adults they did almost everything together with Patrick clearly being the dominant partner in the relationship.

As a child Patrick does not seem to have had much contact with his younger sister Mary Brighid. Being almost five years older and a boy made this quite natural. However, he did display a similar protective and caring attitude towards her as he did towards his brother. Mary Brighid was a sickly child and for a long time he read to her daily upon returning from school, mostly classics such as *Uncle Tom's Cabin*, *Alice in Wonderland* and *Robin Hood*. Only when he became involved in the language movement in his mid-teens did this stop. His extreme dedication to the movement did not leave him time or interest. In later life he nevertheless still liked to please her. When she developed an interest in the harp he bought her a cheap imported one and then saved up to get her a real Irish version.[124]

Patrick clearly stood out among his siblings and spent much of his life socialising almost exclusively with them. When they were adults Margaret was generally considered a hardworking conscientious but fairly uneducated and domineering person. Brighid was a strong willed but excitable woman with a good sense of humour. She was something of a hypochondriac, demanding the full-time presence of a paid companion; she was always overdressed and seen as slightly odd and not very sociable. The two sisters did not really see eye to eye either.[125] During most of his life Patrick's social, personal and working life revolved around his family who participated in his work with the language movement, his school and even in the Volunteers. Some outsiders saw the ever-present Pearse women as stifling. 'P was surrounded by a regiment of monstrous women.'[126]

In contrast Willie was considered pleasant looking, friendly and particularly charming to women: 'He was arty and nice. He liked to help you and did help me with drawing.'[127] Many men, however, were put off by his somewhat weak personality and squeaky voice: 'Willie to us always seemed an imitation of P[atrick]; we called him "Wooly". He was a nincompoop sissy sort of boy.'[128] He paid a lot of attention to his appearance, and had a 'carefully cultivated artistic appearance, complete with flowing dark hair and a floppy tie'.[129] This was an expression of the fashion in Gaelic League circles to sport long hair and rough tweeds as they believed this was the style of the old Gaels.[130] Willie's penchant for nice cloth and particularly for kilts in later life did not enamour him to the more rural elements within the language movement: 'Willie P. was very dressy more so than Pearse. One summer day at 8 Nt. Frederick St. where [the] Keating Branch had rooms I saw him come down, wearing dust coat. He looked at his boots and saw that they were dusty and with the lining of his very swagger dust coat he wiped his shoes of bourgeois touch, most unlike the Gaelic League.'[131] At times he could also be quite truculent; in this respect it was said that he took after his father. 'Willie was clever with his hands but otherwise an ass.'[132]

Willie had inherited some of the artistic talents of his father and grandfather, and was destined to take over his father's sculpting business particularly after his older half-brother James fell out with the rest of the family. Although he was well trained, attending the Metropolitan College of Art in Dublin, the Kensington School of Art in London and some courses in Paris, his abilities as a sculptor were nevertheless questioned: 'Willie was a poor sculptor; everything he did was sentimental.'[133] One of the sons of John Early and fellow student under Oliver Shepherd in Dublin recalls that Willie had difficulties sculpting hands, and that one of the Early employees had to do them for him. Willie was indeed hesitant to emphasise his artistic qualities. In an unsuccessful letter of application for a job in the Dublin School of Art he described himself as 'a practical worker in marble and stone and besides my work at my place of business at Brunswick Street I here execute some small commissions on my own responsibility – so that I am not an amateur but one with the earnest intention of pursuing my craft as a practical sculptor'. Stimulated by Patrick he had applied for the job to develop his artistic side. Apparently weakly motivated he explained the absence of awards and good examining results in a rather awkward way: 'Firstly my temperament would not allow me to go thro' such things with any degree of comfort or success. And I never saw sufficient reason why I should do violence to myself by so doing.'[134]

Some of this hesitance may be explained by the inferiority complex some assigned to him which was possibly associated with having a domineering brother.[135] The actress Maire Nic Shiubhlaigh felt that Willie 'seemed to be overshadowed by P.H. He agreed to his every decision and seldom put forward an argument of his own. This submission could be rather irritating to the onlooker unfamiliar with the brothers. But Willie's deference was not born out of lack of character.' Her judgement was that Willie and Patrick just thought and believed the same.[136] The only time his personality really came out seems to have been in acting, which he loved.[137] He participated in most of the performances staged in St Enda's, the school Patrick later founded, and also acted in theatre productions. Together with his sister Mary Brighid he even set up a theatre company, the Leinster Stage Society, in which he acted and Mary Brighid wrote the plays together with their nephew Alf M'Cloughlin. On stage he showed the same uncertainty about his own abilities as he did elsewhere. The sympathetic Maire Nic Shiubhlaigh was not overtly impressed and felt this was because Willie never lost his self-consciousness on a stage. 'But what he lacked in ability he made up in enthusiasm. At rehearsals he obeyed every command with humility. Often he would draw one aside and whisper: "Do you think I was good? I'm doing my best." One could always gain his gratitude with advice.'[138]

Despite all this, Willie seems to have been a central figure in Patrick's life. They were almost inseparable, often holidayed together in the West of Ireland, had their own private language which appeared as baby-talk to outsiders and Patrick saw Willie as his most important friend. 'William Pearse was the confidant, counsellor, and often critic of his brother. I have known them to spend hours arguing over a pupil's behaviour or character, a new school programme or scheme, and I remember Willie once saying bluntly about a speech: "Pat, you were terrible, you repeated yourself, you were too slow and bored the people!"'[139] According to Desmond Ryan, Patrick's pupil and later biographer, Willie was the only one who Patrick truly listened to. 'Pearse listened most courteously to all critics and went on doing as he liked until Willie lisped his fierce word.'[140]

Patrick's father appears to have been a fairly remote and quiet presence in the children's lives, as was quite common in Victorian society. However, living over the shop for most of their early lives meant he had more contact with the children than the average lower middle-class father. He came up to the family rooms once or twice a day and in the evening. In their early years the two boys had the habit of coming into their sisters' room at night and messing around half undressed like 'silent clowns'; a short sharp knock on the door by their father usually ended this.[141] On their father's arrival the children always became quiet, but Patrick stated they were not afraid of him. Margaret Pearse later described him as 'a great and just man'. According to Patrick he gave a very sad impression to his children and was apparently a somewhat introspective, melancholic almost depressive man at this stage of his life.

> He was big, with broad shoulders that were a little round; he was very silent, and spoke only once or twice during the course of a meal, breaking some reverie to say something kind to my mother or something funny to one of us; Otherwise whether we were by ourselves or one of our rare visitors were there, sitting a little abstracted, always a little lonely we thought, a little sorrowful at times indeed, but these were very seldom, he would in order to please my mother, rouse himself to exercise the wonderful social gift that he had, and then my mother's face would flush with pleasure, and we would laugh in pure happiness or join shyly in the conversation.[142]

James's mindset may well be a personality trait exaggerated by his frustration over not making it as an artist in his own right, but could also be associated with the socially isolated double life he lived in Dublin. He had only a small circle of friends and had to keep his life as an atheist pamphleteer secret to his surroundings. Outsiders claim his reticence was caused by his domineering wife, but there seems to be more at play.[143] In a letter to James written not long after Patrick's birth, Margaret admits to a rift between them. She writes the letter clearly in a distraught state at half past three in the morning from a house called Pembroke Lodge, which was not the family home at that time. It seems to have involved an affair which had made James doubt her devotion to him. In reaction he had obviously said or written something which hurt her deeply, as she threatened him with the ultimate punishment in a lifetime marriage of not having any more children with him if he did not take back what he had said. She was desperate as she claimed that if it had not been for the children she would have been happy to die at that particular point. All this was no doubt an emotional reaction to a clearly traumatic experience. She accused him of not caring enough for her to be jealous, but at the end expressed the desire they would forgive each other and make up.[144]

Indeed, a reconciliation does seem to have taken place. In a letter written a few years later, the two were clearly again in love. James asked her to 'tell wow wow [their daughter Margaret] and Pat to give you some bigy ones [kisses] for papa' and added 'I find you can write a love letter all most as well as you would of old.' In reply Margaret stated: 'I am dreadfully lonely for you. The only consolation I have is I got your photo on Saturday. ... I long to clasp you in my arms once more and think I will be satisfied.' Right up to Patrick's death his mother referred to the beautiful pieces James wrote when her sister and father died in the 1890s.[145] Indeed, following the fallout Margaret and James had another two children. However, some have wondered why they did not have any more. By the time Mary Bridget was born Margaret was after all only 27. The problematic births, particularly of Willie, may have contributed to it, but alternatively this could of course be the result of the use of some form of birth control advocated by James's political guide, Charles Bradlaugh, and practised by many middle-class families at this time. However their relationship developed, the rearing of the children fell mostly to Margaret and her aunt.[146]

All this did not mean James was not involved with the well-being of his children. He kissed the children goodnight every evening, but just like in his relationship with Margaret he did not openly express a great deal of affection for them. In letters to Margaret, however, he does show a great concern for their health and safety, warning her to be mindful of gas and the fire. On hearing she was going to make a trip to the country he implored her to make sure the children were well fed and did not catch a cold.[147] When the family lived over the shop in Great Brunswick Street he also worried about the impact of the dust particularly on his children's health. On a few occasions Patrick recalls a particular concern for them in his father:

> Occasionally at night when he was kissing us, or when going away (he sometimes went away to look after some work he was doing or trying to get to do), the deep reserve of his nature would break down and he would lift one of us and press our face against his rough face and put his arm round us and draw us very close against his stone-dusty blouse.[148]

James was indeed what we would call a reserved person, but this was certainly not uncommon at that time. The only other time Patrick saw his father expressing emotion was when Patrick's grandfather died in 1890: 'I remember that my father cried when the news of his death came and this seemed a strange thing to me, for I had not known that men could cry.'[149] James felt a deep longing for a happy family life, which was exposed in a letter to Margaret in which he expressed a craving for the warmth of his family home and lamented the recent passing of his mother. 'I am glad you feel so comfortable and contended, Maggie, you could not feel otherwise; it is only when we have lost our home for ever that we can fully realise its value, for my own part I am shure the happiest part of my life was spent with the "Old folks at house", but that is all past and gone, my dear mother gone to rest.'[150]

Despite his reserve, James talked fairly freely to his children. He told them about his own poor but happy childhood and had clearly made them aware of his early atheism and probably discussed such issues with friends coming over from England in their presence. The children were also never antagonistic to him. Both Willie and James, the son from his first marriage, were groomed to take over the business, and even Patrick worked for him after he finished his Intermediate Exams. In one of her letters to James while he was away in Birmingham, Margaret refers to the children talking about him 'every moment in the day', and that Willie who had apparently hurt his arm called for him all the time.[151] Desmond Ryan states that Patrick always spoke with great affection and reverence about his father.[152]

Nevertheless, Ruth Dudley Edwards has concluded that Patrick was not very attached to his father. She bases her contention on the fact that Patrick went back to work within a week of his father's death and that there is no mention of his father's death in the Gaelic League transactions. However, the tendency to return to work so quickly probably had more to do with Patrick's dedication to his work, and the fact he now had the responsibility of being the head of the household and the running of a large business trusted upon him. In private he did receive condolences from colleagues in the League. He thanked Edward Martyn in particular for his 'kind words of sympathy on my father's death'.[153]

There are clear indications Patrick was proud of his father and his own English ancestry. His mother claimed he cherished the fact that his father was English, despite occasionally being taunted with being an 'Englishman'.[154] Desmond Ryan recalls how in hours of depression he picked up his father's pamphlet and read the closing lines and said 'For an Englishman, he was not too bad!' Although the family appeared to have objected when Patrick's cousin on his mother's side married the Protestant Sydney Taverner Shovelton, a fellow of Merton College, Oxford, because of his religion, Patrick told Desmond shortly before the Rising to remember that 'If you ever are free, it is the son of an

Englishman who will have freed you!'[155] He did at one point wonder whether his own reserve and somewhat oppressive impact on others was due to his English blood.[156]

Social life

James's disposition meant that the family had few friends and also few visitors apart from Margaret's immediate relations. The family therefore functioned largely as a self-contained social unit. The only outings mentioned are those to visit relatives: 'To spend a day at Uncle Christy's was always a great event in our lives as it had been in our mother's life before us. ... Their generosity was great; great the cheer of their table and their hearth.'[157] For a while they regularly visited their half-sister Emily but at one point they did not see her for a number of years. Patrick had more interaction with his cousins Mary Kate and John Kelly, the children of his maternal aunt Catherine. They often came to the house and joined in the plays the children staged, and even moved in with the Pearse family in the early 1890s after their parents and grandparents had died. Patrick's sister recalls how he and Mary Kate, who was nearly two years younger, spent their hard saved pennies on travelling the newly built loopline connecting the train lines north and south of the river Liffey. This contact ended when Mary Kate was sent to a boarding school. In a letter to his cousin written at Christmas 1895 Patrick refers to the good times they had had: 'often thinks of jolly times we spent at grandfather's – playing in the hay loft, swinging in the yard, and hiding in the bedrooms. Those days I reckoned among the happiest of my life.' In his autobiography Patrick states that he spent part of his childhood in his maternal grandfather's house. He does not explain why.[158]

James Pearse mostly worked with pals from Birmingham and also socialised almost exclusively with them – especially the M'Gloughlin family, who took him and his children in when his first wife was ill, seemed to have remained very close friends. John M'Gloughlin, an Irishman married to an Englishwoman, was James's best man at his wedding, and eventually Patrick's half-sister Emily married one of their sons, Alf, on 5 July 1884. Indicating the relative wealth of the artisan community originating in Birmingham the wedding was a grand affair. The four-year-old Patrick was the page and carried his half-sister's train when she came out of her carriage and into the church. He distinctly remembers that he wore a claret-coloured velvet suit with white socks and a deep lace collar.

Outside the immediate family and the M'Gloughlins no Irish visitors seem to have frequented the house. However, a small but steady stream of often unusual visitors from England did arrive on their doorstep. The artists and bohemians, which James had acquainted while attempting a career as a professional artist in England in his early days, provided Patrick with an unusual experience as a nude model:

> Many of these visitors made drawings and paintings of me, sometimes of my head only and sometimes of my whole body without any clothes on. They said I had a thoughtful face and that I was very finely shaped. I think what they valued me chiefly for was my faculty of remaining still for a long time. I liked to stand, or better still to lie, without my clothes in the warmth of the fire, and to think out my thoughts. Some of the longest stories I have ever made up about myself were made up while a man was making a picture of me stretched on my face at full length with my chin resting on my hands.

The nude modelling continued until his parents considered him 'too big for such things'.[159]

Other English visitors were members of James's immediate family. His father and brothers visited on a number of occasions, which were memorable for the children: 'Uncle Bill taught us how to make shadows on the wall and Uncle Harry [sent us after he had gone home, a wonderful model in wood] of Powerscourt Waterfall.' Sometimes they brought one or two members of their own families with them. Some of these cousins continued to visit the Pearses occasionally even long after James's death. A few other more distant relations also came to Dublin. A somewhat mysterious Aunt Jane made some unexpected and dramatic appearances, and a cousin named Neald who had been an alcoholic tailor but was called by God to found a new religion, which he did in Manchester, came over once sporting a very long dark brown beard.[160]

James also made frequent visits to England, often taking some of his offspring with him. He liked to go home to Birmingham as the son who had made good. When he was a child he was supposed to have promised his younger brother Henry that: 'When I do well I'll see U all right'. He got on well with his brothers and is supposed to have paid for his father and brothers' trips to Dublin.[161] James always maintained a yearning for Birmingham which he considered 'the greatest city in the world' and planned to return to it to live. In the mid-1880s he invested heavily in stocks and bonds associated with the city, lending a total of £510 to the Borough of Birmingham.[162] Around 1890 he developed serious plans to retire there, which if pursued would certainly have changed Irish history. An important factor in this seems to have been the detrimental effect of the dust associated with the stone work on his family's health. His letters to Margaret in the early phases of their courtship indicate continuous throat problems. Once it was so badly ulcerated he could not see her for days.[163]

When his father died in 1890 James inherited the title to a shop on Bristol Street in Birmingham. He paid off the mortgage of £85 in 1891 and had plans drawn up by a Birmingham architect to have a four-storey house built including a shop and five bedrooms. He thought his wife and daughter Margaret could run a newspaper shop downstairs, like his wife had done before they got married, and he might retire. However, ultimately the plan seems to have faltered upon opposition from Margaret.[164] The issue of Irishness versus Englishness seems to have played a part in this decision according to some of those involved.[165] Nevertheless James probably did not give up on the idea altogether as he kept the original house in Birmingham in his possession. However, the retirement idea was ultimately cut short when James himself died suddenly on one of his visits to Birmingham. The house in Birmingham was then sold but the various branches of the family maintained contact and at least for a while Patrick continued to visit his relatives in England.[166]

School life

Patrick's personality, mixed background and peculiar upbringing certainly ensured that he was not an average boy. Particularly in the working class surroundings of Great Brunswick Street Patrick stood out, not least because of his peculiar accent which contained a lot of English inflection and did not blend in very well with the brogue spoken by most children around him.[167] One of his schoolmates 'regarded P as an odd English rather than Irishman'.[168]

Recognising and reaffirming this difference Patrick and his siblings were not sent to the local National School but received their first formal education at a private institution. Patrick and his sister Margaret started to attend Mrs Murphy's school in Wentworth Place (now Fenian Street) in 1886, when Patrick was seven and Margaret eight. Their half-sister Emily who lived with them until her wedding in 1884 had then already taught them how to spell. A few months after starting school the family decided to move their home to the more leafy surroundings of the Dublin suburb of Sandymount near the sea.[169] This may well be caused by James's concerns over the detrimental effect of the dust on his children's health, in particular of the somewhat sickly last born Mary Bridget, but was also a sure sign that the business was doing well. The children liked their new home in Newbridge Avenue as it gave them whole new areas to explore: 'It had a large garden behind it, and a field behind the garden, and another field across the road opposite.' Their father proudly decorated the gate with a Gothic arch and carved caps giving the impression of an entrance to a church.[170] However, they did not have much time to enjoy their new environment as Patrick soon fell ill with scarlatina and also infected his brother Willie. The sisters were sent back to live in Great Brunswick Street and Aunt Margaret again came out to nurse him.[171]

Within less than three years the family moved back into Great Brunswick Street altogether. The exact reasons for this are unknown but it happened around the time that James's father died and the partnership with Edward Sharp broke up. It may therefore have been part of the plan to move to Birmingham or simply for financial reasons due to the cost of the breakup with Sharp. This may also be behind the decision to take the two boys out of private education and send them to the CBS (Christian Brothers School) at Westland Row in August 1891 for their further education, while Margaret was sent to the Holy Faith nuns.[172] Most of their classmates in the CBS felt the Pearse brothers should never have been sent there, as their accent and general demeanour stood out at this school which was mostly populated with fairly rough working-class kids.[173]

I, Pearse, Martin Ryan, and Murray were in the front desk. Murray's father had a pub but most of the boys were working class, parents in gas coy or corn porters with some children of comfortable off shopkeepers. It was a

rough school – slates were thrown at masters. I saw one being thrown at
Bro Burke. It passed over our desk and Pearse's head and mine.[174]

The fact James was able to pay off the mortgage on the house in
Birmingham he inherited from his father in 1891 seems to weaken
the financial argument. J.A. Duffy, the son of one of James Pearse's
employees who was quite friendly with his boss, thought the decision
to send the two boys to Westland Row CBS was due to his own
achievements at that school: 'It was because he heard that I was
doing so well in the school that James decided to send Patrick to
Westland Row.'[175] Another acquaintance suggested a reason which
may tie in with this: 'I don't believe P's father took the least interest
in the two boys, the school was next door and cheap. I think the
mother had the feeling that religion would be better looked after in
CBS than elsewhere.'[176] James's niece recalls how he bragged that
Patrick's education did not cost him anything due to the prizes and
scholarships Patrick won.[177] In the annual exams of each of the
four years of the Intermediate certificate Patrick indeed won a £20
exhibition and book prizes especially in languages.[178] The strong and
unquestioning Catholicism of his mother possibly combined with the
financial situation give this some credence, but James's strong desire
to improve himself and to move up socially as a family suggests that
he also believed the Christian Brothers would prepare his sons for
a professional career. His willingness to support Patrick's university
studies also indicates this. One of his early biographers suggests the
move to the CBS might also have been intended to change Patrick
from a shy and somewhat weak boy into a self-reliant youth.[179]

It appears that Patrick made little effort to get close to his classmates.
In primary school he was described as a 'singularly quiet, unobtrusive
and studious child. Rather inclined to be shy and diffident Padraic
made little or no effort to befriend other children and shrank visibly
from the roughish type of contact sports and the horseplay which
are generally indulged in by children of this age group.'[180] This was
no different in the CBS: 'He never joined in the ordinary games at
playtime and was always studying. He often climbed up on the high
window-ledge of the school-room and sat there reading.'[181] As a result
he did not really befriend anyone at school: 'No one knew Pearse. I sat
beside him for 4 years in Westland Row but knew nothing of him. He
was aloof.'[182] One of his classmates generously explained the Pearse's

lack of social interaction with other boys by pointing to the fact that the school was so close to their home that they had no opportunity to mix with the others.[183] However, some described him as a sissy or expressed a fear that he would become 'effeminate'; to others he was a disinterested, self-centred and introverted child.[184]

The resulting social isolation was, however, clearly aggravated by the family's attitude. Patrick's mother seems to have felt they were socially superior to the other children, as no other boys were ever invited to their house.[185] At primary school they were taught how to dance, but Patrick was never taught an Irish jig or reel.[186] Their mother's tendency to dress them in a kind of public schoolboy outfit consisting of a tight velvet coat and Eton collar made them potential victims of bullying.[187] Photographs in later years showed they were then dressed more in line with the norm at school, but also portray Patrick as a distinctively nerdy young boy.[188] The fact that Patrick was also in many ways a model pupil only increased the potential feelings of aggression towards him. He was always studying even to the dismay of his parents. 'My son was exceedingly fond of study. In fact, his father could not get him to put his books away even at night-time.'[189] In his schoolwork he already displayed the dogged determination which would later characterise him. His sister recalls various hobbies he took very seriously while they lasted, including becoming a vegetarian because he considered it cruel to eat flesh. However, after having eaten in a vegetarian restaurant for a while he gave up on it.[190]

Overall he was considered one of the quietest and best behaved boys in the school and never got involved in any mischief. At one time he participated in a rough game called 'blocking old fellows' which involved knocking top hats off men in the street. He was recognised by one of the victims and told off by his mother. Afterwards he was never bold again.[191] No one in the school could even imagine him being so. When one of the pupils had broken a shop window nearby, the shopkeeper came into the school and was asked to pick out the culprit from a line-up: 'The irate dauber pointed to Paddy Pearse, as the culprit – upon which all, master & boys laughed in incredulity. Impossible! Everyone said.'[192] The accusation was unlikely due to Patrick's general disposition but also because he was not keen on sports: 'He was never an athlete. They started a football team, soccer, and he was in it but useless, running up & down the side line.'[193] Although enjoying the seaside, it was clear he could not swim. As a boy he was often seen at Merrion standing in the sea, never venturing out further than knee deep. He only tried to learn to swim in Loch Eileabhrach in 1910 with the aid of a rubber tyre.[194] This was apparently unsuccessful as in 1915 he still needed a rope held by his brother.[195] In later years the only sport he participated in was chess.[196] However, Patrick did not like being ridiculed about his lack of athleticism. During a match between Westland Row and Bath Avenue in which Patrick participated he miss-kicked the ball: 'A boy in the small crowd there was watching him & laughed when he saw P. fumble it. P. rushed over & hit the boy in the jaw.'[197]

It is not exactly clear how Patrick maintained himself at school. It was rough and the fact he clearly was an exceptional and hardworking scholar and therefore favoured by the brothers would not necessarily have aided him either.[198] He was rarely punished at school possibly due to his father's objections to this, which led to feelings of injustice among his classmates:

> Bro Burke was severe. During an Easter Holiday of 14 days he gave us 2 inter papers to do (ones of 3 hours each) one for each day of the 14 days. … I did only 4 papers. Bro Walsh brought me out & gave me 23 slaps. I was made to kneel down. I could not work for 2 days. He slapped all round on this occasion. He had given us 24 papers in all to do. When it came to Pearse's turn to be slapped Bro Walsh stopped. It was as if he was exhausted. I never saw Pearse slapped. Pearse had done only 4.[199]

What apparently saved Patrick from serious victimisation by his classmates was his upright attitude; he was uncompromising, loyal and did not pretend to be better than his classmates: 'There was no snobbery about him.'[200] He was also praised for the fact he would speak out when he felt it was needed, and would stand up against the brothers if he felt the cause was right:[201] 'There was irreverence at prayers. P. did not say the phrase objected to. P. said something and Brother boxed him. He refused to hold out his hand and then ran to his father.'[202] Another classmate remembers how he, Patrick, Murray and Martin Ryan got a prize of a silver watch for their achievements in one of the exams. The next year he and Patrick again got exhibitions and expected a similar reward:

We expected a watch each. I was hoping for one as I wanted to give it to my brother. We were given a novel and a religious book. I was 1st at the presentation & I did not take them as I wanted a watch. P was next & he said he wanted a watch too. He just stood by me. The brother said I was a stuck up boy. Next day P & I were given a watch in private each of us. P was not blamed for this – it was said that his conduct was due to my bad influence. He stood by me.[203]

Eamonn O'Neill claims that although shy boys like Patrick were usually unpopular they all liked and respected Patrick 'for they felt that his reserve and shyness were not signs of weakness, but of strength'.[204] The Brothers described him later as 'silent and thoughtful and very reserved in manner. Without any effort he always commanded respect from the boys.'[205]

During his time with the Christian Brothers Patrick was not known for his nationalism. Although his mother and grandaunt had inculcated an Irish outlook, the family was clearly not particularly radical. James Pearse's support for home rule was not a rejection of the connection with Britain, and it was commonly known that the family used to finish up parties with 'God save the Queen'. When they entered Westland Row the Pearse boys had clear signs of an English accent and had no strong nationalist views. They were even considered to be pro-British. In the eyes of their school friends they were certainly not destined for martyrdom in the name of Ireland.[206]

Personality

Patrick was thus not a sociable person. As a child he had been largely engrossed in his own fantasy world together with his family, and at school he kept mostly to himself. In most of the reminiscences his friends and acquaintances tend to describe his activities and demeanour, but rarely depict any interaction with him in any detail. He is invariably discussed from a distance, 'he went there', 'he was there' or 'he made a speech'. He apparently rarely engaged with people or activities but tended to be the observer or outsider. No one recalls him making a social visit to a friend at any time. In the early 1900s Sean O'Casey portrayed him as a man who could even be alone while participating in a procession. 'Trudging along in a wide space by himself came Padruig MacPiarais, head down, dreaming a reborn glory for Ireland in every street stone his foot touched.'[207]

As a result his social skills left much to be desired, and he never betrayed a great ability to empathise with other people's feelings while in direct contact with them: 'Once I was writing in the Gaelic League rooms for his paper. As I wrote he came in and stood there. I could not write with him there so I stopped writing in irritation. He stood looking at me and it seemed as if 10 minutes had passed ere he spoke. He seemed not to realise that he had upset me.'[208] Much of the time Patrick lived in his own world and was often unaware of his surroundings or the impression he made.[209]

> Many of my failures have doubtless been due to the fact that my thoughts and emotions of yesterday, my ordeals and triumphs of tomorrow have always been more to me than my deeds of today the remembered or the imagined experience more insistent than the actual. Often in a world which demands swift and ruthless action I have found myself pausing to catch some far-off sound, the echo of a long silent voice, or to anticipate some unspeakable glory of a new sunrise or moonrise. When people have been talking to me about national policies I have been listening to the flickering of the wings of flies on a window-pane that I once knew; in the midst of military plans and organisation I have been watching myself as a child come out of a certain green gate into a certain sunlit field.[210]

To others he came across as an extremely serious and somewhat arrogant man. His demeanour was variously described as aloof, forbidding, unapproachable, dour, etc., and it was considered very hard to get close to him.[211] He was, however, well aware of the oppressive impact he could have on other people, as is testified in an open letter he wrote to himself in 1912. 'Pearse, you are a reserved person! You do not associate with Gaels. You shun their company. On the occasions when you join them, a black cloud accompanies you which as it were settles over them. Those who were talkative before your arrival grow silent and those who were merry become gloomy.'[212] In later life he also confessed that when he was young he was undoubtedly 'a bit of a prig'.[213]

As an adult he was often mistaken for a priest due to his clean shaven appearance, propensity for black clothes and extremely serious outlook on life. Country children in the West often addressed him as

Father, and even a deliberate change into cycling trousers did not alter this.[214] He was always very particular about his appearance, ensuring that his hair or clothes were never out of place. Some considered him vain or a bit of a poseur, but this was probably born out of insecurity over the impression he made on others. From a young age he sleeked back his hair to give himself a learned academic air, to banish 'the thought that he was a clerk in the accountant General's office'.[215]

Basically Patrick was a shy person, particularly in front of women.[216] His growing involvement in the public arena was propelled by a burning desire to advance the causes he believed in. 'Two things have constantly pulled at cross purposes in me; one a deep homing instinct, a desire beyond all words to be at home always with the same beloved faces, the same familiar shapes and sounds about me; the other an impulse to seek hard things to do, to go on far quests and fight for lost causes. And neither thing, neither the quiet home life nor the perilous adventure, has ever brought me any content.'[217] This strong urge to express himself is reminiscent of his father's secret career as a pamphlet writer, but he continued to be pulled towards the quiet life. When he became fully engaged in public debate he lamented: 'Wouldn't it be a grand thing to have no ambition whatsoever, and be a clerk with £2 a week? Yes, I should enjoy that, no worries and ease among my books.'[218]

The opposing forces caused a lot of internal tension in Patrick. His physical behaviour betrayed a constant nervousness, even around his family: 'He had a curious habit, when drinking tea, of walking about a room with quick, nervous steps, and lightly tapping the side of his cup with the middle finger.'[219] The same nervous tick was displayed when speaking to others: 'He would talk starting with a snort & then tap with his foot & then tip right hand on left in front.'[220] He tended to show a hesitancy even when speaking to people socially as if he was on a platform.[221] Much of this tension was due to his self-consciousness: 'I am not sure whether it is a good thing for a man to possess as fully as I have possessed it the faculty of getting, as it were, outside of himself and of contemplating himself as if from a little distance.'[222]

He was particularly shy about his left eye which had a cast which apparently was hereditary in the family.[223] Probably in an effort to be more heroic, he told Jerome Cronin, one of his pupils at St Enda's, that this was caused by an accident while hunting with his father as a boy: '"I got on to the target." He explained. "Then pressed the trigger – like this, click (he made a sucking noise). Instantly there was a flash of red in my eye, and the pain was so intense that I thought I was going to faint. But I recovered, wiped the blood away, and went home to let my mother patch it up."'[224]

For the rest of his life he tried to hide the disfigurement, which appeared as a squint, by bending his head and looking at people sideways, most notoriously reflected in his insistence on only being photographed from the right.[225] In public he raised his chin looking down on people which made him appear arrogant and somewhat sly, not aided by his inability to engage in small talk and repartee:[226] 'A man said to me "I don't like that man. He can't look U straight in the face".'[227] 'He did not repel you consciously but he never looked at you. I once used the phrase "his half averted eyes".'[228] Those who knew him better also saw his human side: 'many people think him very haughty and proud; not, of course, those who know him, but people who meet him casually'.[229] His weak handshake also did not endear him to those he was introduced to: 'He gave a cold, clammy handshake & let one's hand drop.'[230] Apart from his nervous demeanour and eye disfigurement, he had a stutter as a young man[231] and moved around somewhat awkwardly: 'He had a queer springy step when he walked.'[232]

His desire to further his causes made him overcome these impediments, which were particularly strong when speaking in public for larger audiences. A friend observed him at what he thought was Patrick's first speech at an Aeridheacht in Blackrock Park:

> He was obviously nervous and shook in every limb, but was so obviously and terribly in earnest and conquered or disregarded his trembling frame so well that the crowd listened and if not impressed were somewhat edified – at least I was – and I noticed the quavers gradually left his voice though not his legs & he finished forcibly and well.[233]

Although contemporaries claim he could recite well,[234] there is much debate about whether Patrick was a good speaker. His niece in Birmingham remembers him preach a sermon wonderfully at nine years of age standing proudly beside his father.[235] However, not everybody was impressed at Patrick's early speechmaking which made little impact and was considered too contrived.[236] 'The lecturer is quite a young man with a peculiar, jerky, pistol-shot-like delivery that becomes trying to listen to after a time as it makes him hack his sentences into single words and destroys the sense of his remarks.'[237] His slow and intense delivery necessitated by his lisp and stutter could sometimes be painful to listen to. 'I have heard him speak from the platform and I can assure you that the idea that some, who have read but not heard his addresses, have now that he was a passionate and trumpet-toned orator is all wrong, if only for the reason that a powerful voice was not part of his physical endowment.'[238]

His passion nevertheless convinced those with a positive outlook even in his early days, as became clear during one of his first orations for the renowned Irish scholar Fr Eugene O'Growney who died in 1899. His delivery was described as: 'not impressive, being grave, slow and deliberate. At times the pauses were painful, the stresses and the rhetorical questions too pedagogic, the stilted phraseology bordering on the banal.' When the public became restless Patrick became more emotional and with the use of quotations from Shakespeare, Cicero, Grattan, Parnell, Balfour and Birrell he managed to move his audience which showed its appreciation.[239] A similar experience was described by the writer C.P. Curran who attended a lecture in 1897: 'The black he habitually wore added to his youth and gravity. His speech was slow and his rare gestures deliberate. One was held by his evident conviction and I may add by the side-long carriage of his head and the slight cast of one of his eyes. He spoke with apparent authority invoking the great names of Irish history.' Curran found Patrick less impressive in private: 'there was something almost childlike, in the direct simplicity of his talk. There was nothing subtle or brilliant in it but just enough humour to show that he was not simple-minded.'[240]

Although the small successes in his early days stimulated Patrick to study the art of oratory more intensely they also went a bit to his head. After a speech he gave in name of the Gaelic League at a Celtic meeting in Cardiff in 1899 this became obvious in a conversation with Osborn Bergin, one of the Belfast delegates:

> I said in Cardiff 'You speak freely.' He said, 'It is no credit to me to speak well. I have to speak every week at the G.L.' I had not said he had spoken well. He spoke there in Irish and English. The Welsh were aroused at his solemnity and were making up epigrams in Welsh about us. They were asking us what name we would each like. He said Railir (orator). He was no orator.[241]

Later Patrick would concur with Bergin's assessment, remarking to Desmond Ryan: 'Well, I thought then I was an orator.'[242]

Aware of the lack of natural talent, Patrick had always worked hard on improving his skills as a public speaker. He took every opportunity to speak at school, debating societies, the Gaelic League or any other occasion. He also made a distinct effort to improve his presentation, practising in front of a mirror and later with his pupils as an audience. In 1908 he even bought a phonogram on which he recorded his speeches, as well as fake interviews he did with celebrities and business managers.[243] He studied rhetoric and Yeats' use of language closely and changed the pitch of his voice to sound more solemn.[244] In his early speeches he claimed to have shied away from too much rhetoric stating in 1900 that: 'Naked facts speak with an eloquence more moving than the rhetoric of orators.'[245] To overcome his nerves Patrick also prepared his speeches extremely well, unable to speak ad lib.

> In New York P. and I were to speak. The chairman was speaking. I was to speak next, then P. he whispered, 'What line are you taking?' I told him and he grew pale and said 'My God. That is my line.' I said 'change it'. He said 'I can't'. I had begun on a dray in Belfast and had no difficulty. So I said 'I'll change' which I did. He spoke his prepared speech.[246]

Gradually his speeches became more dramatic but they were highly rehearsed and strictly choreographed.[247] 'He had definite views on diction, articulation and the varying tempo of an address. He was convinced that soft-oh, very very soft – and very slow speech, with here and there a flash of drama, or of pathos, travelled farther, deeper. In fact, reached not only the ears of the audience, but their hearts.'[248] He began to excite the audiences, most famously at the oration at the graveside of the old Fenian O'Donovan Rossa in 1915.[249]

Although some were genuinely impressed, the judgement of his biographer, Xavier Carty, of his abilities in this area seems to be accurate: 'It was the conviction and the strength of his personality rather than the quality of his oratory that impressed Pearse upon listeners. Although he worked hard at techniques of public speaking and rehearsed carefully beforehand he never overcame a lisp which forced him to speak slowly and carefully. His delivery was ponderous and heavy.'[250] Nevertheless Patrick was convinced of the impact of his oratory. Speaking about himself in 1912 he stated: 'You have the gift of eloquence. You have the power to move and arouse audiences when you speak publicly. You can make them cry or laugh as you wish.'[251] The only one who would disagree openly at that stage was his brother Willie who berated him for one of his performances around that time. 'Pat, you made a rotten speech this evening. You repeated yourself and dragged on and on until the poor people were bored stiff!'[252]

The picture that emerges from the testimony above of Patrick as a self-centred, somewhat neurotic young man does not explain his success as a Gaelic League activist, schoolmaster and revolutionary leader. Some of the criticism can be accounted for by the fact that particularly in later live he gave his opponents plenty of ammunition to malign him, causing some exaggerated estimations: 'I thought Pearse a degenerate, a witless man with an over-emotionalised nature who really ought to have been certified in his youth. The whole family was mawkish and maudlin.'[253] In an open letter written to himself in May 1912 he already doubted whether anybody liked him: 'I am undecided as to whether I like you or not. I wonder does anyone like you. I do know that many dislike you. I never heard anyone say "I like Pearse".'[254]

However, he was also a man who was appreciated by those around him for his gentleness, energy and unselfishness. This endeared him to his immediate family and friends, many of whom express their fondness for him.[255] Although occasionally showing a bad temper as a young man and getting in a few fights, he was certainly not a violent man.[256] While he claimed to enjoy hunting he detested cruelty to animals. No one who knew him could imagine him killing any living thing, not even a rabbit let alone a human being. He is supposed to have stopped work in the garden for a day after he accidentally killed a worm. One of his pupils in St Enda's remembers how he opposed the use of the cane in the classroom and that when he was convinced there was no alternative he would 'cringe and tremble each time the swish of the cane was heard'.[257]

To appreciate his softer side one had to get close to him, 'many people think him very haughty and proud; not, of course, those who know him, but people who meet him casually'.[258] Mary Hayden later described him as 'most companionable, a really nice fellow'.[259] This discrepancy between his public image and his internal life is expressed quite well by Patrick himself in an article in *Irish Freedom* of June 1913:

I am visibly poor, but am merry only in an esoteric or secret sense, exhibiting to the outer world an austerity of look and speech more befitted my habitation than my heart. Understand that, however harshly I may express myself in the comments and proposals I shall from time to time make here, I am in reality a genial and large-hearted person, and that if I chasten my fellows it is only because I love them.[260]

Sometimes he was able to express these warm feelings in his letters. He responded particularly well to the exuberant hospitality shown him when he visited the United States. 'I am not a very sociable person, but I did feel intimate and at home in your circle, and can hardly imagine now that I did not know any of you three months ago. ... I came home somewhat richer in purse and much richer in memories of friends made in New York.'[261]

Patrick's somewhat pessimistic outlook on life – 'I often think there are far more sorrows than joys in life, and every joy is soon extinguished by a grief' – obviously came across in his dealings with others.[262] There was nevertheless also a lighter side to him. Again this was only seen by those who knew him well. With them he occasionally engaged in light conversation in a jolly atmosphere.[263] His sister asserted that he 'would appreciate a joke against himself more than anyone I ever knew'.[264] Outsiders remarked on the fact that they never heard him joke, but others recognised that he 'had a sense of humour deep down'.[265] Although bright, he was not quick witted. His sense of humour was either simple or intelligent. Close associates like Michael Dowling remember how he 'roared with delight' when his mother put on a mask at Halloween,[266] while others remember his acid wit particularly where it concerned John McNeill in the final stages of his life.[267] He did not like the more bawdy humour of the streets: 'Anything coarse disgusted him; from a doubtful story or jest he shrank as from a blow; never, in all the years I knew him, did I hear from his lips the mildest swear word'.[268] But he frequently used irony in his journalistic and political writings.

His energetic nature also appealed to those around him. He rarely saw the difficulties in the often grand plans he came up with. Throughout his life he considered the objective all important and was rarely concerned about practicalities,[269] for example his tendency to be late for everything, from getting up in the morning to arriving at functions even if he spoke at them himself.[270] To him, trying to achieve something was always more important than the likelihood of success. 'At least we are doing something' was one of his favourite lines. This became apparent when Patrick joined a committee formed in 1907 to organise a national exhibition: 'Pearse always made optimistic suggestions. They would examine them & he would always agree that his suggestion was not workable. He would listen very patiently & reason the thing out and each suggestion was rejected and he would accept the ruling and then make another suggestion equally impracticable.'[271]

Most importantly Patrick seemed to have had a certain draw which made people accept and follow him, despite the less attractive aspects of his personality. There appeared to be something forceful about him and some felt it was difficult to refuse him a request.[272] On meeting him for the first time Desmond Ryan considered him humourless and priggish but when the fire and determination which was hiding within him came out he argued Patrick put a spell on those around him.[273] Even admirers acknowledged this juxtaposition. In a pamphlet commemorating the leaders of the 1916 Rising he was described as not handsome, with no particular charm of manner 'but he won his way almost always and those that had been in the beginning least attracted by his presence or by his proposals were often found to their own astonishment to be very soon his most loyal and obedient henchmen'.[274]

From an early age he had a certain gravity and strength of conviction. During a visit to Wales in 1898 he was remembered for refusing to believe that Pope Adrian IV had handed over Ireland to Henry II to convert the natives despite the existence of a papal bull to that effect.[275] He displayed the same single-mindedness in the Gaelic League: 'He would listen carefully to opinions of Coiste Gnotha [the Gaelic League central committee] and would seem to agree but always did what he liked particularly in regard to the paper no matter how much he seemed to be impressed. He always printed what he liked.'[276] As a teacher he liked to provoke his pupils into all kinds of debates but his own mind was invariably made up: 'Upon certain subjects, political and religious, he adopted a very decided attitude, held them as dogmas, and made those who were rash enough to argue the latter out, feel rather foolish with his emphatic "No, it's not so; it's not so."'[277] Although influenced by arguments put forward, he would rarely change his mind regarding any issue he had decided upon.

Patrick was almost ascetic in his personal habits. His dedication to his causes which was widely appreciated allowed little time for entertainment. In line with his father's motto that labour concurs all, he worked almost constantly, was a member of the Pioneers, did not smoke and had just one cup of tea a day, albeit in a giant willow-patterned mug. He used to wear the same black clothes until they were worn down and rarely indulged himself. His main entertainment consisted of having tea in Mylis on Westland Row and frequent visits to the theatre, where he showed a prolific international taste.[278] He enjoyed drama, particularly Shakespeare, but also operas, in particular Wagner, and the marches of the American composer and conductor John Philip Sousa, who he saw perform in Dublin.[279] During his visits abroad, to Paris in 1900, Brussels in 1905 and frequent visits to England, he showed a great appetite for new cultural experiences. During his visit to Belgium he wore his sister Margaret out with his full programme of visits to museums, art galleries, monuments, etc., and put her to the test with his desire to try new sensations like Chinese food. He told her he went abroad to see 'pictures and people'.[280] In his story *Eoineen of the Birds*, dating from 1905, this interest in far away places combined with a strong celebration of home life is most clearly exposed.[281]

It is clear Patrick had two sides to his personality, one shown to outsiders which often repulsed people and one for intimae which inspired strong feelings of affection and dedication. In the open letter he wrote to himself in May 1912 he showed this was something he was conscious of:

I imagine that there are two Pearses, one a cheerless, wintry person and the other pleasant, calm and serene. The calm serene person is seen all too seldom. On public platforms and in Sgoil Éanna [his school] he is most often seen. The dull cheerless person is frequently to be seen. He is not a pleasant type. I do not like him. I grow chill when I see him. The funny aspect of this is that I am not sure which is the real Pearse, the gloomy or the bright one.[282]

Social engagements with strangers made him feel extremely uncomfortable, but when he felt at home with his company, especially with children, or was in total control of his persona, as during a public speech, he was relatively relaxed. From a young age Patrick had a tendency to want to please those around him and shied away from confrontation. He clearly had a somewhat obsessive personality and when he became involved in something he would be completely dedicated to it. Some of his lack of social skills and awkwardness was probably due to his self-conscious nature. He was clearly very intelligent, and had an unusual tendency for reflection on his own behaviour and personality which made him hard to understand for others. This kind of disturbed socialisation is often associated with those who become involved in political violence motivated by strong ideological conviction.[283]

Sexuality

Patrick's personality and the fact that he never raised a family of his own has brought up the thorny subject of his sexuality. There is no proof he ever had a relationship with a woman. His shyness around women which is mentioned by many observers does, however, seem to indicate a certain amount of internal tension caused by an inability to approach potential objects of his desire. He acknowledged such problems as a sixteen-year-old boy in a letter to his cousin Mary Kate: 'it is natural for a boy to feel a little embarrassed when writing to one of the opposite sex even though she is his cousin'.[284] In the plays he wrote for his siblings as a very young boy heterosexual love and passion were central themes. This was, however, probably simply an imitation of the plays he saw and read. When he became a teenager these themes disappeared from his writings and when he had to act romantic parts in Shakespeare's plays he always had to laugh uncontrollably when he had to use endearing terms to his sister who played the leading female part.[285] This shyness nevertheless indicates a heterosexual development in the maturing Patrick.

As an adult he still exhibited the same features. 'He was always excessively shy in the presence of young women, and soon I had the gloating satisfaction of hearing him, following a magnificent oratorical opening, stammering and "er-er-ing" and shuffling his feet at increasingly frequent intervals. ... "I hope your sister didn't think me an ass," said he to me a few days later.'[286] Patrick was indeed well aware of his own awkwardness in these situations. Michael Dowling recalls Patrick's comment on his brother Liam: 'Liam liked girls &

was at ease with them. "Liam na urban" he called him. "How easy he seems with them" said he of Liam "I never could do that".'[287]

Patrick nevertheless had close friendships with a number of women particularly through the Gaelic League.[288] He even went on a holiday to Connemara with the seventeen years older Mary Hayden in 1903: 'Hester and I dare say others, didn't think my coming with him over proper: however I came and *he* at least seems to have had no hesitation about accepting the situation as a matter of course, which is a blessing. We talk a lot on all sorts of subjects.' Afterwards Patrick picked her up from the train on her return a few days after his and 'wheeled the laden bicycle right across town'.[289] It is, however, clear from their correspondence that there was no sexual aspect to their relationship, and Patrick did not even seem to have considered the possibility.

To explain the absence of romantic liaisons Patrick's extreme idealisation of women has been put forward. 'Akin to his love of children and idealising of them was Pearse's attitude towards women. Their lower or even their lighter side he very little understood, though he had many women friends. ... He looked on the purity, the power of self-sacrifice which is to be found more commonly among women than in men as something divine.'[290] Mary Hayden even felt compelled to stand up for men as he was so hard on them.[291] In his early writings he did indeed idealise the love of a woman: 'Next to love of God and love of country, love of woman is the noblest feeling that can stir men's souls!'[292] To Patrick women could therefore be seen as untouchables, something to worship or love from afar. In his story *The Singer* women are portrayed as higher than men, too full of care. He compared them to teachers, giving all and getting little back. In *The Mother* he portrays mothers as being closer to God. Some have stressed the dominating influence of his mother which stunted his sexual development. Many contemporaries refer to the restrictive influence of the Pearse women whom surrounded Patrick.[293]

The childlike bond he had with his brother Willie, most famously exposed in their private baby language described by Desmond Ryan as 'weird in the extreme', seems to indicate a similar stunted emotional development. In their teens they also had a habit of going into town dressed up as women. This does not necessarily indicate a latent transvestism as it was quite common among young men, but does show an unusual childlike behaviour.[294] It has recently also been suggested that the absence of romantic interest might be explained by a neurological disorder. It is of course impossible to diagnose such a condition retrospectively, and although Patrick displays a number of the symptoms associated with autism or more particular Asperger syndrome to a degree, he also had some character traits which would preclude such a conclusion – in particular his extremely well-developed fantasy life as a child seems to be critical in this regard.[295]

There is nevertheless one woman with whom Patrick is often romantically associated in adult life. This was Eveleen Nicholls, a language enthusiast and UCD (University College Dublin) graduate who had been elected to the Coiste Gnotha and was described as 'tall and stately'.[296] Many believe Patrick was in love with her, feelings she apparently did not reciprocate.[297] The truth of this is hard to ascertain as Eveleen died early in 1909 during a swim with her friend, Kate Crohan, in the sea off the Blasket Islands in Co. Kerry. Kate's brother drowned trying to rescue Eveleen while Kate was rescued by Patrick Kearney. Reports of the events were confused and in Dublin people thought that Eveleen had drowned trying to rescue Kate or even some children. In retrospect some of Patrick's contemporaries are very clear and adamant about Patrick's love. Jerome Cronin, one of Patrick's pupils, recalls how Patrick became emotional when Jerome spoke about his native county Kerry: 'It is my county of grief, as Galway is my county of joy, Kerry. He told me the only woman he loved "lost her life in a gallant attempt to save the lives of little children from the sea that licked the Kerry coast." "Somehow I could never care for another woman as I cared for her", he added simply.'[298] Some have even stated that Pearse was unofficially engaged to Eveleen.

Edwards has pointed to the 'In Memoriam' Patrick wrote for her in the League paper. 'It is not in human nature to write a glib newspaper article on a dead friend. One dare not utter all that is in one's heart, and in the effort at self-restraint one is apt to pen only cold and formal things.' Still under the misapprehension she died saving another girl's life he went on to say:

> Her grand dower of intellect, her gracious gifts of charm and sympathy, her capacity for affairs, were known to all, but those who knew her best know that these were the least of her endowments. What will stand out clear and radiant in their mental picture of her is the loftiness of her soul, the inner sanctity of her life. The close of that life has been worthy of it. If she had

been asked to choose the manner of her death she would surely have chosen it thus. She died to save another, and that other a young Irish-speaking girl … Her life was consecrated to the service of higher things.[299]

Much can be read into this but it was written in his official capacity as editor of the Gaelic League journal writing about a fellow member of the executive whose death had distressed many in the Irish language community. Patrick consequently had to say nice things and it is striking he turns her death into a sacrifice for the cause. This attitude is confirmed by Patrick's sister Mary Brighid who recalls how Patrick took solace in the manner of her dying:

'She was wonderful!' my brother continued. 'The night before she died she had a strange premonition of her death. … She saved a life and made the supreme sacrifice.'

'It was tragic!' I whispered.

'It was glorious – wonderful!' he said, in vibrant tones. 'A weak, delicate girl, yet with so strong a soul! She knew she was going to meet death and went swiftly, gladly. But now she will never come back!'.[300]

Some contemporaries noticed a change in Patrick's behaviour after Eveleen's death: 'P. never laughed afterwards.' They saw a reorientation in his life towards a higher calling which could explain Patrick's apparent lack of interest in romantic liaisons afterwards.[301] This seems to be confirmed in some of his writing. In the poem 'I have not Garnered Gold' he portrays someone that has never looked for fortune and lost fame and love: 'The fame I found hath perished; In love I got but grief That withered my life' points in this direction.[302] In his story *The Singer* the main character MacDara is tempted by physical beauty but sees it as an unholy thing distracting him from his cause: 'I tried to keep my heart virginal; and sometimes in the street of a city when I have stopped to look at the white limbs of some beautiful child, and have felt the pain that the sight of great beauty brings, I have wished that I could blind my eyes so that I might shut out the sight of everything that tempted me.' The same sentiment is expressed in the poem 'Renunciation' where the writer closes himself off from physical beauty, music, lust and desire to dedicate himself to the cause:

> I blinded my eyes,
> And I closed my ears,
> I hardened my heart
> And I smothered my desire

So Patrick can easily be seen as a shy heterosexual whose hesitantly expressed desire for women had been killed off by the death of his great love, and which has been sublimated into a struggle for national independence.[303] However, some historians have claimed that his romantic involvement with Eveleen is a story invented to sanitise the memory of one of the founding fathers of the Irish State. First, they point to the absence of any mention of Eveleen in the first biography of Pearse written in the early 1920s.[304] Second, there is much circumstantial evidence in Patrick's own writings, in which he sets himself against any intention to marry. In an undated reply to such a statement Mary Hayden wrote to him: 'No, I don't want you to have such a future as you plan for yourself. ... There is a part of human nature that asks for human relationships and human sympathies. If I go to Rosmuck as a white haired old lady (the white hair is coming fast already) I hope it will be to find you settled as paterfamilias, with children not adopted. However, there is time enough.'[305] In response to another friend announcing her intention to get married in 1913 Patrick stated: 'I do not intend to follow your advice nor your example. If I go to America, I do hope to bring back some money – but should there be a lady associated with the money, I will abandon both the lady and the money.'[306]

Some writers have also contrasted the 'In Memoriam' Patrick wrote for Eveleen with his description of another Gaelic League activist, Michael Breathnach, president of Connacht College, who died in his late twenties of consumption almost a year before Eveleen. In this Patrick emphasises Michael's physique, an element totally absent in his description of Eveleen. According to Patrick, Michael Walsh was 'a figure slender and almost boyish but held erect with what a grace and dignity! Recall then the kindling red in the pale cheek, the light in the large soft eye, the spirituality of the whole countenance, the noble gesture of the shapely head with its crown of dark brown clustering hair.' 'He was only a boy then, very straight and slender and comely, with a virginal face and a voice that we thought was the softest and sweetest we had ever heard.'[307] The fondness for young men which speaks from these words has been remarked on by many. A similar tendency to describe the physique of male characters, especially boys, and not of female characters can be found in his writing.[308] Much of his prose and poetry also has a homoerotic quality, eulogising the body of young boys as a symbol of innocence, purity or sacrifice. In his play *The Master* Iollann, the central figure, is described as 'more like a little maid, with his fair cheek that reddens when the Master speaks to him. ... He has a beautiful white body and therefore you all love him; aye, the Master and all. We have no woman here and so make love to our little Iollann.'[309] In much of his writing this is combined with Christian symbolism and later on with a yearning for the physical arrival of the body of Christ.

There is only one poem in Patrick's oeuvre that explicitly expresses love for a real woman.[310] 'O Lovely Head', often seen as being about Eveleen:

> O lovely head of the woman that I loved,
> In the middle of the night I remember thee
> But reality returns with the sun's whitening,
> Alas, that the slender worm gnaws thee to-night.
>
> Beloved voice, that wast low and beautiful,
> Is it true that I heard thee in my slumbers!
> Or is the knowledge true that tortures me?
> My grief, the tomb hath no sound or voice?[311]

However, the poem was written five years after her death and Patrick's poetry usually had an immediacy connected to actual events. The only other example of a heterosexual longing is contained in his story *The Singer* in which the hero shields himself from the physical attraction of women to fulfil his destiny. There is also no reason to single out this poem as expressing his personal desire in contrast to the much greater number of examples where Patrick idealises the love of boys.

Ruth Dudley Edwards and others have pointed in particular at Patrick's poem 'Little Lad of the Tricks' in which the following verses leave little to the imagination and clearly seem to point in a paedophile direction:

> Little lad of the tricks,
> Full well I know
> That you have been in mischief:
> Confess your fault truly
>
> I forgive you, child
> Of the soft red mouth:
> I will not condemn anyone
> For a sin not understood
>
> Raise your comely head
> Till I kiss your mouth:
> If either of us is the better of that
> I am the better of it
>
> There is a flagrance in your kiss
> That I have not found yet
> In the kisses of women
> Or in the honey of their bodies[312]

The term 'lad' was associated with homoerotic poetry,[313] while the references to physical love indicate a desire for intimacy with boys. The 'sin not understood' can be read as a reference to homosexual longing, which becomes more obvious in the last two verses:

> Lad of the grey eyes,
> That flush in thy cheek
> Would be white with dread of me
> Could you read my secrets
>
> He who has my secrets
> Is not fit to touch you:
> Is not that a pitiful thing,
> Little lad of the tricks?

Similar 'desires of my heart' torture the character in Patrick's poem 'Why Do Ye Torture Me?' Edwards has famously concluded that Patrick was a homosexual with a liking for young boys, but who was not fully aware of his own orientation. Dick Hayes, a contemporary, concurred. Talking about Patrick he referred to him as 'A mhic og na gcleas' (Little Lad of the Tricks).[314]

Other historians and literary scientists have rejected these claims and stated too much has been read into Patrick's writings. They have pointed at the danger associated with taking too personal an interpretation of poetry and referred to the tradition in the Irish-speaking areas of Ireland of men kissing each other on the lips. This is also often referred to in Patrick's own writings.[315] Furthermore, there was a homoeroticism in much of the literature and poetry of that period which, looking back at ancient Greece and Rome, eulogised, even eroticised, male beauty and youth.[316] Patrick directly refers to this in his writing. He likened the ancient Irish to the ancient Greeks. His description of Irish men of antiquity clearly shows this same eulogising: 'splendid specimens of manhood ... Big boned and sinewy, but without an ounce of spare flesh; broad in the shoulders, thin in the flank ... as tithe as greyhounds.'[317]

According to Patrick pre-Christian Ireland valorised youthful masculinity and appreciated the natural beauty of the nude male body. Men often bathed together, youth wore little or no formal clothing and 'a cultured Gael would no more have been shocked at the sight of ... a nude young lad' or of 'a nude athlete or warrior than would a cultured Greek of the days of Socrates'. He also alleged that the favourite game of the mythological Gaelic hero Cúchulainn and the Red Branch was to try to pull each other's clothes off. He believed the horror of comely nakedness was a British and imperial invention, and indeed many dedicated Irish-Irelanders slept in the nude as they believed the old Gaels had done.[318] To Patrick and the Victorians children were innocent and spiritually pure; the celebration of their bodies and innocence had no sexual connotation. The same had applied to the episodes in the 1880s when Patrick himself posed nude for his father's artist friends. In many of Patrick's stories Irish-speaking boys offer redemption in opposition to spiritual uncertainties of adult monks and saints.

Some of Patrick's friends, however, appear to have made Patrick aware before publication that the intentions of the above-mentioned poem might be misconstrued. Patrick rejected this and refused to stop publication. To him boys represented Irishness and spiritual integrity; the 'Irish speaking child is the most important living thing in Ireland today'. A child is capable of revealing to the rest of Ireland 'the real

Ireland which has hitherto been concealed'.[319] Reactions to the poem were generally positive and the sexual aspect was apparently only mentioned among Irish speakers. In an article published in *The Irish Monthly* in 1922 the poem is quoted as proof of his love of children without any sexual connotation. The kiss on the lips is seen as a way to attain the pure and holy status of children which is unlike the sullied and tainted state of adults.[320]

This points to a very different sensibility concerning the expressions of love for boys and admiration of their physiques than would now be acceptable. Patrick provides a more direct example of his attitude when he explains his reasons for setting up a boys' boarding school in the school magazine:

> Various high and patriotic motives have been assigned to me by generous well-wishers in the press and elsewhere. I am conscious of one motive only, namely, a great love of boys, of their ways, of their society; with a desire, born of that love, to help as many boys as possible to become good men. To me a boy is the most interesting of all living things, and I have for years found myself coveting the privilege of being in a position to mould or help to mould, the lives of boys to noble ends.[321]

Many contemporaries remarked on the fact that the socially challenged Patrick could only relax fully in the presence of children: 'It was in the world of children, animals, birds and flowers that Pearse was most at home. He loved all of these with a love at once intense and general.'[322] It has been argued that this can be explained by his extreme shyness and a sense of social inferiority in company of people like Yeats and Lady Gregory. In his stories he tends to idealise the innocence and sinlessness of boys who can thereby reach a higher stage of spirituality. In his early stories, like *Íosagán*, he consistently argued that the love of boys can one bring closer to God.[323]

However, it is not just an idealisation of young boys that drove Patrick. His special fondness for boys was observed by his pupils. Patrick certainly seemed to have a tendency to favour good looking boys. Following a tour of Donegal in support of the League he wrote to his fellow traveller Francis Joseph Bigger with a request for a photo of one of the boys he had met on the way. 'I should be grateful if you could send me another copy of the photo in which I am standing. I have a gradh for the little boy in the forefront of the group on my right and I should like to send him a copy.'[324] There is a story stemming from 1902 in which he undressed and shared a bed with a boy while in Connemara.[325] In school he also showed clear favouritism: 'Pearse was very attracted by Frank [Dowling] who was very good looking. The women didn't like this and put up rivals and after 1st year he dropped Frank.'[326] Patrick also wrote parts in his plays for specific pupils, and it is striking he never wrote a play for girls. In 1913 he acknowledged this. 'I must write a play with a girl heroine. I have an idea for one in my mind, but am too busy to work it out.'[327]

This favouritism was even more apparent when Jerome Cronin did not return to school from his home in Tralee after the summer holidays because the family was in some disarray after the death of his father. Although Jerome prevailed on his mother to keep him home, Patrick came by train to Kerry to convince him to return. He made this more attractive by offering him a job as paid secretary: 'P did not really require a secretary & could ill afford to pay one',[328] but Jerome agreed. From the testimony of other former pupils it becomes clear that Patrick did express his penchant for boys openly to them: 'Pearse used to kiss the young boys. He tried to kiss me but I would not have it.'[329] Some of the Fianna boys referred to Patrick as 'Kiss me Hardy' after a character in the introduction of *John Bull's other Island*.[330] Seamus O'Sullivan claimed this was widely known: 'Pearse was under a cloud because it was known that he used to kiss boys in his school',[331] putting it more bluntly: 'Pearse made love to his boy pupils.'[332]

Nevertheless, there is no proof that Patrick's activities went beyond kissing, which could still be interpreted as an extreme expression of idealised love and not lust. In his poem 'To a Beloved Child' the kissing of a child expresses the sadness felt over the inevitable aging process. In discussing his connection with the more openly homosexual Roger Casement and Francis Joseph Bigger one of Patrick's pupils never mentioned potential advances from Patrick, indicating his sexuality was not a topic as far as he was concerned: 'I knew Casement. I was good looking. I was with him in Bigger's in Belfast. I never knew Casement to make overtures. They said the same thing about Bigger. I slept with Bigger & there was never anything.'[333] Most recent historians have nevertheless more or less agreed with the conclusion that 'Pearse was a homosexual who sublimated his erotic desire for the male body into his work, his writing and his politics'.[334]

To explain the lack of sexual activity Elaine Sisson has claimed that it is unlikely that Patrick envisioned the possibility of sexual relations between men due to his orthodox Catholic background, his highly principled disciplined life and the sheltered conservative social circles he moved in. In the absence of a gay identity at that time she has even suggested that he probably would not have known what to do or suppressed the possibility of having gay sex.[335] Being well acquainted with the case of Oscar Wilde and the stringent sexual mores of Victorian times, this would make Patrick uncharacteristically naïve, and it is clear he was not interested in men but in boys. It could also be argued that Patrick's interest in boys and their way of life was not sexual but stemmed from his own inability as a young boy to join in with 'the society' of young boys. He thus longed for something he never obtained as a child. In a sense he had fallen in love with boys as a representation of Ireland, a feeling so strong he had to kiss them but not make love to them. In this way Patrick also had a kind of stunted sexual development.[336]

One can thus support several conflicting lines of interpretation on the basis of the sources, including both a heterosexual love and a homoerotic longing for young men and boys. Some of his writing may well be explained by what was current in society at that time, but other aspects have been neglected or highlighted because they do or do not concur with an idealised version of Pearse. As with many gay people in a gay-unfriendly environment Patrick's expressions of love for women may well have been an attempt to show socially more acceptable forms of sexuality – more acceptable to others as well as to himself. He clearly also idealised women although his love for them had no physical aspect. Although it will not be possible to ascertain whether Patrick was a latent or active paedophile, beyond his tendency to kiss boys, it seems most probable he was sexually inclined this way.

Early career

When Patrick finished his Intermediate Exams in 1896 he was sixteen and had no clear direction. Most of his schoolmates joined the civil service but Patrick despised such a career.[337] Fr McGill, one of the priests at City Quay, urged Patrick to do the same, but Patrick considered this 'soul destroying'.[338] He had been awarded a scholarship to university but could only sit the matriculation, the entrance exam to university, when he was eighteen. As this was still two years away he had to find an occupation. In this respect the Christian Brothers came to his aid. They were looking for an Irish teacher; Irish was made a compulsory subject in secondary school in the year Patrick finished his exams. His interest and achievements in the Irish language – he had the second highest mark for 'Celtic' in the country – made him a suitable person to fill this vacancy. Straight after his exams the Christian Brothers appointed him a tutor of Irish. This was his main occupation until he passed the matriculation in June 1898. His job with the Christian Brothers only required him to teach a few hours each day, and allowed him plenty of spare time to aid his father with administrative work, join in with the activities of the language movement and prepare for his studies.[339]

According to his student testimony Patrick became a junior freshman in modern languages at the Royal University in the autumn of 1898. This was solely an examination body and Patrick simply studied by himself, only attending lectures at UCD in his third year. This allowed him to take up a law degree at the King's Inns at the same time, which meant attending lectures at TCD (Trinity College, Dublin). Why he chose law is unclear. It may have been something pushed by his family as a good career path for ambitious educated Catholics. His father's lifelong desire to show his own family back in Birmingham that he had made it professionally probably played a part in this.[340] The speechmaking involved in it may also have appealed to Patrick and concurred with his fondness for recitation and elocution.[341] His mathematical teacher is supposed to have told him that he was no good in maths but that as he was good at argument law would be a good career.[342] According to the records of the King's Inns he kept ten terms there and was allowed one term by grace. He did Feudal and English Law and Criminal and Constitutional Law during 1900 and 1901, and obtained his degree on 3 June 1901, being called to the bar on 8 June 1901.[343]

Pearse did initially participate in college activities, but apparently did not feel at home at the King's Inns. The minutes of the law students' debating society record his presence in the autumn of 1898 but he never spoke.[344] Apparently not much had changed from his demeanour at secondary school. His fellow students recall him as someone who refused to enter into student life: 'a big, shy boy who neither drank nor smoked, nor joined in our adventures or took part in our debates. If one of the wits, who never failed in that company, let fall a jest too risqué over the coffee and the wine, Pearse would hurry away blushing.'[345] He was regarded as 'too serious for levity'. 'He used to come to lectures & the moment they were over, he would walk off speaking to nobody.'[346]

Patrick did not share many interests with the upper middle class, often Protestant, students which populated Trinity. His nationalist outlook and strong interest in the Irish language and literature were not shared there. He found more kindred spirits in his last year at UCD, particularly in his philosophy class, where he struck up a close friendship with the rising star of the Irish Party, Thomas Kettle.[347] Although he did not participate much in proceedings of the Literary and Historical Debating Society, his knack for organisation came to the fore when he became its chairman in 1902.

Apparently Patrick did not exert himself too much in his studies, but did well at his exams.[348] In the matriculation and at all his annual exams he received first class honours for Celtic and a second class exhibition with a monetary reward rising from £15 to £21 in his final exams. In 1901 he received a second class BA degree in modern languages consisting of English, Irish and French in which he came second out of a group of nine students and in his law exams he also came near the top.[349] He took third place in modern literature at his Degree Examination, and won the special prize offered by University College for excellence in Irish.[350] Although he once entertained the thought of practising law in the Connacht circuit, he was quite adamant at the end of his studies that he would not pursue a career as a lawyer, a profession which he later described as parasitical.[351] At the time of graduation this was already clear to his fellow students at TCD who believed a career as a writer would be more appropriate.[352]

After being called to the bar he explained his reasons for not practising to his niece in Birmingham: 'you had to be too big a liar to be successful', describing the law as the 'most wicked of all professions'.[353] Patrick expressed a preference for a trade.[354] Although the freedom of having a trade may have appealed to him, he was notoriously clumsy. One of his friends recalled how: 'I have seen his face and throat covered with terrible gashes, the result of an attempt to shave himself.'[355] Others remember suggestions of becoming an

army school master and his philosophy professor in UCD suggested
he should enter the Indian Civil Services, not an uncommon move
for upwardly mobile middle-class Catholics at that time.[356] However,
according to their own statements there is no proof in the records of
the Irish Civil Service Commission, the India Office, or the Colonial
Office that Patrick even applied for a position.[357]

After graduating Patrick drifted for a while, unsure of what to do
next. After the death of his father in 1900 he had become responsible
for running the family business and the maintenance of his mother
and two sisters. This made it apparently impossible to practise as a
lawyer as engaging in trade or commerce was considered incompatible
with the status of a gentleman of the law.[358] Business initially did
quite well and financially the family was well off, even being able to
send Willie to the College of Art in London and to Paris in 1905.[359]
Patrick and his brother had inherited the largest stone working yard
in Ireland. In the 1880s James Pearse had also invested substantial
amounts of money in stocks and bonds and in 1894 Margaret had
inherited nearly £200 after her father died. James's estate in 1900 was
valued at the very substantial sum of £1470.17.6d, although most of
it was tied up in his business.[360]

Despite this relative wealth the family moved to a smaller home
in Lisreaghan Terrace, Sandymount, in the spring of 1901, soon
renaming it Liosan.[361] Presumably to ensure a continued income for
his family in case of his death Patrick took out life insurance for £300
in January 1901.[362] From this period on there were several members
of the extended family who more or less depended on Patrick and the
business. For a while his half-sister Mary Emily moved in with her
children after her husband had left her, apparently having run off to
the United States with the maid. She eventually moved to Fanad, Co.
Donegal, around 1903 where she got a job as a maternity nurse. One
of her daughters later married James McGarvey, a local man.[363] Her
son Alf continued to live with Patrick's family well into the days of
St Enda's. Another niece of Margaret who had lost her parents also
moved in at around that time.[364]

As far as can be ascertained Patrick only acted as a lawyer on a
couple of occasions. Friends recall a case in which he unsuccessfully
defended a relative or close friend who had been knocked down by a
bread van; in another case he got Michael Scally acquitted, who was

supposed to have been arrested for the unlikely offence of speaking Irish.[365] The latter reference may well relate to a better documented case in which he made a more lasting impression. In 1905 he aided in the defence of Neil MacBride, a celebrated Gaelic poet who was prosecuted for carrying his name on his cart in Irish. At this time all cart owners were required to have their name clearly indicated. The policeman in question had objected to the fact that the name was written as Niall MacGiolla Bhrighde which he considered illegible. When the case came to the high court Pearse was called upon by the defence to aid both as a lawyer and then as a well-known expert on the Irish language. The defending lawyer Dr Walsh recalled in 1942 at the death of Neill MacBride how he had called on Pearse despite the fact that 'he had often told me he would not plead in an English Court of Justice until Ireland was free'.[366]

According to newspaper reports, Patrick defended the case with very rational and sometimes amusing arguments. On the basis of census figures which showed the high number of Irish speakers in the district in Donegal where the alleged offence had taken place he pointed out that the Irish name could hardly be considered illegible. The Lord Chief Justice is reported to have stated at the conclusion of Pearse's speech that 'it was the first time Mr Pearse addressed that court, and he was bound to say he did so with great ability and in a very interesting manner'. Mr Justice Andrews is recorded to have added: 'And very much to the point.'[367] However, some in the movement were very unhappy about this, because losing the court case meant that the prosecution of cart owners was taken up much more vigorously than before. They had wanted to make the use of Irish an established fact instead of making it a *cause célèbre* over the heads of the cart owners. Patrick was undeterred by this and made great mileage out of the case in the pages of *An Claidheamh Soluis*.[368]

Eventually Patrick gave up on a potential career at the bar altogether when he started St Enda's in 1908. One of his aids in the Gaelic League was sent to the courts to retrieve his wig and gown. When handed them, the man at the door said to Patrick's aid: 'Well, I hope that Mr P will do better at this school than he would have done here.'[369] In later years Patrick developed a strong contempt for the legal profession. Although three of his four heroes of Irish nationalism, which included Wolfe Tone, Robert Emmet, Fintan Lalor and John Mitchel, had been lawyers, Patrick referred to Wolfe Tone's 'glorious failure at the bar' and 'His healthy contempt for what he called "a foolish wig and gown"' in an address at Bodenstown in 1913.[370] After his graduation it had quickly become clear his real interest lay with the Irish language, and it was the Gaelic League who provided him with his first regular job outside the family business.

1. Patrick (left) and his siblings

2. Patrick on a rocking horse

3. Patrick's parents James and Margaret

4. Workers in front of James Pearse's shop and family home (courtesy of Deirdre O'Reilly)

5. Patrick in his barrister's outfit

2

Cultural nationalist

Gaelicism is the birthright of us all: of Protestant as of Catholic, of Unionist as of Nationalist, of non-native speaker as of native speaker, as of North as of South.[1]

Early links

In his short autobiographical piece Patrick traces his interest in the Irish language back to his grandaunt Margaret who taught him some Irish songs and stories when he was a small child.[2] However, grandaunt Margaret had little Irish and Patrick did not acquire any competency through her. By the time he came to the Christian Brothers at Westland Row he may have had a warm sentiment but little else. His ability and interest in the language was truly kindled at this school, where he saw written Irish for the first time.[3] Two of the teaching brothers, Maunsell and Craven, are singled out by Patrick for having played a prominent part in this.[4] For a loner like Patrick focusing on a subject like the Irish language could give his school-life direction and purpose. Studying the language became one of his main preoccupations: 'Interested is not the word: his earnestness was the most notable trait of his work.'[5]

Through his tendency to study while others were playing, his ability in Irish grew fast. He worked on his grammar and translation, and even researched the language in various libraries.[6] This enabled him to read Irish mythology, like *The Lay of Oisin in the Land of Youth* and *Pursuit of Diarmuid and Grainne* which had been published by the Society for Preservation of the Irish Language, and also books by Douglas Hyde, the first president of the Gaelic League.[7] One of his classmates recalls how Patrick once presented a lecture on 'some Irish saga', and wrote an article on it for the school paper.[8] His dedication paid off in the shape of prizes at his Irish exams and an appointment as Irish teacher after the language was made compulsory in the curriculum in 1896.[9] In 1899 he was described as having a purity of accent which was most surprising for such a young man.[10]

Actual involvement in the language movement was a direct result of his success at exams. Thomas Flannery's *For the Tongue of the Gael*, which he had received as a prize in the final Intermediate Exam and dealt with contemporary Irish scholars, had led Patrick to join the Gaelic League in October 1896.[11] At the same time he set up the New Ireland Literary Society together with Eamonn O'Neill and some other classmates. In the document announcing its foundation they stated with youthful confidence that the society would focus on reviving old Irish literature because they believed there was no contemporary literature written worth considering.[12] In one of his lectures to the society Patrick described all modern literature in the world as 'carried away by a craving for the unreal, for the extravagant, for the monstrous, for the immoral'. He added that he believed the Irish were particularly suited to provide a new unpolluted source of contemporary literature needed to renew itself.[13]

For two barely seventeen year olds the society was an ambitious venture, and although O'Neill co-signed the initial charter he later claimed Patrick was the one who really started the organisation.[14] Not uncommon for someone with a somewhat obsessive nature Patrick indeed threw himself headlong into the movement. The first meeting was held shortly after his seventeenth birthday on 1 December 1896 with Patrick acting as president. Following this they met most weeks in the Star & Garter Hotel in D'Olier Street, where they read, recited and discussed Gaelic literature and debated all kinds of issues. Patrick frequently recited Shakespeare and one of its members recalls a debate on the proposition 'was Kipling a true poet' in which Patrick took a purely literary stance: 'He did not speak as if he were a Gaelic Leaguer, or in any way interested in things Irish.'[15] At social events Patrick and his siblings played very prominent parts in the performances.

The society did fairly well in its first year and in December 1897 Patrick felt confident enough to invite Eoin MacNeill, then the moving force in the Gaelic League, to present a public lecture to the society. Although he was suitably modest about their organisation, 'neither a very large nor a very important body', the seventeen year old skilfully wooed the busy MacNeill: 'your name was the first that suggested itself to us; for we knew that a lecture by you ... would not only be the most delightful of events to us members but would also attract a larger number of strangers than any other available person'.[16] MacNeill duly complied and gave a lecture on Ossianic Gaelic Poetry on 18 January 1898 in Molesworth Hall.

Apart from his organisational and artistic contributions, Patrick also presented three lectures on Irish literature and folk songs to the regular meetings of the society which were published as *Three Lectures on Gaelic Topics* the following March. Irish-Ireland newspapers such as *Fáinne an Lae*, *Shan Van Vocht* and *Irish Monthly* received them positively. The topics covered were not very original. The main aim of the booklet was to support the profile of the society but also to call upon Irishmen to fight for what Patrick called the survival of Irish nationality. It was written for those to whom Irish language and literature were 'a region as dark and unexplored as the heart of Africa', intended to show that the language was as old as that of 'Homer and Virgil' and as alive and rich as that of 'Dante, Shakespeare and Goethe'.[17] Patrick attempted to highlight what he considered the superior qualities of ancient Irish prose and poetry, its great realism, humour, purity and capacity for alliteration. In the preface Patrick denied publishing the book out of vanity, but he later saw it as a youthful indiscretion: 'the little book I rashly published four years ago. Kindly recollect that its publication was, in every sense what an Irish romanticist would call a "mac-gníomh" or "boyish exploit".'[18] He nevertheless always held to the assertion that old Celtic prose was about as good as the Greek classics, and that if it had been rediscovered in the fifteenth century there would have been a Celtic revival and not a Greek renaissance.[19]

Although the society was relatively successful, proving the existing demand for such activities, Patrick soon became wrapped up in the more prominent Gaelic League. During his studies in the League premises in Dame Street he had become acquainted with many of its leading activists. For a shy and introverted young man the League provided a ready-made social circle, and the relatively high social standing of its leading members in Dublin formed an added attraction to an ambitious lower middle-class Catholic. The importance of his search for respectability was highlighted in a dream he had in 1915 in which he called out to a priest who opposed him: 'I am Director of Organization for the Irish Volunteers. My name is well known. I am a most distinguished person.'[20] He joined the Central Branch, where most of the prominent Dublin language enthusiasts were gathered and which had an undue influence on the leadership of the League. It counted some representatives of the Ascendancy and a number of Catholic and Protestant clergymen among its members. Patrick nevertheless soon came to prominence. Many welcomed his willingness to work for the movement while others felt he was too keen to be noticed and pushed himself forward.[21] His tendency to contradict even the leading figures in the movement in this period dispels the latter assessment. In *Fáinne an Lae* of 19 August 1899 it was reported that 'a boy named Pearse' had insulted Douglas Hyde by claiming his rendering of *The Memory of the Death* was not Irish and refused to qualify or retract his assertion.[22] A few months later Patrick described the work of Eugene O'Growney, professor at Maynooth and a prominent member of the League, at his oration as lasting but not brilliant.[23]

The Gaelic League

The Gaelic League was itself a young organisation, founded in 1893 to promote the use of Irish as a spoken and literary language. The objective went much further than the purely antiquarian interest that had dominated language enthusiasts since the middle of the eighteenth century. These had been mainly involved in recovering the fruits of the high bardic culture which came to an end in the seventeenth century. Although there had been some, mostly devotional, writing and a number of Irish language newspapers were established after 1835, Irish was no longer used as a literary language. By the end of the nineteenth century only one in every hundred Irishmen could speak Irish fluently, and most of these were illiterate. With the establishment of the Society for the Preservation of the Irish Language in 1876 the objective of establishing a modern Irish literature based on contemporary speech had become a serious objective.[24] The Gaelic League took this one step further. They believed the revival of the language should preserve a unique way of life: 'What underlies our contention is the fact that language and thought are inseparably connected, and exert such powerful mutual influence on each other, that it is impossible to represent the Irish spirit and the Irish mind in anything but the Irish language.'[25]

They argued that the Irish had been brought to a state of powerlessness and degeneration by the destruction of the language and the influence of modern industrial society. Many of the League members including Patrick idealised traditional Irish society and saw a clear dichotomy between a democratic rural society based on peasant proprietors and mass industrial urban society. An Irish folk community with heroic and visionary ideals was contrasted with an English class society which was utilitarian and commercial. In their eyes the real Ireland was morally superior and untainted by the vices of positivism, materialism and hedonism, but this was now under threat.[26]

> Two great evils in country places at present are stagnation and drink. The sociability of the people is disappearing. Some years ago, there were in every small town some houses where anecdote, story and good talk were everlasting as the welcome, and where the neighbours constantly foregathered. Now when the young men do not mope their evenings away, they go to the hotel or to the public house bar – of other social recreation there is almost none![27]

This negative view of modernity was shared with many separatist and regionalist movements throughout Europe at this time and was largely a reaction to the process of modernisation and state sponsored nationalism.[28] In Ireland this perception was strongly advocated by the Catholic Truth Society founded in 1899 and by popular authors like Canon Sheehan who portrayed a battle between English materialism and irreligion on one side and Irish nationalism and religious fervour on the other.[29] Even John Redmond, the leader of the Irish Party, shared this outlook and stated in 1900 that 'The process of Anglicising Ireland was an unmixed evil. It was bad for religion, for the moral, for the material and for the national well-being of the nation.'[30] Patrick took this a step further. To him 'the people had lost their souls and were being vulgarised, commercialised, anxious only to imitate the material prosperity of England'.[31]

The detrimental effects on society could, however, be reversed. To regain the golden past the League asserted that it was necessary to turn to the voices of ancient Ireland which could only be known through its language. 'The decay of the native language is everywhere accompanied by industrial and general decadence. The converse holds equally true. Whenever a language revival has taken place material prosperity also has been restored.[32] The introduction of an English-based education system in the 1830s was held responsible for the decline of the language, and the regeneration of the Irish nation could also only take place through the same education system.

> The whole tendency of Irish education for the past sixty years has been to undermine and destroy the self reliance and self respect of the Irish Nation. At the end of sixty years of English education, the nation lies bloodless, waste and helpless, almost powerless to resist patent wrongs or to rebuild the patent wreck of her prosperity. English education has brought us to this. We trust to Irish education to bring us out of it.[33]

For their model they went to those who still spoke Irish. 'We want to preserve the speech and mode of thought of our forefathers and to understand it as they understood it, and this can only be done by making the old Irish-speaking men and women hand over to us their beautiful, expressive and dignified modes of speech.'[34]

Nevertheless, the League accepted that English was so well established that it could not be replaced with Irish. They therefore advocated a bilingual society, which they contended would actually give the Irish an advantage over other peoples.

> To be bi-lingual is educative to the intellect in a very marked degree. In their determination not to abandon their tongue, the Welsh show great prudence. I have no hesitation in saying that a Welsh peasant is much ahead, intellectually, of the English peasant of the same social position and I attribute this mainly to the fact of the greater agility given to his brain in having to think and speak in two languages. When he gives up one of these tongues he abandons mental gymnastics as well as the exercise of the vocal organs in two different modes of speech.[35]

To create this bilingual Ireland the League called for support from all sides of the political spectrum irrespective of views held: 'The League is wedded to one wife – the cause of the Irish language – and being faithful to its bond indulges in no flirtations. It holds that all who aid in carrying out its aims, be they Orangemen on one side of Mr. O'Brien[36] or Irish Republicans on the other, are helping the cause of Irish Nationality.'[37]

Although officially non-political, the revival of the language had nevertheless a very clear nationalist objective. 'The Gaelic League, I take it, is only in a small degree a literary movement. It is a national affair – a movement absolutely necessary if anything like an Irish Nation is to be preserved.'[38] In this they called upon a protestant nationalist icon: 'In the words of Thomas Davis: "A nation should guard its language more than its territories – 'tis a surer barrier and more important frontier than any fortress or river". Our language is not only a safeguard of our nationality, IT IS PART OF OUR NATIONALITY.'[39] Despite such claims, the League was realistic about what could be achieved. 'No people are more conscious than we that when all of us speak Irish, bread will still remain in the staff of life and that the Irish-speaking children of the future will be born in original sin.'[40]

From his writings it becomes clear that the young Patrick was much influenced by the thinking espoused by the League leaders in the early years of the movement. The central role of Irish literature, the importance of a living language, the superiority of an Irish-Ireland, the idea that the education system had been central in the destruction of the language and was central in the recreation of it, the benefits of bilingualism to the brain, and so forth all came back in Patrick's writing. To those who encountered him in this period he seemed to have a one-tracked mind: 'He struck me as being an idealist with his head in the clouds, and he looked the part to perfection. He was completely obsessed with one idea, and that was the cult of the Irish language, which he considered a panacea for all ills that Ireland suffered from.' Once 'he told his audience that if they only learned Irish it would save them from pauperism, lunacy, and crime, which prevailed amongst them in a relatively larger degree than amongst their fellow-citizens'. His audience was none to pleased with the latter assertion even though it was put across as the fatherly advice of a friend and not as the reproach of an enemy.[41] In practice, however, Patrick initially focused more on the aesthetic than the political element of the language.[42]

Patrick and the League

The first time Patrick influenced League policy was at the November 1897 meeting of the Central Branch when he proposed to replace the existing ad hoc arrangement of League activities with a regular programme of lectures and readings which was to be drawn up in advance of each session. On the basis of his positive experiences with the public activities of his literary society he thought that in this way the weekly meetings could be made more popular. He also proposed to hold a series of concerts and lectures under the Gaelic League name during the winter. The motion was carried and Patrick was appointed to a committee set up to popularise the League and make the learning of Irish pleasurable to a wide audience.[43]

The League was already growing in popularity in this period. Its Irish classes and social gatherings attracted ever larger audiences from among the lower middle classes particularly in English-speaking districts. In 1898 the League moved from its two upstairs rooms in Dame Street to prominent premises at 24 Upper O'Connell Street and implemented Patrick's programme.[44] There were still many practical problems in stimulating the use of the language. Irish had long been forbidden by the authorities and was still not an acceptable language for official communication despite the fact that there were still areas in the West where it was the native tongue. The Donegal poet who had written his name in Irish on his cart is a case in point, and there were many other such practical barriers. As a result, the implementation of the lofty ideals of the League often led to very practical struggles with the authorities.

Early in the twentieth century it was thus involved in forcing the post office and railway companies to accept Irish addresses, the banks and postmasters to accept signatures in Irish and Dublin Corporation to introduce bilingual street signs.[45] In this they encountered some stubborn resistance. 'The Railway Companies have so persistently ignored and tabooed Irish as a factor in present-day requirements that they regard docility to their stone-age habits a matter of course.'[46] Most of these issues, however, were fairly quickly resolved with the aid of questions in the House of Commons by Irish Party MPs and some subtle but practical people pressure. 'Our suggestion is that every Gaelic Leaguer when sending letters through the post, should, in all cases where the missives are not of a very urgent nature, address them in Irish only.'[47]

Not all obstacles were that easily overcome. In the case of the right to carry one's name on a cart in Irish, Patrick wanted to turn the conviction in court to their advantage. He felt the stronger enforcement of the law resulting from it should be utilised to display the force and passion behind the language movement. The fact that the decision is bound to go against the Gael is immaterial. Every appearance in Court to answer a charge which calls into question the legality of Irish serves to advertise the movement and to hasten the day when British law must either recognise the national language of this country or give place to a law which does.[48]

In the meantime Patrick became ever more deeply involved in League affairs. In May 1898, he felt confident enough to present his first paper to the Central Branch and many more followed; he frequently took the chair at meetings and generally spoke as often as possible from the floor. Such dedication was much appreciated in a voluntary organisation and this was made apparent when on MacNeill's motion he was co-opted on the Executive Committee or Coiste Gnotha of the League in October of that year just short of his twentieth birthday.[49] The organisation, which had no paid officials at that time, desperately needed enthusiastic members. However, a high profile in the League, studying for two university degrees and teaching Irish at several institutions all at the same time, made it difficult for Patrick to keep his literary society going. Following advice from Fr Yorke, who had lectured to the society, and at Eoin MacNeill's request Patrick wound up the New Ireland Literary Society after just two years and affiliated it to the League, with most members following his example.[50]

Patrick now became the best attendee on the executive, making it to 103 out of 109 meetings in his first two years.[51] He also became assistant editor to Eoin MacNeill of the weekly *Gaelic Journal*; originally set up by the Gaelic Union, an offshoot of the Society for the Preservation of the Irish Language, it was adopted as official organ by the League on its establishment.[52] In 1899 Patrick also became the official delegate to the annual festivals of the Welsh and Scottish counterparts of the League. Furthermore, he functioned as adjudicator in two letter-writing competitions, organised the annual gala event and was bequeathed with the grand title of 'Conductor of the Competitions' at the League's national cultural festival, An tOireachtas, instituted in 1897.[53]

In the preparations for the festival he had made himself less than popular by proposing that there would be no intoxicating drinks served at the reception. The votes in the Coiste were evenly split on this issue but he urged Mrs Bradley, who held the chair, to use her casting vote. As a result the League became more or less temperate overnight. Although Patrick was very pleased, it disgusted some – one member stating that he 'didn't want to be a puritanical dyspeptic'.[54] When later that year the League was asked by the Jesuits of UCD to provide Irish lessons for their students, Patrick again let his name willingly be put forward. For two years from September 1899 onwards he gave classes twice a week in the League's headquarters before receiving a direct appointment from UCD after his own graduation in 1901.[55]

Even most of his social life revolved around the League. He often met other Irish-Irelanders in a conveniently placed tobacco shop, 'An Stad' on Rutland Square, where you dropped in and were sure to meet like-minded people. Among those frequenting were James Joyce, Sean T. O'Kelly, Oliver St John Gogarty and Patrick.[56] Even on his holidays he did not forget to propagate the movement. While on the Aran Islands in 1898 he set up a Gaelic League branch with the aid of the local parish priest, returning the following year to conduct exams in written Irish and present a paper to the new branch. He made efficient use of his initial visit by presenting a paper on Irish in Aran to the Central Branch and publishing his account in the new League paper *Fáinne an Lae*. During his first visit he also became interested in Irish names for birds, flowers and wild animals. He collected them and studied the various dialectic variations between areas, reporting on it in *Irisleabhar na Gaeilge* in 1899. In September 1899 he gave another paper to the Central Branch on Brian Boru, which was also published this time in the newly launched *An Claidheamh Soluis*, and early in 1900 he lectured on the Fiann Saga, which appeared in the *Gaelic Journal* in June 1900.[57]

All Patrick's early writing was principally dedicated to language issues. In his *Three Lectures on Gaelic Topics* written in 1897–1898 he argued that the survival of the Irish nation depended on the success of the language movement: 'Save the language, and the folk-tale, and the folk-song, and all the treasures accumulated in the folk-mind during three thousand years will be saved also. The cause is a holy one – God grant it may succeed! May our language, and our literature, and our folk-lore live; and if they live, then, too, will our race live.'[58] He believed an Irish Ireland would have a great future and could become 'the saviour of idealism in modern intellectual and social life, the regenerator and rejuvenator of the literature of the world, the instructor of the nations, the preacher of the gospel of nature-worship, hero-worship, God-worship'.[59]

In his first leader as editor of *An Claidheamh Soluis* in 1903 he developed this theme: 'On the organisation of the Irish-speaking districts depends the life or death of the language. On the life or death of the language depends the life or death of the nation. That is the issue at stake.' The League played a vital role in this.

> The young men who founded the League grasped primary truths, and clung to them as shipwrecked men cling to a plank. They gripped the fact that the language of this country enshrines the mind and soul of this country. That was the first step. They then grasped that other primary fact, that a language is a living energising force only so long as it is a living idiom on the lips of living men and women.

Being Irish was therefore inevitably connected with the language. The language was shaped by the nation, and the nation could not express itself other than in the language. Without the language the nation could not exist. It was thanks to the movement that the language question had been set high on the public agenda, and considering what was at stake its survival was vital. 'A movement like ours cannot fail. There is something irresistible in sheer conviction, in downright doggedness.'[60]

As indicated Patrick generally followed the official line in his early years. His often quoted attack on the Irish literary movement in which he caricatured W.B. Yeats as 'a mere English poet of the third or fourth rank'[61] was part of a concerted attack. Patrick asserted that what that movement was trying to do, promote an Irish literature and theatre in the English language, was fundamentally impossible:

> Newspapers, politicians, literary societies are all but forms of one gigantic heresy, that like a poison has eaten its way into the vitals of Irish nationality, that has paralysed the nation's energy and intellect. That heresy is the idea that there can be an Ireland, that there can be an Irish literature, an Irish social life whilst the language of Ireland is English.[62]

Just a week earlier Eoin MacNeill had, in less strident tones, argued something similar in a discussion on the opening of the Irish Literary Theatre.

The first play is Mr. Yeats 'Countess Cathleen' of course written in English and to be acted in English. The subject matter is based upon a German legend discovered by John Augustus O'Shea, transferred by him to the Shamrock whence the story found its way to English-reading, English-speaking people in the West of Ireland. There Mr. Yeats re-discovered it, and here it is – the foundation of what is to be our national theatre. The management of the theatre is English, and the cast is English – the actors hailing from London theatres. ... It has been objected that this tale is pagan. It is enough for us that it is un-Irish.[63]

Patrick thus simply followed MacNeill's argument that a national literature had to be written in Irish. How else he wondered could a 'treatise on German metaphysics, or on Japanese pottery, or on the history of Egypt, or on a novel dealing with life in Whitechapel' be part of the national literature of Ireland.[64]

Patrick's uncritical eulogising of the Irish language in this period also extended to the qualities of its ancient literature. In his early lectures this annoyed those in attendance who were not ardent followers of the movement:

He was indiscriminately eulogistic to absurdity over his subject, and the adjectives he employed to describe the extracts which he read from the Sagas were beyond the bounds of reason when the stuff praised became known to his listeners. Woeful exaggeration or absurd grotesqueness were the only merits they possessed as far as I could see, but then I am not a Gaelic speaking maniac (harmless but boresome) which makes all the difference in the world. With them art stopped short in the early ages and nothing outside the Irish language is worth a rap.

At this stage the influence of Gaelic Leaguers like Patrick could still be dismissed: 'It is this absurd unmeaning, almost fanatical, praise that makes the few lovers of the Irish language left to us so unbearable and impractical to all broad minded people.'[65] The denigration of the English language by Patrick in his Irish beginners class for UCD students drove James Joyce, who briefly attended this class around 1900, to take up the study of Norwegian, as he preferred Ibsen to the old Irish writers.[66]

Patrick's inflated appreciation of ancient Irish literature and poetry seems to betray a deep felt insecurity about his own identity. The inability to see any merit in foreign literature may well have been a means of asserting his own Irishness and building up his credentials with the League leaders. When he began to form his own ideas he became more confident and increasingly critical of the narrow-minded insular attitude which led some members to form vigilante committees against evil foreign literature. Patrick began to warn against fanaticism and attacked such nativist philistinism masquerading as moral fervour. By 1904 Patrick still celebrated old Irish literature and prose like the nativists did, but unlike them he now also believed it was necessary to develop a modern literature in Irish which would use contemporary forms and thus lead Ireland away from what he saw as the Anglicised backwaters into the European mainstream. He promoted the learning of European languages and wanted to re-establish connections with Europe and its writings.[67] He strongly criticised the focus on Irish rural life and called upon writers to deal with the modern world: 'Let us move away from the dungheap and the turf-rick; let us throw off the barnyard muck.'[68]

Pan Celtic cooperation

An important influence on the direction of Patrick's thinking stemmed from his visit to Wales in the summer of 1899. He was sent there by the Gaelic League as its designated delegate to the Welsh equivalent and precursor of the Oireachtas, the Eisteddfod. Why they chose Patrick is unclear, he was not yet twenty, and had not shown a particular interest in pan-Celtic cooperation. He may simply have been the only one willing to go. Apart from his representative duties, such as a visit to the Cardiff branch of the Gaelic League and a speech at the public reception, he was asked to collect information on bilingual education, for which he interviewed the secretary of the Cardiff School Board and visited schools.[69] There are no immediate signs of the effects of this visit but bilingual education obtained an ever growing importance in Patrick's thinking.

As an immediate consequence of the visit Patrick became embroiled in a controversy within the League. When the issue of sending a League delegation to Wales came up the suggestion to join a contingent from the Irish Pan-Celtic Movement, which propagated cooperation between the various Celtic races to promote a revival of their cultures, was vigorously discussed. Particularly the protestant element in the League saw affiliation to the Pan-Celtic Movement as a means of countering Catholic clerical influence. Some members of the Coiste Gnotha, however, considered the strong aristocratic element among the Pan-Celts with its cosmopolitan attitudes a threat to a purely Irish stance.[70] They voiced their opposition through the pages of *An Claidheamh Soluis*.

> It is absurd to talk of the 're-union of the Celtic nations'. There was no historical union between this country and Wales or between this country and Brittany. Welsh is not intelligible to Irish people. Wales and Ireland have developed on entirely divergent lines. For instance no two countries could well be farther apart in the matter of religion. Without community of religion or language there exists no such thing as innate racial sympathy.[71]

According to this staunchly Catholic section the language movement should rely on Irish support alone and accused the Pan-Celts of depending on foreigners and fritting away money on 'masquerading and banqueting and processioning'.

Patrick had not clearly spoken out on the issue, as he tended to do on most controversial issues at this stage,[72] but he was not averse to the idea of international cooperation between Celtic language organisations. Although the League had eventually decided not to join the Irish Pan-Celtic contingent, he became close to their thinking while he was in Cardiff after speaking to their leader, Lord Castletown. The pro-Celtic newspaper *Fáinne an Lae* welcomed Patrick's address to the Eisteddfod, which they described as 'of a most advanced and encouraging character'. They acknowledged that he was put in a difficult position as a representative of the League which was seen as hostile to cooperation, but stated that he 'acquitted himself with great tact and courtesy'.[73]

At the same time the opponents of cooperation in the League mounted a vicious attack on the Irish Pan-Celtic movement in *An Claidheamh Soluis*. 'We have been fighting against anglicisation, we should fight as determinedly against institutions unsuited to the conditions and temperament and the needs of the Irish people.'[74] The attack was so vehement that the editor, Eoin MacNeill, considered it necessary to write to the popular daily the *Freeman's Journal*, to disassociate himself from contributions published in his own paper.

This of course was much to the delight of the rival *Fáinne an Lae*, which berated the 'belligerent spirits who have control of the League publications ... and whose arrogance and egotism is fast dragging the movement into the mire'.[75]

The attack explicitly included Patrick who together with his co-delegates sent telegrams of protest home to the Coiste Gnotha.[76] As a result of the embarrassing public washing of dirty linen, the League intervened and the worst offenders, Miss O'Reilly and P.J. Keawell, were forced to tender their resignation from the editorial staff of *An Claidheamh Soluis* and the Coiste Gnotha.[77] The Coiste expressed regret at the publication[78] and devised a compromise solution which stated that the League would maintain 'the fullest and most cordial friendship' with the other Celtic language movements but it would not affiliate to the Pan-Celtic movement. However, its members were free to join if they so wished. Further discussion of the issue was banned as it was deemed 'hurtful to the progress and solidarity of the Language Movement'.[79]

Patrick subsequently met representatives of the Pan-Celtic movement at the Scottish festival, the Highland Mod, in Edinburgh in October that same year, joined a delegation to the Representative Congress in Paris in 1900 and was co-opted on the Irish committee of the Pan-Celtic Congress.[80] This was too much for another fellow member of the Coiste Gnotha, Norma Borthwick, who lodged a complaint with the Coiste and asked for Patrick's resignation. She also tried unsuccessfully to have *An Claidheamh Soluis* suppressed and replaced by an anti-Pan-Celtic weekly to be edited by D.P. Moran, who was known for his staunch Irish Catholic position. When her complaint was rejected in light of the recent compromise, she tried to undermine Patrick's position by asserting that he had drank to the Queen's health when in Wales in his capacity as a League representative: 'the Gaelic League should not send delegates who would do such things in their name'.[81]

Although the accusation was quickly neutralised, Patrick and Douglas Hyde realised their association with the Pan-Celts was detrimental to their position and gradually disassociated themselves from them. At the same time contacts with the Welsh and Scottish counterparts were maintained, and a larger informal international network was slowly established, mainly with foreign scholars of the Irish language in Germany, France, Denmark and England.[82] A few years later Patrick even described the League's rejection of the Pan-Celtic idea in 1899 as 'a gigantic blunder', particularly because of the impression it gave to leaders of kindred movements and international language experts that the Gaelic League was a fraud and 'that no effort is being made to save the language'.[83]

Education

The main preoccupation of the League at the turn of the century became the teaching of Irish in schools. This followed the publication in 1899 of two government-sponsored reports on educational policy in National Schools and on Intermediate education. Since the teaching of Irish had been made possible in Nationals Schools in 1878, Irish was treated as a foreign language similar to Latin and French and could only be taught outside school hours even in the Irish-speaking Gaeltacht. As a token incentive teachers were paid ten shillings for each pupil who obtained a pass in Irish after a three-year course.[84] Consequently there were very few pupils actually taking Irish at this level; in 1885 there were just 161, in 1892 it had grown to 575 and in 1899 there were 1317. In the review which followed the publication of the reports the League campaigned vigorously to have Irish upgraded at primary level. Its two demands were clear:

1. That where Irish is the home language, pupils shall be taught to read and write Irish and their education shall be through the medium of their home language.
2. That where Irish is not the home language, it shall be lawful to teach Irish as a remunerated subject within school hours at the earliest stage at which pupils are capable of learning it.[85]

In an orchestrated campaign four leading members of the League sent letters to the press regarding this issue. Testifying to Patrick's rising star in the organisation he was chosen as one of them, together with Eoin MacNeill, Rev. Dr M. O'Hickey, professor of Irish at Maynooth, and the aforementioned Norma Borthwick. In his closely argued contribution Patrick emphasised that it was impossible to teach pupils who had grown up with Irish through English. They would not understand what was going on and this could only perpetuate illiteracy. 'These children are for the most part mere wrecked intelligences who within a year or two after leaving school will lapse back into illiteracy, will forget the "English" they have spent six years acquiring, and will have lost a large part of their mental nimbleness in and native mastery over Irish.'[86] His simple recommendation was to teach all subjects through Irish.

The League campaign was widely supported. Nearly 200 managers, representing 1007 schools in Irish-speaking areas, had signed a memorial in February 1900 stating that the 'defects of the existing educational system in those districts could be removed only "by teaching the children to read and write, and utilise to the fullest capacity, the language in common use among the grown people in these districts".'[87] When the protest led to only a minor improvement in the status of Irish in the Gaeltacht the campaign was intensified. A large protest meeting was held in the Rotunda in Dublin on 19 July 1900, which was supported by Cardinal Logue and leading members of the Irish Literary Movement like W.B. Yeats, A.E. and Lady Gregory who showed no rancour towards the movement despite the harsh criticism of their attempt to create an Irish literature in the English language.

In particular the attitude of the authorities was challenged. During the meeting one of the education commissioners, Prof. Fitzgerald of Trinity College, was quoted as having said: 'I will use all my influence, as in the past, to ensure that Irish as a spoken language shall die out as quickly as possible'. The public outcry that followed caused Archbishop Walsh, a strong supporter of the language movement, to resign from the Education Board and led to questions in parliament by members of the Irish Party.[88] The Chief Secretary for Ireland took up an ambivalent position: 'As Mr Gerald Balfour I am strongly in favour of bi-lingual education for districts where the children know Irish better than they know English. As Chief Secretary for Ireland, I see that there are innumerable difficulties in the way that the Gaelic League wants to have Irish taught in every school in Ireland.' The issue was then handed back to the Education Board which made some further minor modifications, but the demands of the League were not granted. Even the minor concessions by the National Board, which allowed the teaching of Irish inside school hours as an optional subject and a recognition of schemes for the teaching of Irish outside school hours, were not always implemented by unwilling teachers, school managers and inspectors. It often required further public campaigns before individual schemes would get recognition from the board.[89]

At intermediate level developments were more acceptable to the League. Irish had been made a compulsory subject in the 1890s, and the League had no further demands at that time. However, the newly accorded status of Irish came under serious attack in 1901 from the provost of Trinity College, John Pentland Mahaffy, who wanted to have it removed. Only active lobbying by Douglas Hyde and another public campaign prevented a downgrading in the position of Irish at secondary level.[90] The League continued to experience active opposition particularly from elements in TCD. At the end of 1901 there were insinuations emanating from there that the examiners of Irish in the Intermediate, who included a number of prominent League men such as Hyde, MacNeill and Dr O'Hickey, had consciously tried to benefit pupils sitting Irish by setting an easy paper and marking 'with undue indulgence'.[91]

Although legal improvements in the status of Irish were thus limited, the two campaigns heightened public awareness of the language and of the League itself. The number of National Schools in which Irish was taught grew rapidly in the years that followed, from 88 out of 8684 schools in 1900 to over 2000 in 1903. At the Intermediate level Irish also benefited. In 1903 39 per cent of boys and 28 per cent of girls in Intermediate education were taught Irish. The number of passes in Irish also grew rapidly from 1266 in 1902 to 2103 two years later.[92] However, the fact that those taking Irish in the Intermediate Exam were given fewer credits than those taking other languages ensured that many pupils, with the support of their teachers, did not take it up. Patrick believed teachers should nevertheless insist because their primary object should not be the winning of distinction but the education of their pupils, and Irish children would be better off if they knew Irish.[93] The League itself also benefited from the furore surrounding these campaigns. Its membership doubled around 1900 and its annual income increased from £43 in 1895 to £2000 in 1900. This meant that the League could appoint paid officials such as a secretary general and organisers, and could bring out more publications. By 1904 the League had 600 branches with 50,000 members, growing further to 900 branches in 1905 with 100,000 members.[94]

The growing confidence of the movement associated with the successful campaigns meant that the League kept pushing for further reforms. In April 1904 it recorded its biggest success when the introduction of a bilingual programme was allowed in primary education in Irish and bilingual districts. From then on both languages could be taught or used as a medium of instruction in these areas.[95] This satisfied the League. 'In this particular matter the Board has, to a large extent, met our demands, and the responsibility is shifted. It now lies with the country, the schools and the various Gaelic League bodies throughout Ireland to rise to the occasion and take the fullest advantage of the situation.'[96]

Rising star in the League

The growing stature of Patrick became apparent when his appointment to the Coiste Gnotha was confirmed through elections in November 1898 and again in June 1899, coming tenth out of fourteen members. The strongest recognition to date came a year later in June 1900 when Patrick was appointed honorary secretary to the Publications Committee of the League. His predecessor Joe Clarke had resigned from the unpaid post because he needed the time to earn money. Although he reapplied when the position was advertised with a small remuneration, Patrick was favoured over him.[97] This gave Patrick a central position in the work of the League, but his ambitions went further.

In May 1901 the paid position of general secretary of the Gaelic League was introduced, and Patrick considered applying. He decided against it, apparently because he considered the salary of £200 p.a. too small, and wanted to pay closer attention to the family business after his father's death the September previous. However, when it became clear in October that there was only one suitable candidate, Patrick felt free to let it be known to the Coiste Gnotha that he was interested. O'Hickey acknowledged that 'there can be no second opinion about his fitness for the office', but felt Patrick's application could not be entertained at such a late stage, and thought that it would look bad if the Coiste Gnotha seemed to favour their own. At about the same time the editorship of *An Claidheamh Soluis*, for which Patrick also had aspirations, became vacant but this was considered a job for a native speaker and went to Owen Naughton. Despite these setbacks, Patrick continued to put his name forward whenever it was needed. When a committee system was introduced to professionalise the League's work, Patrick joined those for education and finance, and soon after he was appointed the League's adjudicator for Recitation, Dialogue and Oratory.[98]

Although graduating in the same month he took up his position at the Publications Committee, Patrick remained a very busy man. Besides running the family business, he was an active member of the Central Branch, of several committees and the Coiste Gnotha, taught Irish classes in UCD, the CBS (Christian Brothers School) and elsewhere. He also frequently lectured to local League branches in places as far apart as Tralee, Carrick-on-Suir and Donegal, and for organisations as diverse as the Temperance Movement and St Andrews Catholic Literary Society.[99] He was even involved in efforts to get Protestants into the League. Vicar B.J. Plunket, later bishop of Meath, was apparently very impressed with him.[100] However, he generally did not push himself too hard. When asked to lecture in Donaghmore, Co. Donegal, Patrick suggested a very general topic such as: 'The Gaelic League and its Work'. The Maynooth Gaelic League branch members who did not claim any great expertise requested a similar basic lecture on language and the industrial movement. 'Our branch is young and is not supported at all as it should be. In fact we are badly in need of a little enlightenment on the subject of our language and our duty thereto.'[101] In between his many duties and commitments he still found time to attend the opening of the play *An Posadh* in Ballyhaunis, Co. Mayo, together with Douglas Hyde in April 1901, and write a ten part series on remnants of traditional Irish life for *An Claidheamh Soluis*.[102]

As with all his endeavours, Patrick took his role as secretary of the Publications Committee extremely seriously, and initiated an ambitious publication programme: 'The object of the Comtee. is to place in the hands of students, both of school and colleges and in League classes, a series of carefully selected modern Irish texts, with introductions (where necessary), full vocabularies and no translations.'[103] He based the programme upon existing textbooks produced for the study of French and German. The Irish version should consist of what he called modern classics such as the works of Geoffrey Keating and David Ó Bruadair, and on the later Ossianic tales. In this he could build upon the work done by the League and other organisations in the previous years.[104]

The emphasis on modern Irish literature was an attempt to deal with the deficiency in that area he had observed in the days of the New Ireland Literary Society. He now wanted to generate such a body of modern texts by actively encouraging contemporary writers such as Henry Morris and J.J. Doyle to deliver new material.[105] As a student in UCD he had already argued that 'Gaelic had to be the medium for poetry, fiction, and essay if it were to continue as a living language.'[106] As secretary of the Publications Committee he wanted authors to get away from the forms and conventions of the folk tales and use ancient Irish and contemporary European writing as their example to develop their own style within an Irish environment. For instance, the convention that stories should start with a genealogy of the hero was one he felt was outdated. In an ironic manner he ridiculed this convention by beginning one of his first Irish stories, 'Barbara', with such a description of what turned out to be a doll – even asking the readers directly whether they knew her now.

In this way he firmly positioned himself in the camp of those who rejected the imitation of the seventeenth century Irish writers and called for a modern form of literature which used simple and natural expression and was based on the living language of the people. As such Patrick was in tune with the contemporary literary sensibilities of Europe and America, in their attack on convention and on false sentiments. He pleaded for the use of natural language, conciseness of expression and metrical freedom. However, the nativists who advocated using the seventeenth century form when Irish writing was at its height were influential and in an attempt to bring them on board he added that modern stories should be 'robustly native in tone and texture, richly idiomatic, impregnated with the traditional Irish spirit in literature'.[107]

His own poetry in Irish dealt with contemporary life and personal experience but did largely follow the old conventions concerning syllabic length and stresses, but did this playfully according to his own interpretation.[108] Apart from those who wanted to learn Irish, Patrick believed there was a ready market for such modern Irish stories and poetry among the many Irish speakers who had migrated to the cities and were looking for something to remind them of their home life. To replace the story-telling at the fireside these migrants now liked to read Irish stories. '[Irish writers] may not be producing very exalted literature but at any rate, they are answering the cry of the awakening thousands of Irish Speakers for something to read in their own language – something that they can understand, something that is pleasant and familiar and homely, something that is filling a place in their daily lives.'[109]

In the following years a whole stream of publications, mostly in short pamphlet form, was produced, which encouraged both the writing and reading of Irish.[110] The Publications Committee even made a profit for the League, and Patrick was considered 'a great success'.[111] He was, however, not yet happy with the availability and realistic quality of Irish prose.

> We would love the problems of today fearlessly dealt with in Irish: the loves and hates and desires and doubts of modern men and women. The drama of the land war, the tragedy of the emigration-mania; the stress and poetry and comedy of the language movement; the pathos and vulgarity of Anglo-Ireland; the abounding interest of Irish politics, the relations of priest and people; the perplexing education riddle; the drink evil; the increase in lunacy; such social problems as (say) the loveless marriage; these are matters which loom large in our daily lives; which bulk considerably in our daily consideration but we find not the faintest echoes of them in the Irish books that are being written.[112]

He could not detect much improvement in the following years. At the end of 1912 he still considered contemporary Irish literature poor compared to its modern European counterpart in the way it clung to outworn forms and was afraid to break new ground.[113]

To deal with this deficiency Patrick would eventually be tempted to try writing himself. His stories, the first of which appeared in 1905, were initially aimed at young boys, which required a simpler Irish. This was also an answer to the publicly aired concern in nationalist circles that Irish boys were reading only English stories and comics which promoted an allegiance to the empire.[114] Patrick asked local League branches to start junior branches or Éire Óg Clubs where they could mould the character of the rising generation. In these clubs the love for and duties to the language and Ireland and its culture should be central. 'The other phases of the movement, such as temperance, cleanliness, use of healthy food, uprightness, and good conduct, should be touched upon, and they should be warned against Anglicisation in all shapes and forms, emigration and other evils.'[115]

Apart from regular books on grammar, and elementary textbooks of poetry and prose, the League also produced political pamphlets supporting the cause of the language movement.[116] The letter campaign on Irish in the National Schools to which Patrick had contributed was published as *Irish in the Schools* in the penny pamphlet series. The evidence presented to the Commission on Intermediate Education regarding the position of the Irish language was printed in ten instalments, and sent to all commissioners, bishops, MPs, heads of Intermediate schools and the press. These booklets were attempts to influence politicians and the general public in their thinking on language policy.

The League also appealed directly to school managers and teachers to implement the changes now allowed by the National Board of Education. A lecture by Archbishop Walsh on bilingual education, of which 10,000 copies were printed by the League in January 1901 at the archbishop's own cost, was sent to all managers and teachers at National Schools. In a letter to Dr Walsh, Patrick stated: 'I hope and believe that it will be the means of inducing a number of managers to forthwith put a bilingual system into practice.' In a sequel a number of prize-winning schemes of bilingual education were discussed to provide a practical guide as to the introduction of schemes approved by the national board of education.[117] In light of the strong growth in schools offering bilingual education this was a great success. When the commotion surrounding the reform of education had died down most new pamphlets again contained literary texts and aids in the study of the language, of which copies were simply sent for review to the dailies and chief Dublin and provincial weeklies.

The sudden increase in material brought out by the League under Patrick's stewardship presented its own problems. Most authors wanted their work to be published as soon as possible but Patrick was hesitant to bring out too many pamphlets at the same time. In July 1901 the Publications Committee had thirty-six booklets in preparation or in press and Patrick was withholding another eight. This was largely due to the attempt to salvage all folk stories in Irish. More collections of such stories were published than of original fiction or of instruction booklets, but they sold far less well. Most did not do more than 200–300 copies, while for instance Patrick's own collection of original stories *Íosagán agus Sgéalta Eile* (Iosagan and other stories) still sold 979 copies in 1909, two years after its publication.[118]

Patrick always dealt tactfully with impatient authors. Not slow to blame the printers as: 'elephantine in their slowness and asinine in their stupidity',[119] he explained his policy carefully: 'It would never do to hurl Irish books at the head of the public in too rapid succession. Time must be allowed for each book to be advertised, to get known, to sell. As it is, many believe we are forcing the pace too hard.'[120] The market for the more difficult works the League brought out was also very small. The readers he targeted were mostly non-native speakers who only read basic Irish: 'I believe personally, that even the most accomplished reader of Irish would be glad of a vocabulary of the more difficult words.'[121] This was reflected in the sales. Of O'Growney's simplest Irish lessons 5645 copies were sold in the last nine months of 1908 while of the most difficult fifth part only 90 found a buyer. Similar differences existed between the literary works. Of a popular simple folk story collection 4206 were sold but only 44 of a scholarly anthology, while a comic story did 3106 copies against 145 of the best selling plays and 13 for the worst. Only one person bought a translation of a Greek hero tale.[122]

Patrick tried to ensure his authors were paid adequately, but was not willing to compromise on the quality of the work.[123] Occasionally Patrick's tendency to involve himself with everything without appreciating sensitivities did annoy some. J.H. Lloyd, a Gaelic Leaguer from Howth and the editor of one of the League's publications, complained about Patrick's last minute alterations to his typescript: 'He did this solely on his own responsibility and without authority. You should not have altered my *final editing*. I am the editor and not Mr. P., who, as you know, is secretary to the Publications Committee. This position not giving him any authority to alter an editor's work.'[124] Patrick did not seem to expect such criticism and was fully convinced that everyone appreciated his selfless dedication to the wider interest of any cause he was involved with.

Even in the most trivial affairs the interest of the movement was central to his responses. When Séamus Ó Ceallaigh, a prominent Gaelic Leaguer, asked him whether a pair of trews, held in the National Museum and dating from the sixteenth century, would be a suitability model for his outfit at the Irish cultural festival Patrick was not enthusiastic: 'One would at first sight take them for a rather clumsily made and ill-treated pair of modern gentlemen's drawers. They are tight fitting and reach down to the foot, the extremities being pointed at each side. There is no opening in front and the wearer must hence have found considerable difficulty in putting them on.' He could not imagine 'an Irish gentleman of three or four centuries ago wearing so clumsy an article', and believed that such garments were universal throughout Europe during the Middle Ages and down to the end of the eighteenth century. He was particularly concerned about the impression the outfit would make on its spectators:

> Frankly, I should much prefer to see you arrayed in a kilt, although it may be less authentic, than in a pair of these trews. You would if you appeared in the latter, run the risk of leading the spectators to imagine that you had forgotten to don your trousers and had sallied forth in your drawers. This would be fatal to the dignity of the Feis. If you adopt a costume, let it, at all events, have some elements of picturesqueness.[125]

The diversity within the Irish language with its various dialects and the absence of generally accepted spelling rules caused its own particular problems. Patrick took a fairly lenient attitude towards issues of this kind: 'My own idea is that so long as substantive uniformity and consistency in spelling are secured, a reasonable latitude may be given to individual tastes.'[126] When applying for the editorship Patrick admitted to having obtained a sympathy for the Connacht version of the language but claimed he would not benefit it to the detriment of the others: 'Though circumstances and associations have made me a Connachtman linguistically and in sympathy, I think I can fairly claim to be above all petty provincial jealousies, and to be in a position to see the movement steadily as a whole.' However, he felt it was appropriate to neglect texts written in the dominant Munster dialect: 'I would devote special attention to the development of Ulster and Connacht, as Munster – at least on the matter of literature – can very well look after itself.'[127] In his dealings with writers like Henry Morris, who wrote in the Ulster dialect, he showed himself flexible: 'It would be necessary however to somewhat modify the dialectic peculiarities. I do not mean to destroy altogether its Ulster flavour quite the contrary … nothing like the vandalism or wholesale boycotting of Ulster forms would be attempted.'[128]

His strong connection with Connacht stemmed from the early involvement with the League and became ever stronger. Since his first visit to the Aran Islands in 1898 he frequently held short holidays there. Shortly after his graduation in 1901 he informed his cousins in Birmingham that 'he was not coming here any more that he was going to the peasants who spoke Irish henceforth for his holidays'.[129] He felt very at home in the West because the people seemed to treat him as one of their own.[130] At times he went around the country in old clothes, unshaven and with a big stick to be even closer to them.[131] He was impressed by what he idealistically saw as the carriers of true Irish culture. 'In the kindly Irish west I feel that I am in Ireland.'[132] In line with the idealisation of traditional Irish society Patrick had an overwhelming desire to see only good in Irish speakers. During his early trips he used to give his money away to whoever spoke Irish. Joseph O'Neill recalls how 'The next holiday there he let me look after the cash for the 2 of us.'[133] He was so taken by Connemara that after spending several holidays he bought a plot of land in 1905 in Ros Muc, Co. Galway, where he had befriended the local schoolteacher and parish priest and where 'you could get a clean room and good attendance'. He had a cottage built in Irish vernacular style with a thatch roof. This mirrored a trend among regional movements in Europe to reappraise the traditional architecture of their area.[134] After it was finished in the summer of 1909 it served as a holiday home where he could write and as a Gaeltacht summer centre for the pupils at his school.[135] One of the local women recalled how Patrick always joined in all festivities and really engaged with the local children. He once even brought his magic lantern and gave a performance to hundreds of local people. In the West Patrick was received as the Big Man from Dublin and was accepted by them. They described him as always courteous to all and a good listener, 'but never talked much himself'.[136]

He consciously tried to alter the image of the West created by the Congested District Board and ethnographical studies as backward and destitute. In his stories he avoided fairies and wild hairy men but focused on willowy women and emphasised their cleanliness to show how civilised the West really was.[137] Patrick had quickly realised that the future of the language lay in the hands of the native speakers and not with the language enthusiasts in Dublin. Native speakers in the West, however, did not share his desire to save the language at all costs. They understood that the economic future of their children was tied up with their ability to speak English and therefore the language was under serious threat. Patrick was not blind to this but had little appreciation of it. He blamed the education system which produced children 'who speak no language, who own no country, who have but one ambition in life – to shake the dust of Ireland off their feet as soon as they can'.[138] 'Let us plainly tell the emigrant that he is a traitor to the Irish State, and, if he but knew all, a fool into the bargain.'[139] He was also critical of the influence of Irish-Americans who he felt were encouraging 'desertion'.[140]

This predisposition for Connacht was not appreciated by the particularly well-organised Gaelic League in Munster. They felt, with good reason, that the leadership neglected the, in their eyes superior, Munster dialect, and that the Dublin representatives, few of whom were native speakers, had undue influence over League affairs. Patrick did not fully acknowledge these concerns. One of his fellow Leaguers recalled how he had to laugh when a heated argument broke out at the Ard Fheis between the Munsterman Dick Foley and the Connacht representative Dr Tuomy over the merits of the Munster jig versus the Connacht reel.[141] Others were less sanguine. P.S. O'Hegarty described the attitude of the various factions 'who hated each other like poison, and would almost have assassinated each other if it would advantage the victory of the particular dialect of Irish in which they believed as the master dialect'.[142] He was also amused by 'the wild controversial letters which came – e g one on slender 'r'. He noted on it "Goide deir Gaillmh" [God speaks the truth in print].'[143] However, some felt that allowing too much divergence in spelling gave the Intermediate Board a reason to downgrade Irish as it would not be considered a real language if it did not have an established spelling.[144]

Apart from a certain amount of jealousy and clashing personalities, the conflict between Dublin and Munster can also be related to a difference in outlook between native speakers and language enthusiasts. Patrick's nephew identified a fundamental lack of understanding on Patrick's side: 'Pearse knew nothing of those Irish who play pitch toss in Green Lanes & of the ritual visit to Baldoyle.'[145] While some of the native speakers refused to take the language enthusiasts seriously: 'Too many of the native speakers were uncouth & boorish like the picture of Michael Cusack in Ulysses. One of them said that I had an English mouth & would never learn Irish so I got fed up.'[146] Some of the more uncultured native speakers had difficulties with Patrick's increasingly cosmopolitan taste. His liking for Shakespeare and opera was often alien to them.[147]

Tensions between Dublin and Munster gradually intensified. The powerful Keating branch, dominated by supporters of Fr O'Leary, was considered to be too political by many of the League leaders and under the sway of Sinn Féin. The attempt by the Coiste Gnotha to drive out this political element was much resented in Munster.[148] One of the first open expressions of these tensions was the row which broke out in 1898 between the Coiste Gnotha and Bernard Doyle, a member of the Lee branch of the League, who was believed to profit financially from his association with the League through his newspaper *Fáinne an Lae*. The ties between the League and the newspaper which had only been founded in January were subsequently broken in December 1898 and a number of Lee branch members were expelled.[149]

As the League saw a central role for an Irish language newspaper in its objective of restoring the language, it was immediately decided that the League should establish its own. 'One of the greatest facts we have to face is that Irish has absolutely no chance to hold its own as a spoken language unless it also holds its own and makes good its position as a cultivated, that is, a read and written language.'[150] On basis of estimates from two printing companies it was decided in February 1899 to have the first issue of the new paper out by 18 March. The Coiste was divided over the title. In the end it took the casting vote of the chairman to choose *An Claidheamh Soluis* (Sword of Light) over *Geal Gréine*.[151] Possibly following the refusal of the Postmaster General to register the paper unless the name and date were printed at the head of each page in ordinary Roman characters, the subheading of the paper became 'The Mouthpiece of the Language Revival Movement'.[152]

Running two Irish language newspapers side by side was too much for a small market and *An Claidheamh Soluis* was merged with *Fáinne an Lae* on 28 July 1900. The disagreements between Dublin and Cork nevertheless festered; the latter gradually developed a tendency to oppose anything emanating from Dublin. In February 1902, for instance, the Munster contingent supported the attack on the Publications Committee by Coiste member Norma Borthwick of the Irish Book Company and D.P. Moran, editor of the *Leader*, for providing unfair competition to other publishers by not sticking to textbooks.[153]

The central position Patrick had gradually come to occupy in the League became increasingly clear to all and with that he became the main target for attacks. Fr Dinneen, a leading member of the Keating Branch who also was a member of the Coiste Gnotha and sat on the Publications Committee, became Patrick's main critic.[154] Dudley Edwards described Dinneen as a sharp tongued Munster priest and as one of the League's great eccentrics. Patrick's meteoric rise in the League, his general modernist attitude, his tendency to put himself forward and his neglect of the Munster dialect clearly annoyed many in Munster and beyond. His arrival at the first Ard Fheis after he was appointed to the Coiste Gnotha in frog coat and silk hat did not enamour him to the country element either.[155] Michael Foley considered Patrick overrated and resented how 'He spoke of unsophisticated peasants running the movement.'[156] His mannerisms and shyness also repelled many others in the movement: 'He was always serious and broody. Cttee men usually said "That fathead," after he had gone by at the feis.'[157]

An Claidheamh Soluis

When the editorship of *An Claidheamh Soluis* suddenly became available in February 1903 the animosity of the Munstermen to the non-natives in Dublin like Patrick came to a head. The sitting editor, Owen Naughton, had been forced to retire by the Coiste Gnotha after he had allowed a letter written by Thomas A. Murphy, criticising the lack of attention paid to the Irish language in the Bishops' Lenten Pastoral, to be printed. Naughton was already considered ineffective by many in the League and he now had compromised the organisation, as witnessed by a vicious letter campaign in the *Freeman's Journal*.[158] O'Hickey, one of the most active and influential members of the executive, was exasperated with Naughton: 'What on earth is to be done with O'Neachtain? Such an awful exhibition of vacillation, of alternate strength and weakness, finally ending in utter imbecility and making the League a laughing-stock before all men, has never before been seen … here we have a fool after making a show of fight giving away the whole case.'[159]

   The editorship was now an attractive proposition for Patrick. The job came with an annual salary of £240 and this gave him an attractive career perspective when combined with his other activities. Besides Patrick there were three other serious candidates: William P. Ryan from London, Patrick MacSweeney, supported by Dr O'Hickey, and J.J. O'Kelly (Sceilg), a Munster republican backed by Fr Dinneen. Those opposed to Pearse's candidature emphasised the fact that he was very young and inexperienced and that he was not a native speaker. Partly for that reason some of the major figures in the League, such as Douglas Hyde, Eoin MacNeill and O'Hickey, who had supported Patrick at other occasions, opposed his candidature.[160]

Patrick had not expected this and used it as a pretext to drum up support for himself.[161] In a series of letters to picked members of the Coiste Gnotha he emphasised his long and intimate experience of League work and his acquaintance with all the leading Irish authors and Irish-speaking districts. Realising his weakness in the language department he emphasised the need for other qualities; our editor 'must also bring to the management of the paper a steady level head and a strong hand; clear sane notions of things, the faculty of grasping issues and facts, and being able to gather round him a loyal band of competent writers; he must be able to give a lead to the country, and inspire the country's confidence'. In reply to J.J. Doyle's response that he would still prefer a native speaker Patrick again emphasised the need for experience and argued that the editor did not write the paper himself but mostly needed good contacts.[162]

Other League members, including J.H. Lloyd, Stephen Barrett and George Moonan, actively supported Patrick's candidacy and wrote to members of the Executive themselves: 'the one who would best serve the interest of the League and the one best entitled to the post is Pearse. His talents and abilities are of a very high order. He has done enormous work for the League during the past five years, for all of which he has received not a penny. His knowledge of Irish, spoken and written is very good.'[163] They felt that impartiality as between the districts and an ability to stand up against 'the Munster clique' were major issues in which they trusted Patrick most.[164]

Patrick need not have worried because he handsomely beat the competition, particularly after Ryan, who was a favourite of many Coiste members, withdrew his candidature.[165] He received the support of various influential members including Arthur Griffith, Dr John P. Henry, the League's vice-president, and female activists like Agnes O'Farrelly and Mary Hayden, who in many ways saw Patrick as her protégé and had developed a close friendship with him.[166] The active support of the female section of the League caused their fellow executive member, Stephen Gwynn, to imply ulterior motives: 'I notice all the young ladies are for the twenty-three year old man.'[167] Arthur Griffith preferred Patrick over Sceilg because: 'the help of the clergy will be necessary and Pearse may be more diplomatic'.[168] It was said that Dr Henry swung the Connacht vote, who wanted to keep out a Munster man at all cost.[169] In the election Patrick received nineteen votes against three for MacSweeney and four for O'Kelly. O'Hickey, one of the principal proponents of the argument in favour of a native speaker who had supported MacSweeney, resigned in protest.[170] With him the most active member of the Coiste Gnotha besides Patrick was lost for the movement. The representatives of the Munstermen described Patrick's appointment as the squandering of a great opportunity: 'our hope of a rational literary development, the cultivation of idiomatic Irish' is now gone.[171]

What swayed many was the coherent plan Patrick had put forward as part of his application.[172] In this he showed himself to be attuned to the wishes of a modern audience. His general aim was to make the paper much more attractive to the reader, in its size, make-up and by the use of illustrations. He proposed to convert the Irish section of the paper to a full blown newspaper, dealing with weekly news so that its readers were not necessitated to read an English language newspaper. He wanted to make this section more attractive by including an illustrated leading article dealing with one of the vital problems which confronted the country, and by introducing a series of reading lessons, humorous stories and 'racy anecdotes'. 'Ponderous propagandist or other such articles in Irish should be tabooed.' The English section would still be aimed at the League members itself but should also appeal to the general reader, containing a leader which provided guidance concerning the issues of the day. Instead of the dull reports from local branches and correspondents, only striking issues should be reported on together with fresh and varied notes concerning the language movement and other matters in which the personal and local note should be struck in bright chatty articles. On top of this new books should be promptly reviewed and in a u-turn from his previous criticism of the Irish Literary Society he suggested to have at least one literary article in English appear each week.[173]

Once instated as editor on 10 March 1903 Patrick insisted the changes he had suggested would be implemented immediately. In the first issue under his command the new direction was announced in what he called 'the nationalisation of the League's weekly organ':

> As the organ of militant Gaeldom, this paper has a well-defined mission before it. It will be its duty to put clearly the point of view of the Gael: to make articulate the thoughts and hopes and ambitions of those who dwell in the Gaelic places. It has a further function as the first fighting line of an organisation which has become the dominant force in the land. As the Gael rises to the surface, and that organisation looms larger in the national life, this paper will gradually become the leading organ of opinion in the country.[174]

In one of his next editorials Patrick emphasised that although the paper was dependent for most of its facts on the daily press, mostly continental rather than English, 'three quarters of its news matter was really original comment rather than a résumé of facts and the comment is always that of Gaels with the Gaelic viewpoint'.[175]

The reforms, which included illustrations, typographical changes, the use of Irish typeset, payment of contributors, a private office and extra staff, were, however, too costly for the League to bear. In the first year of his editorship the League had to subsidise the paper by more than £611.[176] After two months the illustrations had to be abolished and the format was modified to cut costs. The change in size was officially inspired by practical reasons: 'the large size of the present page of *An Claidheamh* has involved certain inconveniences; the paper is too large to be comfortably handled, too large for binding, too large for slotting in a drawer of ordinary size'. The financial aspect was, however, not concealed but the readers were assured they would get 'substantially the same amount of reading matter as heretofore. In its new form *An Claidheamh* will contain twelve moderately large pages.'[177]

All the changes did not remain unnoticed and Patrick received a great deal of unwanted and unsolicited advice. He was not altogether pleased with this and made that clear in an ironic comment. 'The amount of interest evinced in this paper by other organs, at home and abroad is really flattering, not to say touching [...] We would throw out the suggestion that the various periodicals interested in our welfare should each open a special department under the heading "Hints to the Editor of the Official Organ as to how to do his business".'[178]

Patrick continued to try other less expensive ways to make the paper more attractive. In October he proposed to divide the local news in four separate sections, one for each province. He asked Henry Morris, schoolteacher and Irish writer from Lisdoonan, Co. Monaghan, to provide three or four paragraphs each week: 'dealing with Ulster affairs – important proceedings of public bodies in the north, big political and other meetings, the more important Gaelic League functions, the state of the weather, crops, markets, etc. – in short everything of specific interest to Ulstermen'.[179] Eventually this division of the news on a provincial basis was successful. In May 1907 he would set up a system of provincial correspondents, offering them £1 a month. With this he considered the paper to have graduated to the status of a real newspaper.[180]

To alleviate the financial strain caused by his initial changes he instructed Sean T. O'Kelly, the new manager appointed on his insistence,[181] to look for more revenue through attracting as many long-term advertisers as possible, even to pressurise local League branches to put in paid ads for their Feiseanna. He considered this the best way of making the paper pay, as production costs per issue were roughly equal to the sale price a rise in circulation did not really add to income. Patrick expressed his fear that if losses continued the Ard Fheis would drop the paper altogether. 'You and I must make a success of this thing at all hazards: our reputation depends on it, and much more, both for us & the League.'[182] Patrick's own tendency to alter proofs continuously even after they had gone to the printers unnecessarily added to the expenses.[183] O'Kelly and Patrick nevertheless reported positively about the changes in a circular to the branches that same month. Noting a 50 per cent increase in circulation and confidently claiming that '*An Claidheamh* now occupies with regard to the Irish-Ireland movement at large the commanding position which rightfully belongs to the official journal of the Gaelic League'.[184] To prevent further losses the Coiste Gnotha was forced to reduce Patrick's budget drastically in March 1904. After that things started to look up. The subsidy for *An Claidheamh Soluis* came to £200 in 1904 and circulation figures reached a peak of 174,044. The following two years the paper managed to pay its own way.[185]

As editor, Patrick gave much space to Irish literature, but did not consider *An Claidheamh Soluis* a language paper in a linguistic sense. Although there would be some discussion of the correctness of various phrases, he did not want it to be a forum for a discussion of grammar and idiom. Expressing regret that there was no real place for that kind of material anywhere, he did not feel obliged to provide it.[186] He did try to put forward new idiom in his own writing and in the contributions by others, but the main task as he saw it was to popularise classic texts and stimulate contemporary writing.[187] The latter proved difficult. By the summer of 1906 he complained that the language movement had not yet produced any modern drama.

> We have the same 'Bean-tighe', the same 'Sean-fhear', the same 'Fear Óg', the same 'Buachaill Aimsire', the same 'Cailín Comhursan' in a dozen plays: and these worthy folk foregather in the kitchen; and dance the same dances and chat in the same way about the same topics, no matter what part of Ireland they hail from, what period they are supposed to be living in, what events – grave or gay – they are taking part in.[188]

In line with his initial proposals he also gave more space to writings in English: 'I am anxious to make the English side of the paper as attractive as possible, and aim at covering the whole ground – literary, linguistic, critical, historical, propagandist, educational, industrial, etc.'[189] He more openly reappraised the work of the Irish Literary Movement and moved away from the days in which he described their work as a heresy and Yeats as a third rate poet. 'As literature, we rate their work high. We regret that it has not been done in Irish that it might be altogether ours. But we prefer that it should be done in English than that it should remain undone. We are broad-minded enough to believe that the world is always the better of the work of a true artist, thinking conscientiously and giving of the best that is in him.'[190]

This largely mirrored Yeats' own position following the attacks by Patrick and Eoin MacNeill in 1899. At a public meeting in Gort Yeats had said that 'For good or for evil he had to write his own books in English, and to content himself with filling them with as much Irish thought and emotion as he could, for no man can get a literary mastery of two languages in one lifetime.' He had remained very positive about the Gaelic League project, and 'foresaw without regret a time when what was the work of his life would be in a foreign language to a great part of the people of this country'. He even agreed that the language was necessary for the preservation of Irish nationhood, and concurred with Patrick's early assertion that Ireland had a role 'to lift up its voice for spirituality, for ideality, for simplicity in the English-speaking world'.[191]

In private Patrick expressed regret for his attacks on Yeats and even publicly defended the significance of John Synge's controversial play *The Playboy of the Western World*.[192] Although he felt it libelled mankind as a 'propagation of a monstrous gospel of animalism, of revolt against sane and sweet ideals, of bitter contempts for all that is fine and worthy, not merely in Christian morality, but in human nature itself', he defended it for its artistic qualities.[193] This may partly be explained by the fact he had built up a professional and sometimes personal relation with many proponents of the Irish Literary Movement. He now also saw a common bond with those trying to create a distinctive Irish literature in the English language: 'I have been trying in *An Claidheamh* to promote a closer comradeship between the Gaelic League and the Irish National Theatre and Anglo-Irish writers generally. After all we are all allies.'[194] He acknowledged that the quality of acting in the Irish Theatre was poor and advised them to go to Yeats' Abbey to learn their craft.[195] The feelings were reciprocated when Yeats attended a play in Patrick's school in 1909 which he then described to Lady Gregory as 'one of the few places where we have friends'.[196]

Patrick was, nevertheless, still convinced that the future of the nation lay with creative Irish writing from the Gaeltacht and could not come from those writing in English: 'Every piece of literature in Irish forms, in our view, part of the national literature whereas no piece of English does, however it may glow with love of Ireland.'[197] He described Anglo-Irish writers as members of the 'Celtic Twilight School' and their movement a movement of defeat, while plays more critical of Irish society stemming from those quarters like those of Synge discouraged him.[198] Ultimately he believed there was no future for Irish writing through English: 'if writers and actors continue to ignore the Irish language, they are doomed to failure as is every other movement that ignores the Gaelic basis of the Irish nation'.[199] When Yeats was described as a member of the Gaelic Revival in the New York newspaper *The Irish World* Patrick also strongly objected.[200]

The disparaging use of the term Celtic Twilight first introduced in a story by Yeats in 1893 came from D.P. Moran whose *The Philosophy of Irish-Ireland* greatly influenced Patrick. Moran believed that Celticism and Anglo-Irish literature perpetuated a relationship with English culture which was harmful and subjugating, and was essentially a form of self-hatred. Celticism was suspiciously urban and feminised, less robust and vigorous than rural Irish culture. Although praising the Anglo-Irish for their work on resurrecting Irish stories, he believed the use of English emasculated the Irish making them unsuitable for self-government. His alternative to the Celts and their personification of it in Hibernia was the Gael, a person close to the land, combining manual labour with scholarship and learning as part of everyday life.[201]

At this stage he clearly foresaw a long and hard road ahead before the language would be restored in Ireland: 'We have a task before us that requires self-sacrifice and exertion as heroic as any nation ever put forth.'[202] 'Belgian Flemish acquired near equality in 75 years, how long will it take for Ireland?'[203] Patrick certainly lived up to this requirement. Although he temporarily resigned his position as Secretary of the Publications Committee when he became editor of *An Claidheamh Soluis*, he continued to teach Irish three mornings a week at the Christian Brothers, gave some classes in Alexandra College and even more privately. From January 1906 he also ran two weekly classes in Irish language and literature at elementary and advanced level parallel with Eoin MacNeill's lectures on Irish history in UCD. Apart from this, he took on several other responsibilities. In 1906 he became board member of the Theatre of Ireland, a breakaway group of the National Theatre, and the following year he became an external examiner in Irish history at Clongowes Wood, the Jesuit College for boys, and also a lecturer in the newly established Leinster College of the Gaelic League.[204]

He also was involved in the foundation of the aforementioned Leinster College. This initiative was inspired by the establishment of a Munster College in Ballingeary, Co. Cork, by the Keating branch in 1904. By 1912 there were eighteen of these colleges which were set up to deal with the immediate shortage of Irish teachers by providing evening classes and summer schools for teachers and other working people. Using modern methods they taught for two evenings a week during term time from October to Easter, with a third evening designated to special lectures by external professors.[205] Patrick particularly liked the summer schools when the teachers were to live with Irish-speaking families, which he compared to 'the bohemian university life of early Christian Ireland', a comparison he would draw upon more and more.[206]

Patrick was well aware of the burden of responsibilities he took upon himself. To Desmond Ryan he jokingly stated that 'He would merely have the Irish people, and not the human race, learn Irish and speak it.'[207] Apart from all these regular activities Patrick continued to promote the League at every possible occasion. He lectured in various places and visited local branches and colleges of the League. Despite his high profile in the organisation, few outsiders knew who he was. During a visit to Cloghaneely, Co. Donegal, where a League College was being opened in 1906, he was not recognised by the large crowd which had expected Douglas Hyde. It was even possible for a group of strangers to impersonate Patrick and his party and eat all the food meant for them at a céilidh organised by the local Irish Party MP.[208] This was possibly due to his late arrival. He had been given a public scolding on lack of punctuality earlier on in the day when he arrived far too late for his lecture in Gortahork. He 'listened with bent head and blushing face – just like an over-grown schoolboy!'[209]

The locals were more impressed when he returned the next summer on a promotion trip through the northwest with high League officials Dr P. MacHenry, Tomás Ó Concheanainn and Francis Joseph Bigger. The latter's open-top car, 'the Gaelic League motor party' in particular, attracted a lot of attention. The schedule was very intensive consisting of various lecture programmes and examinations followed in the evening by social functions. Although finding a good response, Patrick was disappointed by the lack of interest shown by local women and children and the apparently growing habit of Irish speakers to speak English to their children. Unable to understand the economic necessity of such behaviour he was shocked when only two girls in a factory in Killybegs were willing to admit they were able to speak Irish. He also wondered why the locals sold beautiful cloth to England while buying cast-off garments in return.[210] In the poem 'I am Ireland' he would later describe this as Ireland being sold off by the Irish. Nevertheless, Patrick considered the trip very fruitful, having promoted bilingual teaching to the local schools which generally did not spend more than an hour on Irish a week. He expressed a desire to visit Connacht in similar fashion the next year, and wrote to Bigger to thank him, ensuring him that they had done much good work, and that 'I for one enjoyed myself thoroughly'.[211]

The manner in which Patrick fulfilled his tasks as editor was also time consuming. He wrote at least two days a week for the paper. He was responsible for the editorials, the miscellanea section, the Notes and in 1905 let it slip that 'Of course all *unsigned* reviews and articles are written by me.'[212] Sean O Brian, an apprentice with the paper, remembers that 'If you told him that he was a column short he would give it to you almost to a word.'[213] Not shy for work, Patrick also unsuccessfully applied for the government position of Assistant Intermediate Examiner in Irish in 1905. In a letter of recommendation Douglas Hyde indicated the enormous amount of work the just 25-year-old Patrick had done for the League: 'he has probably edited more Irish matter than any other person living'.[214] Sometimes the pressures of all his responsibilities got the better of him. After failing to answer a letter he stated: 'My only excuse must be that amid a multiplicity of pressing and worrying affairs I kept putting it off.'[215]

In 1905 Patrick also began to write fiction, all of which was first published in *An Claidheamh Soluis*. Somewhat uncertain of his abilities and fearful of the criticism of native speakers like Fr Dinneen and Fr O'Leary he published his first story, 'Poll an Phiobaire' (The Piper's Cave), under the pseudonym Colm O Conaire.[216] One of the native Irish speakers associated with the League remembers his constant questioning of the use of Irish in the story.[217] His first five stories came out between March 1905 and December 1906. When four of these were published as a booklet, *Íosagán agus Sgéalta Eile* (Iosagan and other stories), in December 1907 they received widespread praise as 'one of the best attempts at creating a modern Irish literature that the language movement has yet inspired'.[218]

Those who believed Irish writing should be based solely on the forms used in the seventeenth century damned this introduction of the modern form of the short story into Irish literature, particularly in its opening phrases: 'The extract is of very high value as affording a sample to beginners of that which must be shunned in thought, in feeling, in outlook, in expression, in word, punctuation, everything.'[219] They felt there were too many detailed descriptions, and that the introduction of an all-knowing chronicler and the absence of a formal introduction of the characters was 'a betrayal of the Irish tradition'. There was also criticism from native Irish speakers, and before it became known that Patrick had written these stories Fr Dinneen had correctly identified the writer as a city-dweller with acquired Irish.[220]

Some later asserted that 'Poll an Phiobaire' reminded them very much of 'Lost on Duv Corrig', a story by Standish O'Grady.[221] In defence Patrick emphasised he was raising the standard of art: 'I may or may not be a good standard bearer, but at any rate the standard is raised and the writers of Irish are flocking to it.'[222]

Although modern in form, the themes of Patrick's stories were traditional in that they idealised and sentimentalised rural life and failed to reflect real life as many European writers did. It has been argued that he wrote only about the world of children and later of women to avoid criticism that he did not confront social and economic realities. His ultimate objective was to represent ideals not realities.[223] Despite his own denials, Patrick can nevertheless still be seen as a modernist. His rejection of the modernist epitaph and celebration of ancient Irish examples can be seen as a tactic to avoid criticism from traditionalists in the movement.[224]

Campaigns and causes

In his role as editor Patrick went way beyond his immediate duties. He took an interest in almost all aspect of the welfare of the language and as a result became involved in numerous campaigns, causes and also some controversies during his tenure. One of the first of these campaigns was that for the welfare of Gaelic poet Colm Wallace from Gorumna Island in Galway. Shortly after his appointment Patrick became aware that the seventy-year-old Wallace was spending his old age in the workhouse. Wallace, who claimed to be 107, was the author of a well-known Irish poem, 'Cúirt an tSrutháin Bhuidhe'. Patrick felt it was intolerable that such an, in his eyes, important Irish poet had to spent his last years in poverty. He immediately set up a fund widely advertised in *An Claidheamh Soluis* to collect money to provide Wallace with free accommodation and maintenance in his place of birth.

As usual Patrick approached this with great energy. He got the London branch of the League to do some fundraising, and the local Irish class in Camberwell organised a céilidh to raise funds. In Dublin he started collecting Wallace's poetry and had a booklet with his work published in 1904 as *Amhrain Chuilm de Bhailis*, the proceeds going to the fund. At the same time he got the *An Claidheamh Soluis* correspondent in Galway, P. Ó Domhnalláin, to try to make Wallace accept this charity and find a place for him to stay. Patrick showed great sensitivity to the feelings of Wallace: 'I do not know whether he would have any delicacy in accepting our offer. You could mention to him that similar collections have been got up for such men as Parnell and T.D. O'Sullivan. Tell him that the members of the Gaelic League are determined that the author of Cúirt an tSrutháin Bhuidhe shall not die in a workhouse if they can help it.' All this was successful. Within two months after the start of the campaign, Ó Domhnalláin had found a place with a Mrs Toole for Wallace to board and there was enough money to pay her and to fit out Wallace respectably. After spending the next two years in comfort Wallace died; he even got his funeral paid for by the League.[225]

Not just the interest of the language and its proponents lay close to Patrick's heart, but also the wider interests of Ireland were served by him. Usually in response to some request or issue that came to his attention he initiated various other campaigns. Concurrent with the Wallace case, he started an employment agency for Irish-speaking boys and girls through the paper after one of the League's Belfast activists, Mrs Hutton, had asked him for an Irish-speaking maid.[226] In February 1905 he approached the editor of the newly established *Irish Independent* looking for support among editorial staffs of the dailies to set up an Irish Union of Journalists.[227] He was also an avid supporter of the buy Irish campaign initiated by his rival D.P. Moran of the *Leader*. His dedication to the welfare of Irish manufacturers went beyond the practical. His Christmas present of a dolls house with furniture to his goddaughter Síle Bairead was accompanied with the following provision: 'The furniture may be a little too big to place in the house, but it is not possible to get smaller furniture of Irish manufacture.' When he was asked to become her godfather in 1903 the language had also been foremost in his mind. 'No small honour especially to one, who will be, as your daughter will, an Irish speaker from the cradle.'[228] During their visit to Belgium in 1905 he advised his sister to buy only small souvenirs as: 'We must not unnecessarily spend our money outside our own country.'[229]

Patrick's demands on the willingness of the reader to support his often wide-ranging causes was unrelenting. In 1904 he took up a suggestion originally made in the *Gaelic Journal* the year before not to wait for the Board of Education but to establish Irish-speaking primary schools in the Gaeltacht. Fr Dinneen had added that it should be financed by Irish-Irelanders. Patrick took this idea to its extreme and imagined unrealistically that the entire National School system could thus be replaced. 'It is a project that would gladden the heart of every Irish Irelander if it could be accomplished in time to save the living language.' To this end, he set up the Tawin School Fund for which he managed to generate widespread support even from the League's contacts in Wales, English academics and Irish clerics. At the end of 1904 the first school was built in south Galway which later served as a training centre for Irish teachers, but it never went much further than that.[230]

In his final years as editor he became involved in a drive to try to tackle TB by financing a health education programme in Connemara and setting up a Home Improvement Scheme for which *An Claidheamh Soluis* offered prizes.[231] Not everybody trusted the motives in this regard. Sceilg claimed that the League only participated in the fight against TB to keep in with the Aberdeens. Lord Aberdeen, who was then Lord Lieutenant for Ireland, and his wife had shown a strong interest in the matter.[232] One of the last campaigns as editor was the acquisition of Ratra, the estate occupied by Hyde in 1908. The high esteem the sickly Hyde was held in was shown by the fact the required £1000 were raised successfully.[233]

Education and the Church

The most influential of Patrick's activities as editor was no doubt his visit to Belgium in June/July 1905. This fact-finding mission on bilingual education was supported by the Belgian Ministry of Public Instruction. Patrick was an enthusiastic believer in the idea that the English had used the education system in the nineteenth century to kill the Irish language and that the introduction of a bilingual education system in Ireland would reverse this trend. Since his visit to Wales in 1899, Patrick had spent much of his writings on bilingual education. Just before leaving for Brussels he wrote extensively on the state of teaching Welsh, clearly well informed by his contacts there.[234] His trips to Belgium generated further material. 'The schools I have visited were most interesting and will supply copy for a long series of articles.'[235] Between August 1905 and March 1907 he indeed published more than fifty articles in two series in *An Claidheamh Soluis*. These were followed by numerous articles promoting the direct method in language education.[236] One of its readers was somewhat exasperated with this overkill: 'In season and out of season he urged bilingualism, and in season and out of season he brooded on the question of Irish education, seeing in that, as so many have done, the spear-point of English influence in Ireland.'[237]

The demand for a separate government-recognised university for Irish Catholics was the first educational issue in which Patrick became prominent as editor. The establishment of a university of their own was a long-standing wish both of Catholics and of the language movement. Initially the League had simply demanded the establishment of Chairs of Celtic studies in existing universities. However, by 1905 suggestions supported by Archbishop Walsh to make Trinity College into a national university by providing it with a Catholic chapel, a Catholic chair of philosophy, a separate honours degree in Irish and space for Catholics on an elected governing body were no longer seen as sufficient.[238] Instead the League now called for the creation of a National University which it described as 'an intellectual headquarters for Irish Ireland'.[239] In this it was looking to the example set in Wales where a National University had been established in 1895.

The government indeed set up a Royal Commission to study university education in Ireland at the beginning of the twentieth century. The League wanted to ensure that the overall ethos of the university would be national rather than Catholic. In their eyes a Catholic university could conceivably be as un-Irish as 'TCD is today'.[240] Consequently it was looking for a strong influence for laymen in the governing body of the yet to be founded university. 'Of course the nominees of the Hierarchy will, in a sense, represent popular opinion, and will certainly enjoy popular confidence; but their specific function on the Board will be to safeguard the interest of the Church.'[241]

To put pressure on the government a Catholic Graduates and Under-graduates Association was set up with clerical support in October 1903: 'to organise the opinion and influence of Irish University men in regard to this question, and thereby to bring such pressure on the government as to secure an immediate settlement of this question'.[242] Count Plunkett, the Unionist MP known for his advocacy of Irish economic development, presided and a number of other important Irish public figures joined the committee together with many members of the League. Impatient with progress, some of them led by Patrick began to push for the foundation of a National University funded by the Irish nation and independent of government control. A motion to this end was proposed by Patrick in June 1905. Although the motion was carried, Patrick's subsequent proposal to request the General Council of County Councils to summon a conference to discuss the policy was rejected.[243]

Plans were then drawn up to use the Jesuit controlled University College, Dublin, as the base for such a publicly supported university. An attempt by Patrick and his friend Thomas Kettle to give lay Catholics a say in the running of this new university got the two men in hot water. Their motion sounded innocuous enough:

That in view of the scholarships already established at University College & the appeal for further endowment now before the Catholic body of Ireland we beg to suggest to the bishops of Ireland that in order to make such an appeal really fruitful – it will be necessary as soon as there is a reasonable prospect of sufficient funds being available for the conduct of the institution to make its system of government & academic administration more fully representative of the general Catholic body of Ireland.

The motion was defeated by eleven to three votes, but the suggestion was leaked to the papers, who openly accused Patrick and Kettle of anti-clericalism. The *Daily Express* opened with the headline 'Protest against Clerical Control', while the shorter phrase 'Anti-Clerical Protest' appeared on the placards.[244] The committee objected to the headline, but the *Daily Express* claimed it was entirely justified. Of course, public protests against their supposedly anti-Catholic stance followed.

Although it is clear Patrick was not in favour of clerical control over issues beyond the spiritual, he can certainly not be accused of being anti-clerical. Despite his father's lack of sincerity in this matter, Patrick had been strongly influenced by the traditional Catholicism of his mother. He was regarded as an avid church-goer with a special dedication to holy week and the crucifix.[245] He was, however, not too particular about observing religious obligations. He was not involved in any church activities and even in his last letters before his execution he was more concerned with personal and political issues than the afterlife. He held a deeper felt spirituality which was represented better through the essentially pagan legends and imagery of the Celts.[246]

Possibly mirroring his father's apparent religious journey, many of his stories deal with adults losing their faith but nevertheless living a good life, by their lifestyle as in *Íosagán*, through their nationalism as in *The Singer* or even by sinning as in *The Thief* and in the poem 'A Song for Mary Magdalene'. Those involved always regain their faith, usually through the example of children. In *The Master* he provides a convincing rational argument against the existence of God but the hero is ultimately persuaded by miracles. In *The Singer* the main character realises that God is an illusion which takes away the loneliness of the heart. However, God then reveals himself through his own suffering, loneliness and abjection. Patrick's general demeanour and serious attitude to religion made some believe he would or even should have been a priest. Tom MacDonagh's sister, who was a nun, claims to have suggested to him to join a monastery some time before the Rising.[247]

Immediately after the publication in the *Daily Express* Patrick wrote to the secretary of the graduates association protesting against the action of some of the committee members in supplying this 'garbled account of last Thursday's meeting which appeared in Friday's Independent. I thought that everyone understood that the proceedings were confidential.' He expressed his desire that 'the society will take steps to discover the identity of the disloyal member, and will deal with his action in the strongest manner'.[248] What he and Kettle had asked for was indeed not novel. Patrick had already been agitating for a national university that was not British supported for a number of years. In January 1905 he also publicly argued that it should not be 'a water-tight denominational institution with doors rigidly barred against non-Catholics'.[249]

Partly due to the ensuing controversy the call for a university funded by popular subscription did not receive a very strong response. Soon after the coming to power of the new Liberal Government in 1905 the need for such a university also seemed to have disappeared. In their submission to a newly established Royal Commission the Bishops and the Catholic Graduates and Undergraduates Association rejected a reformed Trinity College but suggested three other possible avenues: a separate Catholic University; a new college in the University of Dublin besides Trinity College or a new college in the Royal University.[250] In due course the Liberal Government decided to establish a National University of Ireland based on the old colleges in Cork and Galway together with the Jesuit-run University College in Dublin.

When the new university bill was imminent Patrick called for a positive wait-and-see attitude, and no condemnation in advance. He believed in the good will of the new Chief Secretary Augustine Birrell, and expressed the expectation that once they had their own university the Irish people could fashion it themselves.[251] When the bill was finally published in 1908 Pearse was not overenthusiastic. In his mind the amalgamation of the three colleges had a makeshift feel to it, and warned of a three-way split in Irish university education in which Trinity would be for Episcopalians who 'cannot afford to go to Oxford or Cambridge', Queen's Belfast was for Nonconformists and the new sprawling university with extremities in Dublin, Cork and Galway was for Catholics and perhaps for non-Catholics of Irish sympathies. Although he found it 'impossible to enthuse' there was no ground for dismay or despondency: 'This really seems to be an honest Englishman's honest attempt to settle the Irish University question in the best interest of Ireland as he [Birrell] sees them.'[252]

Initially the question whether the constitution of the new university would allow it to develop an Irish atmosphere and ideals was Patrick's main concern. He felt it was the duty of Irish-Ireland to involve itself in the statutes, personnel and constitution because '[t]hese are the things on which depends the final emergence of an Irish culture in Ireland'. He was doubtful about the democratic credentials and the make-up of the governing body which contained more appointed members than the senate of Queen's. He also expressed his concern about the lack of women on the board.

> Is one woman – would even two women or for that matter six women – be a sufficient representation of the interests of what is, after all, the more important half of Ireland's population, a half, too, which is bound to be largely represented amongst the students of the university? We think that some of the male deadheads might well give place to female brains and educational experience. And we should like to see it made clear that women will be eligible for the professorial chairs.[253]

Very soon, however, his main focus became the status of Irish in the curriculum. In May 1908 when the University Bill went through its second reading Patrick spelled out what he expected from the university. He not only wanted all students to enter with a knowledge of Irish at intermediate level but also wanted to make Irish a compulsory subject at undergraduate level in the same way as English was compulsory. He wanted a system of scholarships and fellowships in Irish, a special degree in Celtic studies for which the League's Training Colleges should be recognised to provide courses at university level. Ample Irish faculty should be appointed with professors and staff in Celtic Philology, Old Irish, Modern Irish Language and Literature, Ancient Irish History and Archaeology, and Modern Irish History. In future all staff should be able to teach through Irish, which he claimed should eventually be no problem when the bilingual programme suggested by the League was introduced throughout the education system.[254]

The issue of making Irish compulsory for the entrance exam of the university, the matriculation, became the most controversial issue in the public debates. At the end of 1908 a majority seemed to form in the senate of the new university against compulsory Irish in matriculation, based on the argument that it would exclude many in Ireland as well as foreigners. Patrick was willing to accept a delay of three years for practical purposes but when a majority including some of the Catholic Church's representatives refused to support a delayed introduction of compulsion Patrick took a very strong line. He stated it was now time to distinguish between friends and foes. 'Their opposition to Ireland's language is their denial of Ireland a nation. They cannot be convinced; they must be fought.'[255]

The League again organised a big protest meeting in the Rotunda, and Patrick called upon Archbishop Walsh to support them as he had done in the past on other issues relating to the language. For Patrick this was not a simple issue, but touched upon the heart of what the League was all about. 'It [the GL] is in protest not against the Union but against the Conquest. Rather, it does not admit the Conquest. It claims that this broken and battered frame is still a Nation, bearing high on its brow all the august marks of Nationality, treasuring still in its heart the unconquerable desire to live its own life, to work out its own destiny.'[256] To him the real question was whether the university was going to be Irish in complexion or foreign. This explains his reaction when the Standing Committee of the bishops declared themselves against compulsory Irish. He felt encouraged by widespread support among the people of Ireland to oppose the Hierarchy. 'Whether the Bishops are for or against us, the people are with us.' He declared that 'It simply meant that their Lordships have not yet appreciated the vastness of the change that has come over Ireland since they were young men.'[257]

When it became clear that the Bishops were actively preventing individual priests to speak out in favour of compulsory Irish while other priests were allowed to silence the public from speaking out in favour, Patrick's stance became openly hostile. Although the Bishops had publicly stated the matter was open for fair discussion, they basically felt everyone should follow their lead once they had spoken. Not afraid to speak his mind Patrick called this attitude 'amazing' and 'bizarre', and denounced it in a rather sarcastic manner. 'So that when the Standing Committee [of the Bishops] said the question was one for fair argument, they really meant that it was no longer anything of the kind, since by a sort of ex-cathedra pronouncement hitherto unknown to theology they were setting it once and for all as finally and irrevocably as if it were a question of faith being pronounced on with all formality and solemnity by the supreme voice of the Church!'[258]

He rejected subsequent charges of anti-clericalism as he felt that this was a subject of neither religion nor morals on which 'the Bishops have no more claim to pronounce with authority than the most ordinary member of that Irish public'.[259] He called upon the Bishops to support the League which was backed by the people and most priests, by Irish-America and many Australians including the head of the Catholic Church there. The people according to Patrick 'have become proud of the name Irishman, or Irishwoman, and they will no longer willingly acquiesce in a campaign of mind murder, character murder, nation murder, which is the end aim of West British education'.[260] To come over to his side would be in the interest of the Bishops and Catholicism, 'we believe that an Irish Ireland freed from the worst influences of English civilisation with its open irreligion and veneered heathenism, would be a truer friend of religion than a West British Ireland'.[261]

Although the campaign for making Irish a compulsory subject in matriculation for the National University of Ireland was ultimately successful, the furore surrounding it led to further conflict between Patrick and the Bishops. This centred around the position of his old adversary on the Coiste Gnotha Dr O'Hickey, who was professor of Irish at Maynooth. O'Hickey had strongly criticised those, including many in the clergy, who had opposed making Irish a compulsory subject in a pamphlet entitled *An Irish University or Else*:

> If we tolerate this thing [optional Irish] we are still a race of helots, deserving the contempt and scorn of mankind. Let us brush flimsy arguments and peddling considerations and specious sophistries aside. Our difficulties are of our own making. More particularly, I grieve to say, are the making of the class to which I belong.[262]

Considering the Bishop's stance that the argument was closed as soon as they had spoken on the subject, the position of O'Hickey was unacceptable. Patrick had already noticed an active campaign run by the Bishops to stifle debate about this issue among the clergy. 'Priests in many instances are constrained now in certain dioceses, to regard themselves as no longer free to argue the question in public.'[263] He claimed that the Bishop had even stopped some ordinations, prevented appointments of priests and sent others who were critical of their policy on foreign missions. In a scathing attack he compared this attitude to the worst excesses of British rule. 'There was a period in Irish history when Dublin Castle allowed no patriotic priest to remain in Ireland. Are the penal laws it administered to be revived by the Irish Bishops?'[264]

Now O'Hickey was threatened with dismissal, Patrick came to his defence. Expressing his disbelief 'that the Bishops of Ireland would dare to lend themselves to the vile work of the suppression, in the interest of West Britain, of Irish intellect and freedom of thought'. Although he claimed the Bishops had done their worst against Irish-Ireland, it was again they who would feel the repercussions. 'It is the good name of the Bishops of Ireland that will suffer; it is, we fear, the good name of the Catholic Church that will pay the penalty of the folly and shortsightedness of those who represented it in Maynooth.' He described the Bishop's threat as a 'piece of tyrannical blundering', and added that the League would fight this decision. 'The hand of God is with us – yea, even though, for the moment, the hands of the Bishops may be raised against us.'[265]

This time the Bishops did respond directly to the charges levied against them in a public statement of 29 July 1909. 'The steps in question were taken solely in discharge of the Episcopal duty of maintaining ecclesiastical discipline in the College, and had no connection whatsoever with the views of anyone as to whether the Irish language should or should not be an obligatory subject at certain examinations, or in certain courses, of the National University of Ireland.' Now they also directly reproached Patrick accusing him of undermining their authority and even of slurring the Pope himself.

> Considering the course which, especially of late, is being pursued in this and similar matters by certain newspapers – including one which is generally reputed to be the official organ of the Gaelic League – the Bishops feel it to be a sacred duty to warn the people committed to their charge against allowing themselves to be misled by writings the clear tendency of which is antagonistic to the exercise of Episcopal authority and which, in some instances, are calculated to bring into contempt all ecclesiastical authority, not even excepting that of the Holy See itself.

The same day O'Hickey was officially dismissed.[266]

Patrick remained undaunted by the Bishop's reproach. In a response he denied *An Claidheamh Soluis* ever stated anything antagonistic to Episcopal authority. 'We are the mouthpiece of a non-sectarian organisation, and as such we have no standing in any matter concerning the exercise of Episcopal authority within its own sphere. But we claim and will always exercise the right to criticise any action of the Bishops, as of any other body of Irishmen, which affects the welfare of the Irish language.'[267] Although Patrick's sentiments in the O'Hickey case were widely shared in the movement outside Munster, his style of attack was not always appreciated and he felt forced to explain himself. 'We spoke out strongly against the recent action of the Bishops, an action which seems to us to have been at once a terrible wrong and a terrible blunder. Our words had in them, as the occasion demanded, a certain passion, but they had in them nothing of disrespect for Episcopal authority, nothing of disrespect for the Bishops.' He concluded that the Bishops' argument that O'Hickey was dismissed not for holding his views but for the way in which he expressed them was a difference nobody would understand.[268] O'Hickey took a case of unfair dismissal all the way to the Pope, but he was never restored in his position.

In this case Patrick again showed himself to be a man who stood for his principles and for a high standard of moral behaviour. As he had done as a schoolboy he fearlessly spoke out against any opposition when he believed he was right, no matter what the consequences might be. This was exactly how he had described his role as editor in 1907. 'When we took charge of this paper we resolved that, though it might cost us our position and – a thing we value far more highly – the friendship of our fellow-Gaels, we would never shrink from taking up an unpopular attitude and never stoop to write a lie.'[269] This was a line he would continue to adhere to.

In a somewhat reminiscent case Patrick had come to the defence of J.O. Hannay another fellow member of the Coiste Gnotha. In 1906 it had come out that Hannay, who was a Protestant clergymen, used the pseudonym George Birmingham, whose fairly innocent works *The Seething Pot* and *Hyacinth* had been under attack for some time for being anti-clerical and showing 'a virulent hatred of the Irish people'. After his authorship came out many League members called upon Hannay to resign. When the local Canon of Tuam subsequently refused Hannay the right to sit on the committee of the Connacht Feis, Patrick sprang to his defence. He stated he did not like the work of Birmingham either but strongly defended Hannay's right to free speech claiming he was 'as good a Gaelic Leaguer as the best of them'. 'We should be untrue to ourselves and to the trust reposed in us by the organisation if we did not protest with all the vehemence of which we are capable.' Patrick's independent line did get enough support in the League to maintain Hannay on the executive, but the latter nevertheless worried about the growing influence of the Catholic Church in the movement: 'I find of late that some of its leaders are becoming cowardly and truckling to priests and politicians.'[270]

The deterioration of Patrick's relationship with the Church was primarily a consequence of his belief that education played a pivotal role in saving the language. The Church ran and controlled most primary and many secondary schools in Ireland so their attitude was crucial. The constant calls on teachers and school management by the League to do more for the language almost automatically meant conflict with church representatives even if they were sympathetic. Some conflicts had ensued with priests, who resented being held to account for a lack of action, even before Patrick became editor of *An Claidheamh Soluis*.[271]

A conflict with the Hierarchy was nevertheless not something Patrick can be accused of having actively sought, but a number of more or less serious collisions occurred as it often failed to live up to his expectations. Underlying this was a different view of the role of religion. Patrick was primarily concerned with maintaining an Irish form of Catholicism while the Church's primary aim was to keep Ireland Catholic. He felt that as soon as Ireland would lose its culture and language it would succumb to the materialism of England and its religion. The Church should therefore defend the language and urge people from the pulpit to use Irish particularly in the Gaeltacht.[272]

In his dealings with churchmen Patrick always took a very practical line. He was always extremely deferential, both in his role as teacher in the Christian Brothers School and UCD, and particularly in his various positions in the Gaelic League. Clerical support was vital to the various causes he was involved in, and he often actively solicited it. In one of his first of many letters to Archbishop Walsh of Dublin in his capacity as secretary of the Publications Committee he asked him to vet the publication of the League regarding the teaching of Irish in National Schools, and assured him that all his suggestions were or would be taken up. He expressed his gratitude generously: 'Your Grace is adding immensely to the debt of gratitude due to you by every one concerned for the progress of the Irish language and Irish education', and signed very respectfully: 'I have the honour to be, Your Grace, Your Grace's obedient servant.'[273]

However, this was also a calculated position to take. Omar Crowley recalls Patrick remarking that it 'was a matter of expediency to keep the clergy on your hands not to antagonise them'.[274] Another contemporary, Greg Murphy, concurred: 'P. held that in Gaelic matters the priest was not the teacher but had his place.'[275] Crowley felt that Patrick's weak support for teachers in the Gaeltacht who wanted to leave the National Board and work directly under the auspice of the League, and for commissioner Starkie, a Protestant Irish-Irelander, against a Catholic on the Education Board was inspired by his fear to antagonise the clergy.[276] This practical attitude is clearly revealed in Patrick's report on the position of Bishop Henry of Down and Conor regarding the League:

> I gather from my observations that the bishop is quite sincere in his support of the movement, but he does not understand it very well. He is

a Churchman, not merely above and beyond all else, but to the exclusion of everything else. I don't imagine he is *consciously* trying to make use of the League as a prop for the Catholic Association but yet in a sort of subconscious way his support of the Gaelic League may spring from his dislike of the U.I.L. [United Irish League] ... personally, I think the support of the Bishop a much more valuable asset than the support of the local U.I.L., and, whilst making it perfectly clear that the League is no mere appendage to the Catholic Association or to the Bishop, I would use the latter for all he is worth, especially as regards the schools.[277]

At occasions when the clergy failed to support the cause of the Irish language, this conditional loyalty to the church became apparent. This went back as far as 1898 when he expressed his disappointment about the clergy's lack of support for the League, and had stated publicly that he hoped 'something would be done ... to point out to them their duty to the National Language'.[278]

Despite his deference, Patrick had frequently come in conflict with Church authorities long before the university question became an issue. In a long series of arguments Patrick had taken an increasingly critical position *vis-à-vis* the clergy. The central role of religion in the virtual dismissal of Owen Naughton as editor of *An Claidheamh Soluis*, which led to Patrick being appointed, should have made clear that he did not have much room to manoeuvre, but Patrick was clearly undaunted by this knowledge. Directly upon his appointment in 1903 he defended a local League branch who had reported on the lack of Irish teaching in Kilkenny schools against strong censure from a local priest.[279]

Much of the conflict with the clergy after 1903 concerned the teaching of Irish in the seminary at Maynooth. Irish had been a compulsory subject until 1901, but it was systematically downgraded in the following years because Maynooth wanted to fall in with the arts degree at the Royal University. The League, which felt that the availability of Irish-speaking priests played a pivotal role in preserving the language, subsequently initiated a campaign to counter this which resulted in Irish being made compulsory for the matriculation and in the junior years at Maynooth. Patrick initially praised this decision, but became concerned when in 1907 the Bishops brought in a provision under which students could ask to be relieved from their obligation to take Irish. He had learned that all such requests were granted and that fifty out of a total of 150 students at Maynooth were now exempted. Patrick understood that the existing system punished students for taking Irish but warned for the consequences of this development: 'What shall it profit Maynooth to cut a fine figure in the Royal University Results List if the Irish language dies in the Gaedhealtacht and with it the old, pure, unquestioning strenuous faith of Ireland?'[280]

The less than cooperative response from Maynooth and the bishops exasperated Patrick. 'It is our own who have struck this blow at us. It is the beloved College of O'Growney that has declared itself with the Gall and against the Gael. Men whom we had thought trusty had failed us. Revered and honoured leaders have seemed to countenance their betrayal.'[281] The president of the college, the young Monsignor Mannix, then bounced the responsibility for maintaining the language back to the League. 'It will be a day of joy and of hope for the friends of the national language when the Gaelic League, in its great work throughout the country, begins to follow the example and to rival the success of Maynooth. The Irish language will then be safe.'[282] In a strongly worded response Patrick demanded in the name of the Irish people to know what was done regarding the secular education of students at Maynooth. 'It is we who sent them to Maynooth; it is we who pay Maynooth for educating them.' He strongly condemned Mannix's attitude. 'This is autocracy with a vengeance.' 'We do not imagine that Dr. Mannix himself, when his little burst of temper has blown over, will seriously maintain the position, into which he has allowed his vexation ... to force him.'[283] This strong line led to public rebukes and a threat by Archbishop Walsh to retract his support for the League, but not to a reversal of Maynooth's policy.[284] Although the Coiste was unhappy with the manner in which Patrick had expressed his objections, they did share his sentiments and kept him in place as editor.

It is in many ways surprising how critical Patrick could be of the Church and how widely that was accepted by most readers of *An Claidheamh Soluis*. His manner of expressing himself regarding church dignitaries was certainly not common among leading nationalists after 1921, showing the growing convergence between them and the Church after independence. Patrick's critical stance towards the clergy was largely inspired by his absolute devotion to furthering the cause of the Irish language, but his willingness to take a strong independent line was in some way also reminiscent of his father. He had not taken his atheism from his father but had obviously inherited the questioning attitude toward hierarchy and authority. In a wider sense the rejection of Church authority in non-religious issues had become more acceptable to many nationalists after the censure by the Church of Parnell in 1890 over the divorce case he was involved in. Some of Patrick's contemporaries claimed that the poor pay in the CBS and the control of the Jesuits in UCD had been resented by Patrick and had been a contributing factor in his attitude to the Hierarchy.[285] Despite the various collisions Patrick managed to maintain a workable relationship with the Church and in particular with Archbishop Walsh.[286]

Irish in schools

It was not only from the Church that Patrick expected the same absolute priority to the furthering of the Irish language that he gave it himself. When Eoin MacNeill, one of the moving forces in the League, announced he was going to get married, Patrick is reported to have been very upset. Instead of rejoicing in his friend's happiness he nearly had to cry and expressed his fear it would take MacNeill away from the movement.[287] His demanding attitude could be harmful to the League and Patrick's own standing in the movement. This became particularly apparent in relation to the payment of fees to teachers for providing Irish classes outside the regular school hours, which ran from 10.30 to 15.00. The fees gave teachers an important extra source of income, but had become a growing burden on the Treasury. After the requirements for the payment of these fees were lowered in 1900 and fees were raised, the number of pupils taking Irish began to rise steeply. By 1904 there were 25,984 pupils who passed the exam as against only 1317 in 1899. The League estimated that another 100,000 children were taught Irish within school hours. In 1905 the number of schools where Irish was taught rose to 2018 while there were just 193 schools which offered French and 109 Latin.[288]

The growing costs involved caused the new Liberal Chief Secretary to announce his intention to abolish the extra fees in 1905. The League, foreseeing a reduction in the numbers taking Irish, called 'for war – war to the knife'.[289] The resulting campaign was again successful winning the League many friends among the teachers. Although Patrick supported the demand, he saw the inconsistency of calling for special treatment of the language, which in his mind should really be an ordinary subject taught in regular school hours.[290] Basing himself on the experience in Belgium he wanted a proper bilingual education system introduced in the whole country, where every child would learn its mother tongue and a second language, 'taught as a living tongue according to sound modern methods'. In such a case special fees for Irish teaching would no longer be necessary.

> In theory, this second language might be anything; in practice, it would in Irish-speaking districts be English, and in English-speaking districts Irish. In some Ulster schools, and in a few Protestant schools elsewhere, French or German would possibly be adopted as the second language, until such time as the language movement should have captured – as it inevitably will capture – even the strongholds of Orangeism.[291]

The government had no lofty ideals concerning the Irish language and still looked for ways to reduce the bill, as the number of pupils taking Irish grew to 31,741 pupils in 1906. A proposal launched that year again fell victim to opposition from the League,[292] as was the amended official scheme launched in 1907, which for the first time made Irish an optional rather than an extra subject inside school hours. This meant it was to be taught by the regular teachers, and measures to improve proficiency in Irish among them were announced. The Chief Secretary suggested he would make Irish compulsory in the Training Colleges, but for the time being only instituted a system of thirty annual prizes in these colleges. Students of the Gaelic League Colleges, where many existing teachers were taking Irish lessons, would also qualify for these.[293]

Patrick was happy with the move to make Irish part of the ordinary curriculum but was worried that there would not be enough time for it. The biggest objection in the League and among teachers against accepting the new scheme was the lowering of the fees and the position of the external teachers which had been employed through the League.[294] Further concessions from the government followed in the autumn of 1907, including Patrick's greatest wish, the introduction of a bilingual programme in Irish districts and districts where both languages were actively spoken. All teachers would henceforth receive fees for bilingual teaching and not anymore solely for Irish.[295] Although fees had thus not been increased to their original levels, Patrick felt there were now reasonable facilities and encouragement for the teaching of Irish.

In *An Claidheamh Soluis* he argued that the new measures were a great advance for the language, and if you accepted Irish as the national language and its teaching as the first duty of a teacher you could on principle not ask for a special payment. He further emphasised that monetary rewards should not constitute the only motivation for teaching Irish but that patriotic reasons, the educational value of having two languages, and what he saw as the growing commercial use of Irish should be sufficient to teachers.[296] Patrick rejected the argument put forward by some that the teachers of Ireland were a mercenary lot that would not teach Irish if they were not paid for it.[297] However, he was fully aware of the lack of commitment among some teachers. 'The young teachers, especially of late years, show a decided disdain for the working population, the company of the policeman is too often preferred to that of the young farmer.'[298]

The teachers who relied on the extra payments were not amused and charged the League with inconsistency. Fellow member of the Coiste, Piaras Béaslai, accused Patrick of acting without sanction in this matter and expressed his anger in a letter to Eoin MacNeill: 'If you think we should leave the editor of the "Claidheamh" to settle the policy of the League according to his own wishes, without permission from anyone, "what is the point of you or me" being on the Coiste Gnotha, "or of the Coiste itself" existing at all?'[299] The influential Cathal Brugha also wrote an angry letter to *An Claidheamh Soluis*, which Patrick published with the reassuring comment: 'The views of Gaels who disagree with us are just as sure of a place in our columns.'[300] Brugha stressed that although Irish should be viewed as an ordinary subject teachers needed to be induced not compelled to teach Irish. He added that in dealing with the government agitation was the only thing that would bring results not a reasoned approach.[301]

In response to these criticisms Patrick denied having acted without the backing of the Coiste Gnotha. He argued that it had decided to give up the agitation about the fees after the government had confirmed rumours that a second language would be made obligatory in the Teacher Training Colleges after 1911.[302] He added that out of 161,740 pupils now studying Irish fees were paid in regard of only 24,712.[303]

Although resistance to the new policy continued within the League, even leading to the resignation of Fr O'Leary, the vice-president of the League, a special Ard Fheis vindicated Patrick's position.[304]

With his principled approach Patrick had built up a great deal of antagonism against him among the bishops, teachers, Irish-Irelanders and many ordinary Catholics. He realised that his tendency to be outspoken had contributed to this. Regarding the fees issue he publicly apologised for calling his opponents cranks but reminded readers of the abuse he himself had suffered. 'During our career as an active Gaelic Leaguer, we have been called pretty everything from a Castle Spy to a Modernist, and it may well be that we under-estimated the sensitiveness of Leaguers who have not occupied so bad an eminence as the editor of the "official organ".'[305] At times the continuous battles in and outside the League made Patrick consider his future as editor. It was not that Patrick was blind for the sacrifices he called upon other people to make and it was not just a simple dedication to furthering the cause of the language or the nation, he truly believed in the benefits for all of his policy.

> The impression prevails that the [Bilingual] Programme will prove immensely more cumbrous and taxing than the existing unilingual programme. We have admitted from the start that the adequate working of a bilingual scheme will at first make larger demands on the thoughts and energies of a teacher than any scheme at present in operation in a national school. The teacher will require to devote more time to thinking out his day's work, to prepare his lessons beforehand, to organise his classes. But increased trouble is incidental to increased efficiency: all good teaching, as we have so often pointed out, makes larger demands on the time and thought and energy and patience of the teacher. Modern teaching techniques, whilst they tend to reduce the drudgery of the pupil to a minimum, do not at all tend in the same degree to reduce the labour of the master; rather to the contrary. But whilst we see that the successful handling of the Bilingual Programme will at first call for special exertions on the part of the teacher, we are convinced that in the long run it will vastly lighten the burden of work both for teachers and pupils. Though it seems paradoxical, it is a profound truth that it is easier to teach two languages than to teach one.[306]

To make matters even worse he subsequently suggested teaching Irish- and English-speaking children in bilingual districts separately in their first few years at school, which would involve a large amount of extra work. He understood the practical objections but saw no other way.[307] On the other hand, in a doubtful Lamarckian interpretation, he claimed that learning Irish was particularly easy for native children. The teaching was immensely facilitated by the 'fact that the child (granting it to be of Irish parentage) was *meant* to speak Irish: his vocal organs have, as the result of heredity working through the generations, got – in Father O'Leary's phrase – the Irish "twist" to begin with'.[308]

Government

Patrick tended to reserve his most outspoken condemnation to those within Ireland who he felt failed to do their duty for the Irish nation. He was easier on government institutions from whom he more or less expected opposition. If they did do the 'right thing' he always expressed his appreciation, but he could also be severely critical. The most consistent object of this was the Irish Board of Education, which in essence decided all educational policy.[309] In the debate over the reform of primary education in 1899 the government had expressed support for the idea of bilingual education in Irish-speaking districts but felt the League's demand to have Irish introduced in every school in Ireland created stumbling blocks. It subsequently handed over responsibility for the status of Irish to the Board, which forced the League to conclude: 'The struggle has now resolved itself into one between Irish Nationality and the National Board. Which shall win?'[310] As all advances in the standing of the language in the education system had to be sanctioned by the Board, it was almost inevitable that they would be seen as the major stumbling block. 'The Board of Intermediate Education seems to delight in crossing the path of the Irish people and in outraging their feelings on every possible occasion. When there is question of the Irish Language it seems to be quite beyond the power of its members to be, we shall say not generous or gracious, but even just or fair.'[311]

Although becoming increasingly sympathetic to the Irish language and being responsible for significant advances in its status, the Board always seemed to short-change the demands of the League. By July 1905 Patrick felt the only solution was a drastic change in its personnel. 'This unrepresentative, irresponsible body appears to be absolutely indifferent to, and out of touch with, the interest of the classes who use the primary schools, as well as being apparently unacquainted with the educational needs and wishes of the country generally.' He asserted the Board should be made up of representatives of the school managers' associations, teachers' organisations, county councils and the League.[312] A month later he went a step further when it became clear that the Board would be overruled by the Treasury if it did support the League in its demand for increased fees. Patrick then declared the Board irrelevant and called for a fight with the Treasury in London.[313] He suspected that the niggardly attitude behind the refusal to provide more funds was an expression of 'the old traditional desire of British and West-British administrators to keep Ireland ignorant and ineffective for the benefit of England'.[314] The constant attacks from the League on its representatives made the government increasingly suspicious of it. It ordered an investigation 'to look into the question of whether the G[aelic] L[eague] was the peaceful educational organization that it professed to be or "a revolutionary party, dedicating the overthrow of English supremacy in Ireland"'. Stories appeared in the papers in 1905 that the League and its leading members were under surveillance by the police.[315]

The continual conflict with government representatives made the language question increasingly political. By the end of 1906 Patrick publicly longed for what he called Educational Home Rule. 'The English Government is unable to settle our grievances for us, for it is unable to understand either us or them. Let us first get control of the educational system: then let us set about solving our problems ourselves. We shall find their solution wonderfully easy.'[316] Gaining some form of control over educational policy had become a distinct possibility with the change of power in Westminster. The new Liberal Government realised that home rule was impossible to pass through parliament, but suggested a form of self-government through the Irish Council Bill.

Although the Council Bill failed due to opposition from all political parties in Ireland, Patrick was satisfied with the educational measures taken by the new government. The status of Irish at primary level had improved rapidly, the bilingual programme was introduced in the Irish-speaking and mixed areas, and the composition of the Board of Education had changed for the better. By July 1907 he even declared that there was now no longer the excuse of a hostile Board to prevent the introduction of Irish in about half the schools which had so far failed to do so.[317] 'Our immediate point of attack must be not the Government, not the National Board, but the recalcitrant schools. In a word, we cannot expect the British Government to thrust Irish down our throats. We must show that we want Irish.' When in 1908 a second language was made obligatory for those entering a Teacher Training College by 1911, Patrick felt the position of Irish in the schools was assured.

There was a general perception in the League that they had reached an important goal. At the end of 1909 Mary Hayden spoke with pride of the great progress the League had made with slender resources. 'Less than ten years ago the few who cried out for common sense in language teaching were looked upon by many as uneasy spirits sent among us to worry honest, earnest workers and prevent progress.' She asserted that since its foundation hundreds of teachers had been trained in the League's colleges, and that tens of thousands of children were now taught Irish through the use of modern methods. Patrick claimed that the language movement was largely responsible. Instead of a fear-based education system children were now filled with a love of the pursuit of knowledge.[318]

According to Patrick the fight to provide Irish children with an Irish language education was essentially won, but that did not mean he would let up. He redirected his attention from increasing numbers to improving the quality and depth of Irish education. 'Our criterion of progress ought to be not the number of children who are enrolled as undergoing a course in Irish, but the number of *educated Irish speakers* who are growing up in the schools.'[319] Further progress of the language thus depended not only on the teachers' willingness but also their ability. If they were unwilling, he stated, local people should demand a proper Irish education, and if a teacher was unable 'it is for him to qualify himself'.[320]

The emphasis on teacher training was not entirely new for the League.[321] Over the years it had built up a number of facilities, including the provincial colleges, in which existing teachers could learn the language at night-time or during intensive summer courses. By 1907 there were sufficient opportunities for all to learn to teach Irish.[322] It was, however, felt the existing Teacher Training Colleges did not pay enough attention to Irish. In 1904 only ninety-one students had finished college qualified to teach Irish, while by 1906 there were just 499 candidates studying it.[323] Patrick claimed that due to the poor pay for teachers the quality of students was low and the best graduates left to teach in Britain.[324] This also meant that few men were willing to contemplate a teaching career, and a majority of those studying were now female.[325] When the League wrote to the managers of the Training Colleges requesting them to receive a deputation 'in reference to the position of Irish on their curricula', only one consented. Patrick dryly reported that 'The correspondence on the whole, does not indicate a very sympathetic attitude on the part of those responsible for the management of the Training Colleges.'[326]

The final element and logical next step in the reform of education was the introduction of a bilingual programme in all schools throughout Ireland. After 1903 it had become widely used in Irish-speaking and mixed areas, but Patrick had developed a great belief in its intellectual advantages to children and wanted to extend it to the rest of the country. The aim of the Bilingual Programme 'is certainly *not* to teach English to Irish speakers. Neither is it precisely to teach Irish or to forward the interest of Irish at the expense of any really useful school subject. Its aim is simply to educate the child through the medium of both Irish and English, applying to him a double intellectual stimulus, bringing him into contact with a two-fold culture, placing before him a view-point at once healthily national and broadly human.'[327] Although he believed all schools would ultimately teach Irish and English, he now seemed to consider the benefits of the bilingual system for the children even more important than the teaching of Irish itself.

Patrick had travelled a long road in his thinking on language education. In the late 1890s he had rejected education through anything but the mother tongue of the children involved. This had of course been a response to the standing practice in schools in Irish-speaking areas to teach through English. Under the influence of his experiences with Welsh and Belgium education and his realisation that an ability in English was a necessity for all children, he began to call for the introduction of a bilingual programme in the Irish-speaking and the mixed districts.[328] By 1903 he still held out little hope for the English-speaking areas, but felt that Irish should be introduced as a 'living spoken tongue' in all schools.[329] His study of the Belgian education system convinced him that bilingualism was not just necessary to the survival of the Irish language but that it was actually beneficial to every child.[330] Early in 1907 he argued that the introduction of the Bilingual Programme in the Gaedhealtacht was the first duty of the proposed Irish Council, but the extension to the whole country would only be a matter of a few years.[331] At the end of 1908 the benefits of the bilingual system even seemed to have taken precedence over the spread of the Irish language. He still viewed the introduction of it throughout Ireland as the only way to make Irish a living vernacular in the non-Irish-speaking areas. If Irish was taught as a second subject children would remain simply English speakers with an Irish ability. As enforcing a purely Irish education system in the English-speaking areas of Ireland was impossible, he asserted the choice was between 'Englishism and Bilingualism'.[332]

In early 1908 he had become very optimistic about the future. He announced that since the sanctioning of the bilingual system by the Board in 1903 there were 110 schools in the Gaeltacht who had started to use the bilingual system and more were preparing to do so.[333] He believed that only one or two minor reforms were necessary to push for bilingualism all round in five years' time.[334] The Board had a tendency to see the Bilingual Programme simply as a way to teach English in Gaeltacht, but they had to be convinced that the two languages were equal.[335] Patrick's optimism at this time may be associated with the excitement that came with the plans to establish his own secondary school, which would of course also be bilingual and not just Irish.

Growing tension

Patrick's somewhat intolerant attitude to those who did not agree with him had always been confined to issues which were directly related to high-minded principles and the interest of the Irish language. In his editorials he often gave it out to opponents and half-hearted supporters, but this was generally done without malice. He seemed to relish a strong debate. When preparing a reply to his critics he asked himself 'how best can I confound them? – that is the question I usually put to myself'.[336]

In his day-to-day dealings with people, particularly in his role as secretary of the Publications Committee and as editor, Patrick showed himself to be much more sensitive to people's feelings.[337] He could indeed be quite direct. When a number of manuscripts compiled by a

Mr Molloy were sent to him by Colonel Maurice Moore he rejected it gracefully but emphatically. After acknowledging it was beautifully written and that a lot of work had gone into it, he stated: 'The books, however, have no scientific value. The philological learning displayed is half a century behind the time, many of the theories fantastic, and the whole characterised by eccentricity.'[338] In response to a complaint by one of the regular writers for the League, Henry Morris, Patrick refused to take responsibility for the slowness with which his book was published: 'You yourself are responsible for whatever delay surrounded *Sean-Fhocla Uladh* and for any related consequences.'[339]

However, he was also encouraging, helpful and aware of how easily grievances developed.[340] On minor issues he could go to great lengths to avoid aggravation. In April 1905 he wrote to Lady Gregory to make sure a letter he had published had not annoyed her: 'When I saw the note in print it occurred to me that (quite unintentionally) it appeared a little carping in tone, and so on my own motion I wrote the correcting note in the following issue.'[341] Later that year he spurred Eoin MacNeill on to finish a review of *Aids to the Pronunciation of Irish*, written by a Christian Brother who had been helpful to the League: 'I would be very grateful, if you could give me the review for the issue of next week. I would not wish to irritate this Brother.'[342] Two years on he tried to ensure that an edition of *An Claidheamh Soluis* in which the names of some artists in the Oireachtas art exhibition were misspelled was not circulated in Dublin: '*above all not sent to Miss O'Brien or anyone connected with the Art Exhibition?*'[343]

Inevitably late publication of material annoyed a number of contributors, besides the above-mentioned Morris. In one letter he refers to an attack on him by a Fr Mullen of Killygordon: 'he has a grievance against me because some letters which he got some friends of his to write for the purpose of boosting his *Key to Ulster Irish* were (unavoidably) held back for a week or two. A personal grievance is almost always at the bottom of such outbreaks.'[344] In retrospect some could appreciate the pressures Patrick was under as editor: 'I knew Pearse as editor of *An Claidheamh Soluis* & was inclined to quarrel with him as he only occasionally put in my long letters telling everyone how to run the language movement. As editor he was sheepish and conciliatory at least to me.'[345] From a letter written in June 1907 to Máire Nic Shíthigh in answer to her query whether he was angry with her it becomes clear that he had become used to attacks: 'Be assured that your other letter did not perturb or anger me – why should it? My skin is not that sensitive after four years as editor!'[346]

Despite his proclivity for Connacht Irish, Patrick was also careful not to aggravate the long-running tensions between the various Irish dialects. In October 1904 he stimulated the Connacht writer Colm Ó Gaora to publish his work, but added that he could not provide space for it yet as he had an adequate supply of Connacht Irish material 'and the Munstermen and Ulstermen would complain if I put more in'.[347] This awareness of how others in the movement perceived his actions as editor also caused him to ask Morris whether he could sign the review Morris wrote as '[I] would not like your fairly strong strictures to appear as editorial'.[348] He expressed the same hesitance concerning the promotion of his own book *Íosagán*. In April 1908 he asked Morris to write a review of the book from a literary point of view for *An Claidheamh Soluis*: 'I cannot promote it in the same manner as I would the books of others.' He also asked him to perhaps 'recommend it to schoolmasters for their students or you may wish to write something about it in one of the papers'.[349]

Apart from the run-ins with the church, impatient contributors and sensitive readers Patrick nevertheless had become involved in several more controversies making many enemies on the way. Most of those were part of the central division within the League between a Munster-orientated group and the rest.[350] The Munster men criticised the alleged undo influence of Connacht Irish over the Munster dialect[351] and made Patrick their main target of attack. They found a ready outlet for this in D.P. Moran's *Leader* and the pages of the *Freeman's Journal*. When the *Irish Independent* was established at the end of 1904 Patrick hoped to have found an ally.[352] In a letter to the editor, W.J. Ryan, he states: 'For reasons which you know, the *Freeman* gives prominence only to the doings of a *section* of the Gaelic League. *The Independent* seems to be starting out on sounder and more patriotic lines.' He then expressed the hope that 'good speeches from John [Eoin] Mac Neill and good articles which happen to appear in *An Claidheamh* will not be boycotted'.[353] P.S. O'Hegarty later described these divisions in no uncertain terms. To him the executive 'was composed of a number of strong-minded people divided into groups, who hated each other like poison, and would almost have assassinated each other if it would advantage the victory of the particular dialect of Irish in which they believed as the master dialect'.[354] The conflict at times indeed became very heated leading to several dismissals from the Coiste and had probably more to do with personal animosities, clashing ambitions and jealousies than the standing of the various dialects.[355]

The group around Fr Dinneen had been unhappy with Patrick's appointment as editor from the start and tried to undermine his position whenever they could. This could be done quite subtly by challenging the integrity of Patrick and the dominant group in the Coiste. Those opposed to Patrick, for instance, always referred to him and other officers of the League as 'our paid officials'.[356] To emphasise Patrick's vanity Fr Dinneen always referred to Patrick as 'babble', based on Patrick's inappropriate pride in using his university titles, BA BL.[357] The main line of attack the Munster group employed, however, was making fun of his abilities in Irish as a non-native speaker. The first story Patrick published in Irish, *Poll an Piobaire*, came in for particular ridicule: 'The Keating crowd regarded P[atrick]'s Irish as a joke. Dr Lynch of Macroom made us all laugh at Poll an Piobaire Irish.'[358] This was not aided by the fact that its title could be translated both as the intended, 'The Piper's Cave', and also as 'The Piper's Hole'. Possibly in answer to this he later renamed the story *An Uaimh*.[359] The same applied to one of his other early stories 'Brigid of the Songs', the original title of which, 'Brigid of the Winds', had caused some in the League to snigger.[360] These negative reactions eventually led to sometimes unfair attacks on his stories as not being Irish or in the Irish tradition.[361]

On the financial side Patrick was also vulnerable. The initial difficulties Patrick's new line with *An Claidheamh Soluis* had caused gave D.P. Moran the opportunity to ridicule Patrick's management by referring to *An Claidheamh Soluis* as 'our kept contemporary'.[362] This was part of a concerted attempt by the Munster group to replace *An Claidheamh Soluis* with the *Leader* as the official organ of the League, of which Patrick was well aware. The charge of mismanagement was, however, somewhat disingenuous as from the summer of 1903 Sean T. O'Kelly, as the newly appointed manager, had become responsible for the financial side of the paper. Despite its difficulties in the early months of Patrick's editorship the paper had also been making a profit since early 1904.[363] When this did not stick, Moran made a big issue over Patrick paying himself £2 as a contributor for *Poll an*

Piobaire. This could be seen as paying himself twice as editor and as contributor.[364] The constant criticism did affect Patrick. His sisters remembered how he tended to respond to criticism with the phrase: 'He said that because he is a Munsterman.'[365] His school friend Liam O Donhnaill recalls that he never mentioned Fr Dinneen after the row over payments, and considered the Munster crowd as 'moral thugs'.[366] In return the Munstermen believed Patrick's antipathy for Fr Dinneen and other Munster representatives was a result of jealousy.[367]

The attacks in the *Leader* became so virulent that in 1905 some boys associated with Patrick prevented Moran from joining the official procession on St Patrick's Day in which the Dublin movement presented itself to the public with all its supporters. The fifty or so Dublin League branches fitted out with banners marched accompanied by pipers and hurlers. They were joined by various sections representing education, business, the corporation and other interests. The League claimed that about 45,000 people including 5000 pupils of the Christian Brothers participated and there were 200,000 onlookers. The boys held up Moran's carriage when he tried to join in: 'we can't allow Mr Moran into the procession. He has tried to spoil our collection.'[368] Afterwards the Coiste Gnotha was called upon to issue an apology. In a public statement they regretted that harmony was disturbed but they felt that no action on their part was called for. The Dublin branch was responsible for the organisation and 'the incident referred to was caused by persons acting without authority and was due to the unauthorised introduction of an individual into the section reserved for the Corporation'. Patrick was apparently not unhappy with the refusal to underwrite an apology.[369]

Although Patrick continued to receive the support of the majority on the Coiste, the divisions in what he believed should be a united movement working for a higher goal and the continuous attacks on his person did get under Patrick's skin in the long run.[370] Right from the beginning of his editorship he had condemned those who seemed to lose sight of the shared objectives. 'Any man who, while professing to support the Irish language, would for personal or extraneous reasons estrange from the movement the support of any person or class, or who would waste the strength of the movement on subsidiary or non-essential matters, must be regarded as a conscious or unconscious traitor.'[371] Although making little headway, Patrick persevered in his attempts to get people to work together for the common goal:

We plead for the return of that old spirit [of comradeship]. What we … deplore is the concurrent existence of a spirit of mistrust which separates district from district, province from province, native speakers from non-native speakers, the supporters of one policy or organisation from the supporters of another … do we not, by our lack of toleration and generosity, by the lightness with which we speak and write hard things of one another, by the readiness with which we take offence and slowness with which we forget, often make work in the movement unnecessarily unpleasant for ourselves and for others? There is need in the Gaelic League for more broadness of view, for a greater fineness of feeling, above all for a more carefully adjusted sense of humour.[372]

This call for unity was certainly not heeded by Fr Dinneen. At the beginning of 1908 following the controversy over the question of paying fees to teachers for teaching Irish during school hours, he started a new series of attacks on Patrick through the pages of the *Leader*: 'No one would care what the *Claidheamh Soluis* says if the Coiste Gnotha weren't paying for it. People think it is the *official organ* of the Coiste Gnotha and Connradh na Gaedilge … but these paragraphs are not the opinion of the Coiste, perhaps it derives from two or three members, or from Cherry and Starkey [the National Board Commissioners].'[373] Dinneen was supported in his calls for the replacement of Patrick in the letter pages of *An Claidheamh Soluis* by advanced nationalists such as Piaras Béaslai and Cathal Brugha. In an attempt to get rid of Patrick and change the make-up of the Coiste Fr Dinneen resigned from it and called for a special Ard Fheis.

Apparently Patrick's patience had worn thin and he answered the allegations with a full page denunciation of what he called the 'Wrecker Party'. He identified them as an unofficial opposition in the League which has tried to destroy everything the Coiste tried to do and supported everything the leaders of the movement felt was unwise and impolitic: 'At each Ard-Fheis these malcontents have mustered in force. Every year has seen them with a new grievance and a fresh shibboleth. … Enmities have grown up; ugly wounds have been given and have festered; bad blood has crept into the system of the movement, welling up from time to time and subsiding only to well up again.' He claimed that this had been steadily worsening and had come to a head in the last year: 'Pretext after pretext has been seized or invented for virulent attacks on the Coiste Gnotha and on individual members of it. Provincial bias had been attributed to it; corruption has been imputed to it; misuse of funds has been broadly hinted at; its members have been accused of climbing backstairs to Government patronage, and finally the whole body has been charged by the leader of the Wrecker Party with "trimming its sails in sympathy with the wishes of a Castle Department".' [374]

Despite these serious charges, Patrick did not want to alienate the supporters of the other side: 'Most of them we believe to be honest and earnest Gaelic Leaguers' who have been misled by Fr Dinneen and the little group of wreckers.' 'Even to this little group – even to its head and leader – we do not attribute base motives.' Adding that when Fr Dinneen says he wants to oust Douglas Hyde from leadership, drive Una O'Farrelly and Dr Henri out of the Coiste, and take over *An Claidheamh Soluis* 'he may be actuated by motives the most lofty and altruistic', but the trend is 'towards the destruction of the movement'.[375] In a private letter to Henry Morris dated around the same time Patrick made it clear he had given up on Fr Dinneen: 'I am glad to hear that you share my view concerning Fr. Dinneen. I believe that there are one or two in that group whose one objective is to break the League. The majority of them are pleasant but they are led by those one or two others.'[376]

At the special Ard Fheis, Fr Dinneen suggested that the editor of *An Claidheamh Soluis* needed a committee to censor his articles. He motivated this by claiming the editor could 'drag after him in his "blunders or worse" Coiste Gnótha, Craobhacha Coistí Ceanntair, Teacher's Congress and unless the Fee-Faw-Fummers look sharp – the special Ard-Fheis itself!'[377] Understandably Patrick was extremely angry about this attempt at censorship and asserted that Dinneen either wanted to bring the leaders of the movement into disrepute or his words 'are the mere meaningless ravings of a diseased imagination'.[378] The majority of the League at the conference clearly gave their support to Patrick and the other members of the Coiste, and Dinneen was effectively sidelined. Patrick was nevertheless greatly hurt by the attacks. As Ruth Dudley-Edwards put it: 'He had been accused of snobbery for wearing morning clothes at League formal functions, of pride because of his reserved manner, of anti-clericalism, and of sucking up to Dublin Castle. His Irish ... was scoffed at by native speakers ... [and he] was abused for giving prominence to non-Munster Irish.'[379]

All this made him deeply disenchanted with the League and contributed to a desire to look for other outlets for his enormous energy. A few weeks after the special Ard Fheis on 19 June 1908 Patrick wrote to Sean T. O'Kelly, the manager of *An Claidheamh Soluis*, informing him that he would put a letter before the Executive Committee the following night announcing his resignation as editor – his primary reason being the opening of his own school the coming September.[380] The lack of effort O'Kelly had displayed in his duties as manager due to his many other commitments also played a part in Patrick's growing disenchantment. He expressed this very clearly in a separate letter to Eoin MacNeill: 'What the Manager is doing I don't know. He is hardly ever at the office. … What occupies him or where he is all day I can't say. He may be at Corporation meetings. He may be doing Sinn Féin work. He may be doing Vincent de Paul work. But I am perfectly sure he is not doing the work he is paid for – managing "*An Claidheamh Soluis*".'[381]

The fact the paper was again running at a loss since 1906 was attributed to this lack of attention: 'The advertisements have been let decrease to a lower point than ever. *Nothing* is done to increase them. *Nothing* is being done to extend the circulation. *Nothing* is being done to collect the debts. At the present moment, there is far more money due to us than would pay all our debts, yet not a penny of it is being collected, and each month Barrett [the League central manager] has to make an advance.'[382] Indeed after the first few successful years of Pearse's editorship the circulation figures had been declining from a top of 174,044 in 1904 to 130,937 in 1908, partly explaining the loss.[383] From 1906 onwards the League again had had to provide money from central funds to keep the paper running, £100 in 1906–1907 and more than £323 the following year.[384]

What happened following Patrick's announcement of a letter of resignation is not entirely clear. Initially the Coiste Gnotha convinced him to take a few months' leave, during which time he was replaced as editor by Séan Mac Einri, a League organiser.[385] This was not unusual as there seems to have been a system in place to replace Patrick in his absence since at least the summer of 1905. At that time Sean T. O'Kelly and George Moonan replaced him for the English section while Tadhg Ó Donnchadha had edited the Irish material.[386] The outcome of the summer discussions was that Patrick postponed his decision and continued as editor for the moment. After the opening of St Enda's he found little time for editorial work:

> our editorial and sub-editorial work is got through either in a crowded class-room, or else after midnight in a certain very icy apartment in the lower regions of Sgoil Eannna, some hours after the professors and pupils have gone off on their nightly visits to Tir na nOg (Land of Youth). To be continuously 'mellow' under these circumstances is a height of heroism towards which we aspire, but which we have not yet attained.[387]

In October 1908 Patrick nevertheless decided he would stay on as editor after he was promised the aid of an assistant editor. He offered this initially to MacHenry who had helped out since the summer. After MacHenry refused, he approached Sean Mac Giollarnath offering him £100 per annum, who accepted by return of post.[388]

Patrick subsequently made a concerted effort to distance himself from the movement. He resigned from several committees including the time-consuming Publications Committee. Even Patrick's editorial involvement became haphazard. Sean Forde states that Patrick wrote very little for *An Claidheamh Soluis* from the end of 1908 onwards and that he gave up coming to the printers to look at articles and help out as he used to do.[389] At the end of 1909 Patrick admitted as much in a letter to Sean Morris: 'I had already resigned the secretaryship of the Publications Committee and I had no connection with the Committee or with the work of the League in any way except that I was nominally the editor of *An Claidheamh Soluis*.' The demands of running St Enda's were clearly responsible for this. 'I am not, as you would say, in touch with the language movement for almost a year and a half, except, that I am devoting all my attention to my business in Sgoil Éanna and neglecting most other things. I hardly open or read any letters which do not bear on the work of the school.'[390] Thomas MacDonagh at that time described Patrick's working habits as killing himself by inches.[391]

The growing demands of running a school eventually forced Patrick to resign his editorship in November 1909. He evidently felt unable to sever his ties completely, rejoined the Publications Committee and he was again co-opted onto the Coiste Gnotha.[392] He also found a new outlet for his writings in the school paper *An Macaomh*. In its

first issue he clearly exposed the frustrations he had felt as editor of
An Claidheamh Soluis.

> It is a luxury to feel that I can set down here any truth, however obvious,
> without being called a liar, any piece of wisdom, however sane, without
> being docketed a lunatic. *An Macaomh* is my own, to do with it as I please;
> and if, through sheer obstinacy in saying in it what I think ought to be said,
> I run it against some obstruction and so wreck it, at least I shall enjoy
> something of the grim satisfaction which I suppose motorists experience
> in wrecking their thousand guinea Panhards through driving them as they
> think they ought to be driven.[393]

An Claidheamh Soluis suffered after Patrick's departure. Circulation
figures dropped to about 100,000 which according to one historian
was directly linked to the end of Patrick's term as editor. 'In hindsight,
we can see a real decline in creative innovation, effort and achievement
after the first years of this century, a decline that to a considerable
extent coincided with the end of Pearse's inspirational and hortatory
tenure as regular and full-time editor of *An Claidheamh Soluis*.'[394]

In the years after his resignation Patrick became increasingly
disillusioned with the League and the way it worked for the language
cause. In an open letter to its president Douglas Hyde in May 1912
he opened a frontal attack. 'I think that the League leadership made a
major mistake from the beginning. Seeking to exhort and persuade the
Irish people, they instituted a structural model of the political parties
of their time in Ireland and proceeded to call it the Gaelic League.'
Despite his own central role in this he now strongly doubted whether it
had been the right way to enable the people to become Irish speakers.

> Which is the more effective to that end, a large organisation with branches,
> committees, motions and regulations, expending its energies making and
> discussing rules or small groups travelling throughout the country, one
> group making music, another group staging new plays, another group
> exhorting the Irish against the foreigner and so on and all this work being
> done through Irish?

Those involved in the League should have done the latter from the
beginning: 'some of us might be poorer than we are, and some of us
suffering from hunger and destitution, but *we would have saved the*

Irish Language. And was that not our objective? I fear that it is too late to undertake all that now.'[395]

By 1913 Patrick became convinced a new phase was starting in the struggle for the survival of the Irish nation. He reiterated that he had never simply fought for the survival of the language but only for the survival of the nation. The language was as he had always said an essential part of the nation for which he had given the best fifteen years of his life. He argued that Gaelic League methods were now no longer effective. By starting to write more and more through English in these last years of his life he effectively acknowledged that the resurrection of the language as a spoken tongue had failed.[396] In his article 'The Coming Revolution', which he published in November 1913, he asserted that the Gaelic League had played an important role but it was now time for direct action.

> I have come to the conclusion that the **Gaelic League**, as the **Gaelic League**, is a spent force; and I am glad of it. I do not mean that no work remains for the **Gaelic League**, or that the **Gaelic League** is no longer equal to work; I mean that the vital work to be done in the new Ireland will be done not so much by the **Gaelic League** itself as by men and movements that have sprung from the **Gaelic League** or have received from the **Gaelic League** a new baptism and a new life of grace. The **Gaelic League** was no reed shaken by the wind, no mere *vox clamantis*: it was a prophet and more than a prophet. But it was not the Messiah.[397]

However, by 1908 there were no organisations yet that could take over the flag from the Gaelic League and Patrick threw all his energy into the running of his school.

6.   Patrick (extreme left on second row) with Gaelic League representatives in Paris

7.   Patrick and League friends

8. Patrick with grey hat at Ros Muc

9. Patrick with Thomas Clery

3 Educationalist

There is no hour of the day during which the teacher cannot, by precept and example, enkindle in his pupils' minds a love of truth and goodness and a hatred of falsehood and baseness. The whole life of a teacher should, indeed, be a sermon to his pupils.[1]

Beginnings

The idea to set up a bilingual school had a long genesis and was the culmination of a fairly natural development. From early on Patrick showed an interest in education which was further stimulated by his appointment as teacher. Although now part of the school system, Patrick was always very critical of it, in particular of intermediate education which in January 1898 he described as of low quality and essentially 'un-Irish'.[2] Through his association with the Gaelic League this critical attitude was sharpened, particularly through his fact-finding mission to Wales. The first coherent expression of Patrick's ideas on education came in February 1900 when Patrick wrote a letter to *The Press* in which he emphasised the importance of teaching through Irish in the Gaeltacht.

At this stage he was very much against the use of English in these areas, believing the children would never acquire a real understanding of the language or a subject taught through it: 'whatever smattering of English and other subjects the child, parrot-like and by mere imitation, happens to acquire at school, is within a year or two after leaving school completely forgotten'. In what he termed the partly anglicised districts, teaching the children through English would even have worse effects: 'There the product of the National Schools is that worst of human monstrosities – the being who has a smattering of two languages, but knows neither sufficiently well to be able adequately to express himself in it.' His advice was to 'teach them to read and write their own language first, teach them English or any other useful subject you choose through the medium of that language and watch the results. Perpetuate the present system, and you perpetuate illiteracy – and worse.'[3]

Although the League promoted a bilingual form of education throughout Ireland, adjusted to local conditions, its primary objective at this stage was to have Irish introduced as a medium of instruction in the Irish-speaking areas. At that stage only voluntary schemes in schools were allowed by the National Board.[4] After taking over the editorship of *An Claidheamh Soluis* in 1903 the issue of bilingual education came at the forefront of Patrick's writings. To him it was central to the whole Irish question. In one of his very first contributions to the paper as editor he made this absolutely clear. 'Take up the Irish problem at what point you may, you inevitably find yourself in the end back at the education question.'[5] In support of bilingual education Patrick called upon successful foreign examples.[6] He explicitly referred to his 'inquiries in to the systems of Bilingual Teaching in vogue on the Continent, notably in Belgium', and on his personal observations in some Welsh primary schools.[7]

His ultimate objective was 'to Irishise education in this country from the smallest National School on a western mountainside, through all the stages of primary, intermediate, and university education, religious and secular, literary, scientific, professional and technical up to the highest educational institutions in the land'.[8] The primary instrument of this was the introduction of bilingual education not just in the Irish-speaking areas but everywhere. However, Irishising did not just mean that. 'We have more than once insisted that the question of Irish in the schools is not disposed of by the mere allotting of so many hours per week to the study of the "National" Boards official programme. It will not do to carefully mark out a special half hour or hour during which children may be Irish – you must Irishise the whole school life and nothing short of this will solve the problem.'[9]

This involved the use of Irish in all kinds of school activities, from the roll call and religious instruction to drill and manual training. Only then would children view it 'not merely as a desirable literary acquirement' but something for everyday use.[10] An Irish atmosphere was thus supposed to permeate the schools: 'the character of a youth is formed and his sympathies determined less by the consciously didactic instruction which he receives, than by, the general atmosphere, the milieu in which he lives'.[11] A special place in this was assigned to the teaching of Irish history and literature.[12] He believed that this would make the pupils form an emotional and intellectual bond with that language, making learning a delight.[13]

Ultimately Patrick's ideal school did not simply teach knowledge but would form children's character: 'the aim of education is not the imparting of knowledge but the training of the child to be a perfect man or woman – to prepare for complete living'. Basing himself on the ideas of the English philosopher Herbert Spencer he stated that 'real education consists in the forming of the child's character, the drawing out of his faculties, the disciplining of his intellect'. 'We conceive that in educating a child the inculcation of truth, manliness, purity, and reverence, is more important than the teaching of vulgar fractions and Latin roots.' A central role was given to the teacher who should be an example to his pupils.[14]

The love of learning underlying Patrick's educational philosophy resembled his father's experience as a self-taught man, but his actual policies were developed slowly by the study of educational theory and the practices in other countries. His ideas were all based on European and North American examples, but this was no slavish copying. Patrick took what suited him and clearly put his own stamp on it. The special place he gave to the inculcation of patriotism was, for instance, the result of his study of the educational system abroad, particularly in Germany and the United States where reference to the flag and the state was a central tenet of educational policy.[15] Patrick had become aware of this through a number of government reports on the educational system in the United States, which had been commissioned to deal with the perception that the huge growth of American industrial power could be explained by their curriculum.

He regarded the teaching of patriotism one of the special duties of a teacher. 'We owe it to our children that they should be taught to know and love their country. If we hide that knowledge from them we commit a crime.' However, it was not to be taught by emphasising the nation itself. Teachers should be men or women of fine character and lofty ideals, who must be warmly Irish in sympathy, but their 'patriotism must not be of a dour and repellent kind, but rather a generous and wholesome enthusiasm which will communicate itself to his pupils without any undue display of propagandism on his part'.[16]

To give children the feeling that they were Irish, more subtle ways were required. 'Far more effective than the mere didactic preaching of patriotism would be well-directed efforts to bring the children into some direct relation with the country they inhabit – its natural beauty, its wild living things, its rocks, its rivers, its ruins.'[17] This emphasis on nature studies included the provision to each child of a small allotment.[18] Following this he demanded that children should be taught a humane attitude to animals. 'They should, above all, be taught that the lives of animals are sacred, and that wantonly to kill or hurt a beast or bird or insect is a wicked and a mean thing.'[19] The absence of corporal punishment, the social mix among the pupils and the absence of rigid barriers between teacher and pupils were other aspects of the American system which appealed to Patrick.

The trip to Belgium in 1905 provided him with the opportunity to study bilingual practices more closely and forced him to formulate his ideas in a more coherent form. Teaching practices in Belgium had been an inspiration to the League for some time.[20] Patrick's interest was probably fanned by T.R. Dawes' pamphlet *Bilingual Teaching in Belgian Schools* which he discussed in *An Claidheamh Soluis* in 1903.[21] Dawes was the headmaster of Pembroke Dock County School and had travelled to Belgium on a University of Wales Travelling Studentship to study education in 1899.[22] Patrick's trip was linked to a week-long visit by the Fontenoy Committee to commemorate the fight of the Irish Brigade at Fontenoy in 1745 during the War of Austrian Succession. He was part of a sixty man strong deputation under the direction of Major John McBride and the old Fenian John O'Leary. Patrick stayed on after the deputation left.[23] According to his League colleague, Eamonn O Donehada, Patrick had wanted them to go together for six months but the board of the primary school at which Eamonn was teaching Irish in Cork city would not give him leave and Patrick took his sister Margaret instead and stayed just for a month.[24]

Patrick had a letter of introduction from Dr W.J.M. Starkie, Resident Commissioner of the National Board of Education in Dublin, to the Minister for Public Instruction in Belgium, M. de Trooz. This ensured cooperation from the Belgian authorities and opened many doors which enabled him to collect a great deal of information. Official policy documents and reports were made available and visits were organised for him to thirty educational institutions at different levels and with different forms of management.[25] Patrick stayed in Brussels, but accompanied by senior inspectors he went to primary schools throughout Flanders, also visited secondary schools in Brussels, Antwerp, Ghent, Malines and Bruges, and a number of small rural schools, two universities, and the College of Industrial Design where he examined design and production of visual aids for language teaching.[26] In a letter to Sean T. O'Kelly Patrick intimated the trip took longer than intended due to red tape and the endless formalities he encountered, but he was impressed with the facilities. 'Some of the large city schools are like huge hotels – only finer and more spacious than any hotel in Dublin, or for that matter in London, Paris or Brussels. The rural schools are more like our own at home.'[27]

In the first of the two series of articles Patrick published on his trip he dealt with Belgian history, its literature and education system and the socio-economic factors influencing it. The second series concerned pedagogical theory and practice, and analysed teaching methods in various subjects and in different school types.[28] It is clear from these articles that Patrick had come home with a greater understanding of pedagogical issues and modern teaching methods, and that he was confirmed in his growing conviction that bilingualism was the appropriate and most effective language policy for Irish schools.[29] He had seen how two languages could coexist and how they could be effectively used side by side as a medium of instruction. He still felt it was a child's right to be taught in its mother tongue but now considered using a second language beneficial for everyone.[30] In 1906 he summarised his demands under four principles: 1. every child ought to be taught his mother tongue; 2. every child ought to be taught one other language as soon as he is capable of learning it; 3. the second language should be gradually introduced as a medium of instruction in other subjects; 4. all language teaching should be conducted, as far as possible, on the direct method.[31]

Due to the problems posed by their demand for bilingual education, the League had always given a lot of attention to modern educational methods and Patrick had become intimately acquainted with them. Fr O'Growney had already published guidelines for language teaching known as 'An Módh Díreach' in 1893. This contained a variation of the Berlitz method, and his simple lessons in Irish had been serialised in *An Claidheamh Soluis* from 1897 to 1900.[32] Patrick's negative experiences at school in which everything was taught by way of cramming, enforced by corporal punishment to ensure a good result in the exams, had made him an ardent supporter of the direct method which taught languages through conversation. The indifferent attitude among most people towards schooling he blamed on the existing system, which was aimed at English urban society and did not teach Irishness. 'It is not then a great wonder that Irish children prefer the freedom of the hills and fields to the stern atmosphere of the Saxonised school.' A better attendance record would be created if more attention was given to Ireland, and the Irish language, history, songs, geography and place names were taught.[33]

Patrick's involvement in propagating bilingual education had brought him in contact with a very lively international debate on educational method taking place in Europe at that time between many of the great names of educational reform. In what is termed the New Education Movement a whole corpus of modern educational ideas, concepts and practices had been formed which he tapped into.[34] Patrick also developed a great interest in the intellectual developments in Europe. He read widely including the main German philosophers of his time like Goethe, Nietzsche, Heine and Hegel, and kept himself informed by perusing newspapers mainly from England, France and the United States, particularly looking for the progress of cultural nationalism.[35] Although not fond of travelling abroad, only having visited Belgium and Paris outside the United Kingdom, he built up a network of international contacts.

In Belgium he had befriended Monseigneur Alfons Tas, a Belgium educationalist, with whom he continued to correspond.[36] Tas was present at the opening day of St Enda's and a student exchange scheme was set up between St Enda's and some of his schools in Belgium, including the leading Catholic day and boarding school where he taught, the College de St Pierre in Uccle. One of these exchange students, Raymond Suetens, was a great success. He became the editor of *An Sgoláire*, the school multi-lingual magazine, within six months of his arrival and handled copy in five languages. His commitment to an Irish-Ireland was put in doubt when he conducted a poll on whether cricket should be one of the summer-term games. Although Patrick 'did not take up an intolerant attitude to non-Irish games', the majority of pupils rejected Suetens' suggestion. At Easter 1914 Patrick's sister Margaret again visited Belgium as part of this exchange.[37]

Patrick's international network clearly influenced his thinking. Through the League he worked together with the Welsh on cultural activities and educational policy, and corresponded with other figures from the New Education Movement like Weygandt in Philadelphia and Grundtvigian of the Folk High School movement in Denmark. He was also in touch with language movements in Finland, France, Wales and Scotland and various academics abroad like the German Kuno Meyer, Professor of Romance Languages in Queens College, Liverpool, who had been largely responsible for the development of Celtic studies and the interest in heroic sagas which Patrick admired so much.[38] Patrick's links with the Slavic countries can be explained by his believe that there was a close association between the Nordic and Celtic myths and iconography. St Enda's also attracted interest abroad. The school was mentioned in the French and Italian press and was visited by English publicists and Egyptian nationalists, and a link was established through Yeats with India.[39]

Although the New Education Movement was not a uniform movement, those involved shared a belief that the needs of individual children should be central and all opposed the traditional payment by result systems, the restriction to the three Rs, and the concentration on rote memory and passive pupils.[40] The reforms in primary and secondary education in Ireland around 1900 were also inspired by this movement and had brought in more so-called hand and eye subjects and modern pedagogy but to Patrick this did not go far enough.[41] In particular the direct method of teaching which gave much more attention to language as a living vernacular had grabbed Patrick's attention as it suited the particular concerns of the Irish language movement which was confronted with a population few of whom could still speak Irish. In 1904 he already promoted the viva voce method and the use of blackboard to teach children a new language.[42] His visit to Belgium where modern techniques were propagated and actually used strengthened these ideas. 'It has been doubted whether a language can be learned at school; I have satisfied myself by observation both in Ireland and in Belgium that it can.'[43] Although Patrick did not say as much, this contradicted his own earlier critique of teaching through the English language in Irish-speaking areas.

Patrick was greatly impressed by the rejection in the official Belgium educational policy of teaching styles which were 'exclusively grammatical, abstract and rule bound exercises in translation, in favour of an intuitive, natural and live method based upon conversational skills'.[44] In 1906 he claimed that teaching should all be by direct method: 'in the ideal secondary school there would never be the slightest necessity for recourse to any other method'.[45] He did not advocate any specific method but felt that the teacher should use whatever suited him. He felt Berlitz was the best conversational technique as it avoided translation of words and phrases but it failed to deal with grammar or writing. Between 1907 and 1909 he formulated his ideas in a series of articles in *An Claidheamh Soluis* under the heading 'An Sgoil' which brought O'Growney's ideas up to date and provided a guide for the use of the direct method. These were later brought out as a *Handbook of the Direct Method*.[46]

By 1907 all legal impediments for the introduction of bilingual teaching were lifted which allowed Patrick to put his ideas about a truly Irish school forward more stridently. The language and its methods became less prominent while the other aspects of Irishness were emphasised. No doubt contrary to the intention of the government behind allowing bilingual teaching in Ireland, patriotism became particularly emphasised by him. 'More important than any programme, more important than any course of formal instruction, more important than any mere "subject", even though that "subject" be the national language, is the creation in the schools of an Irish atmosphere, the Irishing of the hearts and minds of the children, the kindling in their souls of the quenchless fire of patriotism, the setting before them of a great and glowing ideal of *Duty*.'[47] The fire of patriotism could in his mind be stoked by frequent narration of the stirring deeds of Irish heroes. Children should be taught to recite ballads and heroic poetry and the legends of Ireland. 'They should be constantly reminded of and made to realise the fact that they are a separate race from England and that it is a disgrace and a badge of slavery for a race to use the language of any other in preference to its own.'[48]

The positive changes in the primary curriculum after 1903 and his experiences in Belgium also caused Patrick to turn his attention from primary to secondary education.[49] His first editorial specifically dealing with this was published in November 1905. Being reasonably satisfied with the changes in the National Schools he identified serious problems in the secondary system: 'The system of Intermediate Education in Ireland, considered as a system, exemplifies nearly every fault of which a national education scheme could possibly be guilty.' He singled out the recently abolished payment by results system which only rewarded secondary schools for the exam results of their pupils and which stimulated a single-minded focus on results and a concomitant cramming of knowledge. The absence of testing of oral proficiency in languages was another major criticism. In general the system failed 'to appeal boldly to the more generous and exalted sentiments of the children for whom it caters'.[50]

However, even at secondary level the government made some positive reforms. The pay by result system was abolished in 1899, and by 1907 the Board of Education even agreed, to Patrick's surprise, with the use of the Direct Method and adjusted its examination to include oral ability.[51] These changes contributed to his declaration that the fight with a government hostile to Irish was now effectively over.[52] The successful resurrection of the language now depended on the practical implementation of the schemes suggested by the League by school managers and teachers. At primary level this was increasingly successful and there were now a great many schools which used the bilingual approach, but there was not yet any secondary school doing so. It was expensive and the whole system continued to be geared towards exam results despite the abolition of the pay by result system.[53] The lack of action on this front caused Patrick to accuse the Christian Brothers in 1909 of having sacrificed the welfare of the Irish educational system on 'a cross of monetary interest'.[54] It seemed there was only one way to ensure the introduction of bilingualism in secondary education and that was by opening a school of his own.

St Enda's

As it now came down to the practical implementation of an Irish education, about which Patrick had clear ideas, setting up his own school became a viable option when he encountered a less than enthusiastic response from those working in the field. Eamonn O Donehada claims that even before his trip to Belgium in 1905 Patrick had already spoken of beginning his own school.[55] Patrick was indeed named in January 1906 in a scheme to found a secondary school for Catholic Boys led by Tomas P. O'Nowlan, a Gaelic Leaguer and then teacher in Mount Mellary, Co. Waterford. The latter had written to

Archbishop Walsh asking for advice and proposing Patrick as the prospective vice-president of the college. The scheme did not then come to fruition possibly due to the hesitance among the clergy to allow lay secondary schools. Most Bishops still considered education a sole preserve for the Church, and might not have looked too kindly on O'Nowlan who was a former Jesuit priest. The Bishops' spokesman Dr Dwyer of Limerick had shortly before remarked that 'no layman has the right to teach'.[56]

Although it is not known to what extent Patrick had been involved in the above scheme, the plans were not pursued. At the beginning of 1908, however, he suddenly began to take steps to open a school that same year. This may have been inspired by the infant school his sister Margaret opened in 1907 and was possibly in response to the vicious opposition he encountered in the League.[57] The latter cause is hinted at in his request to those he approached for support to keep his plans silent for the moment: 'please observe strict secrecy because there are people in the Gaelic League – you can guess to whom I am referring – who, for sheer malice, would do their best to wreck the scheme before it is started'.[58] At the end of February 1908 Patrick sent out letters to a number of prominent Irish-Irelanders asking for financial support: 'I wonder whether I can interest you in a project which I have had at the back of my head for the past two or three years and which, if I can see my way clear, I am now more than ever anxious to proceed with? It is the project of a High School for boys in Dublin on purely Irish Ireland lines.'[59] Patrick acknowledged that he had initiated this plan with Tomas O'Nowlan but that due to the latter's marriage this had become difficult. Some time later O'Nowlan became professor of Irish in Carysford Teacher Training College.[60]

Patrick claimed the arguments in favour of such a school were irresistible. On the one hand, it would fill the void created by the absence of an Irish High School and of a High School for Catholic boys conducted by laymen. On the other hand, he argued that there were now 'quite a number of Gaelic Leaguers in Dublin and throughout the country who have brought up their children more or less Irish speaking and who are now anxiously on the lookout for a school which would provide those children with an education genuinely Irish while at the same time, up to a high standard generally'.[61]

Those he approached were not that easily persuaded as the scheme required a substantial amount of money. He had already given up on his initial idea to establish the school on the Aran Islands because he needed the supporting network of Irish-Irelanders that existed in Dublin. He had wanted to call the school Sgoil Lorcain in honour of the archdiocese of Dublin, but now that the school was going to be based in Dublin he changed the name to St Enda's or Sgoil Éanna, after the saint associated with Aran.[62] Aran had been first choice because of its early Christian monastic settlements and the pre-Christian civilisation there which symbolically brought together the monastic scholar and pagan hero Patrick wanted to emulate in his school. St Enda was a role model because he had abandoned a heroic warrior life to become a monk and a teacher.[63]

Patrick proposed to open up in Cullenswood House, the building adjoining his own home in Oakley Road, and have two classrooms built in its garden. He thought the house could be bought and adjusted for £510 while another £500 was needed to cover running costs during the first two years. As he had little money himself he was dependent on benefactors.[64] The relatively wealthy patron of the language movement, Edward Martyn, was asked to finance the whole scheme: 'I calculate that a thousand would be ample for equipment and so to provide against a possible loss on the first year or two. Forty pupils would ensure the absolute financial success of the school but I think we should start if we were sure of twenty for the first year. It would be well to commence modestly and feel our way very carefully.'[65]

Martyn reacted with hesitance and expressed doubts about his ability to support it due to the manifold demands on him and his fear of losses which were so common with other Irish-Ireland undertakings. His doubts about the financial basis of the plans were justified. Patrick was not always equally realistic about running a school, even rejecting a friend's suggestion that he would need a salary himself.[66] In response to Martyn's doubts Patrick adjusted his plans: 'by commencing very modestly and by avoiding heavy responsibilities in the matter of large salaries etc, I shall be able to make the scheme pay from the very start'. Showing the less than forthcoming attitude of others he had approached, Patrick tried his utmost to convince Martyn of the viability of the scheme:

> Suppose that in a month's or six weeks time I am in a position to go to you and say: 'I have received definite promises of so many boys; that would represent a net revenue of so much; the corresponding expense on rent,

teaching power, and general working would be so much, leaving clear profit of so much on the whole year's work?' – would you not then be able to consider the whole question of investment with full data before you?[67]

Patrick also suggested some alternative financial schemes in which Martyn would invest £300 against some securities including Pearse's cottage and land in Connemara.

You see, I am so confident of the ultimate success of the project that I am willing to give up my position in the League (worth, as you know, £230 a year) and practically stake my whole worldly future on it. I feel that I am cut out for this particular work and granted a fair start, it seems to me that failure is impossible to a determined man engaged in the work for which, above all others, he feels a natural aptitude and to which he can give all his enthusiasm.[68]

When this did not convince his prospective backers he tried to alleviate doubts further by taking up MacNeill's suggestion to put the emphasis on opening a preparatory school, with a secondary school attached to it at least to show that secondary education in Irish was available. Such a preparatory school would receive a grant from the Board of Education so would be automatically viable. 'I would propose to take boys from 7 or 8 up to 16 or 17 – both boarders & day boys.' Teacher salaries could be reduced by hiring League dignitaries as auxiliary staff.[69]

MacNeill also expressed doubts about the underlying premise of the school that real Irish speakers could be created in a day school:

I cannot at all agree with you that any course of instruction at school will produce really Irish-speaking children, unless there is a domestic foundation, or its equivalent, to build upon. I fear you have in your mind some imaginary state of things which does not exist. Nothing but *life* can teach a whole live language, though an intellectual medium of communication like Esperanto may be thoroughly taught by instruction. You cannot live life in a day-school. You cannot have passions, emotions, cares and endearments, you will not put the children to bed or give them their meals or do the thousand petty things and great things that occur in every normal home, nor will you be able to reproduce the contact with the outer world that a full-blooded language must have. Your school-taught language will never be more than a simulacrum of the living thing.[70]

Patrick did not fully accept MacNeill's criticism, which was not in line with practices in Belgium, but to provide the closer contact MacNeill felt was necessary he concentrated on attracting boarders. In response to a query by Conn Murphy whether his son was old enough for St Enda's Patrick set out his thinking:

> indeed the presence of quite young pupils is necessary to the carrying out of my scheme in its entirety. I want to show that it is possible to make a child a bilingualist in the fullest sense of the word by commencing with him at a sufficiently young age, by teaching him throughout on proper 'direct method' lines, and by placing him for a sufficient number of hours daily in an 'atmosphere' in which he will hear the less familiar language & be induced to speak it.[71]

His early enthusiasm and grand plans were thus toned down somewhat in response to the doubts expressed by these men, but Patrick was not easily dissuaded.[72] Naming his school a college was a deliberate attempt to appeal to the aspirational nationalist middle classes, who were looking for a school on par with the private secondary schools such as Blackrock, Clongowes Wood and Castleknock, but who were reticent to send their children to what they saw as Anglo-Irish institutions. The existing schools for the Catholic middle class were training grounds for service to empire and contemptuous of the Irish language, while the Christian Brothers primarily prepared lower-class pupils for the Irish civil service. Patrick believed he had found a niche among Irish speakers and boys from Ireland and abroad whose parents were looking for a high class education and who wished their children to be educated along bilingual lines. To rival the public schools St Enda's also sported a heavy classical curriculum, but with an emphasis on the Irish language which Patrick believed would better prepare its pupils for a future in Ireland.[73]

Although most of those he approached for financial support appear to have argued against the project, Patrick pressed ahead after he obtained the promise of sufficient prospective pupils and some encouragement from other Gaelic Leaguers.[74] Stephen Barrett and Joseph Dolan, a wealthy merchant from Ardee, Co. Louth, stood as guarantors for the mortgage and Patrick acquired Cullenswood House. As the birthplace of William Lecky, a noted Irish historian, it was a worthy association, even though he was a unionist. Patrick also assigned heroic deeds of resistance to English occupation to the site dating back to 'Black Monday' in 1209.[75]

The building and grounds were well suited for running a school, and the summer was spent adjusting it further for the opening in September. By that time it was well equipped, containing a science lab, playroom, three dormitories and an infirmary with 'fully certified sanitation'. The grounds of five acres included all types of gardens and buildings one would expect with a stately home as well as playing fields, a handball court and an open-air gymnasium.[76] The building was nicely decorated with contemporary Irish art specially made for Patrick by sympathetic artists, such as Beatrice Elvery, Jack B. Yeats, Sarah Purser and George Russell, supplemented by a range of engravings and sculptures by Patrick's father.[77] The cottage he was building in Ros Muc provided a potential summer school in the Gaeltacht open to his pupils.

After the first successful year extensive refurbishment almost doubled Cullenswood House in size. A fifth classroom was added and it then included a study hall for 150 people, an art room, a science laboratory, a museum and refectory, and a library, which already contained 2000 volumes mostly from his father's extensive collection, while a school chapel was furnished by a friend. 'I do not know that we need much else in the way of accommodation or equipment for teaching, except perhaps a special room for Manual Instruction. That will doubtless come in good time.'[78]

Enrolment went well despite the short preparation time. The first advertisements and the prospectus for the school only appeared in July less than two months before opening.[79] However, Patrick had extensively canvassed privately and in September 1908 the senior boys' school started off with 30 pupils of which 10 were boarders and the mixed preparatory school attracted another 30 boys and girls. By November numbers in the senior school had increased to 43 while 2 pupils were added to the preparatory section; 15 or 16 of the total were then native Irish speakers. Children continued to be enrolled during the year and by the end of the year there were 24 girls and 70 boys including 20 boarders.[80] Things went very well but Patrick was not yet content and continued to seek new pupils.[81] The second year began with 30 boarders and 100 day pupils, which was more than the original maximum of 30 boarders and 80 day pupils set to ensure a private and homelike character and to avoid the somewhat harsh discipline of ordinary boarding schools. The overall maximum was increased to 150 pupils but it was nevertheless decided to discontinue the girls section of the preparatory school, which enabled a merger of the junior and senior school into St Enda's College proper. He retained his plan to take in young children but the senior side of the school, which by the end of the second year had 40 boarders and 65 day boys, clearly received most prominence at this time.[82]

Students came from all over Ireland with most counties represented, including three from Connemara. There were also five boys from Britain, one from Buenos Aires, Eamonn Bulfin, the son of the editor of the Argentinean *Southern Cross* newspaper, and one from the Dublin Jewish community, Moynagh Bloom.[83] The high standing of Patrick was shown by the great number of sons and relatives of many of the leading figures in the Irish-Ireland movement in the first roll call of the school. To them St Enda's offered an education based on national principles in which the Irish language and culture were central elements. A sense of being part of an important, even historical experiment was certainly an added element in the attraction provided by St Enda's. The assistant editor of *An Claidheamh Soluis* John Henry eulogised after the opening: 'With such an ideal master, a beautiful school, an original and up-to-date system of Irish education, Sgoil Éanna will be a nursery of character, intellect, patriotism, and virtue, which may eventually exert a benign influence on the private and public life of our school.' The pupils' relatives and other notable cultural figures such as Douglas Hyde, Standish O'Grady, W.B. Yeats, Constance Markievicz, Maud Gonne, Roger Casement and Sean O'Casey actively supported St Enda's in various ways.[84]

The staff in the first year of the running of the college consisted of the ebullient poet and advanced nationalist Thomas MacDonagh as second master and Tomas MacDonnell, a well-known musician who taught dancing, music and athletics, as third master. They were assisted by teachers of mathematics, classics, Irish, music, manual instruction, commercial subjects, and drill and gymnastics. A range of visiting professors also lent a hand. Willie Pearse who still ran Pearse's sculpting business also taught art, and Margaret ran the preparatory school and taught junior French. With her mother and cousin Miss

Brady, Margaret also ran the domestic side. All of them lived in the school while Patrick's younger sister Mary Brighid resided elsewhere but also taught music.

In the second year some teachers left but the staff was strengthened by the addition of Dr Patrick Doody for classics and a science teacher supplemented occasionally by MacDonagh's brother Joseph, Padraic Colum and some others.[85] The closing of the girls' preparatory section meant that Margaret Pearse and her assistant Miss Browner became regular members of staff at St Enda's.[86] The third year opened with a slightly more compact staff. MacDonnell had left and apart from Patrick as headmaster, there were now just five assistant masters; Thomas MacDonagh, Patrick Doody, Frank P. Nolan, Michael Smithwick and Eamonn O'Toole. They were aided by visiting professors Richard J. Feely for physical science, Padraic Colum for English literature and William Pearse for art. During the year MacDonagh left to go to university, but Con Colbert was added for drill and gymnastics.[87]

Religion

Despite the Church's objections to lay involvement in education and MacNeill's advice to avoid antagonising the Church by any kind of emphasis on the lay character of the school, Patrick seemed not to have considered obtaining Church backing very important.[88] He anticipated getting the archbishop and some prominent Catholic laymen as patrons, but showed no great urgency or desire to sign them up.[89] Only after MacNeill had approached the archbishop himself and it was made clear that Dr Walsh felt he could not be associated with or even publicly recommend an institution of which the chances of success were 'more than doubtful', did Patrick approach him. In a letter dated 15 July he simply expressed his understanding for Walsh's position and asked him to go through the prospectus of the school and make sure there was nothing to which he would object. Although not looking for official sanction, Patrick was anxious 'that there should be something in the Prospectus to give parents an assurance that the religious education of their boys will be in proper hands'.[90] His local parish priest, Canon Frisker, had agreed to have one of the local clergy visit the school to test the boys in religious knowledge, but was apparently unwilling to have this stated in the prospectus. Only now that Patrick felt he needed a more direct endorsement did he approach Dr Walsh, asking him to name a priest prominently associated with the language movement who would act as an official chaplain to the school.

Apparently Walsh's reply never reached Patrick and there was also no effort made to tell him about the archbishop's position. Patrick was only made aware of the content of the reply in November through the brother of Fr Curran, Dr Walsh's secretary, who was a colleague of Eoin MacNeill. In his reply Walsh had apparently reiterated he was sympathetic to the project and had agreed to the appointment of any of the priests Patrick had suggested as chaplain.[91] As a result the school had started off without any official sanction from the Church or a chaplain. In November Patrick suggested Fr Landers, curate of St Andrew's Westland Row, which was accepted by Walsh in December. However, as Landers was sick he only took up his duties sometime in 1909 and resigned again in May 1910 due to pressures of parochial work.[92]

Patrick clearly did not want clerical control over the school, but religious instruction was central to his perception of good education. In the prospectus 'the profession and practise of Religion' was described as the most important preparation for life. In school the boys were stimulated to form a guild of the Apostleship of Prayer and an Arch-confraternity of the Sacred Heart or guild of the Sodality of the Sacred Heart.[93] Despite his critical attitude to the hierarchy, Patrick's Catholicism was deep rooted and these statements were certainly not just a front to make the school more acceptable in the eyes of Catholic parents. Apart from the visits of the chaplain, the boarders attended daily mass and the catechism was taught each day from 12 to 12.30. In the first year of operations a group of boys also prepared for first Holy Communion in the school.[94]

The resignation of Fr Landers coincided with the move of the school to new premises in Rathfarnham. These contained a private oratory and in his letter to the archbishop requesting a replacement Patrick expressed his hope that the new chaplain could be a permanent member of the teaching staff and asked whether mass could be served in the school daily. This seemed to have been a step too far as Landers was simply replaced in September 1910 by Fr Michael Burke, the chaplain of nearby Rathfarnham Abbey, who just visited St Enda's once a week.[95] Despite the prominence of religion in the curriculum, the lay character of the school remained a concern to some parents. In a letter to one of them Patrick set out the way religion was taught. '[Fr Burke] visits us at least once a week and gives half an hour's instruction. When classes are preparing for the sacraments or the whole school for the annual Diocesan Examination he visits us more frequently. In addition the smaller boys have half-an-hour's catechism every day, as well as frequent spells at the Irish prayers; the bigger boys half-an-hour's Catechism, Bible History, or Religious Instruction four times a week.' To reassure the parents further he stated that St Enda's devoted more time to religious instruction than any secondary school for boys he knew, and that at last year's Diocesan Examination the school got 99 per cent in Catechism and were very highly praised by the Diocesan Inspectors. He added that he gave frequent 'sermons' himself, 'my discourses while most orthodox, are so framed as to interest and attract boys'.[96]

It is not entirely clear to what extent Fr Burke fulfilled his role. Nuala Moran, the daughter of D.P. Moran, was taken out of the school as she was not being prepared for her first confession, and one of the pupils of St Enda's recalls a somewhat less than rigid adherence to religious teaching. He never saw a priest visiting St Enda's, 'but every evening after study Pearse recited prayers in Irish and on Sundays and Church Holidays we were marched to Rathfarnham Parish Church, and, of course, we were encouraged to go to confession and communion weekly'. The subjects of the after-prayers lecture often dealt with the Fenians.[97] One of the neighbours of St Enda's had the idea in the early years that 'they teach across the road more of the gospel according to Cúchulainn than of the gospel according to Christ'.[98]

Fr Burke's Irish was quite rudimentary and Patrick was not entirely happy with the arrangement. The attendance of daily mass his boarders had enjoyed in Cullenswood House was not possible in the Hermitage because of the distance to the local church, and in May 1911 Patrick came back to his idea to establish a chapel in the college itself.

I feel that a Catholic College is not complete without its Chapel and the presence of the Blessed Sacrament. I think we should interweave religion into our daily lives at every point and that the truest education is that which best combines the spiritual with the heroic inspiration. We have now some sixty boarders and I expect that we shall have a good many more next year; adding masters, servants and day-boys, we are a little community of about a hundred, and quite large enough to have our own little Chapel.

Patrick asked Dr Walsh for a permanent full-time chaplain attached to the school who would say daily mass, hear confessions, give religious instruction, and prepare pupils for communion. The new chaplain could fulfil the same duties for the sister institution St Ita's, the bilingual high school for girls established in Cullenswood House after the move of St Enda's to Rathfarnham in 1910. For practical purposes he suggested the chaplain would reside with the nearby Augustinians a mile or so away.[99] Walsh gave his permission and Fr Philip Doyle was found willing to take on this role. However, faced with the expense of furnishing and consecrating a chapel Patrick drew back from this plan. He was reluctant to ask Rome for permission if he could not guarantee the oratory would be finished and put to use, which was indeed never done.[100] As far as can be ascertained the oratory was never consecrated but Dr Walsh gave permission to say mass in the school chapel which was fitted with an altar during a four-day retreat in the College in 1915.[101] However, in March 1914 Willie noted a less than willing attitude among the local clergy towards the school: 'of course no priest from Rathfarnham came near us'.[102]

Curriculum

Traditional in its religious curriculum, the teaching in St Enda's was to be based on the most modern educational methods and thinking. All the elements of the educational philosophy Patrick had developed in the previous years came together in Patrick's description of his programme for St Enda's:

Chief Points
(a) An Irish standpoint and 'atmosphere'.
(b) *Bilingual teaching* – as far as possible.
(c) All language teaching on *Direct Method*.
(d) Special attention to science and 'modern' subjects generally, while not neglecting the classical side.

(e) Association of pupils with shaping of curriculum, cultivation of observation and reasoning, 'nature study' etc., etc.

(f) Physical culture; Irish games, etc.

(g) Systematic inculcation of patriotism and training in the duties of citizenship.

(h) Above all, *formation of character*.[103]

Combining these elements made St Enda's a very modern and for Ireland a unique experiment.[104] The ideas that Patrick linked into had also caused the establishment of similar schools abroad. The child centred education, modern teaching methods, the emphasis on the development of the whole person including character formation, patriotism and physical training were common denominators. Many private schools in Britain, including the venerable Eton College, had taken on at least some of these elements. A radical version of this was Ruskin School. Although having an agnostic basis, it was very similar to St Enda's in its workings.[105]

From the description of his approach it becomes clear that Patrick's more strident attitudes had mellowed. In the first issue of the school paper *An Macaomh* (The Youth) he sets out the lofty goals he had with the inception of the school: 'which should aim at the making of good men rather than of learned men, but of men truly learned rather than of persons merely qualified to pass examinations'. Each child should be urged to live up to his finest self. In his eyes a good man who was Irish should also be a good Irishman; therefore his school should be an Irish school. 'What I mean by an Irish school is a school that takes Ireland for granted. You need not praise the Irish language – simply speak it; you need not denounce English games – play Irish ones; you need not ignore foreign history, foreign literatures – deal with them from the Irish point of view.' Although Irish should be used as a medium of instruction, he believed that Irish culture and not the language should be central in education. 'An Irish school need no more be a purely Irish-speaking school than an Irish nation need be a purely Irish-speaking nation; but an Irish school, like an Irish nation, must be permeated through and through by Irish culture, the repository of which is the Irish language.' In this he had come a lot closer to the position of those like Yeats who emphasised the possibility of a purely Irish culture in the English language.[106]

In St Enda's Irish would initially be administered 'in homeopathic doses'. In the lower grades he introduced Irish gently 'as to appear always as a pastime to be enjoyed and never as a task to be learned'. In senior grades all classes were bilingual except the sciences for which there were no Irish books available. Patrick always spoke Irish and urged his pupils that until they became proficient they should use such Irish as they knew 'stating that even bad Irish was preferable to no Irish at all'. The existence of various dialects could be a problem to some pupils. On his arrival Joseph McSweeney from Donegal could not understand Patrick's Connacht dialect.[107]

The intended Irish atmosphere was created by wearing the specially designed uniform, the teaching of Irish music, dancing and traditional singing, and the introduction of a clan-based tutorial system, while Irish history and literature were prominent subjects.[108] Otherwise St Enda's curriculum had that British emphasis on the classical subjects added to by modern science and nature studies 'to inspire a real interest in and love for beautiful living things. Practical Gardening and Elementary Agriculture are taught as part of this scheme.' Inevitably Patrick emphasised the exceptional beauty of the Irish countryside both in his writings and the curriculum.[109] To this end the boys were taken on walks in the mountains and occasionally in a horse brake to Co. Wicklow.[110]

The rounded human being Patrick wished to nurture was further developed by paying a lot of attention to extra-curricular activities. A system of weekly lectures was instituted on topics in literature, phonetics, philosophy, physics, botany, archaeology, Egyptology, topography and medieval history. In the first years most of the best-known members of the Irish nationalist intelligentsia and cultural elite visited the school including Yeats and Standish O'Grady.[111] The pupils were also actively involved in the development of the curriculum and the administration of the school, frequently being asked for suggestions 'as to schemes of work and play'. Ideally he felt a school should be run like a 'child-republic', where the desire to learn would come from the children.

Physical fitness, an important element in international discourse, was also central in St Enda's curriculum, 'every day I feel more certain that the hardening of her boys and young men is the work of the movement for Ireland'.[112] This was not in direct preparation for revolution, but a reaction to the widespread fear in Britain and Ireland for the physical decline of men following the problems in finding sufficient men fit to serve in the Boer War. Physical deficiencies were associated with moral weakness and engendered a call to encourage discipline and moral character in young men in popular and academic discourse. The government stimulated attention to physical education in schools after 1900 which took both a gymnastic and a militaristic form. Apart from Irish sports the boys in St Enda's were trained in boxing, fencing, wrestling and swimming. At the same time the Swedish Method was introduced under Con Colbert, which involved drill, marching and shooting.[113]

Patrick's ideas even attracted the attention of Baden-Powell, who wrote to him in 1909 to invite him to set up a branch of his newly founded boy scouts movement in Ireland. Patrick declined as he did not want 'to make potential British soldiers out of Irish boys'. Baden-Powell's letter apparently inspired Countess Markievicz together with Bulmer Hobson to set up Fianna Eireann, the Irish-based boy scouts. Its motto was very close to St Enda's objective of 'training youth of Ireland mentally and physically by scouting and military exercise, and Irish history and language'. A branch of the Fianna was founded in the school by two pupils, Eamonn Bulfin and Desmond Ryan, in 1910: 'with the object of encouraging moral, mental and physical fitness'. They called it 'An Chraobh Ruadh' or The Red Branch after the heroes of the Ulster Cycle in Irish mythology. The Pearse brothers, who were not very physical, were not involved in this.[114]

The formation of character, however, was considered the foremost task of the school. It was highlighted in the school prospectus even before religious education and the Irish language. In Patrick's thinking the figure of the teacher took a central role in this. 'I think that the true work of the teacher may be said to be to induce the child to realise himself at his best and worthiest.' The teacher should be an example to the pupils in conduct and duty, but only to foster the individual child taking account of the various backgrounds: 'One does not want to make each of one's pupils into a replica of oneself (God forbid).' He saw elements of this in the Montessori system where the spontaneous efforts of the children were the main motive power and the teacher should inspire.

The attempt to foster boys into men in an all male environment was not unusual in secondary education elsewhere. This had become an explicit objective after 1904 when the term adolescent came into vogue following the publication of the book *Adolescence* by psychologist G. Stanley Hall.[115] In contrast to his contemporaries, however, Patrick claimed to base himself on an Irish not a Greek tradition.[116] He mirrored his own role on the idealised image he had of the teacher in ancient Celtic culture, whom he believed had truly fostered the unique abilities of each individual child rather than to implant 'excellences exotic to its nature'. In medieval Christian education a master and disciples relationship had existed, where the master inspired and fostered. Not directed and constrained by what the state believed a child should learn, but with a freedom to learn: 'freedom to bring themselves, as I have put it, to their own perfection'. This emphasis on developing the best in each pupil was impossible in the existing exam-based system where there was no room for more than the set programme. As one teacher put it: 'Culture is all very well in its way, but if you don't stick to your programme your boys won't pass.' To Patrick school was the university of life at home, where interdisciplinary learning, primacy of pupil over curriculum, and the outdoors were important.[117]

Another feature of contemporary education which Patrick wanted to overcome was the rigid social distinctions it perpetuated. He believed that the medieval system of education was a much more democratic system where social background did not affect a pupil's chances to excel. Socially Patrick was somewhat of a radical. He opposed the influence of the Church on anything beyond spiritual matters and freely supported issues such as women's rights. He blamed the inequality and poverty in current society on the influence of Adam Smith's political economy which he believed was 'invented by the devil'. One should not live by economic books, as life 'is a matter not of conflicting tariffs, but of conflicting powers of good and evil'. The solution to contemporary problems could, he felt, always be found by going back to Irish sagas.[118]

all the really important problems, were long ago solved by our ancestors, only their solutions have been forgotten. There have been states in which the rich did not grind the poor, although there are few such democracies now; there have been free self-governing democracies, although there are few such democracies now; there have been rich and beautiful social organisations, with an art and a culture, and a religion in every man's house, though for such a thing today we have to search out some sequestered people living by a desolate seashore or in a high forgotten valley among lonely hills.[119]

He also imbued his pupils with socially subversive attitudes. To him 'The great enemy of practical Christianity has always been respectable society.'[120] He believed one should stick to the ten commandments of Christianity and not add to them as many people did. He particularly abhorred the stifling respectability associated with the Catholic middle classes in Dublin's suburbs, who lived up to what he called 'The Commandments of the Respectable':

1. Thou shalt not be extreme in anything – in wrong doing lest thou be put in gaol, in right doing lest thou be deemed a saint
2. Thou shalt not give away thy substance lest thou become a pauper
3. Thou shalt not engage in trade or manufacture lest thy hands become grimy
4. Thou shalt not carry a brown paper parcel lest thou shock Rathgar
5. Thou shalt not have an enthusiasm lest solicitors and their clerks call thee a fool
6. Thou shalt not endanger thy job[121]

Patrick can certainly be seen as a radical democrat and a modernist but despite his rejection of respectable society and social inequality he was not a socialist. He was sympathetic to the plight of the working classes and their advocates but saw the future of the nation clearly in the hands of the Irish-speaking peasant led by representatives of the class he and many of his pupils belonged to. A certain paradox is present there as well. While idealising the life of Irish-speaking farmers in the West he himself sought respectability and acceptance from higher society. This was clearly expressed in the frequent use of his academic titles and by wearing a top hat and frock coat.

Medieval Irish education was his desired model because it combined the pagan Gaelic ideals of strength and truth with the Christian ideals of love and humility. Inspiration for the children should therefore be drawn from religion and hero stories to show that doing something for the nation is inspiring. In the first edition of *An Macaomh* Patrick stated he had found his inspiration for this in the story his aunt had told him when he was young called 'The Boy-Corps of Eamhain-Macha', about a king who gathered young boys around him and taught them simply because he enjoyed it so much.[122] The heroic model always remained central to Patrick's educational ideal. Already in his very first writings he had described hero-worship as 'a soul-lifting and an ennobling thing', which was central to all cultures. 'What would the world be without its heroes? Greece without her Hercules and Achilles, Rome without her Romulus and her Camillus, England without her Arthur and her Richard, Ireland without her Cúchulainn and Fionn, Christianity without its Loyolas and its Xaviers?'[123] He saw the potential of mythological and historic narratives to teach self-control, greatness and patriotism, which was again in line with many other nationalist movements throughout Europe.[124]

In St Enda's the Irish saint Colmcille but especially the hero Cúchulainn obtained a central role. Patrick was much influenced by St Colmcille who as a respected poet, a teacher with his own school, and an exile had expressed a great love of Ireland and provided a suitable model of manliness. Colmcille's phrase: 'If I die it shall be from an excess of love for the Gael' provided an inspiration for Patrick's pupils. Many publications had appeared on Colmcille at the end of the nineteenth century due to the commemoration in 1897 of his death. The Bishop of Raphoe had stated that Colmcille was the patron of the exiled, the patriots and the total abstainer but above all of schools. All issues close to Patrick's heart.[125] In his appreciation of Ireland's mythological past he was more influenced by Standish O'Grady's sagas than by genuine historical studies of Eoin MacNeill and others.[126]

The one Irish hero who stood out as an example above all was Cúchulainn.[127] Already in Patrick's first publication he asserted 'that the noble personality of a Cúchulainn forms a true type of Gaelic nationality, full as it is of a youthful life and vigour and hope'.[128] He represented the ideal Gael who possessed the qualities of 'what would be now called a thorough gentleman' with a chivalrous love of what was great and noble. Every day after religious devotions Patrick told his pupils a tale of the Cúchulainn saga which he saw as the Irish alternative to the Arthurian cycle. It has become clear that he fed them with a sanitised version in which he had excised the womanising, arrogance, violence, trickery and non-national elements of Cúchulainn.[129] As a model for his students he needed to be beyond reproach. 'Cúchulainn may never have lived, and there may never have been a Boy-Corps at Eamhain; but the picture endures as the Gael's idealisation of the kind of environment and the kind of fostering which go to the making of a perfect hero.'[130] Although students jokingly stated Cúchulainn was 'an important if invisible member of staff', they took on board the intended message: 'we understood that it was Pearse's goal to make every student a Cúchulainn for Cúchulainn was his exemplar'.[131]

This celebration of the hero was something that was widespread throughout Europe at this time as witnessed by the popularity of Wagner and mythology, but also in intellectual currents such as futurism.[132] This was part of a rejection of what were seen as feminised nineteenth century Christian ideals of moral earnestness, purity of feeling, privileged asexuality, self-denial and passivity. Instead a celebration of manliness in the heroic warriors of earlier times, who represented physical prowess, beauty, vigour and moral courage became prominent. This accompanied the militarisation of western society prior to the First World War. The most influential early manifestation of this in Ireland can be found in Standish O'Grady's hero-based history of Ireland.[133] Patrick linked the Celtic and Gaelic vision, and made the feminised attributes of Celticism into a masculine ideal of pagan Irish civilisation. He sought indigenous male role models in bardic past and Celtic Church history who were both pagan and Christian, warrior and scholar at the same time.[134] In Patrick's writing the loss of manhood was linked to the alienation from Ireland's heroic past. The purpose of St Enda's was not just a cultural regeneration but also 'to restore manhood to a race that has been deprived of it'.[135]

This identification with the heroic Irish past permeated the life of the pupils in the school. Cullenswood House was decorated with mythological images. A fresco by the Morrow brothers of the Setanta, the young Cúchulainn, with uplifted spear and shield dominated the front hall with around it in old Irish lettering his famous choice between life and fame: 'I care not though I live but one day and one night if only my name and deeds live after me.' The wainscoting of the main classroom was adorned with the names of heroes and saints, impressing upon the pupils not to live a mediocre life but to be inspired to act.[136] The omnipresence of Cúchulainn caused visitors to remark that 'the kids in there are being taught according to the commandments of Cú Chulainn rather than the ten commandments of God'.[137] Oddly enough one visitor to Cullenswood House recalls being met by a red banner which stated in white letters: 'Fear God & honour the king.'[138]

Images of Cúchulainn were used as well for the illustration of the school exercise book, the primer and the Módh Díreach lesson charts and reader published by Dundalgan Press. The motto of St Enda's was identical to that of the warrior band of another Irish hero Finn McCool, 'Strength in our hands, Truth in our tongues, and Purity in our hearts.' The flag used by St Enda's and the Fianna boy scouts was also based on the ancient Fianna, a 'blue poplin adorned with the gold sun disc of the Fianna'. The uniform of the boys also referred back to the heroic age. The parents were told that a kilt was preferred as a distinctively national form of dress, but the minimum requirement was that it was Irish made. The kilt was popular with Irish-Irelanders and some of the teachers like Thomas MacDonagh and Willie Pearse in particular wore them often.[139]

A central position in the expression of literary and educational opinion of pupils and staff members was intended for *An Macaomh*, the official objective of which was to be 'a rallying point for the thought and aspirations of all those who would bring back again in Ireland that Heroic Age which reserved the highest honour for the hero who had the most childlike heart, for the king who had the largest pity, and for the poet who visioned the truest image of beauty'. In reality it was particularly important as a vehicle for Patrick's own ideas. 'I do find the possession of a School and of an organ [a publication] necessary at once to my happiness and to my usefulness; a School for bringing me into contact with the wisdom of children, and an organ for the purpose of disseminating the glad and noble things I learn from that contact.'[140] Although supposed to appear twice yearly, only four issues were published; in the summer of 1909, at Christmas 1909, Christmas 1910, and in May 1913.[141]

The most visible element of the heroic cult in St Enda's were the many plays its pupils and teachers performed both in the school and in various other venues including the Abbey Theatre. The first public performances took place in the school from 20 March 1909 when Standish O'Grady's *The Coming of Fionn* and Douglas Hyde's *An Naomh ar Iarraidh* (The Lost Saint) were staged on three consecutive days. They were very well received by a mixed audience; Standish O'Grady who attended one of the performances even mounted a chair afterwards for an impromptu speech.[142] The end of the year pageant in the grounds of St Enda's on 22 June was a rendition of *The Boy-deeds of Cúchulainn* which was also performed for Sir Henry Bellingham at a summer feis in Castlebellingham. The choice of topic could have been expected, as Patrick remarked, 'we are anxious to crown our first year's work with something worthy and symbolic; anxious to send our boys home with the knightly image of Cúchulainn in their hearts and his knightly words ringing in their ears. They will leave St. Enda's under the spell of the magic of their most beloved hero.'[143]

In the second year an adaptation of Patrick's own story *Íosagán* was performed with Padraig Colum's *The Destruction of Da Dearga's Hostel*, Dr Hyde's *An Naomh ar Iarraidh* and Mr O'Grady's *The Coming of Fionn* for three days in St Enda's and once in the Abbey Theatre. Every year one or more plays were performed at St Enda's. All eight dramatic works Patrick wrote between 1909 and 1916 were designed with the pupils of St Enda's in mind. They included two outdoor pageants, a three-act passion play, one short skit, and four one-act plays. All of his works were attempts at introducing contemporary conventions in dramatic life and were intended to inspire spirituality and heroism both in the players and in the audience. 'I have always felt vaguely the potency for good or evil of the tremendous spirits whom the bards have taught us to know under the famous names of Lugh and Aongus, Cúchulainn and Meadhbh. But it is only since I have been working among the boys of St. Enda's that I have been able to realize how effective an influence their memory may yet become in shaping character and giving an intellectual or an imaginative stimulus.'[144] The actual staging of the plays and pageants were mostly directed by Willie, who took a great interest in acting. Alf M'Cloughlin, the son of Willie's half-sister, helped in costumes and production. 'He is at our service whenever we want anything done which requires artistic insight and plastic dexterity of hand, be it the making of plans for an Aula Maxima or the construction of a chariot for Cúchulainn.'[145]

The popularity of public pageant and dramas based on historical themes was also a pan-European phenomenon at that time. In *An Macaomh* of Christmas 1909 an article from *The Freeman's Journal* was reprinted on the return of pageants in Europe, arguing people were again seeing the merits of this medieval form.[146] Patrick certainly enjoyed the impact his heroic re-enactments had in Ireland. When the whole cast of *The Boy-deeds of Cúchulainn* marched through Dublin in costume in June 1909 on their way back from Castlebellingham, a crowd gathered spontaneously around them starting to sing the popular nationalist ballad *Who Fears to Speak of '98*. This gave Thomas MacDonagh the feeling that the crowd 'expect us to lead them against the Castle [the seat of government]'.[147] Critics were not always that impressed. Patrick once snapped at a journalist of one of the leading daily papers who had been pestering him for information during the staging of one of these pageants, leading the journalist to the retort 'I have endured your Pageant but I will not endure your abuse'.[148]

Culturally the boys of St Enda's played a major part in the Dublin of the pre-war period. They made their presence felt through their successful involvement in Gaelic games, and their parades through town in ancient dress. They performed in seven different plays in the Abbey Theatre between 1908 and 1912, organised numerous public pageants and plays in St Enda's and around the country at League events, which aroused widespread interest and were invariable well received.[149] The passion play 'An País', written and directed by Patrick and staged on Good Friday and Holy Saturday 1911 in the Abbey Theatre in particular, had a great impact: 'Probably the most outstanding Gaelic production seen in Dublin before 1916 was Padraic Pearse's Passion play ... In its own way this created something of a minor sensation in Dublin, reports of it travelling across the Atlantic, and some of them finding their way into the continental press. ... It was probably the first really serious piece of Gaelic dramatic writing produced.'[150] The cast was formed by students and staff of St Enda's and its sister school St Ita's, with Willie Pearse playing Pontius Pilatus. The commentary of spectators showed there was a great sense among them of being at an important Irish cultural event, not just because of the use of the Irish language and because it drew upon Irish folk tradition, but also in its expressions, the keening of the women in the lament and the use of uileann pipes. Photographs of its characters were sold in relatively large numbers showing a public demand. In the way it created new forms based on old styles it mirrored continental modern drama and can even be seen as an example of Celtic modernity.[151]

Patrick as teacher

Before the school opened some doubts were aired whether Patrick was suited for the job of headteacher. Lady Gleneary was not very impressed. 'P[earse] seemed reserved, too shy for a schoolmaster. Mrs Purcell said after he left if he was going to start a school it would be a ["poor" erased] queer school.'[152] Patrick, however, had no doubts about his qualifications: 'I suppose you know that I have had considerable experience as a secondary & as a university teacher, and that for the past 6 or 7 years my chief hobby has been the study of education in most of its phases. In a word, I feel that I have ideas on the subject of the education of boys which are worth putting into practice.'[153]

There are conflicting reports of Patrick's abilities as a teacher in his early years. The recollection of one of his pupils in the CBS testifies to his use of traditional methods in his first years of teaching: 'He would hit us with knuckles on back of neck if we made mistakes. He used to call this a "dullier".' He used the direct method in teaching with 'conversational phrases repeated time and time again, without emphasis on formal grammar'. Each phrase was repeated by every boy in class until he was word-perfect. 'Padraic moved around among them, making stabbing gestures with his stick of chalk, keeping everyone lively and alert.'[154]

He nevertheless showed a certain empathy for his pupils and his manner enamoured them: 'A boy named Molloy made a sop of bread and ink & fired it at another. P was rear [facing] blackboard as usual turned for us. That thing hit him. He at once lit on Molloy "Why did you throw that?" asked he. "I meant it for Byrne" said Molloy "Well next time see that I am not in your line of fire." He showed no bad temper & made the right retort.' Despite the use of physical incentives, which he probably felt he needed as a sixteen-year-old teacher to keep order, he was liked by his pupils: 'We bought him 2 vols as a present when he went to UCD … We all liked him – we were good students – but feared him a little.'[155] A similar combination of respect for and unusual liking of Patrick as a teacher is provided by other students. 'Without any effort he always commanded respect from Brothers and boys.'[156] In Alexandra College, where he started to teach some years later, his teaching ability and enthusiasm were publicly acknowledged.[157]

The more mature pupils in his early days in UCD and in private classes were less universally impressed. The classes in UCD seemed to have been miscast in the first instance: 'I have no recollection of the subject-matter of the lectures, except that they were not very advanced. I think the lectures were originally intended for persons taking up the study of Irish, and when Michael Christie and myself who had taken the full intermediate courses in the language, turned up as the only candidates, the scheme went somewhat awry, and the lectures took the form, more or less, of a refresher course.' He did come across to them as well as a very gentle teacher: 'I remember the man, soft spoken, and dreamy and gentle, almost timid, he gave me the impression of being a man naturally reserved & shy whose shyness was overcome by intense convictions. I never heard him raise his voice above the conversational level at any time.'[158]

The presence of women appears to have had a particularly detrimental effect on Patrick's teaching. One of his female students was particularly critical: 'The girls called him "My Lord Conceit", after a novel so called by Rhoda Broughton. He was conceited. ... He would read O'Growney & corrected our pronunciation. He was a very poor teacher. He would just read the lessons. He was uninspiring.'[159] A fellow student claimed that Patrick's natural shyness was exacerbated by the presence of women: 'There were ladies present. This seems to have made him shy.' This student was, however, much more impressed with Patrick as a teacher: 'He stimulated enthusiasm. He was an attractive teacher very serious & reserved.' Possibly this was due to the introduction of the direct method in his teaching early in the twentieth century: 'He was all for conversation ... He would try to organise conversation by asking questions. "What do you do in the morning?" "What do you do after breakfast?" When I heard this I began to grin & so did a lady girl student present. P had no humour & I think the presence of the girls made him shy.'[160]

His trip to Belgium seems to have inspired further innovation of his teaching methods. In particular the introduction of cardboard marionettes of people, animals, household articles, garments, toys instruments, etc., which were an invention of the College of Industrial Design in Belgium, enlivened his lessons. With this he could portray situations and conversation topics suited to various aspects of language teaching. 'He had cardboard figures movable. He used these figures during lecture. A hat was put over figure & you were asked where it was then it was taken off &c &c.'[161] The same emphasis on modern aids can be found in his articles on the Belgian education system.[162] This stimulated other teachers and possibly also the introduction of coloured wall charts in his *An Sgoil* teaching method.[163]

The appreciation of his teaching at St Enda's was more unanimous. Michael Dowling stated that Patrick's 'marvellous teaching faculty got the confidence of boys and drew them out'.[164] Patrick's enthusiasm and ability to interest his pupils were particularly liked. 'I left my two boys in his school. I was then lecturing on education in Girls Training College. I thought his theories of education 1st rate. I spent a day there. I remember hearing him lecture on Julius Caesar. I knew the play well but was genuinely interested and noticed that the boys too were.'[165] Joseph O'Neill, the school inspector, got a similar impression of Patrick's abilities to capture the pupils attention.[166] Even the far more hostile inspector Ernest Ansor, who objected to the use of the Irish language and had stated that Patrick's school was the sort of one he loathed, said after his inspection: 'I saw the best English teaching I've ever met out there in that Gaelic fellow's school at Rathfarnham.'[167] One of his pupils recalls that Patrick had the ability to bring a class around, and get in the mind of the most backward pupil.[168] The positive response from pupils also greatly inspired him.[169]

The students generally also remember encountering a loving environment at St Enda's: 'I was, as I say, very young when I knew Pearse – we always called him that, he had no nickname as far as I remember, but I can still see him tall, broad shouldered, slight cast in one eye with a great "gradh" for boys and they for him; love and admiration. I think we would all have done anything we could for him if he asked us.'[170] Although initially coming across as distant and fearful to new pupils, this did not last: 'My first sight of Pearse was overpowering. He swept into his study where my perfectly composed sister and my quivering self waited. I noticed his stature, the strong build, powerful shoulders, quick, impatient step, the half-shy look, with its half-shy flicker of a smile. ... But Pearse soon lost his terror for me.'[171] He nevertheless always inspired a certain awe, and students later recalled how 'the mere sound of his footsteps in a corridor instantly brought most of their activities to a halt. The horseplay and the romping froze, speech and chatter petrified, the students responded to his Gaelic greeting and waited for him to pass by before relaxing again.'[172]

Patrick idealised children and in particular Irish speakers who he saw as 'the fairest thing that springs up from the soil of Ireland – more beautiful than any flower, more graceful than any wild creature of the fields or the woods, purer than any monk or nun, wiser than any seer'.[173] He had a great admiration for the moral, emotional and imaginative standards of the young. He believed they were superior to adults who had been tainted by life's experiences. In most of his dramatic works small boys in particular are portrayed as sinless and close to God.[174] Adults often find redemption through the innocence, strength and morality of a young boy. Through his own contact with his pupils he received a great amount of pleasure and in their company the shy retiring Patrick was transformed. 'When he was in their company he had a sort of boyish enthusiasm which set him on a level with all of them.' They could also raise him above his natural gloominess: 'if we share in the[ir] joy it is by rising to their height from our own slough of despond'. He could be greatly touched by expressions of their appreciation. After receiving an umbrella as a present on his birthday he broke out 'in one of his rare bursts of self-revelation, spoke to us of his friendship and intimacies with pupils in the school past and present'.[175]

Patrick believed children were essentially truthful, and asserted that when his boys lied or bullied this was something they had learned in other schools.[176] He therefore avoided punishment, particularly corporal, as much as possible unlike most other intermediate schools. 'We have frequently seen masters – many of them wearing religious habits – systematically punishing boys for faults in their home work on the delightfully simple principle, "one slap for each mistake".'[177] To Patrick this was a basic error. 'To inflict corporal punishment *for a mistake* is surely the very acme of stupid and purposeless folly.' He strongly believed that 'The teacher should not be a man of terror to his pupils [but] ... a wise and tolerant friend.'[178] Patrick had a presence which did not necessitate punishment, and he did seem to have had a close relationship with his pupils who often came to him for advice.[179] One student who was taken out of St Enda's by his mother on the 'behest of certain rather pro-British friends of my mother who believed in a more "practical" form of education than that offered by the Pearse family', actually ran away from his new boarding school and walked three days through the Dublin mountains to get back to St Enda's.

Patrick nevertheless sent him back after impinging on him that his parental wishes were paramount.[180]

He did not reject physical punishment altogether. Most teachers at St Enda's rarely used the cane, but the classics teacher Dr Doody sometimes felt it to be necessary.[181] In a letter of recommendation Patrick called him, possibly with a touch of irony, 'an admirable disciplinarian'.[182] If the cane was used Patrick allowed this with some difficulty: 'Pearse shrank from violence. I have seen him dash out of the long study hall at St Enda's when a favourite scholar of his came under the sting of the cane in a neighbouring class. When circumstances gave him no other alternative but to "stick it", I have seen him cringe and tremble each time the swish of the cane was heard.' When he was put in a position to use the cane himself he often failed to do so, sometimes making the boy in question promise not to tell the others.[183] He publicly celebrated the fact 'that he had only ever chastised one pupil for dishonesty in his entire career in St Enda's', when one of the boys from the Gaeltacht stole a cake. His sister Margaret is reported to have rebuked him for the punishment.[184]

The pupils did not always live up to his expectations. Even in 1914 he could still be shocked if he encountered lying. In a letter to the father of Eugene Cronin he reported that the boy told lies if he wanted to get things done, and 'does not regard it as a serious matter even if the lie is such as to get another into trouble. I have had a long talk with him about this, and have no doubt that I shall in the end be able to get him to see how wrong it is to tell even the semblance of an untruth.'[185] The other major fault he found in children was cruelty. Possibly based on his own experiences as a child, Patrick abhorred all forms of cruelty, in particular to weaker children and animals. 'The two gravest faults of Irish children, as we have known them, is a certain lack of veneration for the truth, and a certain thoughtlessness in their treatment of weaker or more sensitive companions, as well as of dumb animals, often amounting to primitive cruelty.'[186] Although he believed such behaviour was not innate to children but learned at school, one of the few pupils expelled was for cruelty to a cat.[187]

Patrick approached his boys not as an awe inspiring figure but one who called upon their honour not their fear to maintain discipline.[188] The fact there was no constant monitoring of their behaviour seems to have been instrumental in maintaining discipline.

At other schools I had perpetually one eye on a Prefect and the other on what I wanted to do. It tended to give me a squint. The prefect had one already. That is why he was a Prefect. In St Enda's there were no Prefects in that sense of the word. You were not watched, or kept under constant observation. And on your first transgression Pearse called you to his study; you gave your word not to offend again, and you usually kept your word. If you didn't, you knew somewhere at the back of your mind that you were doing something shabby on the Ard-Mhaighistir [headmaster]; that you were letting down him, letting St Enda's down, and letting yourself down too.[189]

Although Willie believed that Patrick was 'never deceived in trusting to honour', former pupils tell a different story. 'Perhaps he was prone to trust too much to honour, and pretty often he was deceived, but his very trustfulness appealed to the lads. "It is no fun to tell lies to Pearse, he always believes you," said one young culprit.'[190] Particularly when new children came in they attempted to use the system to their advantage but in time his approach nevertheless seemed to have worked well for most of them:

When we were punished for some wrong act or omission we were ashamed rather than annoyed. I think the whole school felt that way. You could not be mean, you could not tell a lie – not often anyway; I remember telling one once and feeling utterly miserable after it especially as my two companions in 'crime' had owned up to 'smoking' and 'mitching'. I went back to P.H.P. and told him, I was commended for coming back but got a couple of strokes to bring my mitching admission and punishment up to their double admission.[191]

And as one former pupil stated: 'Though school-keeping somewhat lowered his former conception of the human boy, it in no way diminished his interest or rocked his affection.'[192]

This does not mean the St Enda's boys were without exception well behaved. One of the neighbours of Cullenswood House complained about the conduct of the boys when their ball went over the wall separating the two properties. They were rude and when the neighbour refused to return the ball this was 'resented, with language and demeanour towards my wife which I prefer not to describe'. The boys also broke some of his windows by stone throwing. This was apparently not a new problem as previous assurances by Patrick and his mother had not helped.[193] One of the American pupils is alleged to have been ejected after running off with a widow.[194]

Giving students responsibility for running the school was a further aspect of Patrick's philosophy. St Enda's was described as a self-regulating child-republic, with various offices elected at the beginning of each year, including a school captain, vice-captain, secretary, librarian, keeper of the museum, captain of hurling, captain of football and a house committee.[195] Self-organisation was part of the educational philosophy, witnessed by the setting up of various clubs and societies including some Catholic and a Gaelic League youth club, and self-reliance and self-discipline were encouraged.[196]

The, for that time, very exceptional child-centred approach confused some visitors. 'There was never any restriction to speak of on the boys of St. Enda's. To the casual observer the pupils ran wild. Inside the school gates was an empire of their own, administered by themselves.'[197] Some were shocked by the untidiness, particularly the prevalence of dirty boots lying around in the drawing room and on the beds, which was considered: 'very bad training for boys'.[198] Whether the lack of hygiene was responsible is unclear, but in September 1909 and in November 1911 boys were removed from St Enda's under the Public Health Act.[199] The manner of teaching also bewildered both pupils and inspectors: 'I went to Enda's in 1909, 1st year in the new premises. It was like a university. There was no order or discipline. The idea of lecturer more than teacher prevailed both in P[earse] & MacDonagh. The classes would tend to degenerate into discussions on language and literature.'[200] The sympathetic inspector of schools Joseph O'Neill was surprised by the conditions but nevertheless impressed with the results: 'There was no discipline everyone did what he liked but it seemed to work out all right.'[201]

Initially there were some problems regarding the attainment of the children. When O'Neill inspected the preparatory section of the school to ascertain whether they were entitled to a grant from the board of education he found that they were good at English but could not speak one word of Irish. 'I told him I would not pass them and this would have disgraced the school. He asked for a month and said he would make them as good as the best.'[202] The class was brought up to scratch quickly and although some complaints were voiced afterwards,[203] eventually many of the pupils of St Enda's went on to obtain prizes in their intermediate exams and a successful academic career. Patrick always remained optimistic about the progress of his boys in Irish. Four months after the opening of the school he calculated that at the present rate of progress the quicker of the purely English-speaking boys would be Irish speakers within twelve months.[204] By 1913 he reported that most had learned to speak Irish well, but a few had been disappointing.[205]

In his dealings with the pupils a genuine concern was shown for their welfare. They were fed the same food as the staff and the lavatories were clean, neither of which was apparently common in other schools.[206] Patrick kept overall numbers of students low so that he could get to know the boarders individually. Particularly in the early years he made a concerted effort and while sitting on the edge of their bed spoke to a different boarder each night.[207] He also kept very extensive records on his pupils, writing frequent reports on the development of their disposition, character, abilities, etc. In these detailed reports and in many letters to parents he showed himself to be very caring towards them, concerned for their well-being and academic progress and displayed a great empathy.[208]

The letters to the parents of Eugene Cronin, an Irish-American whom he was taking home with him to Ireland after his visit to the United States in 1914, show this close association with and care for his pupils: 'He and I are already friends and I anticipate that we shall be very close friends indeed by the time we reach Queenstown. There will, of course, be a wrench when he is parting with you and his mother, but my experience of boys makes me know that as soon as he settles down among his new friends and fits into the homelike surroundings of St. Enda's there will be nothing like loneliness.'[209] He also emphasised that, contrary to the practise in other schools, he did not read the letters which boys sent home. However, Eugene apparently complained of loneliness to his parents to such an extent that Patrick felt forced to suppress his letter home and inform his father of this.[210]

The primacy given to the welfare of the children also comes to the fore in the role that pupils were given in determining their own curriculum. In the school paper it is stated that each pupil has a suitable course selected from the available subjects: 'No pupil of St. Enda's is forced into a groove of study for which he evinces no special talent or native inclination.'[211] This was not mere padding. On a number of occasions he adapted pupil's curriculum to suit their ability.

In March 1909 and in September 1911 he suggested to parents to have their son drop French in middle grade: 'He has asked to be allowed to drop French and as he seems positively to dislike the language there is no use in keeping him at it. He will devote the time saved to Latin.'[212] Parents of another pupil were consulted extensively about holding him back for a year because 'we believe that at Dick's present stage of mental development it would be better to excel in one thing than put him where he is out of his depth'.[213]

The individual attention to the boys and the fact that the domestic side of the school was run by 'ladies' made the school in Patrick's mind 'specially suited for the education of sensitive or delicate boys'. In this there may well be some resonances of his and Willie's experiences at school. However, all this did not mean Patrick was particularly soft on his pupils. He did expect serious dedication and hard work:

> I do not plead for making school-life one long grand picnic: I have no sympathy with sentimentalists who hold that we should surround children with an artificial happiness, shutting out from their ken pain and sorrow and retribution and the world's law of unending strife; the key-note of the school-life I desiderate is effort on the part of the child itself, struggle, self-sacrifice, self-discipline, for by these only does the soul rise to perfection. I believe in gentleness, but not in softness.[214]

Patrick's efforts and expression of concern were not always motivated purely by the pupils' welfare but sometimes mixed with the interest of the school. He made great efforts to convince the father of Kevin Henehan, another Irish-American pupil, to keep his son in school after the boy had asked his father to be allowed home due to feelings of homesickness. Patrick keenly identified the fact that every child in the first few months at a boarding school would express such feelings in his letters home and if he did not it would be a bad reflection on the situation at home. He stressed that Kevin did not show any sign of unhappiness in the school and would lose a once-off opportunity to become an Irish speaker like his parents. He also felt it would not be good to give in to the boy's demands and believed it had more to do with the presence of the boy's mother in Europe: 'you will do a permanent injury to the boy's character if you do not help him to fight his first temptation. I assure you honestly that he is happy here all the time and that his homesickness is purely due to his knowledge that his mother is near and will soon be returning without him. Once his mother sails he will settle down as contentedly as possible till June.'[215] The repeated attempts to convince Kevin's parents, however, do seem to contain a fear on Patrick's part of losing out on the fees.

A similar ambivalent motivation comes through in Patrick's dealings with the case of the very talented Denis Gwynn who forgot to sit one of his maths tests in 1910 and as a result failed his whole intermediate exam. A letter to his mother makes this clear, describing it as a 'terrible calamity for this school, for a high exhibition in Senior Grade in our first year would have made our reputation as an intermediate school. But I am still more concerned for the disappointment to Denis.' The two issues together had a great impact on Patrick's peace of mind: 'need I tell you how the mishap about the Intermediate grieves me? I have not slept since.'[216] He does not leave it at this and in the same month he wrote several times to the Board of Education, initially asking for a special exemption in the interest of the school and Denis. Later he claimed that the rules allowed for the interpretation Denis and the second master had based themselves on that there was no need for a second examination for a pass. Patrick threatened he would fight the case but expressed the hope the Board would agree with their interpretation. How the case ended is unclear but after his appeal was rejected Patrick proposed to start legal proceedings against the Board.[217] To gain recognition of Denis Gwynn's excellent results was particularly important to the school as its grant from the Board was based on examination results. Pearse made similar efforts in challenging the results of the English exam in 1913.[218]

For Denis Gwynn, who later became Professor of History at UCC (University College Cork), this was of lesser importance. He obtained first place in the matriculation for NUI (National Univerity of Ireland) and won several scholarships, including the first Entrance Classical Scholarship in Greek, Latin and Irish worth £50, and also a £30 Universty College London scholarship and entrance to London University with a Scholarship of £40 p.a. for two years. Not only did Denis do well but all told nine students did their matriculation for NUI in 1910.[219] And by June 1912 the academic distinctions of the school included: an Exhibition in Modern Literature, a Special Prize in Science, and a Composition Prize in Irish for the Intermediate; eleven successful matriculations for NUI and a First Kildare Co. Council Scholarship. The pupils also won a Taylor Memorial Art

Scholarship, gold and silver medals at the Gaelic League's Feis Ceoil, and the Dublin School Championship and Cup in hurling and football – leading Patrick to justifiably conclude that 'we more than held our own in public competitions with other schools and colleges'.[220]

Financial consideration also affected Patrick's attitude towards more serious issues. In 1913 there was pressure put on him to eject Jim Larkin's son from the school, because many of the middle-class parents objected to his presence after the Labour leader had become involved in the Dublin lockout of 1913. Patrick could not afford to lose the middle-class clientele, but felt it was 'Most unfair, one of the most pious boys in the school. Goes to Holy Communion every morning.' Larkin's son was not expelled and later on his siblings also came to the school.[221] Similar concerns were behind Patrick's approach to the intermediate exam. Considering his criticism of the exam system and the emphasis on cramming it entailed, it is not surprising that he was initially hesitant to put his pupils forward for the exams. However, as the Inter was a vital marker in the career of young men and grants were paid by the Board of Education on the basis of exam results there was considerable pressure to allow pupils of St Enda's to go up for it. Patrick had foreseen this and initially stated that he was inclined to agree with the idea that it could be taken up without materially interfering with the Irish character of the school.[222] In the original prospectus it was stated that the children would only sit the intermediate if parents requested it.[223] When the first school year was up and running Patrick made clear that none of the students would go forward: 'we do not propose, however, to send our pupils forward for the Intermediate Examinations, but are working rather on the lines of the Matriculation Examination of the R.U.I. – our intention being, if possible to send forward our best pupils for matriculation at the new University.'[224]

His original attitude towards the Inter turned more negative when he came to realise the disadvantage at which pupils of St Enda's stood with its emphasis on bilingualism and oral skills. He felt the low status of Irish and absence of a test for oral skills would make proper Irish or bilingual teaching impossible, and penalise 'sound teaching in modern languages generally, and relegates to the limbo of the impracticable and fantastic all that more important part of education which aims not at the mere imparting of knowledge but at the formation of the character and the kindling of the imagination'.

The demands of the intermediate exams were unacceptable to him. 'At Sgoil Éanna we take the view that we alone, in consultation with our pupils and their parents, have the right to decide what subjects we shall study, what books we shall read; and we have been willing to sacrifice to this precious liberty the certainty of valuable fees and possible fame as a successful Intermediate school.'[225]

A few months later, however, Patrick came around and was ready to introduce the intermediate. The main reasons for this were the lure of financial compensation and the changes the Board of Education introduced to the format of the exam: 'the establishment of a system of oral inspection by the Intermediate Board has brought about a new state of affairs which makes it possible for us to avail of the Board's grants, without sacrificing any of our principles'.[226] His assessment of the new intermediate exams was substantially better: 'The programme itself is a magnificent one – wider and better than Matric. or 1st Arts – and I believe that we here at Sgoil Éanna are strong enough and competent enough to make use of it without being led away into a scramble for honours or in to "cramming" our boys.'[227]

The St Enda's boys were indeed reasonably successful. John Dowling won several prizes and Patrick was content: 'If we had concentrated on Intermediate work, and adopted Intermediate methods I have no doubt we should have done even better. But we have not concentrated on Intermediate work, and have no intention of doing so.'[228] From 1910 onwards the policy was summed up as follows: 'We refuse to worship the gods of Hume Street [Board of Education], though we send forward boys for the Intermediate Examination when their parents so desire.'[229] At the same time the higher forms continued to be prepared for the matriculation examination of the National University of Ireland or other professional entrance exams.[230] In his famous essay 'The Murder Machine' of 1913 Patrick would nevertheless again rail against the intermediate system.[231]

The move to the Hermitage

The first years of the school in Cullenswood House were extremely successful. The educational attainment of the pupils had been good, many moved on to university and some won prestigious scholarships. Their pageants and plays had made a significant impact on the cultural life of Dublin and in Irish games they had won a number of important prizes. As a result student numbers had grown rapidly and they were forced to hire additional space opposite the school in Sunnyside for housing senior boarders and Willie. Although Cullenswood House had been refurbished extensively at great cost, Patrick had already begun to look around for larger premises at the beginning of 1910.

From his correspondence and other sources it becomes clear a number of reasons can be identified for this. The fact the existing school building was too small to accommodate rising numbers was an important element. Patrick claimed that if they had to rent another additional property to house boarders the total costs would be equal to that of renting a new place of sufficient size. Moving the senior boys' school out to other premises would also allow him to open up a secondary school for girls in Cullenswood House, which a number of parents had requested. In this way the expensive refurbishments of Cullenswood House would not go to waste. Furthermore he felt that the beneficial effect of moving the school out of town would be a reduction in the numbers of day pupils and a concomitant increase in the proportion of boarders. This would allow him to pay more attention to creating a totally Irish atmosphere in the school which would enable the making of real Irish speakers. A final element seems to have been Patrick's ideological preference for rural living over urban.

> I had convinced myself that the work I had planned to do for my pupils was impossible of accomplishment at Cullenswood. We were, so to speak, too much in the Suburban Groove. The city was too near; the hills were too far. The house itself, beautiful and roomy though it was, was not large enough for our swelling numbers. The playfield, though our boys had trained themselves there to be the cleverest hurlers in Dublin, gave no scope for that spacious outdoor life, that intercourse with the wild things of the woods and the wastes (the only things in Ireland that know what Freedom is), that daily adventure face to face with the elemental Life and Force, with its moral discipline, with its physical hardening, which ought to play so large a part in the education of a boy.[232]

An important final consideration for Patrick was the desire to bring the housing and surroundings of St Enda's on par with the other great Irish secondary schools such as Clongowes Wood or Castleknock. 'I feel that if we are to hold our own we must offer boys as beautiful a home, as much room, as much fresh air, as much accommodation for games, as they get in other places.'[233]

Soon Patrick's eye fell on the Hermitage, an estate located in Rathfarnham.[234] Rumours had been circulating of Patrick taking several other properties but 'as soon as I saw the "Hermitage" I set my heart on it, and it would take a great deal to keep me from it'.[235] The Hermitage was owned by the Woodbyrne family, and originally built in the eighteenth century for Edward Hudson. The fact that his son William Elliot Hudson had been one of the founders of the Celtic and the Ossianic Society and a friend of the famous Young Irelanders Gavan Duffy and Thomas Davis made the property especially attractive.[236] There were initially some problems obtaining the lease early enough for refurbishing the building as the property had been leased for the summer of 1910, but as soon as it was clear that a permanent letting was involved the summer contract was dissolved.[237]

Financially the move was a great gamble and was advised against by many. St Enda's had already borrowed extensively to make Cullenswood House suitable as a school and now Patrick estimated that another £10,000 was needed to buy the property, refurbish the building and equip the school. A four-page circular was sent out on 10 May 1910 to try to raise this money. Patrick expressed the hope that 'the Irish Ireland public has sufficient faith in the possibility of regenerating Ireland through her schools to endow this great undertaking' and secure 'a permanent and entirely worthy centre for the great educational work we are attempting'.[238] Any funds provided would be repayable with an interest of 4 per cent per annum.[239]

Patrick was realistic enough to admit that the £10,000 would not come in on time for opening in September, but he hoped he would raise enough to rent the house with the option of buying it later. He stated he had arranged to go to the United States in two years' time to bring in further funds from a lecturing tour on behalf of the school with Shane Leslie, a League member from a prominent Anglo-Irish background. In the meantime he would increase the fees slightly and expressed the hope student numbers would not drop too far as a consequence of moving out of town: 'True we stand to lose most of our day-boys. But against this, I believe that some of our best day-boys will come to us as boarders; that others will be able to cycle or tram out; and that we shall get a certain number of new dayboys there.'[240] Ultimately Patrick felt that despite the financial risks it was important to try to make the venture a success: 'if one can feel that one has striven faithfully to do a right thing does not one stand ultimately justified, no matter what the issue of one's attempt, no matter what the sentence of the street?'[241]

In financing and setting up St Enda's in Cullenswood House Patrick had also largely been guided by this principle. As Thomas MacDonagh remarked, Patrick first looked at what the school needed, committed himself to it and looked for money to pay for it afterwards.[242] Patrick concurred: 'Prudence is the only vice.'[243] Money was nevertheless needed upfront and financial support from the movement had always been difficult to obtain. He had started the school originally with only about £150 of his own money, had spent liberally on refurbishments and charged low fees. As a result he had already been in serious financial difficulties by Christmas 1908. In January 1909 he had written to Joseph Dolan asking for an additional loan of £300 to pay off a threatening contractor. Dolan duly complied as he had done the previous summer when he lent £50 to enable the opening of the school.[244]

This was not the end but merely the beginning of the financial troubles. In May 1909 Dolan was asked for another £105 to pay off existing debts while Patrick took out a bank loan of £400 for further improvements to the school for which his friend Stephen Barrett stood as guarantor.[245] In November 1909 Patrick was behind with the rent and gas payments, the potato dealer threatened with solicitors over a bill of £3, while the mother superior of the Magdalen laundry warned she would retain the laundry if the bill was not paid promptly.[246] This caused Patrick to lament his troubles. 'Sometimes I wish that a millionaire would endow us with a princely foundation, and sometimes I feel that it is better to build things up slowly and toilsomely ourselves.'[247] In January 1910 he even turned to the much maligned Board of Education for an advance of £300 to finance the building of a laboratory in Cullenswood House which he received in April in lieu of the next ten years grant of £44.5.6d per annum.[248] At the same time Patrick gave up his editorship of *An Claidheamh Soluis* which had provided the only steady income, leaving only some incidental revenue from lecturing, teaching and royalties on his books.

With such large debts it was extremely difficult to find enough money to pay for the move to Rathfarnham. Although many influential Irish-Irelanders had agreed to join a board of governors, the money raised following the initial circular in May 1910 was indeed not enough to buy the estate.[249] There are several letters from people turning down Patrick's request for aid, while most others donated small sums of less than £10.[250] In June Patrick issued a second appeal, trying to raise at least another £1200 pounds in loans which 'in addition to the amount already promised, will enable me to transform the new premises into the most perfectly planned and equipped school in Ireland'.[251] At the end of June he had indeed collected enough promises of money to make the necessary deposit, though not yet enough to allow him to go on with the entire building scheme, making him increasingly anxious.[252] When the lease for the Hermitage was finally signed in the middle of July Patrick had undertakings for £2356.3.8d including £500 from the dissolution of the family business, £600 from Joseph Dolan, £350 from Seamus Macmanus, £200 from Alex Wilson, and £130 from Dr Henry. The remaining £576 came from sixty-nine different people who had donated sums ranging from five shillings to £50.[253] Most of these were just promises. When the date came to sign the lease he did not actually have enough money in hand to pay the deposit. At the last moment the two sisters of The O'Rahilly gave him another £100 under condition their gift would remain anonymous.[254]

Possession of the Hermitage and 24 acres and ten perches (5.5 yards in length) of land of late Irish plantation measure was handed over on 1 August.[255] A condition of the lease was that the main house could only be used as a private residence not as dormitories, school, class or playrooms for the boys. Although Patrick received an exemption on a yearly basis for using the residence as a dormitory, this meant that the billiards room at the back of the house would have to be replaced with an extension at a cost of £700.[256] He modelled the rebuilding of the Hermitage on the development of Rockwell College near Cashel, a good Catholic school where Thomas MacDonagh had taught.[257] He claimed that 'In beauty of site and suitability of surroundings the new St. Enda's will be the finest school in Ireland.'[258] That the refurbishment could not be fully paid for with the money he had collected meant that a building debt would remain which he hoped he would devise a means of paying off later.[259]

Patrick was indeed not certain that the school would survive the move. In June 1910 he was devising a legal scheme to ensure that the subscribers to the St Enda's fund would be repaid in 'the (I hope) unlikely event of a financial smash', while leaving them free from all financial responsibility.[260] The interest he had to pay on all the loans was a heavy burden on the school. He had not made life easier for himself by establishing St Ita's, a girls senior school, and a mixed preparatory school in Cullenswood, and running them side by side with the senior boys' school in the Hermitage. It was of course worthwhile trying to obtain a return for all the investments in Cullenswood House but it did add another financial risk. There was also a mortgage on the house and a rent of £96.15.10d p.a. The same applied to Glanmire, the house next door to St Ita's where the Pearse's used to live, which had a rent of £22.10.0d p.a. and an equitable mortgage, but they managed to rent it out with a small profit.

The expected loss of most of the day pupils for which the school was now too far out of town, and the expense of the conversion and upkeep of the new building, meant that the school soon ran into further financial difficulties. Only two months into the new academic year of 1910–1911 Patrick was urgently looking for more money to pay the rent, builders and other expenses.[261] To this end he organised a meeting of subscribers to St Enda's and St Ita's 'To discuss means for raising funds for the completion of an absolutely necessary building scheme and if possible for the purchase of the freehold of the Hermitage.'[262] The meeting resulted in a scheme devised to keep Patrick, as the person who was bearing the sole financial liability, in effective executive control while protecting the interest of the subscribers. A board of patrons was to be created in which all those who had donated £1 or more towards its development since May 1909 would be seated. It would elect a consultative committee from those who had subscribed more than £20 which would audit the accounts, visit the College, receive a quarterly report from the headmaster and offer suggestions as to the working of the Colleges, submit a report to the patrons' annual meeting, and organise further financial support.[263]

The objective of the board was to raise another £1500 but this did not have any immediate success and in December 1910 Patrick was again forced to approach his greatest benefactor, Joseph Dolan, for another loan of £500 to ward off another builder threatening to sue. Dolan had to borrow this money from the bank himself so needed extra security. Patrick promised to repay the £500 in six months with interest of 5 per cent. His solicitor suggested taking out a mortgage on Patrick's interest in the Hermitage in Dolan's name; in case of failure Dolan would then have the right to take over the school as a going concern. This would ensure repayment above any other possible claims. As additional security Patrick suggested taking out a life insurance on himself with Dolan as benefactor. The other £500 Dolan had lent him previously remained on the same par as the loans of all the other contributors.[264] When the money came through and some of the bills were paid in January Patrick was suitably grateful to Dolan. 'I need not labour my gratitude to you for coming in this way to the rescue of Sgoil Éanna. It is one of the generous noble things which make great movements possible, and which great movements always call forth.'[265] However, in June 1911 Dolan was in urgent need of some of the money he had provided to St Enda's. His bank wanted him to reduce his overdraft, but Patrick was not able to pay him back until September. In the meantime Patrick again suggested getting another life insurance on himself and handing it over to Dolan.[266]

None of these initiatives ever substantially alleviated the financial problems of the colleges. Patrick had a tendency to live from hand to mouth and borrow from one to pay off a loan from another. At the same time Dolan asked unsuccessfully for some of his money back; Patrick approached Mrs Hutton for a loan of £100 to pay off another creditor. If this was not paid St Enda's would become public property and other creditors would come down on them and banks would refuse further credit.[267] Patrick realised the danger of this but remained optimistic. In a letter to Archbishop Walsh he discussed his financial constraints in relation to obtaining a paid chaplain: 'I am trying to do a great deal on a very small capital, and there are moments when I have grave anxiety as to how exactly I am to make ends meet – though they generally *do* meet in the long run.'[268]

The most dangerous element of the way Patrick ran his financial affairs was the absolute priority he gave to providing facilities for the school. He even used money needed to pay off debts to start new building projects in the school.[269] On top of this the apparently cheaply built handball alley blew down in a storm in February 1911 three months after its erection.[270] At the same time that Dolan was looking for some of his money and Patrick was desperately trying to borrow money to pay off other creditors,[271] he still attempted to hire a specialised teacher from a commercial school because he was 'not satisfied with the handwriting, spelling, etc., of several of our boys, and I feel that I and the members of my staff – specialists in classics, modern languages, science and so on are not the people to correct these defects'.[272] The same priority given to the interest of the pupils made him apply successfully to the government for money for a drawing teacher in St Ita's, and a science teacher and an instructor for manual instruction in St Enda's. In his application he stated he could afford little in equipment but wanted 'to teach boys to be useful in their own homes'.[273]

Patrick rarely spent any money on himself. He did not even pay himself a salary, just drawing £1 a week from the school accounts for expenses. Everything he made was put towards furthering the cause. Buying an occasional book initiated a strong internal struggle. 'He loved his books: that much-read edition of the *Cattle Spoil of Cuailgne* and his many editions of Shakespeare, all of which he had watched in the booksellers' windows, nobly renounced, entered, fingered, steeled himself, fled whole streets away, lingered, wavered, turned back and purchased, radiant and ashamed until he saw the next.'[274] One of his pupils remembers how after three years at St Enda's Patrick was 'still garbed, I suspected, in the same well-worn mourning black suit, still draped in the same gauzy gown'.[275] He expected a similar austere attitude from others. Some felt financial support for his efforts to educate the youth of Ireland was demanded as an obligation rather than as a gift.[276] 'He depended on his friends to give him money & he made it clear that it was a duty to give him money. He considered he was supplying the energy & the leadership & that others should give him the cash & that it was no compliment.'[277] In his letters, however, he does show a realisation of the financial impact his demands could have, he genuinely tried to convince prospective backers of the viability of his scheme and offered the payment of interest on their investments. What he did take for granted was that they would consider the scheme worthwhile, and many indeed did.[278]

Even the suppliers of goods to the school were not exempted from this. When asked for payment by the butcher he replied that he had more important things to think of.[279] Some suppliers were willing to oblige. The baker from Rathfarnham often sent bread in without being paid because he 'didn't want to see the boys go short'.[280] Most suppliers were indeed supportive of his venture and easily swayed by Patrick's enthusiasm: 'He would come into the shop after it was closed with his little brief bag. He looked like an archbishop dressed in black looking impressive and tell me all the wonderful things he was going to do.'[281] However, not all were this lenient. The photographer Lafayette took him to court while the gas company cut off St Enda's.[282] They were reconnected on condition payment was made in advance. D.P. Moran took the same line with advertisements for St Enda's in *The Nation*. Patrick was unwilling to accept the logic behind the refusal to supply goods without payment. When Whelan, a bookshop and retailer in hurleys, failed to provide any more hurleys because they were not paid despite repeated requests, a comment in the newspaper appeared: 'no doubt supplied by Pearse, that hurling in Enda's was meeting with opposition from most unexpected quarters'.[283]

What prevented many willing supporters from investing was the poor reputation Patrick had built up as a businessman.[284] Patrick acknowledged his weaknesses in the area of financial management. At the time his family sculpting business went under in 1910, as a result of a combination of bad business sense and a slump in the building trade, he commented to a fellow member of the Publication Committee: 'they are not very good as businessmen – some of them at least, of which I may be the worst offender!'[285] However, Patrick was a born optimist. To justify his move to Rathfarnham and the huge financial burdens he had taken upon himself, he wrote: 'I have constantly found that to desire is to hope, to hope is to believe, & to believe is to accomplish.'[286] However, his realisation that he was a poor manager did not change his attitude.

Running St Enda's

The move to Rathfarnham and the financial difficulties did not at first affect the attainment of the College. It could well be argued that in 1911 it stood at the height of its academic and cultural success, and also won several distinctions on the sports field. In 1910 St Enda's had taken the initiative in organising a Leinster school's League in Hurling and Gaelic Football, which they won in its first and third year. Their hurling and football teams also reached the inter-colleges league finals.[287] St Enda's also played its part in curriculum development. In November 1911 the first of a series of textbooks for Irish schools written by its masters was published called *Leabhráin Éanna*.[288]

At the end of the second year in the Hermitage Patrick expressed his satisfaction. 'We have accomplished the miracle of making boys so love school that they hate to leave it. I do not think that any boy has ever come to St. Enda's who has not in a short time grown fond of it. It is not that we make things unduly easy for our lads; they work as hard in the study hall and on the games' field as it is healthy for any lads to work.' He attributed this success on the 'real comradeship' that existed between teachers and pupils. 'I mean not merely that we masters fraternise with the boys when off duty, but that we have put ourselves definitely into such a relationship with them that every boy is always sure that his point of view will be seen by the master and his difficulties sympathetically considered.'[289] He was also now convinced that the broader goals of St Enda's were attainable. 'After four years I am more than ever convinced of the importance of the work we have taken in hand, and have satisfied myself of the absolute feasibility of regenerating Ireland nationally and socially, as well as saving the Irish language, through the medium of the schools and colleges of the country.'[290]

Much of St Enda's success had been dependent on the widely held respect for Patrick's achievements among Irish language enthusiasts. 'I think that all who were eager to help with Sgoil Éanna were moved first by admiration for your personality and confidence that your ideal of training and developing character was a high one. Secondly by the knowledge that you are a fine Gaelic scholar. And thirdly (at least in my case) by the wish to get children taught without the hampering influence of intermediate exams.' The always critical MacNeill doubted whether it was possible to achieve the same standard in the girl's school, St Ita's. 'I do not think a girls school will command the same support unless the Principal is well known as an enthusiast for education not mere book learning, but the training of character as well as intellect.' He also doubted whether a headmistress could be found with sufficient experience, personality and idealism to make the Irish teaching better than in existing schools.[291]

Patrick had first considered Miss Louise Gavan Duffy and Miss Eleanor Butler as headmistresses, who were both experienced teachers, but finally decided to appoint Mrs Bloomer, a musician from Derry. It is not entirely clear why this was so. Butler had not been allowed to combine the position with her role as examiner for the Commissioners of Intermediate Education, but why Bloomer was favoured over Duffy remains unclear. A willingness of Bloomer to invest money in the schools may have played a part. Patrick functioned as director of St

Ita's, with Mrs Bloomer as house mistress. Patrick expressed the hope that Miss Butler would function as an occasional visiting mistress.[292]

Ties between St Ita's and St Enda's were strong in every sense, even the prospectuses were virtually identical. Instead of the concentration on physical training St Ita's spent much more time on domestic economy, needlework, drawing, dancing and other 'lady-like activities'. However, it did give a lot of attention to academic subjects which was uncommon in other schools for girls. As witnessed in his writings Patrick saw women primarily as moulders of the next generation,[293] but nevertheless championed their fight for recognition as useful members of society. His support for various women's rights also extended to his girls' school, and he did not shy away from being involved in their development. Every Wednesday afternoon he lectured to them in similar fashion as to his boys, exhorting them to develop themselves and not be hampered by duty or anything else, 'if your way of life or your profession in life does not allow you to live up to that best that is in you, then you must *change* your way of life, or your profession'.[294]

The first signs that the financial difficulties were starting to affect the academic achievement became visible in the increasing difficulties to staff both places. Doody and Smithwick stayed with the Colleges throughout these years but otherwise there was a high turnover in staff. Of the original members Thomas MacDonnell and the energetic MacDonagh had left in 1910. The latter primarily to prepare for his university examinations, but he also had some unspecified concerns. 'I was dissatisfied in certain things in the teaching and the staff, but I should be dissatisfied in Heaven.'[295] The erratic payment of salaries only exacerbated such feelings of discontent.[296] Yet Pearse did not hold a grudge against these teachers as he wrote several positive references for them.[297]

The colleges were basically run by idealistic young teachers who were attracted by the new ideas and idealism of the new school and for a while at least were willing to sacrifice much for this. Mary Maguire, who taught in St Ita's, recalls the atmosphere of the time:

> it seems incredible that so many young people were eager to devote their lives to the service of causes and ideals rather than to normal things of youth. That they should take on themselves the arduous task of running a school, of bringing up and educating boys and girls, a task so full of drudgery

and routine, seems unbelievable. But then it seemed equally incredible to some that parents would want to entrust their children to a group of young people whose chief recommendation was their ideals, their scholarship, their sense of art, and in other ways their lack of experience.[298]

However, it proved difficult to keep up this dedication for any length of time, particularly when financial rewards were low. As a result Patrick came to rely more and more on his own family. After the winding up of the family business Willie became a full-time teacher. In 1911 he acted as art and drawing master, but he also had enough Irish to become a regular master in 1913 and even acted as assistant headmaster in 1914.[299] He turned out to be central in keeping things going: 'He it was who made the young idea wipe its boots on the mat and keep its fork in its left hand and answer all bells promptly. He it was who managed plays and pageant and guided clumsy fingers round circles and curves in the drawing class.'[300]

The growing involvement of Patrick's family lowered the wage bill but as head of the family Patrick was now responsible for his mother and two sisters as well as a small array of relatives who had moved in with them.[301] This included Alf M'Cloughlin, his cousin Maggie and some other cousins on his mother's side. After the move to the Hermitage in 1910 a Miss Byrne moved into Cullenswood House, who apparently also had a close relationship with the family. She might have been the wife of his deceased half-brother James who died in 1912. The foray of Willie, Mary Brighid and Alf in acting through the Leinster Stage Society added more demands in the midst of a new financial crisis St Enda's faced in the spring of 1912. They had staged some moderately successful plays in Dublin but when they took their production to the Cork Opera House they encountered bad reviews and an almost empty theatre, losing most of the money Patrick had put up for it.[302]

By 1911 the running of the school was at breakeven point. The move to the Hermitage had lost the school sixty of its 130 boys but the addition of the girls' section meant that by January 1911 there were 150 pupils of which seventy were boarders.[303] Patrick painted a fairly positive picture of the future: 'St. Ita's has ample accommodation for many years to come, and is practically free from debt, having inherited the classrooms, etc., originally erected for St. Enda's, and already paid for, or virtually so.'[304] On basis of the accounts for 1910–1911 and the estimates for 1911–1912 Patrick concluded that they had reached a point where the college as a whole was actually paying for itself.[305] However, he acknowledged that he had never kept regular accounts and the burden of debts was increasingly difficult to bear. So much so that Patrick was forced to replace his regular telephone line with a penny in the slot telephone as the cost of calls became too high.[306] By January 1912 Patrick had spent £2066 on building and decorating the new house, another £350 on furniture and fittings and £250 on a laboratory. He had also promised the landlord, who had incorporated very clear restrictions on the boys' entrance to the house, to build a dormitory.[307]

Various efforts were made to raise additional funds including the organisation of a Gaelic tournament by Cathal Brugha and Sean Forde,[308] but these initiatives never brought in enough to reduce the large debts. A more structural solution had to be found, and during a meeting with George Cavan Duffy and others in London in October 1911 the idea was put forward to bring the schools into a limited company.[309] Such a company could give out shares in lieu of the existing loans and give everyone interested in the ideal represented by St Enda's a chance of associating him or herself with their work. They hoped most debts would be converted to shares while this would also bring in sufficient money to pay off the remaining debts and complete a new wing for the boarders.[310]

Although the limited company was not formed until April 1912, Patrick already assigned shares in lieu of loans from October 1911 onwards. By January 1912 there was, however, little more than £200 collected and the directors decided to postpone the establishment of the company until they had at least £500.[311] To facilitate this Patrick launched the idea to engage organisers to sell shares against a commission of 10 per cent. Sean T. O'Kelly, the former manager of *An Claidheamh Soluis*, was subsequently appointed on that basis. 'Do your level best for us among Leaguers, public men and business circles in Dublin.'[312] Patrick also made every effort to try to sell shares in the new company. Liam O Donhnaill remembers how 'Pearse & Eamonn O'Neill used come to town on roller skates. I gave him £5 for school as a subscription. He insisted on regarding it as a share and gave me a registered stamped share certificate.'[313] A number of prominent Gaelic Leaguers had been approached to form a board of directors and an academic council. The first prospective director was

Dolan: 'You and I would seem to be the obvious first two, as I am practically Sgoil Éanna and so much of your money is involved.'[314] In June 512 shares had finally been sold and a board of directors and an academic council were officially installed.[315]

When the company was set up the prospectus showed liabilities of £6685 and assets of £566. Various creditors had agreed to take shares in the company accounting for £1990 leaving £4130 to be paid. The small surplus on the running of the schools in 1911–1912 was certainly not enough to do so. The accounts for 1911–1912 show that the annual income of both colleges in fees, grants and proceeds from the garden was £3688, while the expenditure was £3559, leaving a surplus of £129.[316] In the official Statement of Income and Expenditure of St Enda's College for year ending 30 June 1912 a profit of £149.10.3d was recorded. Patrick claims that with efficiency, saving on lights of 5 per cent and with ten more pupils the profit could go up to £300–£400. He could then pay the interest on the debts.[317]

Progress in solving the debt situation was, however, very slow and the situation became critical in June 1912 with the whole school threatening to go under. The financial accounts of St Enda's published in various papers in that month showed total liabilities of St Enda's had increased again to £4344.0.8d of which £2362.0.8d was urgent. St Ita's had liabilities of £728.1.9d, all of them urgent. On 7 June Patrick wrote to one of the teachers informing her he was unable to give her any money he owed her, and added: 'At all costs we must keep the food bills paid each week till the girls go home.'[318] The following week he was even more desperate:

> The financial affairs of St. Ita's have reached a desperate stage. I have not been able to pay Magees for the past three weeks. Eastman, Lucan Dairy, Ferguson, O'Dwyer, and the landlord are exercising constant pressure. Worst of all, Bolands served a writ on me yesterday for the amount of their a/c – some £37 I think. This is very serious, as if it is not paid in ten days they can mark judgement which means that we shall be in the 'black list' and that the credit of St. Enda's and St. Ita's is gone. Indeed it will be a signal for everyone to come down upon us.[319]

As a way out of the situation Patrick apparently urged Mrs Bloomer to stand as guarantor for another bank loan. This was part of an overall scheme designed by Alec Wilson to refinance the debts.

Bloomer who had already leant a considerable amount of money to the school refused and Miss Gavan Duffy, who had previously been suggested as headmistress, then suggested she would lease St Ita's as a going concern at £180 per annum for a term of three years. She would pay two years' rent upfront and bear all losses as long as the agreement lasted. This advance together with some of the 'assets outstanding would enable the directors to clear all the pressing liabilities of St Ita's', and gave Patrick renewed optimism: 'Now that the future of St. Ita's is secured by Miss Gavan Duffy and that St. Enda's is actually paying its way, nothing is needed but a sum of money, whether by way of endowment or of loan for a period of years, sufficient to meet the outstanding obligations from the early years, in order to ensure the permanent success of the tremendously important work for Irish education undertaken by the two colleges.'[320]

To allow this new arrangement to be put in operation it was necessary to get Wilson's refinancing scheme working. Some progress was made in repayments but by July there was still more than £3000 outstanding and the creditors were getting impatient. 'My fellow directors regard the situation so seriously that they have come to the opinion that unless we can raise £3,000 immediately we cannot go on.'[321] Patrick even expressed a willingness to sell the school but continue as headmaster without any payment.[322] Wilson assessed the situation and concluded that so far probably £8000 was spent on the school. Patrick had sunk every penny he possessed into it, and besides the larger benefactors, nearly £3000 had been contributed by 200 others, 'nearly all poor people' 'for the most part without any expectation that the money would ever be repaid'.[323]

Wilson himself now agreed to stand as guarantor for £1000 if others could be found for the remaining £2000. In July Patrick approached several people, including George Berkeley and Archbishop Walsh, but none were willing to cooperate.[324] The continuous demands on his friends for money had wearied some and financially exhausted others. Patrick's goddaughter Sígle Barrett claims that her father sold a house without telling her mother to clear a debt of Patrick's of about £300.[325] Finances were coming under further threat when Mrs Bloomer demanded her loans back after she was, as she claimed, ousted from St Ita's by Ms Gavan Duffy.[326] It was clear Patrick had run out of financial options and bankruptcy was imminent.[327]

He was nevertheless unwilling to let the school go under out of a combination of commitment to the cause and fear of personal humiliation. 'If I don't save the school, I won't walk round Dublin to be pointed out as the man who founded it and failed: no, I shall go to America and work until I have paid off the last penny of debt.' He blamed the richer members of the public for their lack of support, and considered starting a fast on the doorstep of a wealthy Dubliner until the school was endowed. 'I think I will be a Socialist, for the rich have failed me!'[328] Later he emphasised that the main reason why he kept the school alive was that it was the only way he would ever be able to pay off his debts to his friends. 'St. Enda's is losing every year, but I dare not let it die, as its continued existence is the sole condition on which I shall be able to pay off the old liabilities.'[329]

As a final measure the directors decided to put the company into voluntary liquidation and try to come to an arrangement with the creditors which would allow the college to make a restart. On 2 September a meeting of Sgoil Éanna Limited was held to wind up the company and D. O'Connor was appointed as liquidator. On 6 September he met the creditors to try to find a way forward and allow the college to reopen on the 9th. On the 3rd Patrick offered to pay the liquidator £500 and the interest in Glanmire, the house formerly occupied by the Pearses on Oakley Road[330] to buy back the Hermitage subject to rent and a mortgage of £1500[331] including all moveable property. The creditors were asked to accept not less than 2 shillings for every pound they were owed, and suspend proceedings against Patrick for twelve months. After that further payments would be made if possible.[332]

There were more than 120 creditors in total including many large firms as well as some of the teachers. There were 35 creditors subject to this agreement, most of whom were not very happy with what was on offer: 'You have treated us very badly and for no other reason that we can see but just because we have been too lenient with you.' Bolands were particularly indignant and at first refused to accept the offer: 'The position appears to be that your friends will provide 2/- in the £ but that you yourself will undertake nothing. Looking to our experience of you, we submit that such a proposition on your part goes beyond all reason. We have nothing to add to our letter of the 13th inst. [threatening legal action].'[333] However, Patrick's assets totalled only £123 and it was estimated that the proceeds of a sale of assets would only bring in another £173. So what was on offer would give the creditors more than a bankruptcy would do. All of the thirty-five companies and individuals had to agree to the deal otherwise the friends of Pearses would not put up the money to pay even the £500. The creditors therefore had not much choice and they eventually all agreed.

Even raising the necessary £500 to buy back St Enda's had not been easy. Wilson had agreed to put up £300 if the remainder could be found elsewhere. At the end of August, shortly before the meeting with the liquidator on 6 September, Patrick was still sending out desperate requests for money. 'It would be a national calamity if the work of St. Enda's were to cease, and a tragedy beyond telling if we were prevented from reaping the fruit of what we have sown during the past four years in capital expenditure and in toil.'[334] Initially asking for an extra £400 he eventually had to settle for £200.[335] Douglas Hyde spelled out why some were still willing to put more money in the project: 'It would be worth any money to the cause of Irish nationhood to have such a school, quite independent, quite Irish, taught by laymen, and Gaelic Leaguers, in giving a good education. Indeed I would go so far as to say that such a school would be a prime necessity in the new Ireland which we are building up.'[336]

After the sale Patrick was in full control of the school and free of any immediate financial threat for the next twelve months. To oversee his directorship the academic council was reinstituted.[337] Patrick again turned from despair to optimism. 'We have pulled through all right, and though I realise that there is an uphill fight before us I am fairly confident as to the future.'[338] However, others doubted his ability to run the school by himself. Edward Martyn stated the settlement was only staving off the inevitable. 'I am sorry you would never listen to prudent advice ... you have now made impossible what with care and foresight might have become a permanent success.'[339] The school did reopen on the 13th only a few days late, it was still not free of debts and St Ita's had fallen victim of the difficulties. The scheme mooted in July under which Louise Gavan Duffy would lease St Ita's had apparently fallen through and St Ita's was not reopened. Cullenswood House, on which they had a ten year lease, was continued as a hostel for female university students.[340] St Ita's was not mentioned in any of Patrick's proposals over the summer and a year later he stated that

'As the yearly loss on St. Ita's was very heavy, it was decided in the general interests not to re-open it.'[341]

Patrick had a year's respite but repayments would have to be taken up again in the summer of 1913. Although his creditors could not ask too much as their only chance to be repaid fully was if St Enda's stayed open, Patrick still needed to give them more than a bankruptcy would provide. To enable this he made renewed efforts to attract more pupils and a flurry of fundraising activities was started early in 1913.[342] As part of this *An Macaomh*, which had not been published since 1910, was resurrected in May 1913: 'To be plain, St. Enda's College has now been at work five years, and we propose to commemorate the achievement of the lustrum by making a very determined effort to reduce the wholly preposterous debt which we incurred in our early months for buildings.' In retrospect he stated he should not have started the project, but 'There are some adventures so perilous that no one would ever go into them except with the gay laughing irresponsibility of a boy; they are not to be "scanned" beforehand; one does one's deed without thinking.' The fact that those involved had not been motivated by money explains its survival: 'Such burdens as we undertook five years ago would assuredly have crushed us if we had been worldlings, persons oppressed with bank balances and anxious about the rise and fall of stocks or the starting prices of racehorses. Fortunately the cares of competency have never existed for us, hermits of a happy hermitage.' Nevertheless he admitted they were 'worldly enough to desire to lighten our burdens, and generous enough to admit others to share in our perils'.[343]

The main elements of the drive to raise money were the staging of a performance in the Abbey, a week long fete and a raffle. Patrick approached Yeats, then the director of the Abbey, in April asking him if he would stage a fundraiser. The idea had come up after Yeats had called the school of the Bengali nationalist and 1913 Nobel Prize winner for literature Rabindranath Tagore 'the Indian St Enda's'. Yeats responded more than positively. 'We had hardly time to frame our project in words when Mr. Yeats assented to it; and then he did a more generous thing still, for he offered to produce for the benefit of St. Enda's the play of Mr. Tagore's to the production of which he had been looking forward as to an important epoch in the life of the Abbey – the first presentation to Europe of a poet who, he thinks, is possibly the greatest now living. And he invited me to produce a St.

Enda's play along with Mr. Tagore's.' The performance was set for 17 May. Yeats directed *Dak-ghar* (The Post Office) by Tagore while Patrick decided to put on his own play *An Ri* (The King) which he had also staged the previous summer in St Enda's. He called upon the existing cast including Mrs Bloomer and some of the former St Ita's girls, who willingly obliged.[344] Tagore subsequently requested Patrick to allow him to perform *An Ri* in his school. This was done and Tagore wrote he was delighted with the play.[345]

The most substantial element of the fundraising effort consisted of a week long fete. Every evening of the week commencing Monday 9 June a series of open air entertainments in aid of the St Enda's Building Fund would be staged. A field on Jones' Road had been chosen as the venue because the more attractive setting of St Enda's College was felt to be too far out of town. The object was to gather all of Dublin for a week's Irish revel with 'open air concerts, pageants & pageant plays by the St. Enda's boys, and display of drill, tent-pitching, skirmishing, 1st aid by the Fianna Eireann'. Money was collected by charging admission and for participation in various games such as 'aiming with missiles at graven images representing Mr Birrell [chief-secretary for Ireland], Dr. Starkie, the President of the Gaelic League [Douglas Hyde], and the Headmaster of St. Enda's'. Support was provided from all sides. Sinn Féin lent out an ass and cart and Jim Larkin supplied turf and paraffin and helped print 5000 handbills. There was also a wealth of publicity and *An Claidheamh Soluis* tried its best to extol the virtues of the St Enda's performances. 'It may be assumed that the pageants & pageant plays will be the most beautiful things of the kind that have been in Dublin. The St. Enda players have mastered the art of grave and measured speaking in Irish as no other players.'[346]

The opening night, however, was a big disappointment. It was pouring with rain and Sean O'Casey remembers how the crowds were 'saturated, gloomy and low in heart'. Patrick was the 'nadir of dejection', particularly after the pupils accidentally set fire to a dressing room tent and the manageress of the fancy fair which had been allowed to set up in a corner of the field to help pay the rent refused to silence her steam organ during the pageant. Still the weather improved, attendance was good overall, and people were impressed with the performances.[347]

The fundraisers brought in enough money to reduce the debt somewhat further. The liquidator had been able to pay each creditor

2 shillings and 6 pence in the pound, and Patrick now paid another 2/6 in the pound and promised more in February 1914. He expressed the hope he would eventually be able to pay all in full. A little late and a little less than promised, 2 shillings in the pound was indeed paid in March 1914 bringing the most pressing debts back from £3000 to about £1950. In October 1913 Patrick claimed that the year without debt repayments had been very successful. Financially the school had paid its way, not having incurred any new liabilities, but he acknowledged they were not out of their difficulties yet.[348]

The United States and the war

To try to facilitate a more substantial improvement in the debt position Patrick finally took up his long-standing plan to go on a fundraising tour to the United States at the end of 1913. 'If I can at all manage it I will go to America either before or after Christmas to lecture and collect for St. Enda's. It seems the only chance of placing the school on a sound financial basis; and it is only a chance.'[349] Although organised on short notice, Patrick made serious efforts to ensure his trip had impact. In October he asked a friend for a 'somewhat absurd' favour in the shape of a couple of articles to heighten his profile in the American newspaper. 'I am told that it is absolutely necessary to get myself "boomed" in the American and Irish-American papers beforehand.' He added that these 'will gather the impression in America that I am a most interesting character!'[350] To ensure cooperation from the Irish-American organisations Patrick was also sworn into the IRB (Irish Republican Brotherhood) by Bulmer Hobson, on condition that some of the funds collected would be diverted to that organisation.[351]

Patrick set sail to New York from Cobh on 8 February 1914 still uncertain whether the trip would bring any financial rewards.[352] He had received a great deal of publicity in the radical *Gaelic American* and enough lectures were organised for him in advance to last at least a few weeks, but much of the itinerary had to be made up while there. A few weeks after his arrival he wrote to Joe McGarrity, one of the directors of Clann na nGael, that he had not made much progress, although several people were working for him 'in various directions'.[353] At that point he was even thinking of going home and returning better prepared later in the year for an extensive lecture tour. However, the initial slow response improved and towards the end of March a St Enda's Building Fund had been set up to coordinate donations and Patrick became more optimistic about the possibilities of raising money and decided to extend his stay.

To American audiences St Enda's was advertised as 'modern in the best sense', wholly Irish in complexion, bilingual in method, and supported by many influential Gaels. While emphasising the nice building with historic associations and the good achievement in education and sports of its pupils, much was made of the educational approach that was used. Some attention was paid to the role it could play in creating an independent Ireland, something most dear to the heart of Irish-American organisations. 'We believe not only that we are training useful citizens for a free Ireland, but that we are kindling in our pupils something of the old spiritual and heroic enthusiasm of the Gael.'[354] Ultimately this would strike 'at the root of anglicisation'. Money was asked for 'to ensure the permanence of the ONE national education effort in Ireland'. 'The whole experiment of Irishising education in Ireland must stand or fall with St. Enda's.'[355]

Patrick's final weeks were spent lecturing in places with large Irish communities in and around New York. There was a large field day organised at Celtic Park in New York on Sunday 19 April. Despite an impressive programme and good attendance the day brought in less than £60 after expenses.[356] He also tried to raise money in other ways. Against better judgement he advertised for boys to attend St Enda's. Although he did not believe many would 'send boys 3,000 miles away from home to school', three American boys came to him that summer. He also tried to rent out the Hermitage as a summer residence to Americans but was not convinced it was luxurious enough. Overall he did raise substantial amounts of money, but not the £2000 ($10,000) he hoped for.[357] He came home in May to a rousing reception by St Enda's boys with about £800 of which £230 was raised in Philadelphia with the aid of McGarrity and £100 had been donated by a Mr Garvin, the son-in-law of a deceased cousin of his mother.[358] Although proceeds had thus been somewhat disappointing, he had seen a large potential and planned to return later to try to raise more money.[359]

The funds from the United States only provided temporary relief and did not substantially alter St Enda's financial position. Patrick spelled out the position to the tax office in reply to a tax assessment he received on his return from the States: 'I do not know on what grounds you assess me for income Tax on "Profits of trade, etc." amounting to £150. I have no income, and make no profits. I am the proprietor of St. Enda's College, but the College is losing money at the rate of about £200 a year, which I have to eke out by subscriptions from friends. I have no salary as Headmaster, but board at the College, and draw £1 a week for personal expenses. I have no other income of any sort.' He added 'the thing is grotesque. I am obviously a pauper.'[360] Although he had in the meantime been engaged as external examiner in the League's Connacht College for a fee of £10, he painted an even bleaker picture in an official appeal against this tax bill lodged in October, while simultaneously explaining what happened to the money he collected in the States: 'The College itself is run at a loss of about £500 a year, but I keep no books and am not in a position to furnish you any particulars. The fact that I had to go to America and collect funds last spring, and that £800 collected was swallowed up before the end of the year – £250 in reducing old liabilities and £450 in making up year's deficit is sufficient proof of this.' He ended his appeal somewhat dramatically: 'My total liabilities are £6,000 and I have no assets except a suit of clothes, a uniform, a rifle, and a sword.'[361]

Although Patrick probably exaggerated as indicated by the year's losses mounting from £200 to £500 between his letter in May and October, it is clear that St Enda's position had not improved substantially since the liquidator had been called two years earlier. In November 1914 he made a more reliable private statement to cover his finances in case of his death. It set his debts at approximately £6000, most of it loans from friends. He wrote optimistically: 'I hope and believe that, if I live, I shall be able to discharge all these liabilities.'[362] In the case of his death, however, the debts would remain unpaid and in such an eventuality he could only declare his regret for having involved so many generous friends.

The finances of the school did not improve after the outbreak of the First World War. Despite attempts to recruit new pupils, attendance figures declined from sixty in 1913, to forty in 1914–1915 and twenty-eight in 1915–1916.[363] This was largely due to Patrick's growing involvement in radical politics, and meant that annual income was reduced and the school incurred a growing deficit.[364] It was only kept open in September 1914 by the personal generosity of McGarrity who sent over some of his own money: 'We duly opened on September 7th.

I was able to keep things steady until your message came. We have fewer boys than last year: my political opinions are looked upon as too extreme and dangerous, and parents are nervous. The war, too makes everything dearer.'[365] The same happened in the spring and the summer of 1915 when a last minute donation by McGarrity of £300 enabled the school to function for another year after financial demands had been put upon the school for political reasons.[366] Despite the continuous problems, Patrick expressed renewed optimism each time money came in at the last minute to save him.[367]

During the war Patrick was unable to pay off any of his creditors. Following his visit McGarrity had promised a lot more money but a split in the Irish-American organisation supporting St Enda's had hampered fundraising.[368] As a result Patrick was not able to reduce the debt stemming from the arrangement of 1912 with more than the 25 per cent he had paid off before the war. In October 1915 he informed his creditors that he would not pay any more until the end of the war after which he would take up his lecture tour again, claiming he could raise $100 a week that way. He argued that the decision to continue after the crisis of 1912 had proven itself to be correct since everyone had received something.[369] He made an exception for the former headmistress of St Ita's who was owed more than £150 and apparently was in financial difficulties. In December 1915, he gave her £5 and promised to send more out of what he earned with 'literary or semi-literary work'.[370] Indeed on Easter Sunday 1916 during the confusion surrounding the start of the Easter Rising, Patrick managed to find time to send another £5 and wished her a very happy Easter.[371] In a statement on his financial affairs written shortly before his execution he stated that his 'one source of personal regret in embarking on this enterprise' was that 'its failure will involve loss, more or less considerable, to various persons'.[372]

The continuous attention required to financial affairs and Patrick's growing involvement in radical politics also affected the way the school was run. Pupils noticed how Patrick became gradually less involved.[373] Some of the best teachers had left and with fewer pupils the teaching of a range of subjects became more and more dependent on the few remaining staff. The vibrant intellectual environment of the first years created by the visits of dignitaries and lectures by leading intellectuals gradually became more stagnant. The quality of pupils after the first badge of talented sons from leading League intellectuals also affected the general atmosphere.[374] Michael Dowling remembers how his father took his sons out of the school because he felt Patrick neglected them and that the school deteriorated.[375] Indeed in the final years some of the boys left school without any degree of fluency in Irish.[376]

Its overall success in creating Irish speakers is hard to measure. The initial optimism expressed a few months after opening about turning boys from English-speaking backgrounds into Irish speakers within twelve months proved to have been too optimistic.[377] By 1913 it was clear that Irish was not that much spoken by the pupils. Writing from the United States Patrick tried to coax them into doing so by calling upon their honour and by referring to the unusual price for the one who best spoke Irish. 'I do hope finally that you are making efforts to speak Irish. Remember that that rifle is still unwon. I want to give it away this summer, but it can only be given on condition that some boy wins it by genuine effort to speak Irish.'[378] Most pupils were nevertheless successful in their exams and Patrick showed no signs of real concern.[379] The presence of Irish-speaking boys from the Gaeltacht was, however, generally not a successful element in the school. They were meant to help the others with their Irish while obtaining a broad education they otherwise would not get. Yeats recalls how MacDonagh noticed that they were often ashamed to speak Irish and did not fulfil their role: 'He watches the Irish-speaking boys at his school and when nobody is looking, or when they are alone with the Irish-speaking gardener, they are merry, clever and talkative. When they meet an English speaker or one who has learned Gaelic they are stupid. They are in a different world.'[380]

Part of the disquiet felt about the development of the school had less to do with slipping standards than with the increasing militarism Patrick displayed from 1913 onwards.[381] The turn to a more overtly militaristic character of the curriculum had already started in 1910 with the move to the Hermitage. Where the child warrior Cúchulainn was the ideal held up to the pupils in Cullenswood House, the national revolutionary Robert Emmet became the hero in the Hermitage.

I am not sure whether it is symptomatic of some development within me, or is merely a passing phase, or comes naturally from the associations that cling about these old stones and trees, that whereas Cullenswood House I spoke oftenest to our boys of Cúchulainn and his compeers of the Gaelic prime, I

have been speaking to them oftenest here of Robert Emmet and the heroes
of the last stand, Cúchulainn was our greatest inspiration at Cullenswood;
Robert Emmet has been our greatest inspiration here.[382]

There was indeed a strong connection between the grounds of the
Hermitage and Emmet, who was supposed to have walked the grounds
with his ill-fated love, Sarah Curran. The Currans had lived across the
road in The Priory but the Hermitage was considered safer to meet in.
The association was so powerful that people had named a path and an
old fort in the grounds after Emmet. Patrick's growing involvement in
politics also meant he paid less attention to the running of the school.
Already in May 1912 he called upon himself to concentrate solely
on the school and make a success of it. 'Take my advice; devote your
attention to Sgoil Éanna and to Sgoil Íde and disregard political affairs.
You have more than sufficient cares to occupy you.'[383] However, after
the establishment of the Irish Volunteers in October 1913 he neglected
the school more and more. 'Yes, we are having a struggle, but other
interests distract my attention from St. Enda's and then it does not
seem so bad.'[384]

The pupils also noticed Patrick's changing outlook. Desmond Ryan
felt that the Hermitage haunted the mind and personality of Patrick.[385]
Alf White recalls how Patrick bought books on military tactics and
'liked to show us Emmet's death mask and Lord Edward's sword
stick with which he had tried to defend himself'.[386] Patrick started
to prepare his pupils more directly for service to Ireland. Developing
patriotism to such an extent that pupils would be willing to dedicate
their lives to Ireland had already been an aspect of the original
prospectus of St Enda's in 1908 but now became more explicitly
strived for. The idea of service to one's country was an integral part
of the curriculum, but few direct references were made to fighting for
Ireland. Desmond Ryan only remembers one allusion to this during
the years in Cullenswood House when Patrick claimed that no nation
in history had won independence without a fight except Norway.[387] In
the stories Patrick wrote at this time this theme was, however, often
central. In particular, in *The King* written in 1912 the boy who is most
willing to serve becomes king and the sacrifice of his life ultimately
brings victory to the cause. Such an attitude he stresses should not be
mourned but celebrated. Already in *Eoineen of the Birds* (1905–1906)

doing your 'duty' was stimulated while sacrifice was celebrated in *Brigid of the Songs* written shortly before 1916.

Yet in 1913 Patrick was still surprised by the reaction of his pupils to a dream he had in which one of his boys stood proud and joyous in front of a silent unsympathetic crowd while it was clear he was going to die for some august cause:

> when I said that I could not wish for any of them a happier destiny than to die thus in the defence of some true thing, they did not seem in any way surprised, for it fitted in with all we had been teaching them at St. Enda's. I do not mean that we have ever carried on anything like a political or revolutionary propaganda among the boys, but simply that we have always allowed them to feel that no one can finely live who hoards life too jealously; that one must be generous in service, and withal joyous, accounting even supreme sacrifices slight.[388]

His worship of military discipline became stronger, beginning with the introduction in 1913 of a rifle as a prize. The play they performed in 1915 was also much more militaristic than their previous artistic endeavours. One of his pupils recalled his dedication as 'fanatical to the point of absurdity'.[389]

Not all pupils responded equally well to the attention to heroes and service to Ireland. One of them called Cúchulainn a bowsie, while another is reported to have ended up as a Black and Tan.[390] Most, however, were more responsive. Writing to Eugene Cronin's father in America, Patrick proudly reported: 'I am glad to find him stoutly taking the extreme Irish side in every discussion with the companions about the war, the Volunteers, etc.'[391] Con Colbert, the instructor of the Fianna branch in St Enda's, even brought some of its members, Desmond Ryan, Eamonn Bulfin, Frank Burke and Joseph Sweeney, into the IRB without Patrick's knowledge and many fought in the 1916 Rising.[392] Father Augustine, the local priest, was distressed over the connection with the IRB in particular because 'They were actually told that they must not tell the priest.'[393] This instruction probably came from Colbert.

In the last speech to his pupils before going out to fight in 1916 on St Enda's Day, one of those present remembers how he declared the school 'had gone on for 8 years he hoped it would continue for 80 but so far as he was concerned its work was done. He had founded Sg E [St Enda's] to make Irish boys efficient soldiers in the battles spiritual & temporal of their country. In the Irish Volunteers that day were many such soldiers. It had taken the blood of the son of God to redeem the world. It would take the blood of the sons of Ireland to redeem Ireland.'[394] Patrick's priority had obviously moved on from saving the nation through education to a military assault on the British presence.

10. St Enda's Boys in front of Cullenswood House

11. Open day at St Enda's at the Hermitage

12. Boys gardening at the Hermitage

13. St Enda's hurling team

14. Enacting *Fionn* at St Enda's

15. St Enda's boys at drill class in Cullenswood House

4 Politician

Some of us are in danger of yielding to the vulgar notion prevalent in pre-Gaelic League days that the whole duty of an Irishman is to be 'agin the Govirmint'.[1]

Early nationalism

In his short autobiographical fragment written in 1915 Patrick traces the source of his militant nationalism back to his grandaunt Margaret who told him of his ancestors' involvement in radical movements.[2] Ruth Dudley-Edwards concluded that Aunt Margaret 'stirred his romantic soul with patriotic ballads of death and exile, tales of mythological Irish heroes, and hagiographical accounts of such doomed revolutionary leaders as Wolfe Tone and Robert Emmet'.[3] Patrick also claimed retrospectively to have been fully nationalistic when he entered school: 'if any boy should have carried into the school a faith in Ireland and a love for Ireland I was that boy'.[4] However, many Irish children at the end of the nineteenth century would have had an older relative who still had some Irish and most nationalist families claimed to have ancestors with a history of radical politics. The Fenians of the 1860s in particular had been a widespread organisation and in 1901 language enthusiasts in Carrickmacross, Co. Monaghan, were still able to collect 200 Irish proverbs even though nobody actively spoke Irish there.[5] The census records also show that a growing number of young men and women were taught Irish by this time. Patrick's background therefore did not in any way predestine him to an active career in the language movement or to becoming a revolutionary republican. The songs and stories about Irish rebels which Patrick's grandaunt familiarised him with probably only obtained significance because of Patrick's later career not because of their actual causal effect.

By the end of the nineteenth century Patrick's maternal family were followers of Parnell. His father's radical English background also sheds some doubt on the idea of a linear development from early childhood to the GPO in 1916. James Pearse had become a supporter of the self-reliance idea of Parnell. The pamphlet he wrote in support of home rule in 1885 did seem to create a heightened sense of political awareness in the young Patrick. His mother recalled how as a seven-year-old Patrick mounted a chair waving a green flag and chanting loudly at the top of his voice: 'Home Rule and Liberty, that is our demand. Nothing else will satisfy the people of our land.'[6] Innocently the young Patrick even believed 'that Parnell would be King of Ireland'.[7] This did, however, not entail a rejection of the ties with Britain. The family was known for singing *God Save the Queen* after social events and most of the family friends were from England. The plays Patrick wrote for his siblings from around the age of ten were filled with a willingness to fight for a good cause but did not contain Irish rebellious elements. One of the first was based on *Uncle Tom's Cabin* in which a slave calls to fight for liberty, while in a story about the crusaders all knights were called to arms to fight to the death. These were all imaginary activities as he did not like playing soldiers like other boys, but preferred board games like halma and draughts and the very English 'Dick Turpin's ride from London to York'.[8]

It is clear that contrary to his own description the young Patrick was far from an Irish radical. When Patrick first entered the Christian Brothers School as an eleven-year-old in 1891 his contemporaries saw no signs of any radical politics. According to one of his classmates 'He was not the type to cut down Union Jacks. There were boys in the school who had strong views on politics no doubt reproduced from what they had heard at home, but he was not among them.'[9] Partly due to Patrick's English accent his school friends even saw Patrick as English. 'I regarded P[earce] as an odd English rather than Irishman.'[10] Another fellow pupil went further: 'In early youth the two Pearses were very pro British.'[11] Patrick never really rejected his English ancestry. Even at the time he had become intimately associated with radical nationalism Patrick did not object when he was introduced to a unionist as 'a man half English' and was always proud of his father's background.[12]

Later in life Patrick acknowledged his lack of overt nationalism as a child but laid the responsibility for this at the feet of the school itself: 'The system of education that I was subjected to grappled me insensibly and by degrees. The books that were put into my hands ignored Ireland. They did not attack Ireland; they simply ignored Ireland. ... I began to write composition about OUR empire, and OUR fleet, and OUR army and OUR colonies. I remember reaching the limit in one composition when I said that our empire would weather this storm as she had weathered many storms before.' In light of his own description of the reaction of some of the Brothers these ideas did not emanate from them but were probably fostered at home and in the private primary school he attended: 'My teacher, a Christian Brother, took my composition and wrote on it "No marks". He said to me "Do try to be Irish." The teacher saved me in spite of the system. After that I did try to be Irish.'[13] However, Patrick's interpretation of being Irish at this stage still did not concur with mainstream nationalism. Another classmate remembers how 'Bro Craven it was who told him to write of an Irish hero and this set him off. The subject "Was Napoleon or Wellington the greater general?" P. spoke for Wellington and praised him qua Irishman.'[14] Although Wellington had an Irish background, he can hardly be seen as a role model for nationalist Ireland.

In his younger years Patrick was thus made aware and may even have identified with the heroics of nationalist figures, but at the same time he was raised in a family which celebrated the connection with Britain. As a young teenager he clearly was seen and acted as someone wholeheartedly endorsing the idea of home rule within the empire. At the height of the division on the second Home Rule Bill in 1893 Patrick was seen 'trudging and pushing with pride through the crowds in Dublin streets, a penny in his hand, trying in vain to buy an evening paper' in the hope of finding that Parnell had finally been successful.[15]

The most important long-term influence on Patrick's political thinking towards a more openly nationalist interpretation came from his involvement with the Irish language. There is no sign that his maternal family's teachings made any significant impact in this regard. In one of the political debates of his New Ireland Literary Society Patrick appeared to have taken on board Brother Craven's comments on his paper when he argued 'They talk about our Navy & our Army. It's the British Navy & the British Army.'[16] The society was nevertheless clearly positioned in the context of the development of public debating within the United Kingdom. In explaining the reason for setting up the society in its founding document Patrick and

Eamonn O'Neill positioned Dublin on a par with other cities in the United Kingdom. 'It is an inexplicable fact that Dublin, which must necessarily contain many young men of ability and culture, should possess fewer literary and debating societies than any city of equal importance in Great Britain.'[17] This comparison between Dublin and cities in Great Britain indicates that they did not perceive a direct opposition between Ireland and England but saw Ireland as an integral part of the United Kingdom.

One of the incentives for Patrick to set up the society may well have been his desire to practise public speaking. It may be tempting to see this as a conscious attempt to become a leading propagandist of the nationalist cause, but considering his ideas and ambitions at that time it is more likely he was thinking of his career prospects as a lawyer. Patrick was politicised through his involvement in the Gaelic League. It brought him in contact with many active and advanced nationalists and the simple *raison d'être* of the League begged the question why the Irish language should be kept alive. For Patrick it was not just because it was ancient, venerable, rich, beautiful or because it enshrined a valuable and unique literature, but simply because it was the language of the Irish, an essential part of their nationality.[18] Already in his inaugural address to the 1897–1898 session of the New Ireland Literary Society Patrick made this clear. 'May our language, and our literature, and our folk-lore live; and if they live, then, too, will our race live.' The subject of a lecture he was invited to give on 15 February 1900, 'The battle of two civilisations', also makes clear that he did accept a fundamental distinction between Britain and Ireland.[19] In a similarly entitled lecture he gave a year later to the Catholic Commercial Club he identified Ireland with the spirit, mind, intellect, and with good manners and piety, against the English civilisation of the body, worldly force, the strength and power of money, and the comfort of life.[20] In the following years he emphasised this dichotomy by referring to Britain as 'abroad' and describing Irish people moving there as 'emigrating'.[21]

This implicit acceptance of the idea of the existence of a separate Irish and English or British nation would of course ultimately legitimise a political separation, but he already took it a step further. He described the emancipation of the Gaelic race as the cause most worthy of success, and described Ireland as a nation which had suffered, bled and endured agony more than any nation, and had fought for eight centuries against oppression.[22] Nevertheless, he never called for political action or violent rebellion at this stage. He felt it was a forlorn hope to believe Ireland would ever achieve independence because the Irish were neither a military nor a commercial or manufacturing race, and the divisions in the home rule party meant they were now 'further off than ever from the goal towards which we have struggled'.[23] Even in 1915 when he was already heavily involved in revolutionary activities he described the use of force as something particularly English in his story *The Keening Woman*. The hopelessness of obtaining full independence through force also underlay the demand for home rule of the Irish Party for most of its members.

In the absence of possible political progress he believed the Irish should concentrate on their special role in the intellectual advancement of mankind. To him the restoration of the language was the essence of being Irish, political nationalism should and could only come second. The emphasis on political nationalism was only a distraction of the real struggle, and he did not involve himself directly in any of the political commotion at that time surrounding the Boer War or the visit of Queen Victoria to Ireland in 1900.[24] In one of his first political statements in 1899 he makes clear he had no time for those who did not understand this.

> Apparently the only thing necessary to make a man or an institution Irish is a little dab of green displayed now and again to relieve the monotony, a little eloquent twaddle about the '*children of the Gael*' or a little meaningless vapouring about some unknown quantity termed 'Celtic Glamour'. Take away the dab of green, strip off the leafy luxury of words and what have you? The man or the institution is as English as Lord Salisbury.[25] Newspapers, politicians, literary societies are all but forms of one gigantic heresy, that like a poison has eaten its way into the vitals of Irish nationality, that has paralysed the nation's energy and intellect. That heresy is the idea that there can be an Ireland, that there can be an Irish literature, an Irish social life whilst the language of Ireland is English.[26]

Although he would never again put it this bluntly, fundamentally he adhered to this statement. In 1904, for instance, he stated that 'Political autonomy can be lost and recovered' and was 'not an essential of nationality'.[27] A year later in reply to Thomas Kettle, who had argued the case for political independence, he elaborated on this:

'In truth, the language movement is not merely more important than the political movement, but it is on a different and altogether higher plane. … Political autonomy … may … be necessary to the continued existence of the Nation – in the case of Ireland it probably is – but it is not, in itself, an essential of nationality.' He clearly believed that a truly independent Ireland began with the restoration of the language; political independence would then follow automatically. 'All phases of a nation's life will most assuredly adjust themselves on national lines as best suited to the national character once that national character is safeguarded by its strongest bulwark [the language].'[28]

In giving primacy to the language over independence he based himself on how he believed Hungarian and Flemish emancipation had come about. Commenting in 1904 on Arthur Griffith's *The Resurrection of Hungary* he asserted: 'The moral of the whole story is that the Hungarian language revival of 1825 laid the foundation of the great, strong and progressive Hungarian nation of 1904. And so it shall fall out in Ireland.'[29] He took the same lesson from the Belgian example he studied in 1905, where he identified a cultural reawakening of Flemish intellectual life after the revolution of 1830. He believed the Flemish culturalist Hendrik Conscience 'raised a decayed and despised speech to the dignity of a literary language' and inspired a movement of national revival. Belgians had managed to make Flemish from a language unused in government to one which was a compulsory requirement for every public and municipal office. All public documentation in Belgium had been made bilingual, legal cases in High Court were transacted in either language, and in larger urban parishes both French- and Flemish-speaking priests were appointed.[30]

This was not a simplistic belief that the language was the nation. To Patrick the nation was made up of various things but the language was the most important element of it, 'it is a preservative not merely of the literature and the folklore of the nation, but of the nation's habits of thought, the nation's popular beliefs, the nation's manifold bents, prepossessions, idiosyncrasies of various sorts. It is a preservative also of nationalism in art, in industry, in pastimes, in social and civic customs.'[31] He nevertheless believed that political independence was sure to come once the nation was saved, 'that it [a National University] will ultimately be realised is as certain as that the Gael will yet rule in this land'.[32] The study of the education system in countries such as Denmark, Flanders, Germany and the United States had also made him a strong advocate of the need to stimulate the teaching of patriotism to children as another step to independence of the mind.[33] By 1909 he added that 'the battle of the two civilisations should be explained in every school until the pupils all become conscious workers in Ireland's cause'.[34]

He thus never rejected political nationalism but simply believed it was subordinate to cultural regeneration. It is therefore also too simplistic to accept his other later claim to have been a harmless cultural nationalist in his youth.[35] The lack of importance he assigned to political activity meant he refused to take sides in the debate, which was heating up early in the twentieth century, between constitutional and revolutionary nationalists. He fell in with League policy which supported Irish Party members if they spoke out in favour of the language. 'The attitude of the Irish Party was all that could be desired. Sixteen of its members spoke in favour of bilingual education and the speeches generally were able and eloquent and showed a good grasp of the subject.'[36] However, if the opposite was true the League also spoke out. As was the case when the Irish Party canvassed in English in Irish-speaking districts: 'We say deliberately that in thus boycotting Irish, the Parliamentary Party is nothing less than a huge Anglicising agency, that it tramples and despises Irish, in fact, and that it is in a large measure responsible for the contempt with which Irish is regarded by thousands of those whom it addresses.'[37] In a subsequent editorial in the League paper it was emphasised that it would 'not lower its flag nor be intimidated into silence until every body, party and organisation in Ireland claiming to be national and patriotic adopts to the full, not only in programmes and sympathies, but in actual and consistent practice, the principle and the policy of an Irish Ireland'.[38]

Attempts to politicise the league by constitutional and advanced nationalists were also rejected by Patrick. 'At such a moment it is essential, even at the risk of hurting people, that the Gaelic League should make it absolutely clear that it, as a corporate body, is to be captured by neither one political party nor the other.' He added that individual members were free to sympathise with whom they liked as much as they liked, but made it clear that he and most of the League members were sympathetic to Arthur Griffiths policy of abstention, which he believed would soon overtake the parliamentarianism of the Irish Party. 'The leaders of the Parliamentary Party see clearly that the majority of Leaguers are sympathetic towards the Hungarian Policy. They fear, and justly – that in a few years Parliamentarianism as a policy may have to fight for its existence. Hence their anxiety to capture the young men of the metropolis for their policy.[39] Although clearly sympathising with it, Patrick did not at this stage seriously contemplate a non-parliamentary form of politics.

Despite this neutral position in relation to politics, he did associate with political radicals. In 1902 he wrote an article for Griffith's paper *The United Irishman: A weekly journal established to promote the principles of Wolfe Tone and Thomas Davis.*[40] He also attended the founding meeting of Sinn Féin in 1905 in a private capacity but did not join.[41] Although thus showing his nationalism had become of a separatist nature, the focus on the language was so strong that at a meeting of the Celtic Literary Society Patrick objected when one of the participants began to sing *Who Fears to Speak* and asked him whether he had not an Irish song. The singer walked out in disgust and it was subsequently written that Patrick did not want a national song, although it was the language it was sung in he objected to.[42] Incidents like this explain why few people in the first decade of the twentieth century saw Patrick as an advanced nationalist and some even doubted whether he could be described as national.[43]

This perception was further strengthened by his active engagement with the government. His position first as editor of the League newspaper and later as headmaster of St Enda's school forced him to seek reform, redress and support in relation to educational policy from them. As a consequence of his ideas on how national regeneration could be achieved, Patrick had also been one of the very few nationalists who supported the Irish Council Bill of 1907. Those focusing on political power felt that the limited degree of autonomy this measure gave had to be rejected. To Patrick's disappointment even Sinn Féin joined in the chorus of disapproval: 'The very Ishmaelites of Irish politics have come in from the wilderness and are howling in concert with the pack.' The fact that the Bill would give Ireland control over education was Patrick's rationale for supporting it. The educational clauses in the Bill would give what the Gaelic League wanted 'an education authority representative of the people of Ireland, answerable to Irish public opinion, and free from the domination of the British Treasury. Whosoever has reason to be disappointed with the Bill, the Gaelic League has none.'[44]

Patrick had long deplored the British influence in education, which forced the League to involve itself in British politics. 'The shadow of the Palace of Westminster falls on Connacht hillsides and darkens the sunlight in Munster valleys. ... Morally they were no more entitled to dictate what should be taught to children in Connemara than they were to dictate what should be taught to children in Yokohama.'[45] After the election of 1905 he had expressed his hope that the new Liberal Government, which he believed was favourably disposed to the use of the Irish language, would transfer power over education to the Irish regardless of its ability to grant Ireland home rule.[46] Not only would an Irish body understand Irish problems better it would also solve its problems with greater ease. 'The English Government is unable to settle our grievances for us, for it is unable to understand either us or them. Let us first get control of the educational system: then let us set about solving our problems ourselves. We shall find their solution wonderfully easy.'[47]

When the Irish Council Bill was brought before the House Patrick saw it as a revolution. If it will 'reach the Statute Book, we shall be on the eve of the greatest and most beneficent revolution in the modern history of Ireland. *The schools will be ours.* The shadows of Death and the Nightmare Death-in-Life will have passed away from the Irish landscape.'[48] When the Bill failed to pass he believed a chance of a lifetime had passed for perhaps twenty years.

Miracles, we suppose, are always possible. The British Liberals may withdraw their Bill and introduce a Home Rule Bill. They may go to the country and the country may give them that 'mandate' for Home Rule which it refused at the last General Election. The House of Lords may be converted, reformed, bullied, or abolished. The Sinn Fein party in Ireland may rouse the nation against the Parliamentarians; the latter may withdraw from Westminster; the General Council of County Councils may develop into an Irish Parliament. All things, we say, are possible. But we are dealing now with probabilities.[49]

Waiting another twenty years before they were again in the same position meant, 'of course, a diminished population and fuller work-houses and lunatic asylums'.

As was often the case Patrick had shown not to be afraid to go against mainstream thinking. As one of his friends said, he appeared little interested in actual politics at this time but simply reasoned from the interest of the League and the language.[50] He was, however, aware that his 'attitude has been a scandal and a stumbling-block to many valued friends'. There had been resolutions passed by League branches disassociating themselves from Patrick's statements on the Bill and many long letters reached *An Claidheamh Soluis* opposing his position. Although he publicly acknowledged them, he refused to publish these as the Bill was already dead and he felt the writers used the issue as an 'excuse for their own inveterate distrust or hate'. He further stressed that the opinion expressed in the paper had been his own and not necessarily that of the Coiste Gnotha: 'we are the Editor of this paper, we are not in the habit of consulting with anyone as to what should appear and what should not appear in it'.[51] Many in the League had abhorred Patrick's support of the Bill and the impression which was created was that he spoke for them. There were several calls for him to be removed as the paper would suffer due to his controversial stance.[52] In particular the ever critical Keating Branch of the League around Fr Dinneen called for Patrick's resignation and was supported by Sinn Feiners who were trying to take over the League and politicise it.[53] Circulation of *An Claidheamh Soluis* did indeed go down from a high of 158,756 in 1906 to 125,840 in 1907, before rising again to 130,936 in 1908.

In the following year Patrick was a bit more careful in expressing his opinion regarding the new University Bill which was being framed. Although he was satisfied with the policies of the new Liberal Government regarding Irish education, asking people to refrain from 'would-be-heroic resolutions against it', he included an implicit attack on British control of Irish policy. 'Once more the fates and fortunes of unborn generations of Irish people are being discussed and settled by permanent secretaries and their clerks in Whitehall. Non-political as we are in these columns, we are not railing at or bewailing these facts: we are merely stating them.'[54] The opportunities the new government policy gave also lay at the heart of his decision to set up St Enda's in 1908. It showed that in his mind the process of saving the Irish nation was still a long-term goal, which was now possible to achieve.

There had thus been no fundamental shift in Patrick's stance concerning the primacy of cultural regeneration over political independence in the first decade of the century. In July 1909 he again stated that 'Whatever be the political fate of our country, there can only be stagnation in national affairs until there be a more general recognition of the essentials of nationality.' He made clear that to him these essentials were still the Irish language and history.[55] The teaching of these could also 'be a link of unity between the followers' of nationalism and unionism. After all regardless of the political situation it was the duty of every Irishman protestant or catholic to work for the language.

> National progress we cannot make while we remain divided within ourselves, and while the Catholic and Nationalist should be willing to allow the Protestant and Unionist full freedom for political and religious opinions, the Protestant should recognise that outside of religion and politics there are duties to Ireland, the observance of which is as binding on the Unionist as on the Nationalist. Loyalty to the language is one of these. Neglect of it implies that Protestants mean to isolate themselves from their fellow countrymen and to remain a British garrison.[56]

He of course realised that most Protestants did not accept the need and value of a national language, but he believed that they were 'foolish' in thinking that their personal liberty was threatened by home rule and had not the least doubt that their conversion would come, if necessarily gradually.[57]

Political action

After his school opened Patrick retreated from public life, but following the move of St Enda's to the Hermitage in 1910 Patrick's thinking developed a more radical edge. The historical connections of the new building to Robert Emmet in particular seem to have motivated him in this.[58] Due to the lack of original material from Emmet's hand he began to read Wolfe Tone's *Autobiography* and John Mitchel's *Jail Journal*, which at a later stage he often carried around with him.[59] This fascination also brought him in contact with more radical circles as he started to attend meetings of organisations like the Wolfe Tone Club where lectures were presented on Emmet or Tone and where patriotism was celebrated. Although the radical members of these clubs were critical of Patrick's moderate stance, their willingness to advocate strong action for the cause of Ireland seems to have been particularly influential.[60]

In *An Macaomh* of Christmas 1910 the effects of this already became evident. He now openly rejected the belief he had formulated in 1898 that force could not play a role in freeing Ireland. 'No dream is more foolish than the dream of some sentimentalists that the reign of force is past, or passing; that the world's ancient law of unending strife has been repealed.' He was looking for the clear-cut battles of the ancient world, and believed these were again imminent in Ireland. 'There will be battles, silent and terrible, or loud and catastrophic, while the earth and heavens last; and woe to him who flinches when his enemy compasses him about, for to him alone damnation is due.' Every day he wrote he became more certain that to be prepared for such eventualities was the work of the moment in Ireland and therefore it was 'of the uttermost importance that we should train every child to be an efficient soldier, efficient to fight, when need is, his own, his people's, and the world's battles, spiritual and temporal'. In a non-specific sense he already wondered to what extent his pupils would be willing to follow him in one of the possible battles of the future. 'Sometimes I wonder whether, if ever I need them for any great service, they will rally, as many of them have promised to do, from wherever they may be, holding faith to the inspiration and the tradition I have tried to give them.'[61] At a later stage when Patrick had become a major figure in the Volunteers movement, four of his students indeed came out with guns to protect him when they heard he was to be arrested on his way home.[62]

Although Patrick's thinking developed towards a more radical stance this did not have any practical translation yet, apart from attending the odd meeting of the radical Freedom or Wolfe Tone Clubs. It has been asserted that another phrase in his 1910 *An Macaomh* article, 'life springs from death', which he also used in his O'Donovan Rossa oration, indicates that Patrick was already thinking of the need to sacrifice himself to reawaken the Irish nation. However, this phrase is part of a discourse on the wildlife on the estate around the Hermitage. After discussing frolicking rabbits being caught and eaten, he muses on death in nature. 'It is murder and death that make possible the terrible thing we call physical life. Life springs from death, life lives on death. Why do we loath worms and vultures? We all batten on dead things, even as they do.'[63] Although an evocative phrase in light of his later writings on the need for a bloody sacrifice, he does not in any way connect this to a national struggle or the future of his pupils in 1910.

The two poems he wrote in the period between 1910 and 1912 provide a somewhat despondent but divided picture. 'Nior Cruinnigheadh Liom-sa Or' (I Have Not Garnered Gold) written at the same time as the above-mentioned edition of *An Macaomh* reflect the financial strain he was under at that time. It expresses the willingness to forego riches and laments the loss of fame and love but celebrates the ability of a teacher to impress himself 'in the heart of a child'. In 'Fornocht do Chonnach' (Naked I Saw Thee) he takes this willingness to sacrifice a step further by describing someone who has openly forsaken beauty, music, love and lust to fulfil the task he has set.[64]

All this indicates that looking back Patrick considers his life a form of sacrifice for a higher purpose and is already starting to toy with the idea that a struggle for freedom will be needed in the future. The emphasis on this theme also shows Patrick is struggling himself with the realisation that he has foregone a career for his dream. In *The Fool* and *The Master*, two plays he wrote during 1915, the same theme is developed. In the former the unlikely possibility of success is emphasised while in the latter a schoolteacher is cured from his doubts by a child. As we saw in the previous chapter he is still unclear in 1912 about the form a future struggle should take, and certainly about his own role in it.[65]

The first sign of a more active role for Patrick in politics was initiated by his attempt to raise funds for St Enda's. One of those Patrick had approached to aid him in 1910 was Patrick McCartan a language enthusiast, and also an active member of Sinn Féin and the IRB (Irish Republican Brotherhood). McCartan got the old Fenian activist Tom Clarke, who had recently returned to Ireland, involved. Patrick was subsequently invited by them to deliver the oration at an Emmet Commemoration Concert. His fascination with Emmet had become known and he was by now a fairly experienced speaker. The lecture delivered in March 1911 was very well received: 'The oration like all of Pearse's set orations electrified the large audience. McCartan had been particularly impressed by Patrick's assertion that 'Dublin would have to do some great act to atone for the shame of not producing a man to dash his head against a stone wall in an effort to rescue Robert Emmet.'[66] One of the others present recalls how Patrick took the recital of the poem on Emmet by John B. O'Reilly extremely seriously, standing with his arms folded and later made everyone 'stand up and pledge ourselves to be true to the principles of Emmett'.[67]

The lecture had no direct consequences for Patrick, although around Christmas 1911 he was invited by the labour leader Cathal O'Shannon to deliver another Emmet Memorial Lecture in Belfast.[68] It was the prospect of the introduction of a Home Rule Bill at the end of 1911 which seems to have spurred him into political activity. Contrary to the primacy he had always given to the language question over all other issues he now implored the language movement to get involved in politics. 'It appears to me to be a severe loss to Ireland that those who are active in the language movement are not interested in political matters.'[69]

Having taken the decision that political action was necessary he went for it wholeheartedly. Early in 1912 he initiated the establishment of an Irish-speaking political society, Cumann na Saoirse (The Freedom Association), and an associated newspaper *An Barr Buadh* (The Trumpet of Victory). This referred to the trumpet of the legendary hero Fionn which he blew to rouse the Fianna for battle. Hobson recalled later that Patrick had told him that setting up *An Barr Buadh* was an idea which came up when walking around the grounds of St Enda's and was immediately acted upon without contemplating the financial implications.[70] When the first issue came out he castigated Desmond Ryan for not preventing him from starting the paper. However, the prospect of again having an outlet for his opinions in *An Barr Buadh* also enthused him. Ryan also recalls how Patrick was looking forward to the furious reactions of Gaelic Leaguers and to his own caustic letters to political celebrities.[71]

The advent of home rule had apparently reawakened Patrick's hope that control over Irish education could be obtained through the political system. To his pupils he emphasised the possibility of placing local administration in Irish hands.[72] However, he felt that the interests of Irish speakers were not adequately represented in the debates and this made him invite a number of his friends to form Cumann na Saoirse. 'In which Irish-speakers can analyse and express their political sentiments and initiate political action.'[73] He hoped this could unite all those in favour of a progressive nationalist movement, who were now divided between Sinn Féin which talked too much, the Irish Party which cared too little for Ireland, and Labour which was too internationalist.

Some mistrusted the motives behind all this sudden activity in the wake of the possible introduction of home rule. There was talk that Patrick wanted to become Minister of Education in a home rule government.[74] Although Desmond Ryan acknowledges that Patrick imagined himself Minister of Education, he was insulted when he was accused of using *An Barr Buadh* to promote himself.[75] Apparently Patrick had indicated he was willing to contemplate standing as a candidate for parliament and his name had been mentioned as a possible minister along with that of Starkie and Dillon.[76] The idea to stand for parliament may well have been a reaction to a note from the young radical Belfast Irish Party MP Joseph Devlin following a speech by Patrick in support of home rule in which he expressed the hope Patrick would continue to give 'his eloquent aid in future'.[77]

Contrary to his slightly defeatist approach at the time of the Irish Council Bill Patrick made clear in his invitation to join the new society that he believed the Home Rule Bill was a matter of make or break. 'If a Home Rule stature is implemented Irish-speaking members will be needed in the Irish Parliament and if Home Rule is not introduced a sustained agitation will be needed, in which we must ensure that the battle cry is not sounded in the foreign tongue.'[78] In a debate with Hyde in June 1911 he had told his pupils that if home rule would come in the next few years they would have a part to play in directing Irish affairs, but if it did not come they would have to use force to attain independence.[79] He was willing to give home rule a chance and was, unlike other advanced nationalists, willing to appear in public to support it. In this Patrick was not unique, his successor as editor of *An Claidheamh Soluis*, Sean MacGiollamath, also extolled the economic benefits of home rule in the paper.

An Irish Government would find means of effecting great economic improvements. Re-afforestation, arterial drainage, the nationalisation of Irish coal mines and their development, the building of harbours and the development of Irish fisheries would give employment on a scale that would check emigration in the first year of home government. Radical improvements in national education and in industrial training would soon place Ireland abreast of small resurgent European nations. For these reasons we believe that the Home Rule proposals now before the English Parliament will meet with no opposition from the Gaelic League.[80]

This was based on the widespread idea at that time, which Patrick adhered to, that Ireland was held back economically by England and that if it had full control over its destiny it would thrive and sustain a population of twenty million.[81]

The main opportunity for Patrick to express his support for the Bill was at a huge mass meeting organised by Joseph Devlin in O'Connell Street on 31 March 1912. There were several platforms at the rally to accommodate speakers from various interest groups. The League was represented by Eoin MacNeill and Patrick.[82] Devlin was the main attraction on platform three, where Patrick also spoke. Indicating his minor importance in national politics Patrick was not even listed in the *Freeman's Journal* as being among the eighteen principal speakers on that particular platform. He gave a short speech in Irish in which he gave his conditional support for the Bill which he believed would be for the good of Ireland. Contrary to other speakers, however, Patrick warned of the consequences of a failure to implement it:

> I think a good measure can be gained if we have enough courage. But if we are tricked again, there is a band in Ireland, and I am one of them, who will advise the Irish people never again to consult with the Gall, but to answer them with violence and the edge of the sword. Let the English understand that if we are again betrayed there shall be red war throughout Ireland.[83]

The *Freeman's Journal* was hesitant to print his speech and decided to do so in Irish which meant most readers would be unable to understand it fully. Their simple introduction to the speech was certainly somewhat deceptive, stating that Patrick 'supported the resolution in a vigorous speech in Irish'.[84]

Despite his support, Patrick saw home rule only as a first step. In *An Barr Buadh* he compared it to a prisoner being released from one of his two manacles. In answer to those who had opposed the Bill because it did not give enough freedom, he emphasised that releasing a prisoner from one manacle would 'make it easier for him to escape'. It was clear to him that this was what the Home Rule Bill was doing.[85] Unlike Devlin Patrick had made clear he had no intention to become a loyal subject of the English Crown once the act was passed. 'Some of your words, I found distasteful. Will you be loyal to the British crown when Dublin has a Home Rule parliament? I do not think that you will.'[86] The threat of force was not just platform rhetoric as Patrick took a similar line at the first private meeting of Cumann na Saoirse two days later. According to one of those present Patrick emphasised the need to arm the Irish and set up a military organisation. Although those present were in principle in favour they were uneasy with Patrick's desire to make this more than just a theoretical notion.[87]

In the preceding years Patrick had apparently become convinced that at least the threat of force was a necessary element in asserting a nation's political rights. He defined the objective of *An Barr Buadh* as preaching 'the elementary political truth that the liberty of a people can only be guaranteed by its readiness and ability to vindicate it in arms'.[88] Such ideas were shared by advanced nationalists in and outside the IRB and even by suffragettes. The unattached radical The O'Rahilly elaborated on it in 1912 in *Irish Freedom*, and already in 1910 the idea that arms were 'the free man's first essential' and that freedom should and could only be won by force of arms was widely aired in this paper. In September 1911 it had chastised the present generation for being in danger of becoming the first since Cromwell to pass away 'without an armed denial of England's right to rule it'.[89] In the March issue of *An Barr Buadh* Patrick published a poem *Mionn* ('Oath') which called upon the memory of the sacrifices of the old patriots and ended with the lines:

> We swear the oaths our ancestors swore,
> That we will free our race from bondage,
> Or that we will fall fighting hand to hand.
> Amen

Although initially this was mainly a theoretical notion it developed a more practical expression in the period hereafter. During a visit to Dungloe, Co. Donegal, in February 1914 to raise a local Volunteers unit Patrick used the same arguments. Influenced by Wolfe Tone and the existing Fenian conception he asserted that true citizenship implied the enjoyment of certain rights and the acceptance of certain duties.[90] Rights could only be enjoyed if they accepted and discharged the duties, the first of which was to be armed in defence of the country. After referring to the successes of the Volunteers movement in the 1780s he argued that their mistake had been to hand in their arms. If they had not done so the union with England, the famine and emigration would not have happened. 'The lesson that history taught them was that it was only by strong men with courage and determination with guns in their hands that freedom could be won, and when won, guarded.'[91] By 1912 Patrick thus had come to share many of the ideas with revolutionaries but was not yet involved in any underground activity, mainly due to his qualified support for home rule which had isolated him politically.[92]

Patrick was still unsure to what extent his ideas were accepted. He felt that at the mass rally Joe Devlin had been the 'idol of the crowds' and that T.P. O'Connor, who had argued that the Irish did not wish to separate from England and would not ever do so as long as the English wanted to buy their pigs, may well 'understand the mind of the Irish people better than I do'. If they did he did not rate the people highly as he ridiculed O'Connor's argument by pointing out that it would mean that if the English continued to buy French wine they should want their countries to unite.[93] He nevertheless gave some credence to the economic argument as he expressed his fear that too many people in Ireland including the Catholic Church were tied to England by money. In *An Barr Buadh* he addressed himself to the few who had not been bought. This of course included himself who had forsaken a career as a lawyer for an uncertain existence. The golden chain that tied most people to England could only be broken by the iron of force.[94]

The picture of Patrick as a somewhat lonely figure in the political landscape is confirmed by the description of him in an advertisement for his lecture on 'Education under Home Rule' in the Dublin Mansion House on 11 December 1912: 'One does not always agree with Mr. Pearse who is occasionally metaphysical and occasionally irritating but one always carries away from his addresses new points of view, new funds of inspiration, a new glow of enthusiasm.' His contribution to the discussion on the spirit and object of education was welcomed, particularly as 'Mr Pearse's contribution to the various issues of "An Macaomh" show a boldness and a generosity of outlook which we look for in vain in the contributions of others to the ever present education discussion.'[95]

Patrick did not let them down. In his lecture he dealt in a humorous and ironic fashion with the question whether Protestants would be forced to learn Irish under home rule: 'the prospect of the children of Sandy Row being taught to curse the Pope in Irish, pronounced with a Belfast accent is rich and soul-satisfying. These things we may, or may not, see when Home Rule comes.' He continued to stress the advantages of having control over education, comparing the existing system to a slave education which bred a slave mentality. 'Some of us even think our chains ornamental, and are a little doubtful as to whether we shall be quite as comfortable and quite as respectable when a few of the links are knocked off by the passing of the Home Rule Bill. It remains the crowning achievement of the National and of the Intermediate systems that they have wrought such a change in this people that once loved freedom so passionately.' He had become somewhat less convinced that the language could actually still be saved. After three-quarters of a century's education under English control he believed that a national consciousness enshrined mainly in a national language was nearly lost, 'so nearly, indeed, in these recent years, that it sometimes seems that Home Rule, if come it does, will come too late to save it'.[96]

A similar disenchantment had spoken from his letter to Douglas Hyde in May 1912 in which he had stated that the League had gone about the regeneration of the language in the wrong way, relying on structures and organisations instead of actually going out to the people and teaching them by example.[97] In his public statements he never indicated he believed that the struggle which he deemed necessary was anything else but a moral fight, although the idea that a threat of arms was necessary had taken hold in his mind.[98] In a separate letter he urged John Redmond to not let the apprehension of old age stop him and accomplish what Parnell set out to do against Irish as well as English opponents. Patrick made clear he admired Redmond for his support of Parnell when he was removed from the leadership of the Irish Party in 1890. 'You were, at one period in your career, the idol of the Gaels. Those of us who opposed you, admitted that you had shown unusual courage on that day when you stood on Parnell's right hand when the baying of savaging hounds was loud in his ears.'[99]

Despite the reports on his political ambitions, Patrick showed no signs of any intention to take an active political role himself. He had no desire to join Sinn Féin, which he claimed never to have had much love for, and did not play an active part in other political initiatives such as the United National Societies Committee, which had been formed after the rally in O'Connell Street. In fact he severely criticised Arthur Griffith for his disparaging propaganda against members of the Irish Party which had scared off Irish-Ireland members and he believed Sinn Féin had become moribund due to Griffith's egotistical manner.[100] The unsuccessful campaign by Sinn Feiners in 1913 to oust Hyde as President of the League was another bone of contention.[101] 'The anonymous critics who have abused their position on the Coiste Gnotha by vilification of the Executive and of the League president have been true to their kind – they remain in the dark. They still employ the anonymous letter and the communication signed with a plausible but bogus or unknown name to keep suspicion in the air. Mr Arthur Griffith, we regret to see, champions all the anonymous tribe and makes a regular muddle of charges on his own behalf, from which a little acquaintance with the Gaelic League would have saved him.'[102]

The financial crisis which befell his schools in the spring of 1912 made political activity increasingly difficult. In a published letter he implored himself to concentrate on the school's survival. 'Take my advice; devote your attention to Sgoil Éanna and to Sgoil Íde and disregard political affairs. You have more than sufficient cares to occupy you. Cast from you the Trumpet of Victory [*An Barr Buadh*] shoot the trumpeter, disband the new society without a name and do well that which you set out to do four years ago.'[103] *An Barr Buadh* was indeed discontinued after eleven issues, 'the poor trumpet of Victory will not be played again for some time!',[104] and he let Cumann na Saoirse die a silent death. Some also believed a reason for closing down the paper was that it irritated the clergy because Patrick had taken up his old habit to criticise the Bishops, and Patrick could not afford to have them against him while his school was in difficulty.[105]

Although not actively engaged in politics from the summer of 1912 on, he did occasionally lecture, such as the one he gave on education in the Mansion House in December. In an address to the League branch in Carrick-on-Suir the month before, he indicated that his hopes that home rule would pass had diminished and his threat of the consequences became more direct. However, he did not yet anticipate a role for himself in fulfilling this threat and believed the younger generation would do so. 'If Home Rule does not come then momentous events may happen soon. The people of Ireland may be called upon sooner than they may expect to make great sacrifices for the country. What will happen if Home Rule does not come can be left to the younger generation to settle and he could assure them that the younger generation would know what to do if the crisis comes.'[106]

In the spring of 1913 he resurrected the school paper *An Macaomh*. In it he developed a new aspect of his thinking.

> It has been sung of the Gael that his fighting is always merry and his feasting always sad. Several recent books by foreigners have recorded the impression of Ireland as a sad, an unutterably sad country, because their writers have seen the Gael chiefly at his festivals: at the Oireachtas, at a race meeting, at a political dinner addressed by Mr. John Dillon. And it is a true impression, for the exhilaration of fighting has gone out of Ireland.

The necessity of a rejuvenation of this fighting spirit had become evident to him. 'Here at St Enda's we have tried to keep before us the image of Fionn during his battles – careless and laughing, with that gesture of the head, that gallant smiling gesture, which has been an eternal gesture in Irish history; it was most memorably made by Emmet when he mounted the scaffold in Thomas Street, smiling.' The last example of this was the Manchester Martyrs in 1867, but he saw few signs of one materialising now: 'I know that Ireland will not be happy again until she recollects that old proud gesture of hers, and that laughing gesture of a young man that is going into battle or climbing to a gibbet.'[107]

In the early summer when bankruptcy was staved off Patrick again became more actively involved in politics. He agreed to give the Wolfe Tone Memorial Lecture in Bodenstown on 22 June, and started a series of articles in the republican newspaper *Irish Freedom* commencing in June 1913 and extending to January 1914. His letters reveal that he held meetings in April and May in the office of IRB leader Bulmer Hobson who was then editor of that paper, probably in preparation of these articles.[108] Two years later he claimed he started this 'series with the deliberate intention, by argument, invective, and satire, of goading those who shared my political views to commit themselves definitely to an armed movement. I felt quite sure that the hour was ripe for such a movement, but did not in the beginning foresee the precise form it was to assume.'[109] However, in his first article he was much less clear about his commitment to armed insurrection and still saw potential in home rule. 'This generation of Irishmen will be called upon in the near future to make a very passionate assertion of nationality. The form in which that assertion shall be made must depend upon many things, more especially upon the passage or non-passage of the present

Home Rule Bill.'[110] In his July contribution he made clear what should happen in case home rule came and called for 'the creation of what we may call a Gaelic party within the Home Rule Parliament ... which shall determinedly set about the rehabilitation of this nation, resting not until it has eliminated every vestige of foreign interference with its concerns'.[111] Although other measures thus might become necessary, his policy was still largely peaceful.

Even in his Wolfe Tone memorial lecture with its necessary celebration of Tone's ideas and rebellious actions he was unclear about the type of fight he was expecting from the people. Like Tone he made clear he was striving 'To break the connection with England, the never-failing source of all our political evils, and to assert the independence of my country.' He expressed his hope that this would happen in their lifetime. 'My brothers, were it not an unspeakable privilege if to our generation it should be granted to accomplish that which Tone's generation, so much worthier than ours, failed to accomplish!' And called upon the Irish to unite and to fight for freedom 'whether victory seems near or far, never lowering our ideal, never bartering one jot or title of our birthright, holding faith to the memory and the inspiration of Tone, and accounting ourselves base as long as we endure the evil thing against which he testified with his blood.' He nevertheless did not openly call for an armed insurrection as he would later do.[112]

At the end of 1913 Patrick's contributions to *Irish Freedom* became more outspoken. In September he put Mitchel, the man behind the 1848 rebellion, next to Tone for his realism and his willingness to arm the people: 'a Man cannot save his people unless the people themselves have some manhood'. In October he asserted that 'There are only two ways of righting wrongs: reform and revolution. Reform is possible when those who inflict the wrong can be got to see things from the point of view of those who suffer the wrong.' He said this in relation to the plight of the poor during the Dublin lockout of 1913, but it had clear overtones for the national struggle.[113]

The lockout, in which some 20,000 workers were either refused entry to their place of work by their employers or were on supporting strikes, was an attempt by employers to squeeze the Irish Transport and General Workers' Union. The concomitant suffering among the working classes clearly awakened a social consciousness in Patrick. As a child he had already shown a concern for the poor. One time he went around dressed as a beggar to see how it felt, and on another occasion he tried to sell apples in their aid. This failed because he and his brother were attacked by children who sold apples for a living and feared unwanted competition.[114] As part of a League effort to stem the tide of emigration from the Gaeltacht in 1903 he advocated some proto-socialist ideas about redistribution of land and the obligation of a state to provide the people with a means of supporting themselves.[115] In 1912 he nevertheless had still called upon all elderly, including the poor and infirm, to reject the newly introduced old-age pension, as a sign of selling out to the enemy.[116] Now he openly supported the workers and was particularly hurt by the suffering of the poor.[117]

Where he had previously criticised Labour for its links with British trade unions, he now defended the strikers against attacks from advanced nationalists who objected to them receiving support from British trade unions by pointing out that the employers relied on British armed forced to protect their interests.[118] When Frank Fahey once suggested taking a short cut home via the working class area around Christ Church, Patrick refused, saying 'I can't go home that way and see the people looking hungry when we can do nothing to remedy it.'[119] In October he criticised the opposition of the rich to the strike and called upon them to try to live on £1 a week like the poor. In response to the violent clashes in O'Connell Street on 31 August in which two men were beaten to death by the police he asked whether the rich would be willing to 'kiss the chastening baton' 'when policemen smash in their skulls' or perhaps 'they may come to see that there is something to be said for the hungry man's hazy idea that there is something wrong somewhere'.[120]

Although after his financial problems in 1912 he had jokingly remarked 'I think I will be a Socialist, for the rich have failed me!',[121] he now made clear he was not in any way a social revolutionary. 'Personally I am in a position to protest my respectability. I do all the orthodox things. My wild oats were sown and reaped years ago. I am nothing so new-fangled as a socialist or a syndicalist. I am old-fashioned enough to be both a Catholic and a Nationalist. I am not smarting under any burning personal wrong – except the personal wrong I endure in being a member of an enslaved nation.'[122] He did certainly believe in the differences between the classes and on a few occasions he displayed a strong sense of social superiority over the poor working classes. He once mistook a new maid for a distinguished lady-caller he expected and approached her in a lordly manner. When the mistake was pointed out to him afterwards he roared with laughter for the 'inappropriate treatment of a lower person'. At the opening of one of his nephew's plays in St Enda's he found a badly dressed woman backstage. He became very angry to find such a person there before it became clear it was his sister dressed up for the play.[123]

The genuine concern for the plight of the poor he felt was, almost inevitably, ultimately connected with English rule as was shown in his life-long attachment to reciting 'Seamus O'Brien' which he was taught by his father and which recalled the suffering of the people and country.[124] He argued that if there was no 'foreign domination', emigration and poverty would be eradicated.[125] Privately he was unsure whether the outcome of the labour trouble would be good or bad for Ireland, but expressed his concern for the people involved.[126] He did admire Larkin for his willingness to take control, and claimed that the methods of Larkin may be wise or unwise: 'but this I know, that here is a most hideous wrong to be righted, and that the man who attempts honestly to right it is a good man and a brave man'.

There were obviously a number of ideas and concepts fermenting in Patrick's mind in the period before the start of the Irish Volunteers in October 1913. He had moved from his idea that fundamentally a cultural regeneration was paramount to a belief that a political struggle was necessary. He still expected that a political compromise could be the first step to a peaceful resolution of Ireland's dispute with England. At the same time influenced by the apparent success of the Ulster Volunteers he had become convinced that Ireland's demands needed to be backed up with a threat of force. In the manifesto issued at the launch of the Irish Volunteers it was stated that the Unionist had made 'the display of military force and the menace of armed violence the determining factor in the future relations of this country and Great Britain'.[127] Probably based on his study of the Volunteer movement and the United Irishmen of the late eighteenth century Patrick legitimised the need for a threat of force by rejuvenating their concept of citizenship which involved the assertion of one's political rights by bearing arms. This would also enable Irish men to recover their manhood.[128] In the late nineteenth century an identification of males with strength, violence, decisiveness, success, and a lack of emotion had grown up which was strongly associated with conforming to military ideals and doing one's duty.[129] In Ireland a dichotomy between a feminine Celticism and a masculine fighting Gall was put forward in the work of Arthur Griffith and particularly D.P. Moran, and was later taken up by Patrick.[130]

Initially the threat of force in Ireland was thus mainly a means to obtain home rule, but it gradually came to obtain a life of its own. Following the example of Robert Emmet and Wolfe Tone the idea of a blood sacrifice for the cause of Ireland seems to have taken hold of Patrick. 'My father visited him after he had taken the boys away and found him sitting on the steps outside looking away towards Emmett's fort brooding. My father said "I suppose you are thinking about Emmett." "I am thinking blood must be shed to save the Nation," answered Pearse.'[131] In his writing there are also a number of comparisons made between Ireland and the sacrifice of Christ. Allegorically this can be read in his 1911 passion play, An Rí, in which a child dies to save his people.[132] Although he simultaneously seems to have developed an ambition to die for Ireland,[133] there are no direct signs Patrick identified himself with Christ as has been asserted.

During 1913 Patrick slowly became involved in active politics. He verbalised more clearly that he saw a role for him and his generation in preparing the minds for strong action. 'I keep drifting more and more to politics and away from books. I feel that we of the Gaelic League generation must be ready for strong political action, leading up to *other* actions within the next few years, whether under Home Rule or in its absence.'[134] The militarisation of Irish politics, which was initiated by the founding of the scouting organisation Fianna Eireann in 1909 and other local militia groups since,[135] became evident after the founding of the Ulster Volunteers which provided advanced nationalists with the incentive to start a militia of their own.

To Patrick the militarisation of Irish society was part of a two-phased revolution. He had begun to see the Gaelic League as having provided the first phase in which the minds of the Irish had been made ready for a revolution, and the Irish Volunteers as forming the second providing a generation ready to fight for Ireland. He expressed this most clearly in his article 'The Coming Revolution' which he wrote in November 1913.[136] In it he described the League as a school which had made Irishmen nationalists. If it had been aimed solely at regenerating the language they would have struck a deal with the British and benefited from it materially. 'Now we did not turn our backs upon all these desirable things for the sake of *is* and *tá*. We did it for the sake of

Ireland. In other words, we had one and all of us (at least, I had, and I hope that all you had) an ulterior motive in joining the Gaelic League.' This was to get to know the real Ireland. The League was a good school, but he added 'we do not propose to remain schoolboys forever'. Just as education was a preparation for complete living, now that they had graduated from the League they were ready for complete living as Irish Nationalists. 'As to what your work as an Irish Nationalist is to be, I cannot conjecture; I know what mine is to be.'

Patrick was now ready for revolution. To him the League had been a prophet but not the Messiah. Its role was over but the vital work which was to be done in the new Ireland would be done by 'men and movements that have sprung from the Gaelic League or have received from the Gaelic League a new baptism and a new life of grace'. This new generation like every generation had its own task. 'The deed of the generation that has now reached middle life was the Gaelic League: the beginning of the Irish Revolution. Let our generation not shirk *its* deed, which is to accomplish the revolution.' The organisations which were to accomplish this task were groups like the Freedom Clubs, Young Republican Parties, Labour Organisations, and Socialist groups. These may take contradictory trajectories but they all had a common objective: 'the Irish Revolution'. He was not sure whether any of these groups were the Messiah, but the people itself will perhaps be its own Messiah, 'the people labouring, scourged, crowned with thorns, agonising and dying, to rise again immortal and impassable'.

With the start of this second phase the significance of the passing of home rule clearly rescinded in Patrick's mind.

Whether Home Rule means a loosening or a tightening of England's grip upon Ireland remains yet to be seen. But the coming of Home Rule, if come it does, will make no material difference in the nature of the work that lies before us: it will affect only the means we are to employ, our plan of campaign. There remains, under Home Rule as in its absence, the substantial task of achieving the Irish Nation.

He now accepted that the regeneration of the Irish nation could follow political independence and did not necessarily have to predate it. To achieve independence it was necessary to be armed although at this stage he felt it might not be necessary to fight. 'A thing that stands demonstrable is that nationhood is not achieved otherwise than in arms: in one or two instances there may have been no actual bloodshed, but the arms were there and the ability to use them. Ireland unarmed will attain just as much freedom as it is convenient for England to give her; Ireland armed will attain ultimately just as much freedom as she wants.' He became more and more strident in his rejection of the link with Britain and called for a war of all Irishmen against the foreign force that occupied them. 'It is evident that there can be no peace between the body politic and a foreign substance that has intruded itself into its system: between them war only until the foreign substance is expelled or assimilated.' What form that war should take is still left undefined. It was, however, clear that the objective was not going to be achieved without hard work, suffering and probably bloodshed. In other words without men's work. For that it was necessary to become men and real men were armed. In this context he expressed his joy for the fact the Protestants in the North had armed themselves, that the North had 'begun' as Hyde had asserted.

> I am glad that the Orangemen have armed, for it is a goodly thing to see arms in Irish hands. I should like to see the A.O.H. armed. I should like to see the Transport Workers armed. I should like to see any and every body of Irish citizens armed. We must accustom ourselves to the thought of arms, to the sight of arms, to the use of arms. We may make mistakes in the beginning and shoot the wrong people; but bloodshed is a cleansing and a sanctifying thing, and the nation which regards it as the final horror has lost its manhood. There are many things more horrible than bloodshed; and slavery is one of them.[137]

This concept of the cleansing and healing power of bloodshed found its origin in the Jacobins of the French Revolution who believed it could lead to a better society and was taken up by many revolutionary movements since.[138]

The Irish Volunteers

The growing importance Patrick assigned to the carrying of arms in the assertion of Irish nationhood had led him to partake in the founding of the Irish Volunteers in November 1913. Although there seems to have been no mention yet in the September meeting of the IRB Supreme Council of the setting-up of a paramilitary volunteer corps, the initiative to start the Irish Volunteers was taken by a group of advanced nationalists some of whom were members of the IRB while others like Patrick were active in a parallel circuit of radical politics.[139] A number of advanced nationalists of different hues like The O'Rahilly, Roger Casement and Sean O'Casey had called for it during 1913.[140] After Eoin MacNeill wrote his famous article 'The North Began', Bulmer Hobson, one of the prime movers in the IRB, and the unattached The O'Rahilly seem to have approached MacNeill and with him invited nine other men from a broad nationalist spectrum, including Patrick and D.P. Moran, for a meeting on 11 November in Wynn's Hotel, Abbey Street. It was decided to set up a provisional committee which would be dominated by separatists but also contain a number of representatives from other nationalist bodies to ensure that a cross-section of society could be attracted. It was also decided not to have any prominent IRB men on the executive to avoid being suppressed.[141] According to Patrick, Eoin MacNeill was then approached as prospective leader.

> When I wrote the article for November 1913 a group of Nationalists with whom I was in touch had decided to found the Irish Volunteers, and we were looking about for a leader who would command the adhesion of men less 'advanced' than we were known to be: of our own followers we were sure. When I wrote the article for December 1913, Eoin MacNeill had (quite unexpectedly) published his article 'The North Began' in *An Claidheamh Soluis*, and we had agreed to invite him to put himself at our head.[142]

In four subsequent meetings this Provisional Committee, with the exception of Moran and two others, was extended to about thirty men, including twelve IRB men, eight associated with the Irish Party and ten formally unattached men such as Pearse, MacDonagh, Joseph Plunkett, Roger Casement, The O'Rahilly and MacNeill. They organised the founding meeting on 25 November in the Rotunda.[143] The committee which presented itself there consisted of fairly moderate non-IRB men; besides MacNeill these were Laurence Kettle and John Gore who were associated with the Ancient Order of Hibernians and The O'Rahilly. There had been good publicity with hand bills distributed all over town, and many organisations including Labour having been involved. Although the Rotunda could take 4000 people, the meeting had an overflow of 3000. In his address MacNeill referred to the inaugural meeting of the Gaelic League twenty years earlier which was attended by only seven men but had led to great things.

Patrick spoke about the rights and duties of citizenship, in particular the essential duty of being armed to qualify for citizenship. The last hundred years he argued had seen unorganised attempts to realise a nation which resembled a mob, but now they went 'back to the policy of the Volunteers, to the policy of co-operation of Irishmen of every class and creed, and every shade of political belief'. He emphasised that the Irish Volunteers were not set up to fight the Ulster Volunteers in North-East Ulster, he even conceived of cooperation with them as they both agreed that it was for Ireland herself and not England to determine the degree of autonomy. He believed, however, 'that for Ireland there would be no true freedom within the British Empire'.[144]

Although the Executive had no IRB men on it, they were well represented on the Provisional Committee and on the four subcommittees which were set up in February 1914. The prominent IRB man Sean MacDermott was one of the four members of the finance committee, Eamonn Ceannt was the single representative on the six-men strong Dublin City and County Committee, while MacDermott, Hobson, Macken and Patrick Ryan dominated the six-men-strong Country Committee, and Ceannt, Plunkett and Robert Page formed the majority in the Uniform Committee.[145] Patrick was on the Provisional Committee and was also appointed Director of Organisation. As with any venture he became involved in Patrick threw himself into the organisation with great enthusiasm. One of his first suggestions was to set up a scouting organisation called 'Buachaillí na hEireann' for the sons of Volunteers from moderate nationalist backgrounds for whom the Fianna was too extreme. This was indeed done by Mrs Eamonn Ceannt, Mrs Clarke and Mr Keddy Reddin. The first meeting was in Sheriff St National School and the boys were addressed by Patrick. However, it soon ran into difficulty because some in the Fianna objected.[146] A newspaper, the *Irish Volunteer*, was also founded. According to Frank Henderson: 'The publicity from that newspaper and Pearse's pamphlets succeeded in getting a number of men into the movement and these were of a very good type.'[147]

Within a couple of days after the founding meeting of the Volunteers Patrick was approached over the role women could play in the organisation, something that had been called for in the Volunteers manifesto. On 30 November he answered a query on this from Miss G. Doyle. He apologised for not having had time to consider the work of women but felt that 'First of all there will be ambulance and Red Cross work for them; and then I think a women's rifle club is desirable. I would not like the idea of women drilling and marching in the ordinary way but there is no reason why they should not learn to shoot. The matter will be taken up by the Committee as soon as possible.'[148] Eventually a women's auxiliary organisation, Cumann na mBan (League of Women) was founded in April 1914. It is doubtful whether Patrick really anticipated a military role for women. Although he had long supported women's rights, he portrayed their role as a supporting one in most of his creative writing. Particularly in *The Singer* the men go out to fight and the women stay at home and are implored upon not to grudge. The men's task is to do and sacrifice; the women are there to serve and suffer.

As Director of Organisation Patrick now assumed a public role in the organisation. He made every effort to make the Volunteers into a success, touring the country to try to induce the formation of local units of the Volunteers as far a field as Dungloe in Donegal.[149] In January 1914 he and Roger Casement were selected as the two representatives for a big public meeting in Limerick, and he even took precedence over Casement at another meeting in Limerick later that year.[150] He was also made responsible for devising an organisational structure. The basic unit in this would be the company defined as all the men in a certain area. Ideally it consisted of three officers and a hundred men, with special sections for Scouting, Transport and Supply, and Ambulance services. Above that there were territorially based battalions and brigades also with specialised services.[151]

The start of the Volunteers and all the associated initiatives clearly brought Patrick into an elated state. In his article in *Irish Freedom* of January 1914 he made fun of what had been achieved, and expressed his disbelief that the Irish had armed themselves so quickly. 'I could have believed such a rapport of any generation of young Irishmen of which I have read; but of the generation that I have known I hesitate to believe it.' After all, his generation had been taught in the English education system that rebellion in all its forms is silly, and that these things may happen 'in other countries and in other times; but surely not in our own country and in our own time'. With a touch of irony he pointed out the consequences. 'Consider the dislocating effect of such a movement. In the first place, it would make Home Rule, now about to be abandoned in deference to armed Ulster, almost a certainty; in a second place, should Home Rule miscarry, it would give us a policy to fall back upon.' It would also make Irishmen citizens, and

> it would unite us in one all-Ireland movement of brotherly co-operation, whereas we derive infinite pleasure from quarrelling with one another. The comfortable feeling that we are safe behind the guns of the British Army, like an infant in its mother's arms, the precious liberty of confuting one another before the British public and thus gaining empire-wide reputations for caustic Celtic humour and brilliant Celtic repartee – these are things that we will not lightly sacrifice. For these privileges have we not cheerfully allowed our population to be halved and our taxation to be quadrupled? Enough said. Volunteering is undesirable, Volunteering is impossible. Volunteering is dangerous.[152]

In an address to prospective Volunteers in January 1914 he emphasised that the Volunteers should unite all nationalists in defence of home rule which was under threat from the Ulster Volunteers. He admired the manliness of Ulster Protestants for arming themselves, but the rest of Ireland should now do their bit and 'realise themselves as men'. In the same month he wrote in *Irish Freedom* that 'it will be for the people to say when and against whom the Volunteers shall draw the sword and point the rifle'. In the Volunteer movement he argued they were giving Mr Redmond a weapon which will enable him to enforce the demand for home rule. He did not expect him to lead a revolution but 'we can lead it and aid Redmond'.[153] In February he wrote in *The Irish Volunteer* that Ireland had renewed its youth, and to be young is to be a hero: 'we are about to attempt impossible things, for we know that it is only impossible things that are worth doing'.[154]

He wanted to dispel the impression that the conflict with the Ulster Volunteers would lead to dissension within Ireland. In his article 'The Psychology of a Volunteer' he warned against a separation between an Irish-speaking and an English-speaking Ireland, each with its own history. To him they were all Irish. He felt compelled to explain his own position and that of the Gaelic League on the issue of the language and nationality. To them the language was not just a sort of stimulant for nationhood but they had fought for the language like Parnell fought for the land to assert their right to independence. He made clear he had not changed his attitude. 'I have spent the best fifteen years of my life teaching and working for the idea that the language is an essential part of the nation. I have not modified my attitude in anything that I have recently said or written. I have only confessed that in the Gaelic League I have all along been working not for the language merely, but for the nation.' To him anyone who solely worked for the language had never had the true Gaelic League spirit.[155]

In testimony to his dedication to the language he composed an Irish marching song for the Volunteers which was published in one of the first issues of their newspaper. In three verses he described Ireland's grief at being dispossessed, then the preparations for a big battle, and finally promises the invading force that Gaels will tout the oppressor.[156] However, as few Volunteers knew Irish it was rarely used. Patrick nevertheless continued to try to connect Volunteering with the language. Early in 1915 he wrote a number of weekly columns in Irish, *Mo Thuairim Fein* (My Own Opinion), in the *Irish Volunteer*, and continued to urge Volunteers to learn Irish.[157]

He was still doubtful over the actual role of the Volunteers in a revolution. He believed that it was up to the youth, now trained in the Fianna, to actually fight it. In an article written in February 1914 he described his high hopes for them in the future. Contrary to his recent statements to the Volunteers which implied a willingness to accept some form of independence within the empire, he asserted that the Fianna believed that their country ought to be free. 'We do not see why Ireland should allow England to govern her, either through Englishmen, as at present, or through Irishmen under an appearance of self-government.' The object of the Fianna was to train the boys of Ireland to fight Ireland's battle when they were men. In the past Irishmen had heroically struggled but lost 'because they were not SOLDIERS'. He believed that the Fianna had kept the military spirit alive in Ireland and without them the Volunteers of 1913 would never have arisen. He finished his article with the hope that 'the man who shall lead the Irish Volunteers to victory come forth from Na Fianna Eireann'. Again implying he did not yet see an immediate rebellion taking place.[158]

To facilitate the development of the Fianna into a more efficient organisation, Patrick opened up the grounds of St Enda's for their training and manoeuvres, particularly during holidays. Several former Fianna members recall they were always welcome,[159] despite occasionally abusing the privilege. 'We usually went to St. Enda's or Sgoil Eanna's as we called it, if the weather was bad so that we could get shelter. Padraig Pearse was very good to us and used to give us every facility. We had permission to swim in the pool he had constructed for his boys. Sometimes we would camp in the big field in front of the house. I remember one week-end we were camping there and some of the boys were found stealing apples in the orchard and we were ordered out at once.'[160]

United States tour

The lecture tour to the United States for fundraising purposes interfered with Patrick's growing role in advanced nationalist politics. First suggested by Patrick McCartan in 1910 the trip had been on the cards at least from the middle of 1912 onwards, but finally came to fruition in February 1914.[161] Initially Patrick tried to establish contact with moderate Irish Americans like John Quinn, who had organised a fundraising tour by Douglas Hyde in 1905, but Quinn refused to help because of what he called the continuous demands from Irish 'spongers' who rarely delivered on their promises. As a result Patrick had to turn to the radicals. For this the support of the IRB was vital. He already had some contact with their American branch through their newspaper *The Gaelic American* which had published some of his articles from *An Claidheamh Soluis*, but he now needed a direct introduction. This was provided by Bulmer Hobson who assured leading Irish-American radicals as Devoy and McGarrity that Patrick was 'all right and in line with us here', adding that Tom Clarke and Sean MacDermott agreed. To provide him with stronger credentials Patrick was finally initiated into the IRB.[162]

Historians and contemporaries have often regarded Patrick's visit, which commenced on 18 February 1914, as having had a radicalising effect on him. One of his associates asserted that 'After he came back from U.S.A. nothing was too extreme for him.'[163] However, although now being part of a radical circle in the United States, there is no significant change in the content of his speeches. The topics he dealt with in the US were largely literary and historical, 'The Heroic Literature of Early Ireland: Its Scope and Value', 'Irish Folk Songs',

'Wolfe Tone and '98', 'John Mitchel and '48', 'The Irish Volunteers: 1778–1914', 'The Fight for the Language', 'An Ideal in Education' and 'Ireland To-day: the People and the Movements'.[164] In a speech on St Patrick's Day Patrick reiterated his view that home rule would only be a slight improvement on the present situation, and that full nationhood would still have to be accomplished and could only be achieved by armed men. Although he again stated that 'to the majority of Irish Nationalists its passing or nonpassing is almost a matter of indifference', he still felt that the future attitude of the Irish people depended on it. 'If Home Rule does not come, the whole nation will automatically swing back to the policy and methods of the Fenians. In either event the year 1914 will mark, not the beginning of a peace with England, but the beginning of a new and stirring chapter in the Irish struggle for independence.'[165]

He did not see an immediate prospect of action. He still perceived the idea of several phases in the development towards national independence which he had first postulated on the basis of his view of Hungarian and Flemish history in 1904. In this the founding of the Gaelic League in 1893 had been the start of the first phase of the revolution. When a 'few clear-sighted young men saw that Ireland could be saved by saving her traditional culture which is its unsilent language'. Now that the Volunteers had been started by a mixture of the Gaelic League and the Fenians, the second phase of the revolution had begun. In an Emmet Memorial Lecture given in New York he argued that his own generation was in the Gaelic League, the younger generation was in the Volunteers learning about the use of arms while the next generation, now 'being trained to be finished soldiers of Ireland' in the Fianna, 'will one day take – or make – an opportunity of putting their [the Fenians] teaching into practice'. He did believe, however, that a rebellion would not be too far away: 'before this generation has passed the Volunteers will draw the sword of Ireland'.[166] For the moment he did not foresee immediate action but hard work with all its disappointments: 'the routine of correspondence and committees and organising'.[167]

Thus the various elements of his thought as it had developed over the years came to the fore in his lectures in the United States.[168] Fundamentally he saw the struggle in Ireland not as a political one but as a battle between two civilisations. Simply erecting free political institutions was not enough; the cultural conquest had to be undone.

To do this the Irish had to re-establish their own civilisation, remnants of which could still be found in the West. 'The Ireland, immemorial Ireland, that broods by the western sea, the Ireland that still preserves something of that gracious native civilisation.' There had always been 'some unconquerable thing' in Ireland despite every attempt by England through the education system to make 'our boys and our girls slaves' by ignoring the Irish language and history and teaching them to be sleek, active and dexterous instead of gracious and noble, self-reliant, brave, strong, and true.

If it was not for the efforts of previous generations of separatists the current movement would not be possible. 'It may be that in the goodness of God it shall be given to us, that though so unworthy to complete the work that they, so worthy, left uncompleted.' To be armed was a central necessity for Ireland to achieve its nationhood. Ireland also had a duty to those who died for it in the past. Dublin in particular had a duty to Robert Emmet to atone for its lack of support it gave him in 1803. 'Dublin must one day wash out in blood the shameful memory of that quiescence.' Although the Irish Party believed home rule would be a final settlement, Tone and Emmet would not have accepted it and even England does not believe the Irish will accept it. They have shown this by forbidding the importation of arms since the Irish Volunteers started while they have 'given the Ulster faction which is used as a catspaw by one of the English parties two years to organise and arm against that Home Rule Bill which they profess themselves so anxious to pass'. The reality is that Britain is afraid of Irishmen with arms, and they should be.

He did not believe it would be necessary to fight the Ulster Unionist leader Edward Carson. 'I can even conceive circumstances in which we can fraternise with Sir Edward Carson to guard the right and liberties of all the people of Ireland against outside invasions.' The Volunteers would fight the empire everywhere in South Africa, Washington, the Senate House, and will win eventually. They cannot be at peace with wrong, falsehood and oppression, and should never give up their arms now they have them. If the Volunteers of the 1780s had not handed back their arms then, he claimed, 1798, the Union, the sacrifice of Emmet, the Famine, and emigration would not have happened. 'We might have had in Ireland to-day a free people numbering twenty million, instead of being, as we are, a dwindling remnant of four million.'[169]

His time in the US was exciting to Patrick. He was widely respected and treated as an important man. On the poster advertising one of his lectures he was announced as 'P.H. Pearse President St. Enda's College B.L and member of the Provisional Committee of the new "Irish Volunteers"'. Bulmer Hobson, who also spoke, only received a minor mention on the same placard.[170] Patrick was also asked to inspect the dress parade of the First Regiment Irish Volunteers in New York. His speeches received some references in the moderate Irish-American press, and he was entertained by some of the Redmondites, including Thomas Addis Emmet the grand nephew of Robert Emmet and also by Quinn. However, his close association with advanced nationalism also made him the brunt of hostility by those supporting the Irish Party. At the Field Day in New York Patrick was physically attacked by supporters of Redmond and had to be protected by members of the New York Irish Volunteers.[171] As a result, most of his contacts were with radicals, and in response to their calls for action he emphasised the radical elements in his thinking. Patrick greatly admired John Devoy and came very close to the leading Clann's man in Philadelphia Joe McGarrity and his family who nursed him when he fell ill during his visit. The warmth of the reception he encountered throughout, in particular by the McGarrity family, also did him much good. When he sailed for home on 7 May he had not only collected about £1000 but had gained a lot of experience speaking to large audiences using extreme rhetoric.[172]

The IRB and Volunteers

From his writings it appears that the concept of living a short but heroic life in service to Ireland, which he had long advocated to his pupils in St Enda's, became a realistic possibility after the Volunteers were set up. Upon his return from the United States Patrick became increasingly involved in the Volunteers and the IRB. Apart from his functions at the top level of the Volunteers organisation Patrick also became Captain of the Rathfarnham Company. Many of his former pupils, who were still boarding at St Enda's after entering university and who had already been secretly recruited into the IRB by Con Colbert, joined.[173] The obsession with Emmet took on more strident forms. One of his boys recalls an address to a small group of boy scouts: 'you come from the streets of Dublin bedecked with blood of Irish martyrs'. He also referred to the blood of Emmet being lapped up by dogs.[174] This story was told to him by Mary Hayden, whose nursemaid claimed to have seen 'dogs licking up Robert Emmet's blood under the scaffold in Thomas Street, and women soaking it up with their handkerchiefs'.[175] Desmond Ryan was later critical of what he termed Patrick's worship of military discipline becoming 'fanatical to the point of absurdity'. He also mentioned Patrick's long-standing admiration for Napoleon, having turned into the conviction that he had a kinship with Napoleon.[176] Among the relics of his heroes which Patrick collected there was also supposedly a lock of Napoleon's hair.[177]

The successes of the Volunteers during 1914 greatly impressed Patrick. 'The Volunteers are growing amazingly. It is the biggest thing in Irish movements since the Land League.'[178] On 12 June he claimed they had at least 140,000 members and that 'The whole country is organising and drilling and clamouring for arms.' The biggest threat to the role Patrick was foreseeing for the Volunteers at that stage came from John Redmond.[179] Although initially staying shy of the movement, Redmond gradually became convinced he could no longer ignore it. Eoin MacNeill is alleged to have invited him to get involved, but he publicly denied this afterwards. Nevertheless, secret negotiations took place between the Volunteers and the Irish Party in April and May but failed partly due to Redmond's objections to the presence of known radicals such as Pearse and Hobson on the Executive.[180] Although MacNeill also distrusted Pearse's influence, he had already taken his sons out of St Enda's, the Provisional Committee did not accept his removal. Redmond then publicly demanded that he would get twenty-five of his nominees appointed on the Provisional Committee and threatened to set up a rival body of Volunteers. MacNeill subsequently convinced opponents on the Executive that they needed to avoid a split in the nationalist camp. This eventually helped carry the motion to accept Redmond's nominees by eighteen to nine votes.

Among the dissidents were seven IRB men including Pearse, Ceannt, Colbert, MacDermott, Béaslai, Liam Mellows and Eamonn Martin. Michael Judge, a prominent member of the powerful nationalist benevolent society the AOH, and Sean Fitzgibbon also voted against. Three IRB men including Hobson and Joseph Plunkett voted in favour. In particular Hobson's stance was resented by the radicals.

His erstwhile friends Clarke and MacDermott distrusted his motives. They even seem to have asked him how much Dublin Castle had paid him. Hobson, however, had been fearful of the consequences of a split which would 'have meant that the Volunteers would have degenerated into an unarmed parade at political meetings, and we of the I.R.B. would have been back to a little secret movement meeting in back rooms, which is all we were before the Volunteers were started'.[181] The accusations caused Hobson to resign from the Supreme Council of the IRB and he was sacked as correspondent for *The Gaelic American*. He nevertheless kept a prominent role in the Volunteers.

The dissidents on the executive published a statement the next day in which they motivated their opposition 'on the grounds that it was a violation of the basic principles which up to the present have carried the Irish Volunteer movement to success'. This alluded to the Volunteers being a body open to all parties and not aligned with any particular one. They further announced they nevertheless wanted to stay in the movement and appealed to all others who shared their view to stay 'and persist in their efforts to make the Irish Volunteers an efficient, armed, National Defence Force'.[182] This was partly inspired by the fact that they knew an arms shipment was heading their way.

Apparently Patrick played only a minor part in these deliberations but in his letters he made clear what motivated him to stay on. He believed the majority of ordinary Volunteers were with the dissidents. His biggest fear was that Redmond on instigation of the Liberal Government was trying to get control to keep the movement unarmed. In a letter to McGarrity Patrick declared that they would remain in the movement and 'be watchful to checkmate any attempt on Redmond's part to prevent us from arming. This is the real danger. The future of the movement depends upon our remaining at our posts to see to it that the Volunteers are a real army, not a stage army.' He even saw a potential benefit of the involvement of the Irish Party in the Volunteers. 'If the Parliamentarians help us to arm it will be well worth while having surrendered to them.'[183] A couple of weeks later this seemed to have become reality. 'Recent information would go to show that Redmond is acting in good faith and would really like to see us armed. Once we are armed our position will be impregnable; and the watchword then must be *never to disband or to surrender our arms* no matter at whose bidding.'[184] In a speech in Tralee he made clear the Volunteers would have the power to determine the political future of

Ireland. 'When they had an Irish Parliament in College Green the work of the Irish Volunteers would be only then commencing. It would be a national defence force which was not going to be disbanded at the bidding of any politicians in Ireland or in England.'[185]

Obtaining arms became the obsession in the summer of 1914. In Patrick's requests to Irish-America the depth of the differences between those who had supported Redmond's demands and those that had opposed it clearly came to the fore. On 17 July Patrick asked McGarrity for 1000 rifles and ammunition to arm the men in Dublin. 'We want this request to take precedence over any other request that may have been made by MacNeill or by anyone else.' He also made it clear his optimism over Redmond's intention was not justified. Now he believed the danger from Redmond was of a graver kind. 'He wants *to arm them, not against England, but against the Orangemen.* The Volunteers are to be used to force Home Rule on Ulster, and possibly to enforce the *dismemberment of Ireland.* Some semblance of Home Rule must, at all costs, be placed on the statute books; the Volunteers have been captured in order to secure this, no matter how humiliating the terms.'[186] He had noticed that Redmond tried to prevent arms reaching those in the Volunteers that were against him and that most of the arms were diverted to Ulster. As a result, Patrick concluded, Unionists and Redmondites were armed 'while Nationalists (Sinn Feiners and Separatists) remain unarmed' – ironically leaving physical force men as the only group without weapons. In the meantime a new Standing Committee of thirteen men had been appointed of which at most five were considered trustworthy. Patrick felt he could rely totally on Hobson, who was in the process of being sidelined by the IRB, and Fitzgibbon, and maybe on Judge. MacNeill and The O'Rahilly he considered 'honest, but weak, and frightfully subject to panic'.[187]

Hobson later became very bitter about Patrick's role in sidelining him, but this appears to be unfounded. Hobson frequently alluded to Patrick's opposition to him when forming the Volunteers, but this was probably part of the decision not to have known radicals on the Provisional Committee to avoid opposition from mainstream nationalists.[188] He also referred to messages Patrick sent to McGarrity at the end of 1914: 'He was writing to my friends in US that I was not revolutionary enough and asked that funds be not sent to me.'[189] Although Patrick had indeed asked McGarrity not to send arms to those around MacNeill, he actually defended Hobson in these letters.

After having been fired from *The Gaelic American* by advanced nationalists in the United States for his acceptance of Redmond's nominees, Patrick wrote: 'I think they have been too harsh on Hobson on your side.' Hobson was left with no income and may therefore have to leave Dublin which Patrick described as an incalculable loss.[190] Even in October 1915 Patrick still showed he fully trusted Hobson when he asked McGarrity to send money for arms to radicals like him and Hobson and explicitly not to MacNeill.[191] This may also have been part of ensuring McGarrity's trust as Hobson had always been close to him.

The most successful initiative to arm the Volunteers had, however, been taken by elements in the Volunteers led by Hobson. With the cooperation of Roger Casement and Mary Spring Rice who had put up the money, Darrel Figgis and Erskine Childers had gone to buy arms in Hamburg, which were subsequently imported into Ireland on Sunday 26 July 1914.[192] About 1200 were landed very publicly at Howth near Dublin in Childers' yacht, the *Asgard*. Although Patrick had only become involved at a late stage, some of the ammunition was to be hidden at St Enda's.[193] Frank Fahey, who came to deliver the first lot of ammunition, remembers Patrick's agitation that day. 'He asked me how things were going & I said "not too good," I had seen movements of DMP. He said "What will I do? I must be there?" I asked him what were his orders & he said to receive ammunition & store it. I said to obey his orders but he wanted to be in the fight.'[194] Indeed the crowd bringing the arms down from Howth to Dublin was stopped by the police who unsuccessfully attempted to seize the weapons. In a subsequent scuffle at Bachelor Walk in Dublin three civilians were killed by soldiers. Another consignment of 600 rifles was landed a week later at Kilcoole in Co. Wicklow. The collection and distribution of these arms were organised from St Enda's where those participating came together in a more relaxed atmosphere. 'During our stay there I saw Padraig and Willie P. there. They gave us a talk on the grounds of the College and they showed us Philpott Curran's house and some semaphore work.'[195]

Afterwards Patrick told McGarrity that the, to him somewhat unexpected, landing of arms had utterly changed the situation. Most Dublin Volunteers were now armed and there was less haste with sending more arms. He stated this might be an opportunity for their American supporters to prepare better and send more weapons to their section in the Volunteers so that Dublin county and then the rest of the country could also be armed. He felt the shooting at Bachelor Walk was a god's gift. Dublin had seen 'nothing like it since 1798'. It was a great coup for the Volunteers, who were seen as the heroes of the hour. 'The whole movement, the whole country, has been re-baptised by bloodshed for Ireland.'[196] The Bachelor Walk funerals, when the Volunteers took over Dublin, were an 'excellent piece of training' and he even detected a 'wave of nationalism among the police and among the Irish regiments of the British Army'.[197]

The whole affair and the way the arms were distributed led to renewed conflict in the leadership of the Volunteers between supporters of Redmond and more advanced nationalists like Patrick. 'Nugent made a violent speech in which he challenged us to deny that the aim of the movement was to back up Redmond and the P[arliamentary].P[arty]. I replied by saying that the aim of the movement was to secure and maintain the freedom of Ireland, and that it must be kept open to all who were willing to work and fight for that end whether followers of Redmond or not.' The division in the Standing Committee was now well defined. The majority of Redmond supporters decided to send all recently imported arms to Ulster, much to the annoyance of the more radical side who had other plans. 'We are determined not to acquiesce in this: independently of the Provisional Committee we must arm our men in every part of Ireland and bid them never to part with their arms.'[198] Subsequently, Plunkett tried to hide the arms imported at Howth to avoid being sent North, and some were placed in St Enda's.[199]

First World War

When England declared war on Germany and the central powers, Patrick saw new opportunities. He was attracted to the idea Carson had put forward that his Volunteers would take charge of the whole country: 'We must fight any move on Redmond's part to offer their services to the English Government but we should be fools if we let slip an opportunity of taking over from the British Army the task of defending the soil of Ireland.' He saw an analogy with the Volunteer movement of 1779–1782 and the potential for a rising. 'If the British Army is engaged elsewhere, Ireland falls to the Volunteers, and then –

well then we must rise to the occasion.' He had already foreseen the possibilities presented by an outbreak of war between England and Germany during his visit to the United States. Joe McGarrity later recalled how he spoke with Patrick and Hobson of the expected war. Hobson believed Britain would be smashed, but Pearse 'was by no means sanguine that she was going to meet an overwhelming defeat. He was quite positive, however, that war was swiftly approaching, and that Ireland's long looked-for opportunity would follow.'[200] When hostilities commenced Patrick prepared for action, and implored McGarrity to make sure he ate and slept enough. 'I attribute my own capacity for getting through work to my always taking enough sleep and never neglecting meals. I have seen many break down, and am determined not to break down myself. We must hoard our strength and vitality against a possible greater demand than even the present one.'[201]

The final change in Patrick's political thinking and what he perceived to be his own role in the advancement of Irish independence seem to have been precipitated by the events surrounding the Howth gun-running and the outbreak of the First World War and not so much his American trip. Having already become convinced a violent gesture was necessary and possible within his lifetime he now saw the prospect of leading a rebellion himself come distinctly nearer:

> the young men of the nation stand organised and disciplined, and are rapidly arming themselves; blood has flowed in Dublin Streets, and the cause of the Volunteers has been consecrated by a holocaust. A European war has brought about a crisis which may contain, as yet hidden within it, the moment for which the generations have been waiting. It remains to be seen whether, if that moment reveals itself, we shall have the sight to see and the courage to do, or whether it shall be written of this generation, alone of all generations of Ireland, that it had none among it who dared to make the ultimate sacrifice.[202]

For the moment, however, he had to contend with the conflicting interests in the Volunteer Executive in which the radicals were increasingly marginalised. A squabble broke out over the allocation of the smuggled arms when the Redmondites, with good cause, accused advanced nationalists of stealing them. A subcommittee was appointed to ascertain where the arms were and to ensure that as many as possible were sent up North. Redmondites were desperately trying to avoid giving the government the impression that nationalists were unreliable, and tried to clamp down on any radical expression. When Patrick made clear to the members of his own company in Rathfarnham that he did not intend to let any more arms go North this caused a furore. 'The rifles which are now in my possession will, when served out to the men, be used for the sole end of the Irish Volunteers – the defence of Irish liberties against aggression, which is obviously a task in which all creeds and classes can join. I shall be the last man in Ireland to seek to divert the Volunteers from their original aim.'[203]

The radical tendencies in the Dublin Volunteers were another cause of concern for the Redmondites. In the first week of the war, three of the five Dublin Battalions of the Volunteers adopted a resolution drafted by the Dublin County Board 'expressing readiness to cooperate with Ulster for the defence of Ireland but unwillingness to support the British Government against foreign nations with which Ireland has no quarrel'. After they paraded at Volunteers headquarters the Provisional Committee ordered the 'county board and all concerned to apologize and promise not to adopt resolutions dealing with matters of policy again on pain of suspension'. At the same time other Volunteers units were allowed to adopt resolutions supporting Redmond's offer of help to Britain.

The control of the Executive by the Redmondites made Patrick desperate. By mid-August he felt he had ceased to be of any use on the Committee and considered resigning. 'I can never carry a single point. I am scarcely allowed to speak. The moment I stand up there are cries of "Put the question" etc. – after the last meeting I had half determined to resign, but have decided to stick on a little longer in the hope of being useful at a later stage.' There were even suggestions to bring the Volunteers under the British War Office which had offered to arm and train them, which would surely precipitate a split. Patrick blamed MacNeill, who was still president of the Volunteers, for allowing the marginalisation of those who were not associated with the Irish Party, but he hesitated to condemn him. 'He never makes a fight except when they assail his personal honour, when he bridles up at once. Perhaps I am wronging him, as I am smarting under the remembrance of what I regard as very unfair treatment of me personally and of all who agree with me at the last meeting. He is in a very delicate position and he is weak, hopelessly weak. I knew that all along.'[204] After Patrick had become convinced there was a deal with the War Office he came to blows on 9 September with the strident Redmondite Nugent. Patrick had reacted to being called a 'contemptible cur' and ended up with a bruised face. In the following confusion revolvers were drawn and the two camps in the Committee only just avoided fighting it out.[205] One of the Executive members, Liam Gogan, believed this had serious consequences for Patrick's attitude. 'I still remember with horror the blow delivered at Pearse in the City Hall, and have often wondered if he was not then receiving his new accolade as leader.'[206]

Patrick's optimism following the gun-running efforts of July had clearly rescinded. There had been far fewer guns imported than expected and they were antiquated 11 mm rifles without magazines. Some of the ammunition that had been delivered turned out to be explosive bullets which Patrick considered useless because they were 'against the rules of civilised war and which therefore, we are not serving out to the men'.[207] Many of the arms were sent North and the need for more was therefore again paramount for most units. Patrick was nevertheless kept going by a belief in the Volunteers themselves. 'Men are sound, especially in Dublin. We could at any moment rally the best of them to our support by a *coup d'état*; and rally the whole country if the *coup d'état* were successful. But a *coup d'état* while the men are still unarmed is unthinkable.'[208] This was confirmed by Greg Murphy who claimed a rising would even have taken place without Clarke, Connolly or Pearse.[209] The tensions in the movement came to a head when Redmond called upon Irishmen in a speech at Woodenbridge on 20 September to help Britain and fight 'wherever the firing line extends in defence of right, freedom and religion'.[210]

This was unacceptable to the original founders of the Volunteers who had set it up to defend Irish interests. They declared Redmond's call as 'fundamentally at variance with their own published and accepted aims and objects'. Redmond's nominees on the Provisional Committee were expelled and the committee reverted to its original form ensuring control over the Volunteers headquarters. A number of proposals were then formulated which included a reaffirmation of the original Volunteers manifesto, a pledge to oppose any diminution of the Home Rule Bill on Statute and in particular partition, a declaration that stated that Ireland could not take part in foreign quarrels unless it had a national government which could speak and act for the people of Ireland, and a call to establish such a national government immediately and abolish 'the present system of governing Ireland through Dublin Castle and the British military power'.[211] Public opinion was, however, largely in favour of Redmond, who had after all just achieved the passing of a Home Rule Act the implementation of which was nonetheless suspended till the end of the war.

Only a small minority of the 180,000 Volunteers supported the original committee. Probably about 10,000 to 15,000 were in sympathy with them but only a couple of thousand actually remained in the Irish Volunteers after the split. Patrick tried to ensure that this minority was 'pulled straight', but even in his own company in Rathfarnham many went with Redmond to the newly formed National Volunteers. This included one of the two treasurers who refused to share the funds with Pearse whom he dubbed a 'Sinn Feiner'. This association between the radical section of the Irish Volunteers and Sinn Féin was a persuasive one. Immediately after the split the authorities referred to them as the 'Sinn Féin Volunteers', which they continued to do right up to the Rising. In private Patrick acknowledged this although he asserted that he was 'something beside a Sinn Feiner'.[212] Shortly before the Volunteers Convention of 25 October 1914 he showed his relief over the ending of the acrimony in the leadership and expressed his belief that they were now stronger than ever: 'the Volunteers have been bought and sold but – happily – redeemed again, and we are now much stronger and more hopeful than ever, having a compact and disciplined body on which we can absolutely rely'.[213]

Redmond's action was, he believed, very unpopular and had multiplied the number of actual separatists by a hundred. 'The whole body of Volunteers that has supported our stand against recruiting may be looked upon as a separatist body.' The main strength of the movement was now in Dublin where according to Patrick about 2500 men were 'admirably disciplined, drilled, intelligent and partly armed'. Outside the capital 'large minorities support us everywhere, especially in the towns and in the extreme south and west. We expect to have 150 companies, representing 10,000 to 15,000 men represented by delegates at next Sunday's Convention.'[214] The image of recovered unity was, however, very deceptive. There were still great differences of opinion about the purpose of the Volunteers among those who had remained in the organisation. Men like MacNeill objected to Irish participation in a European war but to them force was only a last resort. Others like Hobson wanted to use the Volunteers for an uprising but only if that was the expressed will of the people as was required under the IRB constitution, while men like Clarke and MacDermott wanted a rising at all costs.

Although initially not being allowed into the convention by characteristically forgetting his admission ticket, Patrick's position on the executive was easily secured. A new General Council of 62 members was elected, one member representing each county and nine of the biggest cities plus the 21 members of the original Provisional Committee. The insurrectionists had obtained influential positions. The moderates MacNeill and O'Rahilly were returned as chair and treasurer, Hobson was chosen as general secretary and his associates Patrick Ryan and Seamus O'Connor as publications secretary and musketry training officer. The IRB man Eamonn Ceannt was appointed financial secretary, Pearse as press secretary, and Plunkett as co-treasurer.[215] Patrick was very pleased with the proceedings and particularly with the setting up of a small daily newspaper, *Eire – Ireland*, which would enable an outlet for extreme opinion.[216]

The inability of this convention to accommodate an alliance with the Irish Citizens Army (ICA), the militia of the Labour movement, spelled difficulties for the future. The relationship with the ICA, which had been founded two days before the Irish Volunteers in reaction to police brutality during the lockout, had always been fraught. This originated in the objection of Labour men to the presence on the platform at the foundation meeting of moderate nationalists such as Laurence Kettle, who as Director of the Dublin Corporation Electricity Works opposed them during the lockout. The subsequent public fray with ICA members had made some turn away in disgust 'saying that Irishmen could never agree'.[217] Afterwards the leaders of the ICA, Jim Larkin and Sean O'Casey, were very critical of the lack of social revolutionary content of the Volunteers. On 24 January 1914 O'Casey asked workers who had joined the Volunteers: 'Are you going to be satisfied with a crowd of chattering well-fed aristocrats and commercial bugs?'[218] Before the split in the Volunteers James Connolly was equally critical: 'We believe that there are no real Nationalists in Ireland outside of the Irish Labour movement. All others merely reject one part or other of the British conquest, the Labour movement alone rejects it in its entirety, and sets itself ... the reconquest of Ireland as its aim.'[219] But after the split he became more interested in cooperation.

Pearse was sympathetic to the workers, and admired Larkin as a man of action. However, there was no alliance formed at the convention of October 1914. Suggestions to have two members of the ICA co-opted on the Provisional Committee or even to incorporate the ICA into the Volunteers had been rejected.[220] This caused friction between the two organisations, and a desire on Connolly's side to go it alone.

In the subsequent months Patrick made it clear that a rebellion was on the cards and that he was going to take part in it himself.[221] His growing stature in radical circles made him an outcast to respectable society. A public furore developed in November over the actions of Professor Mahaffy, vice-provost of Trinity College, who banned a meeting of the Trinity College Gaelic Society because of the presence of 'a man called Pearse' who had been invited together with Yeats and Thomas Kettle to speak on Thomas Davis, an alumnus of the College. The meeting was subsequently held outside the College and Patrick got a highly publicised opportunity to spread his new found gospel of hatred of England which had replaced his earlier commitment to love of Ireland.[222] In his speech he described Mitchel's *Jail Journal* as the last gospel of the New Testament of Irish nationality in a long and 'deadly monotonous' speech.[223] This highly publicised meeting only enhanced Patrick's public profile. In the same month he sealed his commitment to armed action when he drew up instructions of what should be done in case of his death or incapacitation.[224]

In response to the immediate threat to the Volunteers from the government Patrick drew up a plan of resistance in case an attempt was made to implement conscription or repress the organisation. The plan involved an ever-increasing level of resistance evolving into guerrilla tactics similar to those later used in the Anglo-Irish War.[225] To implement this plan a military headquarters staff was created in December with MacNeill as Chief of Staff, Patrick as Director of Organisation, O'Rahilly as Director of Arms, MacDonagh as Director of Training, Joseph Plunkett as Director of Military Operation, and Hobson as Quartermaster General. In August 1915 Ceannt was added as Director of Communications and in November Ginger O'Connell as Chief of Inspection. The insurrectionists now occupied the positions which involved direct contact with ordinary Volunteers, allowing them to control the organisation throughout the country. Patrick reorganised the structure of the Volunteers according to a very elaborate scheme based on his original design which involved a structure of companies, battalions and brigades.[226]

In early 1915 the leadership attempted to implement this scheme and professionalise the organisation. In March Dublin was given a battalion structure and a brigade commander in the person of Thomas MacDonagh. Hobson, Plunkett and Patrick were made independent commandants which gave them the freedom to involve themselves in all units throughout the country. At the first meeting of the new Dublin staff on 13 March it was discussed whether a rising could take place in September. Afterwards Patrick made sure he could rely on Eamon de Valera, the only Dublin Battalion Commander who was not a member of the IRB, to participate in such a venture. Despite his efforts, Patrick retained doubts over the future. 'I am busier and more anxious than ever, for things are not going as they should.'[227] While in March 1915 he wrote to Desmond Ryan's father. 'Yes, we are having a struggle, but other interests distract my attention from St. Enda's and then it does not seem so bad. St. Enda's is now only a part of a bigger thing, and that bigger thing – the Irish movement that you and I have known – is in danger of going out ingloriously; unless something terrific saves it, which may happen. The public situation is more disheartening than ever before in our time, but there is always a germ of hope.'[228]

The biggest problem concerned the military abilities of the Volunteers. At Easter 1915 large manoeuvres were held in which the Dublin Brigade attacked the Volunteers in Fingal. Patrick was in charge, observing the procedures in his new officer's uniform and carrying a sword.[229] Ginger O'Connell, an ex-soldier who had joined the Irish Volunteers staff, was not impressed with their accomplishment. 'The fact is that Pearse and MacDonagh, Plunkett also, believed that the art of war could be studied in books.'[230] Although a lot went wrong in the manoeuvres, including a lack of men showing up, an attacking force that began its assault far too early and could not find the enemy's headquarters, Patrick was satisfied with the results.[231]

It was clear that the organisation was plagued by lack of military abilities and men, particularly outside Dublin. In one of his major articles in this period, 'Why We Want Recruits', published in May 1915 Patrick unintentionally made clear that there was a lot left to be desired. After calling for recruits to join he emphasised that the Volunteers were able to train them. Revealing that there were great doubts in the public mind about this he stated: 'The great majority of our officers are now fully competent to undertake the training of Irish Volunteers for active service ... Those officers who are not so competent will be made competent in our training camps during the next few months.' The same doubts existed concerning the ability of the Volunteers to arm its recruits. After assuring the reader that in 'a rough way of speaking, we have succeeded already in placing a gun and ammunition ... in the hands of every Irish Volunteer that has undertaken to endeavour to pay for them', he added: 'We are in a position to do as much for every man that joins us. We may not always have the popular pattern of gun, but we undertake to produce a gun of some sort for every genuine Irish Volunteer; with some ammunition to boot.' In other words the professionalism of the officers was questionable and the ability to arm the Volunteers very limited. An arms fund seems to have been unavailable so the men had to pay for their own weapons. Apparently the public perception of the Volunteers was so low that these deficiencies had to be acknowledged in a major recruiting effort in order to be taken seriously.[232]

The organisation also encountered hostility from other nationalists. The day after this article appeared a recruiting meeting in Limerick in which 1000 Volunteers from Dublin and Cork paraded through the town led by Patrick was jeered and pelted with garbage by sections of the crowd of onlookers. This certainly led to doubts that the country would rise in support of a revolution, and even caused fear that a confrontation between the Volunteers and supporters of Redmond would lead to the suppression of the Volunteers and scupper a rising. To avoid the likelihood of such a confrontation erupting, Patrick sent out an order in June forbidding any unauthorised discharge of firearms on pain of suspension.[233]

Whether or not the organisation was supported by the population became increasingly irrelevant to Patrick. In 'Why We Want Recruits' he made clear he no longer had any doubts about the righteousness of his course. 'We have no mis-givings, no self-questionings. While others have been doubting, timorous, ill at ease, we have been serenely at peace with our consciences. ... We have the strength and the peace of mind of those who never compromise.' Ironically considering their experience in Limerick the next day, he made clear he believed the tide was turning to them, 'to the party and to the men that stand *by Ireland only*', and that the destiny of Ireland was in their hands.

More members were needed because they were to free Ireland which is 'worthy of all love and all homage and all service that may lawfully be paid to any earthly thing'. He meant lawful to divine not to English law. Those who joined would get a definite task involving military action, as this would inevitably be forced upon the Volunteers. 'We do not anticipate such a moment in the very near future; but we live at a time when it may come swiftly and terribly.' He did not intimate any plans for an uprising but stuck to the official Volunteers' policy that they would not hesitate to act if conscription or partition would be forced upon them, the Home Rule Act repudiated or the Volunteers were disarmed. Although the IRB had now a very strong position on the Executive of the Volunteers they did not hold all levers of power. Eoin MacNeill was still the leader and together with the influential Hobson they opposed a rebellion without a direct cause.

Despite the certainty expressed in 'Why We Want Recruits' Patrick tried to broaden their base of supporters. The recruiting effort for the British Army and the formation of a coalition government, which involved the Conservatives and Ulster Unionists, undermined the position of the Irish Party and would he hoped turn people away from them. 'Redmond will not be in a position to make Asquith toe the line and it is very likely we might say good-by to the Home Rule Bill.'[234] In April 1915 he supported a protest meeting against a ban by the government on women activists attending an International Women's Peace Conference in The Hague. He called it 'another example of British policy to exclude Ireland from international debate' and added that much good would be done if the incident ranged more of the women definitely with the nationalist forces. This caused Margaret Connery of the Irish Women's Franchise League to reply that it should range more of the nationalist forces definitely with the women.[235] Ironically the meeting in The Hague was organised by pacifist suffragettes who rejected the call for nationalism and militarism, two themes Patrick wholeheartedly supported when they applied to Ireland.[236] Following a suggestion by a J.A. Lyons in December 1915 to set up a political organisation, Patrick tried to convince him to form an 'information bureau whose duty would be to diffuse information and educate public opinion by leaflets, pamphlets, press letters, etc.'.[237]

Patrick's growing radicalism lost him many friends he had made through the language movement. 'I saw nothing of him from the time he went into the volunteers & revolution. He seemed to be a different man altogether.'[238] His relationship with Eoin MacNeill was increasingly strained, but particularly his relationship with Douglas Hyde had deteriorated. Radicals within the movement had frequently attacked Hyde's apolitical attitude, and numerous attempts had been made to oust him from his position as president of the Gaelic League from the beginning of the century. Patrick always continued to support his presidency, although Hyde, who wanted to keep the League strictly apolitical, was appalled by his radicalism.[239] By August 1915 the forces railed against Hyde became too strong. At the Ard Fheis in Dundalk two imprisoned radicals were elected on the Coiste Gnotha apparently with the use of doubtful methods, and a motion declaring independence for Ireland the League objective was accepted against Hyde's will. Republicans claimed this was done to prevent an Irish Party takeover of the League, but Hyde was appalled by this politicisation of the organisation and resigned: 'I will never attach myself nor allow myself to be attached to any body of men which I might think wished to use the Irish language as a cloak for politics, I don't care what kind of politics.'[240]

Patrick's response seems to have been double edged. In the reprint of his 1913 articles from *Irish Freedom* he shortened the phrase 'I love and honour Douglas Hyde above all men who are leading us Irish today' to 'I love and honour Douglas Hyde', but he still defended Hyde in his fight to remain president of the League. 'O ye of little sense, know ye not when ye have got a good captain for a good cause? And know ye not that it is the duty of the soldier to follow his captain, unfaltering, unquestioning, "seeing obedience in the bond of rule"? If ye know not this, ye know not the first thing that a fighting man should know.'[241] This call for unquestioning loyalty was at least somewhat disingenuous considering the fact Patrick was planning an uprising behind MacNeill's back. Omar Crowley also believed Patrick's support for Hyde was insincere. Although Patrick had not been at the 1915 Ard Fheis, Crowley recalled meeting up with Patrick and some others after the resignation finding them in jubilant spirits, while at the same time sending out a deputation to Hyde to ask him to come back and refusing to appoint another president. 'This was sheer hypocrisy. The IRB had got control of G[aelic]League and was delighted.'[242] Patrick's ambivalence may well be associated with his loyalty to friends and an admiration for principled behaviour even if he disagreed with it. In a similar vain he defended Thomas Kettle's decision to join the British Army at a Volunteers' meeting. 'Whatever Kettle's faults were he had acted up to his own convictions and had joined up.'[243] This was also in line with the inclusive nature of Patrick's thinking and his abhorrence of divisions among the Irish.

> I propose that we take *service* as our touchstone, and reject all other touchstones: and that, without bothering our heads about sorting out, segregating and labelling Irishmen and Irish women according to their opinions, we agree to accept as fellow nationalists all who specifically or virtually recognize this Irish nation as an entity and, being part of it, owe it and give it their service.[244]

The most influential development in Patrick's political thinking in 1915 was his rapprochement with James Connolly. They met first in 1911 but had not then impressed each other.[245] The 1913 lockout caused Patrick to study James Connolly's *Labour in Irish History* and made him more aware of the plight of the poor. This was further strengthened by the rising food prices during the war. He argued that after the war 'nations can never again afford to despise the worth of the poor worker and the workers themselves will realise much better the purpose for which many of their lives have been sacrificed'.[246] Pearse, who had long admired Connolly's support for women's suffrage, also began to read his newspaper the *Workers' Republic*, and was increasingly influenced by the thinking of Fintan Lalor, one of the few nationalist icons who had shown a genuine concern for the welfare of the people and was advocated by Connolly.[247]

Patrick supported a number of socialist policies towards the end of his life which put the interest of the people as a whole over the individual, for instance in relation to the common ownership of means of production, distribution and exchange. In this way he fused his organic nationalism with a romantic socialism, which was reminiscent of the ideas of Rabindranath Tagore, the Indian nationalist and writer with which he had become acquainted. The ideas on independence of Indian nationalists were very similar to Patrick's.[248] They also celebrated a glorious past, the holy soil of India and advocated sacrifice. Patrick also admired the radicalism of labour and suffragettes in Britain and the progress of democracy as a forceful expression of the will of the people.[249] In the reprints of his articles from *Irish Freedom* he listed incongruities which ought to disgust:

'A millionaire promoting universal peace is such an incongruity; an employer who accepts the aid of foreign bayonets to enforce a lockout of his workmen and accuses the workmen of national dereliction because they accept foreign alms for their starving wives and children, is such an incongruity.'[250] The pamphlet was well received by Connolly who appreciated that Patrick was 'widely sympathetic to the struggles of the workers'.[251] During the war Connolly had left the internationalism of the socialist movement behind him and adhered to the belief that a social revolution in Ireland also must involve a separation from Britain. He also moved closer to Patrick's thinking on the need to shed blood: 'we recognise that of us, as of mankind before Calvary, it may truly be said "without the shedding of blood there is no redemption".'[252]

Connolly was also adamant Ireland was ready for a revolution. At the end of 1915 he described Ireland as a tinderbox which only needed a spark. This could be provided by an attack of a small group of men which would lead to a general uprising. The realistic Hobson famously replied that Ireland was a wet bog in which any spark would immediately be extinguished. His commitment to an uprising, however, brought Connolly increasingly closer to the IRB. An opportunity for a united purpose came with the funeral of the old Fenian leader Jeremiah O'Donovan Rossa in August 1915. The funeral was used to promote the Fenian cause and provided an opportunity to show a united front of the IRB, ICA and Volunteers. Tom Clarke who organised the proceedings made sure all prominent advanced nationalists were involved including Arthur Griffith, James Connolly, Eoin MacNeill and Constance Markievicz.

In an ultimate recognition of Patrick's prominence in the movement and acceptance of his propagandist talents he was chosen to give the graveside oration. In an opinion poll published in the newly launched and fiercely separatist paper *The Spark* in February 1915 Patrick had come out the sixth most prominent Irish nationalist whom Dublin most wished to honour, ahead of any other IRB man. He had clearly become the movement's biggest public asset. Upon asking Clarke how far he should go in the oration he was told: 'As far as you can. Make it as hot as hell, throw all discretion to the winds.' Patrick went to his cottage in Ros Muc to write the script in all tranquillity. He returned to a buzzing city excited in expectation of what was to come with thousands of uniformed Volunteers and ICA men and hundreds of thousands of spectators lining the streets. Patrick arrived in Dublin for the oration in an aggravated state mostly caused by a drunken countryman who kept insulting Patrick after he had asked him to stop smoking in a non-smoking carriage.[253]

O'Donovan Rossa was an ideal subject for Patrick to advertise his own thinking at this time. Not gifted with great intellectual powers Rossa's attraction to Patrick lay in his hatred for England, his uncompromising adherence to physical force and his advocacy of an Irish-Ireland. Clarke's choice was justified by Patrick's performance, as the oration had a great impact. In it he made clear the objective of all Irishmen could only be a totally free Ireland to be obtained through 'carrying out the **Fenian** programme'. He called upon all present to emulate Rossa's unshakable purpose, high and gallant courage, and unbreakable strength of soul to create the Ireland he envisioned: 'not free merely, but Gaelic as well; not Gaelic merely, but free as well'. And turned Rossa's hate of England into a Christian ideal to strive for: 'to hate evil, to hate untruth, to hate oppression, and, hating them, to strive to overthrow them'. He did not underestimate the strength of England but it would be unable to overcome the strength of the seeds sown by the young men of 1865 and 1867 which had come to their miraculous God-given ripening today. He ended his speech with the now famous words.

> Life springs from death; and from the graves of patriot men and women spring living nations. The Defenders of this Realm have worked well in secret and in the open. They think that they have pacified Ireland. They think that they have purchased half of us and intimidated the other half. They think that they have foreseen everything, think that they have provided against everything; but the fools, the fools, the fools! – they have left us our **Fenian** dead, and while Ireland holds these graves, Ireland unfree shall never be at peace.

Patrick was very happy with the proceedings, 'O'Donovan Rossa's funeral has been wonderful', and it affected those who witnessed it.[254] 'There is one memory I shall always treasure, it is the mental picture of him as he delivered his now famous oration on the graveside of O'Donovan Rossa. By sheer accident I was privileged to stand opposite to him at the grave as he uttered the words "The fools, the fools they have left us our Fenian dead". It would take an abler pen than mine to paint the picture of the speaker or the effect of his words on the crowd.'[255] But the oration not only stirred those present, it had a wide impact: 'its effect on the listener who was present and on the masses in the country who read it was tremendous. The oration soon became the favourite recitation at concerts and social entertainments all over the country. I have heard it recited in railway journeys to football and hurling matches. It was accepted everywhere as a brilliant exposition of our national faith.'[256]

The proceedings further enhanced Patrick's public standing and value to the movement. The oration was even published in full in the *Freeman's Journal*.[257] To others, however, he became increasingly unacceptable. This caused some Redmond supporters to initiate an attempt to bankrupt him. Apparently on instigation of the Lord Chancellor the solicitor acting for the owners, Sir John Robert O'Connell, demanded the rent for the Hermitage upfront. This was not established practice and only occurred after O'Connell was told that Patrick was 'in a very dangerous position'. After consultation with leading Redmondites he had decided to take out a legal writ. The affair brought Patrick immediately down to earth and with some humour Patrick wrote to McGarrity that the Lord Chancellor must have been 'referring to my political rather than my financial position'. Nevertheless, Patrick did not have the £300 he needed to pay within fourteen days to stave off bankruptcy. 'We are all convinced that it is part of a move to discredit me in the eyes of the public. It is their way of hitting at me. They will represent me as a bankrupt and discredited man who takes refuge in "advanced" politics and hides his failure to meet his creditors by preaching sedition.' Without the money it was not only Patrick and the school which would suffer, but it would 'discredit the whole cause' and 'impair most seriously, if not fatally, my public influence and utility'.[258]

To keep St Enda's open Patrick already increasingly relied on financial support from Clan na Gael, but now he was forced to turn to them again. In his efforts to convince McGarrity, Patrick did not rely anymore on his references to the vital role St Enda's played in the regeneration of the Irish nation, but now also used political arguments. Letting St Enda's die he claimed did not scare him anymore at this point, as his political work had overtaken his educational mission. 'I could bear to see it [St Enda's] go down gloriously by my imprisonment for a political offence, but to see it go down squalidly as the result of such a plot would be heart breaking.'[259] He also made clear that going over to the States to earn the money himself by lecturing would at this point be a desertion of the cause. McGarrity duly complied with Patrick's request, who then again moved quickly from despair to optimism. He thanked McGarrity profusely and assured him no more money was needed the rest of the year. 'We have a bigger school than last year, and on the whole a more promising lot of boys. So I am full of hope.'[260]

The growing public attention to advanced nationalists did not benefit the IRB's position in the Volunteers. At the Convention of 31 October 1915, the insurrectionists took fourteen out of twenty seats on the Executive, but there was no clear takeover and MacNeill and Hobson remained in function.[261] Neither had the public enthusiasm led to strong growth in the number of Volunteers. Although Hobson reported an increased strength, most counties still did not have a representation on the General Council. Four organisers had been appointed at the beginning of 1915, but in July two of them, Ernest Blythe and Liam Mellows, were arrested after failing to obey an order to leave the country. MacNeill was still able to prevent the attempt by some Volunteers and ICA members to take action in response to the arrests. New organisers were then appointed. The fortunes of the Irish Volunteers, however, experienced a positive turn towards the end of 1915. In particular their anti-recruiting stance following the introduction of conscription in Great Britain found increasing support.

During 1915 Patrick started in some way to clear the deck. In a letter to Desmond Ryan's father of 5 March he remarked: 'I am keeping myself sane by working a little at intervals at old plays and stories of mine; I am, so to speak, setting my literary affairs in order.'[262] The following week he tried to interest an English publisher to bring out an English translation of three of his Irish plays, *An Rí*, *Íosogán* and a third up to then unpublished one. He is, however, not very hopeful about this. 'I suppose they would hardly be in fashion at the moment.'[263] During his stay in Ros Muc to write the graveside oration for O'Donovan Rossa in the summer he had also put together a collection of his short stories. In November he republished two pamphlets with older work, *From a Hermitage* and *How Does She Stand?*. The latter originally published in 1914 brought together the Emmet Commemoration addresses he had given in Brooklyn and New York in March 1914 with his Wolfe Tone Commemoration of

22 June 1913 in Bodenstown. He had 2000 copies printed of both pamphlets which were distributed through James Whelan, a bookseller specialised in separatist literature.[264] He also continued to write new material. Between February 1915 and January 1916 he contributed a serial to *The Fianna* about boys in a boarding school called 'The Wandering Hawk', and also wrote a play and three new stories with a religious theme for a collection of Irish short stories for adults published in January 1916.

The final exposé of Patrick's thinking on Irish nationality came in a set of four pamphlets he completed around Christmas 1915. These can be seen as an attempt to secure his legacy and also played a further part in bringing Patrick closer together with James Connolly by the elevation of Lalor to the pantheon of Irish nationalist heroes next to Wolfe Tone, John Mitchel and Thomas Davis. In the months before the Rising Patrick's political activity in public confined itself to presenting some lectures and keeping in touch with activists in the country and abroad.[265] However, most of his doings involved secret work in preparation of a rising.

16.   Pearse family

17. Patrick and Willie in conversation

18. Patrick during a public speech

19.   Patrick in military uniform

20.   The surrender by Patrick after Easter week

5 Revolutionary

When I was a child of ten I went down on my bare knees by my bedside one night and promised God that I should devote my life to an effort to free my country.[1]

Early life

Shortly before his execution Patrick made this direct link between his early years and his involvement in the Rising. We have, however, seen that his political ideas did not show such a connection. When in 1915 his brother Willie recalled taking the above-mentioned oath Patrick had to laugh heartily but admitted he had forgotten about it.[2] In line with his father's active campaign for home rule within the British Empire the oath possibly referred to his youthful desire to help achieve that objective. In his later teens he became more explicitly nationalistic but was convinced, as many others were then, that it was hopeless to fight the military might of the British Empire. In 1898 he asserted that the Irish were not a fighting race and would never become powerful enough to overcome the English militarily. Consequently he concentrated on efforts to gain freedom through a process of cultural regeneration and asserted that political independence was ultimately unimportant.

The concentration on the language over all other issues struck James Mullin, who met Patrick at the Pan-Celtic Congress in Cardiff in 1899. 'He was a young man and neither in appearance nor in manner a revolutionary or even a political partisan, and the very last man whom I should have taken to be a leader in rebellion. He struck me as being an idealist with his head in the clouds, and he looked the part to perfection.' He did add that Patrick appeared to him as 'a man of one idea, and such a man is always dangerous, if not to others, to himself, even though their motives are most pure and patriotic'.[3]

The first hints of a more activist attitude came at the time of the first Boer War (1899–1902). The military successes of the Boers influenced many nationalists in thinking that the British might be vulnerable after all. James Connolly, the fellow leader of the 1916 Rising, wrote in the *Workers Republic* of 18 November 1899: 'the Boers have pricked the bubble of England's fighting reputation'.[4] In 1900 Fr Francis McEnerney could warn an audience of language enthusiasts to great laughter and applause, that if the influence of the English language was allowed to come into Ireland unchecked the youth of Ireland would soon become 'like the little effeminate corner boys of the English cities who would run away from the sight of a Boer, aye, even of a black'.[5] Even the leading Gaelic Leaguer Prof. O'Growney argued in 1899 that: 'We have now a literary movement, it is not very important; it will be followed by a political movement, that will not be very important; then must come a military movement, that will be important indeed.'[6]

The excitement surrounding the Boer War and the centenary of the 1798 Rebellion did inspire a certain rise in the fortunes of the Gaelic League and advanced nationalists. Sentiments ran so high that the authorities even began to fear an insurrection. Although not part of any organisation, Patrick became got caught up in the excitement. During a visit to Birmingham he told his cousin that: 'he was not coming here any more that he was going to the peasants who spoke Irish henceforth for his holidays and the first one he would teach Irish to he would give him a gun'. In a direct reference to events in the Boer War he informed her of his plans to import pianos from America. When she asked him 'Can't you get pianos from England?' He said 'Yes, but these pianos are full of guns.' This mirrored a story going around that Cecil Rhodes had smuggled guns into Johannesburg under the guise of bringing in pianos.[7] Apart from this there are few signs of an interest in political action at this time.

As a rule Patrick was unimpressed with either overt or covert separatists prior to 1913. He accused them of all talk and no action. The IRB (Irish Repulican Brotherhood) had indeed become not much more than a socialising platform for old men who had been involved in radical politics in the 1860s: 'Fenians of Pearse's time were impressive wise looking bearded figures like Hebrew prophets much more sapient looking than they really were.'[8] When he started to attend republican meetings around 1910 he did not hesitate to make his disdain for them clear. At one of these he was heavily criticised after he called from the floor for a fair treatment of Irish Party members whom he described as fellow Irishmen. This attack led Patrick to a stinging reply: 'what do we do in our meetings but talk, talk, talk and carp at the Parliamentarians who are, after all, Irishmen like ourselves? You want to free Ireland without taking into account the people, without which you are helpless. And, once more, how will you know the people if you do not steep yourselves in the Gaelic sources of the Irish Nation?' He finished up with a rousing call: 'Yes, give me a hundred men and I will free Ireland!' On his way home from the meeting he told Desmond Ryan: 'Let them talk! I am the most dangerous revolutionary of the whole lot of them!'[9] Although this probably referred to the effect of his work for the Gaelic League and in St Enda's, it showed a clear contempt for the revolutionary credentials of those professing to work towards an independent republic.

Despite the early flirt with the use of force, Patrick did not have any inclination to join or instigate an actual revolutionary movement in the first decade of the twentieth century. He realised that the public enthusiasm generated by the Boer successes had not fundamentally altered the military position of Ireland. However, he did apparently see a possibility of future action. In the Irish language prospectus for St Enda's of 1908 a line was added which did not appear in the English version: 'It will be attempted to inculcate in them [the pupils] the desire to spend their lives working hard and zealously for their fatherland and, if it should ever be necessary, to die for it.'[10] Although not an overt part of the curriculum, such an ethos became increasingly prevalent in the school after 1910. Patrick 'believed that every man should know how to use a rifle. In his talks to his students, he always stressed the fact that every generation of Irishmen should have a rising in arms. He stressed it in such a way that you felt impelled to believe that he did actually believe there should be some attempt.'[11]

Only after the move of St Enda's to the Hermitage and the advent of the home rule crisis did Patrick come into close contact with the IRB. This seems to have been initiated by his attempt to obtain financial support for the school from Patrick McCartan. Tom Clarke, who had been approached by McCartan for support, made clear that from what he had heard he did not trust Patrick's type of nationalism. Patrick was subsequently forced to articulate and defend his stance. He managed to convince McCartan, but Clarke continued to distrust him.[12] Although the first contact was thus fraught, this episode nevertheless seems to have been the lead-up to the invitation speech at the Emmet Commemoration Concert they planned to hold in the Dublin Rotunda in March 1911. Sean MacDermott, the IRB's national organiser and close associate of Tom Clarke, suggested that Patrick might be the person to give the oration. It was again Clarke who seems to have objected. 'Pearse, he said, might be a good Gaelic Leaguer but he had never been identified with the separatists.' MacDermott then brought the two together to talk. Patrick emphasised to Clarke that his support for home rule was only on the basis that 'if we can get complete control of Education we can get a Republic'. This apparently convinced Clarke and he withdrew his opposition.[13]

Patrick did not disappoint. The audience was enthused and even Clarke remarked afterwards: 'I never thought there was such stuff in Pearse.' In the excitement following the speech McCartan jumped on the platform and proposed a resolution condemning the proposed visit of the King of England to Dublin. Tom Clarke supported McCartan and the resolution was passed by a cheering audience.[14] This seems to have precipitated a crisis in the IRB itself, which had become divided between the veterans of the nineteenth century movement and a group of young activists led by Clarke. The old leadership had forbidden any explicit provocations of the authorities, but after some hesitation Clarke had judged this might be a good opportunity to take them on.

For some time the radical young men had been trying to get the organisation more openly involved in political activity. This had resulted in the launch of their newspaper *Irish Freedom* in 1911, but they were still forbidden to act openly. Following the Emmet commemoration Clarke and McCartan were court-martialled for breach of discipline, but they were acquitted and the old leadership was then ousted.[15] The new Supreme Council was filled with young radicals, with Clarke as treasurer, and MacDermott as secretary.[16] The oration had made clear to the new leaders of the IRB that Patrick was a powerful asset as a public speaker, and could be of use in the future. He was able to articulate the need for action and was also acceptable to most nationalists. Clarke nevertheless remained suspicious of Patrick. When his wife asked him and MacDermott later why they did not get rid of Patrick if they did not trust him they argued that he represented a certain class whose support they needed.[17]

Patrick was not as pliable as Clarke may have hoped. His conditional support for home rule expressed on a public platform in Dublin's O'Connell Street a year later only confirmed suspicion concerning his reliability. Although St Enda's physical education teacher, Con Colbert, was a member of the IRB who recruited many of the older pupils around this time, Patrick was not yet deemed acceptable. Eamonn Bulfin, one of Patrick's former students who resided at St Enda's, claims to have proposed Patrick as a member in 1912 but various objections were raised. His political support for the Irish Council Bill in 1907 and the current Home Rule Bill had made him a controversial figure in IRB circles, but his obsession with the language to the detriment of political activity, his financial dealings and even the fact his father was an Englishman were also held against him.[18]

Between 1911 and 1913 Patrick nevertheless gradually grew closer to IRB circles. With MacDermott he was involved in setting up an Irish-Ireland benefit society. A kind of insurance company created to serve as an Irish alternative for working men who were obliged to take out cover under the new Insurance Act. At the same time his brother Willie became a member of the Wolfe Tone and United Irishmen Memorial Committee together with most of the members of the Supreme Council of the IRB.[19] Patrick became convinced something had to change. To his pupils he referred to the need for a rebellion: 'I would rather see all Dublin in ruins than that we should go on living as we are at present.'[20] The poems he collected in this period for his anthology *Songs of the Irish Rebels* were mostly about exile and death.[21] During 1913 plans were becoming increasingly real and Patrick was again considered as someone who could be functional for propaganda purposes. One of the first expressions of this was the request to write a series of articles for *Irish Freedom* starting in June 1913 followed by a demand from the editor of *An Claidheamh Soluis* for a political analysis in July.[22]

Patrick's role in founding the Irish Volunteers in October 1913 and his position on its Provisional Committee and as Director of Organisation enhanced his usefulness for the insurrectionists, but considerable doubts remained whether he could become a member of the IRB. The actual reason for eventually swearing Patrick in was simply to give him easier access to the Irish-American organisation

Clan na Gael.[23] At the confirmation meeting Patrick's name was apparently omitted when the list of candidates for membership was read out for fear it might encounter opposition and the officer in charge was anxious to get him through to help him collect in the United States.[24]

Patrick was initially not an enthusiastic member. At the first meeting he attended he sat quietly at the back, and he was kept out of further meetings of his own circle because of his by then high public profile and the consequent risks of detection by the police.[25] Apparently he was not entirely happy with the secretive underground nature of the movement. Shortly before the Rising he told Frank Fahey that 'The IRB is necessary because we must keep our counsel, but as soon as an Irishman can declare himself a republican openly there should be an end of the IRB.'[26] In the early months of 1914 he nevertheless became more and more convinced the use of force was necessary. Early in 1914 he was doubtful when Hobson reiterated the idea mooted by Roger Casement in 1912 that there would be a major war within ten years which would give them an opportunity for insurrection.[27] During their conversations in the US where Patrick and Hobson again met it appears their differences concerned the military strength of the British and not so much whether or not a war would break out.[28]

After his return from the United States in May 1914 Patrick got closely involved in the planning of a rising. Many have argued that his confrontation with unreconstructed Fenians in the US had convinced him his generation was in danger of failing where the previous generations all had their attempt.[29] However, although these meetings may well have inspired Patrick, he had already advertised his conviction that Ireland should be liberated before going to the United States. It was the founding of the Volunteers which seems to have made this a real possibility in his mind. Before his trip to the US he had publicly advocated an armed Ireland.[30] He emphasised this further in a speech to Tralee Volunteers on 4 July 1914: 'They in Ireland to-day were again learning the nobility and dignity of military discipline and military service. It seemed almost like a dream coming true – they had at long last an Irish army.' The present generation could therewith realise the dream of the generations before them, and determine Ireland's political future.[31]

Within the IRB it was the foundation of the Volunteers and increasingly the looming war that spurred the men into action.

Plans for an uprising seem to have moved fairly quickly. There were apparently calls to have a rebellion in 1914, but this was rejected by the casting vote of Clarke who wanted to build up their hold on the Volunteers first.[32] In a confidential letter to McGarrity Patrick indicated that a rising starting in Dublin was already on the cards in July, a month before the outbreak of the First World War. 'We owe it to these men to arm them; we shall be stultified forever if we allow the chance to go by. We propose to commence in Dublin, which is the soundest, and where we have most influence.' Apart from Dublin he believed they could rely on the Volunteers in Cork City and County, Limerick City, Waterford City, Galway City, Co. Kerry and 'a large minority everywhere, including all the best men – the young, active men'. To facilitate the importation of arms he asked the Americans to send someone to Europe to purchase them there and pass them on. 'Of course you would not land guns until we had completed all arrangements for receiving and distributing them.' He offered to pay for part of the cost by having companies keep their arms funds away from the Provisional or Standing Committees which were then still controlled by Redmondites.[33]

The actual outbreak of the Great War was the final push. At a meeting in September it was decided to have a rebellion during the war.[34] However, their hold on the Volunteers was tenuous and had been further eroded by the resignation of Bulmer Hobson from the IRB's Supreme Council following his support for the acceptance of Redmond's nominees on the Executive Committee of the Volunteers. To ensure a strong turn-out attempts were now made to forge an alliance with the Irish Citizens Army led by James Connolly who was very keen to initiate a rebellion. A meeting was held on 9 September between leading ICA and IRB men, which included Patrick.[35] Apart from confirming the commitment to a rising during the war with the objective of strengthening the Irish case at a post-war peace conference, it was decided to try to develop various organisations including Fianna Eireann and Cumann na mBan, to assist a German invasion if it occurred, and to resist any attempt to disarm the Volunteers. In preparation two subcommittees were formed in relation to securing German aid and for planning an armed insurrection.[36]

The subcommittee or advisory committee organising an insurrection was formed by Eamonn Ceannt, Joseph Plunkett and Patrick Pearse. Patrick's membership was primarily based on his central position in the Volunteers organisation and surprised some in the IRB as he was not yet on the Supreme Council. As Director of Organisation Patrick was also responsible for drawing up plans for the Volunteers to resist the possible introduction of conscription.[37] An important function of the committee was to control the ICA which was likely to strike out by itself in the belief that if an uprising was started the people would follow.[38] The optimism generated by the cooperation between radical forces was thrown in disarray by the split in the Irish Volunteers following Redmond's call on 20 September to support the British war effort wherever the firing line extended. Those who believed that the defence of Ireland itself was the real task of the Volunteers only formed a small section of the organisation. This faction was still led by MacNeill and Hobson neither of whom supported an uprising.

The end to the wrangling in the Volunteers organisation following the split certainly pleased Patrick, but the likelihood of a successful attempt to overthrow the government with the aid of the Volunteers had diminished. The following months, however, Patrick became more optimistic and more openly committed to a rising. The positive united attitude in the movement after the split exhilarated him: 'A meeting of Dublin officers the other night was as exhilarating as a draught of wine.' Obtaining arms was the main obsession of the movement at this time because action might be forced upon them soon, by a German invasion, the introduction of conscription, a shortage of food, or by a government attempt to disarm them or arrest their leaders. In private Patrick also left room for proactive action once they were properly armed.[39]

The Irish Volunteers had held on to about 500–600 of the 1500 illegally imported rifles following the split. In October Patrick turned to McGarrity for funds. He informed him that he knew from reading the *Gaelic American* that the Clan na Gael had collected at least $27,000 for the Volunteers but that they had received only $5000. Getting arms, he emphasised, may mean the difference between failure and success. Without it a rising would be 'either a bloody debacle like '98 or a dreary fizzling out like '48 or '67.' He implored him not to send the money to MacNeill or other men of his thinking. 'Not that I doubt their honesty but simply that they are not in or of our counsels and they are not formally pledged to strike, if the chance comes, for the complete thing.' Possibly in an attempt to convince McGarrity he expressed a lot of faith in the ordinary members of the movement which he optimistically estimated had grown to 10,000–15,000 men as a result of the popularity of their anti-recruitment stance: 'It seems a big thing to say, but I do honestly believe that, with arms for these men we shall be ready to *act* with tremendous effect if the war brings us the moment.'[40] In the end the Clan sent over money to Ireland totalling about $100,000 between 1913 and 1916, but arms were difficult to obtain and even at the start of the Rising in 1916 the Volunteers had just 2000 guns.[41]

In the meantime the organisation was forced to concentrate again on its three official aims to 'arm, train and organise the men of Ireland'. Arming was done not only through Patrick's attempt to obtain money from Irish-Americans, but unknown to him also by contacting Germany directly. The Clan had approached the German ambassador in the US and had sent Roger Casement to Germany to try to convince them to send troops, provide arms for a rising, to define Irish independence as a German war aim and to raise a brigade from among the Irish prisoners of war in Germany. Patrick was not keen on a direct link with the Germans as he rejected foreign interference of any kind, but he accepted their support for practical purposes. Later he would even contemplate the enthronement of a German prince as Irish king to facilitate de-anglicisation.[42]

Increasing attention was also paid to training the men, as most members of the Volunteers had no military experience. This applied both to separatists and those simply committed to defending Ireland. As Patrick put it fairly grandly: 'We are daily perfecting their fighting effectiveness and mobilising power.'[43] In reality this merely meant that the Volunteers were drilling and marching. In early 1915 an intensive course of special lectures for Dublin brigade officers was introduced. Patrick gave some and James Connolly provided a number on street fighting, which Piaras Béaslaí considered very useful and practical. It was said by some that these were based on Connolly's experience in Mexico.[44] In June and July these were published in the *Workers' Republic*. Some large-scale manoeuvres were also undertaken including a night training exercise in the city, and an Aeridheacht on 6 September at St Enda's.[45] This was really a military display with Volunteers drill and shooting competitions, Cumann na mBan displays, marches, and pipe bands. With a deputation of the Irish Citizens Army and the Hibernian Rifles, the military wing of a small radical faction of the Ancient Order of Hibernians, it brought together all those who later participated in the rising.[46]

At the same time the number of Volunteers organisers was raised to six to create a nationwide network of units, and a general council of Volunteers officers was established to enable direct contact with country units.[47] Piaras Béaslaí states on the basis of his diary entries that a great deal of attention was paid to discussing plans for action early in 1915. Various positions were visited armed with maps, and Béaslaí and Thomas Ashe submitted various schemes to Plunkett on 15 February.[48] Information was also collected by the various battalions on the military barracks in Dublin. Michael Staines even got inside Islandeady Barracks with the aid of a soldier.[49]

Patrick also toured the country to mobilise Volunteers. In his speeches he became increasingly explicit about their objectives. On 26 September 1915 he returned to his favoured theme of armed citizenship in Enniscorthy calling 'unarmed citizens' a contradiction in terms. Being a citizen to him implied rights and duties, including the duty to secure and maintain the rights and liberties of the country, and only an armed person could do so. He implored his audience never to give up their arms, 'the guarantee of your citizenship, and the symbol of your manhood', and defined their goal as the same as their fathers': 'We ask no more, and we will take no less.' The use of force he argued had aided the Ulster Volunteers to prevent the introduction of home rule and so it will help the Irish Volunteers. He also called upon the principle of self-determination which was obviously already public knowledge even before the entry of the United States into the war. 'In the near future new nations will be written on the map, so what about Ireland?'[50]

These activities did worry the authorities. The mounting casualties and lack of progress in the war in Europe meant recruiting had become increasingly unpopular. The Irish Volunteers, who were closely associated with the anti-recruiting campaign, witnessed a rise in support. However, it was felt suppressing them was too difficult. Only those who were conspicuously active against the government such as those engaged in the anti-recruiting campaign were prosecuted. In this manner, two Volunteers organisers were banished from Ireland in July 1915. In many ways this only aided the separatists as it papered over the internal differences and united the leaders. Patrick was afraid he would be arrested too, but instead of taking direct action, the authorities instigated the unsuccessful attempt in August to bankrupt him by demanding the rent for his school buildings upfront.[51]

Planning a rising

The plans to start an uprising became more concrete during 1915. In May the time was fixed for September and a Military Committee was formed which superseded the Advisory Committee but had the same line-up which included Patrick. According to Alec McCabe, a member of the Supreme Council: 'The purpose of this committee was to look after military organisation. I understood the appointments were to be in the nature of a Military Staff.' Another member saw its task as 'drafting plans for an Insurrection'.[52] Subsequently the idea of an uprising was also raised in a meeting of the Irish Volunteers' Executive held on 30 May. According to British intelligence Bulmer Hobson proposed a motion in favour of an immediate resurrection which was only defeated by the casting vote of Eoin MacNeill.[53] This seems unlikely as Hobson was a proponent of those who felt a rising required the support of the majority of the people. It is nevertheless conceivable that the clampdown by the authorities on the Volunteers initiated this idea. However, the September date passed apparently due to the absence of arms.[54]

In a meeting of the IRB Supreme Council that month, new plans were drawn up. The insurrection policy was now formally adopted despite some discussion of its legality according to the IRB constitution. The composition of the council was reshuffled after its president Deakin retired and due to some imprisonments and releases. Dennis McCullough was elected President. McCullough who was based in Belfast felt he was unsuitable and had wanted to propose Patrick but MacDermott had prevented this arguing that Patrick could not be controlled. McCullough's enforced absence from Dublin gave Clarke and MacDermott, the treasurer and secretary respectively, the freedom to run the organisation to their own designs.[55]

Patrick had been made a member of the Supreme Council shortly before this meeting. He was there as the direct representative of the Irish Volunteers, being the highest officer in the IRB. The exact timing of his cooptation is somewhat unclear. Members recall a different sequence of events, placing it either in May, August or September. It is clear, however, that the Military Committee was extended by the appointment of Clarke and MacDermott at the meeting in September, which effectively meant that they together with Patrick were running the show. The committee started to meet in Ceantt's house and was possibly renamed the Military Council at this time, although this may also have been done retrospectively. One member does remember discussing whether having a Military Council was constitutional, which may have led to an official redesignation.[56]

Subsequently plans became more tangible and were based on three propositions. First, the success of the rising was made contingent on arms coming from Germany. Patrick sent Diarmuid Lynch to identify suitable places for an arms landing in the southwest and Joseph Plunkett went to the United States to get support for procuring German arms.[57] In August 1915 Robert Monteith was sent over to Germany via New York.[58] The actual details of the rising also started to take shape. The focus on Dublin in the initial plans of early 1915, when the rising was meant as means to awaken the people, was substituted with an effort to stage an all Ireland rising. Patrick had been a strong proponent of the centrality of Dublin, inspired by his conviction that Dublin had to atone for the shame of failing to aid Robert Emmet when he staged his rebellion in 1803.[59] There was also a current in IRB thinking which emphasised that the control of Dublin and Dublin Castle was central to the success of an uprising. Already in September 1913 an article had appeared in *Irish Freedom* which suggested that had Emmet taken Dublin Castle the country would have risen.[60] From September onwards attempts were made to involve country officers by frequent visits of the Volunteers Executive, Patrick being particularly prominent in this. The final proposition was the idea to use the Easter manoeuvres as a cover for staging the rising, based on the experiences of those held at Easter 1915.[61] The seriousness with which the preparations were engaged in was witnessed by the decision at the September meeting to provide all members of the Military Council with bodyguards.[62]

The increasingly visible preparations for a rising brought the insurrectionists in growing conflict with the section of the Volunteers which opposed this. In September 1915 MacNeill had overheard Patrick giving instructions of a military nature to a local officer in Limerick, which kindled his suspicions about the intentions of the radicals. However, maybe partly due to his long-standing friendship with

Patrick and his tendency to avoid conflict, he accepted the assertion that there were no plans to initiate a rising but that they were just preparing for the eventuality of conflict with the authorities. Others in the Volunteers Executive increasingly opposed the idea of a *coup d'état* in the form of an open insurrection. Hobson, supported by the military experts J.J. O'Connell and Eimar Duffy, suggested in the *Irish Volunteer* that guerrilla warfare would stand a much greater chance of success. An alternative plan designed by Ginger O'Connell gained support in late 1915 among the Volunteers, but Hobson claimed Patrick was unwilling to be convinced: 'I cannot answer your arguments, but I feel that we must have insurrection.'[63] A similar conviction that at some point practical considerations, intellectual arguments, and personal soul-searching must give way to commitment, based on an unquestioning faith, is also very much apparent in his contemporary play 'The Master'.[64] Others recall Patrick emphasising more explicitly at this time that they 'must have a sacrifice'.[65]

Clearing the deck

By the end of 1915 Patrick started clearing the deck intellectually by setting out his thinking on nationalism in a series of four pamphlets which were all published shortly before the rising. In *Ghosts*, the first of these pamphlets finished on Christmas Day 1915, he challenges the attitude of the previous generation in relation to Irish independence. Their emphasis on political independence over spiritual nationality had given them the false idea that freedom could be bargained over. To Patrick freedom had become a spiritual necessity which could not be given up for wealth or easy living, a by-product of a negotiated settlement such as home rule. Freedom to him was like a divine religion. It 'bears the marks of unity, of sanctity, of catholicity, and of apostolic succession'. He thus considered the nation as one, as holy, as embracing all the men and women of the nation, and it or the aspiration for it as passed down from generation to generation. The substance of freedom was to him also unchanging like a religious truth. 'A nation's fundamental idea of freedom is not affected by the accidents of time and circumstance. It does not vary with the centuries, or with the comings and goings of men or of empires.' Therefore Patrick's conception of freedom was and should be exactly the same as that of those before him, most importantly like Wolfe Tone's, Thomas Davis's, Fintan Lalor's and John Mitchel's whom he defined as the four fathers of Irish freedom. To them only total freedom was acceptable; a freedom achieved not conceded.

In the pamphlet he then traced the history of Irish resistance since 1169 and asserted the presence of a continuous link both in thought and in person in the rejection of the English presence which had ensured the continued existence of the Irish nation. Those who had repudiated the need for separation, like Grattan, O'Connell and most recently Redmond, had, he claimed, ultimately been rejected by the people. Now that home rule had become unlikely to materialise and support for it had diminished during the war, the Irish Party had failed, not nobly like the other generations before them but shamefully: 'The men who have led Ireland for twenty-five years have done evil, and they are bankrupt. They are bankrupt in policy, bankrupt in credit, bankrupt now even in words. They have nothing to propose to Ireland, no way of wisdom, no counsel of courage.' In a reference to his own and his family's support of Parnell he wondered whether it was the Irish Party's attitude to Parnell that was punished with their loss of manhood. It has been argued that by thus retracing past experience he was establishing a legal precedent for his own actions.[66]

In the other three pamphlets Patrick discussed the importance of the thinking of what he termed 'the four gospels of the new testament of Irish nationality', that is the writings of the fathers of Irish freedom. 'Now, the truth as to what a nation's nationality is, what a nation's freedom, is not to be found in the statute-book of the nation's enemy. It is to be found in the books of the nation's fathers.' Tone, Davis, Lalor and Mitchel had laid down the conception of Irish nationality, anyone else should simply be seen as commentators on them except maybe Parnell 'who saw most deeply and who spoke most splendidly for the Irish nation'.

In *The Separatist Idea* Wolfe Tone is put forward as 'the greatest man of our nation'. He is portrayed as the original founder of Irish nationality, as a separatist and the first Irish democrat. Basing his thinking closely on the ideas of the Enlightenment he drew a comparison between the rights of nations and the rights of men in that every nation should be free to pursue welfare and happiness. Tone believed that England stood in the way of Ireland's happiness, and that the connection with England was inherently detrimental to

Ireland. Patrick summed up Tone's thinking in a number of simple propositions: the people are the nation and the Irish nation was one. It had an indefeasible right to freedom, which was necessary for its happiness and prosperity. A free nation would guarantee true personal freedom and the pursuit of happiness of the nation and of the individuals that compose that nation. Sovereignty was upheld against other nations and over all parts of the nation, therefore the nation had jurisdiction over lives and property within the nation. Patrick believed God thus spoke through Tone, and therefore everyone should accept his thinking.

The main contribution of Thomas Davis, according to Patrick, was set out in *The Spiritual Nation* and concerned the idea that a nation was not just a group of people but had a spirit of its own. A spirit which could be compared to the soul of a person, and which lived within the language in its broadest sense, consisting not only of the sounds and idiom but also of its literature and folklore. This national spirit could only reveal itself entirely in a free nation, in its institutions, the arts and the inner life and actions of the nation. Whether Ireland was a truly great nation could only be known when it was entirely free. The suppression of old nations like the Irish therefore was a terrible thing. This concept also accounts for Patrick's original conviction that cultural regeneration was more important than political independence. After all independence could be gained and lost, but once a nation had died out it could never be revived.

The final pamphlet, *The Sovereign People*, discussed the contributions of Lalor and Mitchel. It developed the idea of external and internal sovereignty originally put forward by Tone. Lalor had made clear to Pearse that physical freedom was necessary to keep a nation alive. That only a particularly vigorous nation like the Irish could survive being subjugated by another nation for a length of time, but there now was a danger the Irish nation would succumb like the Maya's or Etruscan's of the past. In a sense this mirrors Patrick's development from a cultural nationalist in the style of Davis to a political activist in the early part of the 1910s.

Particularly influential was also Lalor's assertion that the public right of the nation stood above the private right of the individual, and that the nation should control the conditions for life including the nation's soil and its resources. This relates directly to Patrick's growing sympathy for the poor and the labour movement between

1913 and 1916. Falling short of becoming a socialist Patrick accepted that the nation, which meant all men and women in it, had the right to determine the extent of private property and political rights. The right of private property was 'the right of man to possess, enjoy, and transfer the substance and use of whatever HE HAS HIMSELF CREATED', which excluded ownership of the soil or natural resources. This concept made all kinds of arrangements to organise society possible, even a socialist form. To him such practicalities were human and not divine or sacrosanct and therefore should be freely decided upon by the people.

He was convinced that working in the interest of the nation was also in the interest of the individual. The pursuit of prosperity and happiness for the nation was nothing more than the pursuit of prosperity and happiness of all the individuals which made up the nation. To him the nation was a natural unit with a common bond given by God, just like the family. In a free nation everybody would be equal, with no class of people having more rights or powers. He contrasted this positively with an empire which was held together only by mutual interest or brute force and was manmade, if not by the devil.

The second half of the last pamphlet reflects Patrick's final acceptance of the necessity of the use of physical force. It discusses Mitchel's writings, in particular his jail journal, which strongly advocated a peasant revolution and expressed an almost irrational hatred of England. At a debate on Thomas Davis for the Trinity College Gaelic Society in November 1914 Patrick had argued that Mitchel's gospel was higher than that of Davis's, which had caused Yeats to lament that Pearse had now elevated Mitchel's hatred of England above Davis's love for Ireland.[67] Patrick now directly confronted this allegation. He asserted that hate is not just evil or barren, but that love and hate are complementary and similar. A love of good is a hate of evil, and they can both be pure or evil. Mitchel did not hate England but hated England's government of Ireland, hated empire and English commercialism supported by militarism. These things needed to be destroyed, and destruction was not always bad. Like physical force, high winds or lightning were not bad but did have the power to destroy. In the end destruction was needed for construction in the same way as life springs from death.

In his summing up Patrick defined his four idols. Tone should be seen as the intellectual father of Irish nationalism, Davis as the father of the spiritual and imaginative part of that movement, embodied in the Gaelic League, Lalor as the father of the democratic strain, embodied in the Labour movement, and Mitchel as the father of Fenianism: 'the noblest and most terrible manifestation of this unconquered nation'. They were all parts of a whole which came together in Patrick himself. He had been part of all these movements and now brought their thinking together in a synthesis. In his judgement Patrick clearly describes the development of his own thinking from a Parnellite to a cultural nationalist, and his recent move towards social radicalism and finally to rebellion. He asked all who accepted his analysis to stand with him under the Irish flag and fight for freedom. Finishing up with the assertion that Mitchel had not lived to see this day as he had wished, but 'the day of the Lord is here, and you and I have lived to see it. And we are young. And God has given us strength and courage and counsel. May He give us victory.'

At the time of writing this ideological testament the militarisation of his thinking had become manifest in an article he published in the separatist paper the *Spark* in December 1915. In it he analysed the fighting in the First World War, which he believed was a fight between Germany and England over the freedom of the seas, with the latter attempting to uphold its three-century-old tyranny. The people involved, however, fought for love of country, which inspired him greatly. The return of this kind of heroism led him to his infamous quotation on sacrifice. 'It is good for the world that such things should be done. The old heart of the earth needed to be warmed with the red wine of the battlefields. Such august homage was never before offered to God as this, the homage of millions of lives given gladly for love of country.' This was, however, not a simple celebration of bloodshed. He clearly stated war was a terrible thing, and that this was the most terrible of wars. However, as he had already put forward in 1913 he felt there were things more terrible than bloodshed, such as the exploitation of the English masses by cruel plutocrats, the infidelity of the French masses to their old spiritual ideals, and the enslavement of the Poles by Russia or of the Irish by England. If this war could put an end to these wrongs by bringing a workers' revolution to England, making the French return to their altars, and free the Poles and the Irish, then all the terrible suffering would have been worthwhile.

The Irish fight for freedom also had a religious component. The peace that existed, the Pax Britannica, was peace with sin, peace with dishonour, the devil's peace. Christ's peace would not come to Ireland until she had taken Christ's sword. The Irish were not used anymore to 'the exhilaration of war' but should not now shy away from the shedding of blood and welcome war when it comes as she would welcome the Angel of God. To alleviate concerns about the strength of England he stressed that it was always the few who fought for the good thing and the many for the evil thing, but that with God's help the few would ultimately win. That they had not always won in the past was because they had 'been guilty of some secret faltering, some infidelity to their best selves, some shrinking back in the face of a tremendous duty'. If they fought now he forecasted that this would be the last Christmas in which Ireland would be ruled by England, and that they would bequeath the Peace of the Gael to their sons.

Although the underlying argument that righting certain wrongs can justify the use of force was reasonable enough in the context of the time, the language in which it was put forward certainly did not enamour all. James Connolly famously commented: 'No, we do not think the old heart of the earth needs to be warmed with the red wine of millions of lives. We think anyone who does is a blithering idiot. We are sick of such teaching, and the world is sick of such teaching.'[68] However, the use of such language was not confined to romantic revolutionaries in Ireland. Poets throughout Europe preached the heroism of war. To them dying in battle was preferable to the horrors of modern life. Even writers like Thomas Mann saw the war in 1914 as 'a purification, a liberation, an enormous hope'.[69] In his 'War Sonnets' written at the end of 1914 the famous English poet Rupert Brooke also used the metaphor of a 'world grown old and cold and weary' and celebrated the blood of young lives given for honour.[70] Even James Joyce, who rejected the narrow nationalism of the Irish language movement, has the main character in his short story 'The Dead' dating from before 1913 argue that it is better to 'pass boldly into that other World, in full glory of some passion, than fade and wither dismally with age'.[71]

During the war the glorification of bloodshed as a cleansing experience was common to English women and many politicians including Bonar Law, Churchill and unionist leaders in the North.[72] Much of Patrick's rhetoric can also be found among nineteenth century nationalists. Thomas Davis wrote of the fighting during the rebellion of 1798 where 'The red rain made Wexford's harvest grow.'[73]

The very popular writer Canon Sheehan wrote in a similar vein in his novel *The Graves at Kilmorna* published in 1914: 'As the blood of martyrs was the seed of saints, so the blood of the patriot is the seed from which alone can spring fresh life, into a nation that is drifting into the putrescence of decay.'[74] This was taken up almost literally by Parnell's sister: 'The blood of martyrs is the choicest seed God sows.'[75]

To most readers these words were essentially rhetorical, but Patrick was increasingly convinced that they needed to be translated into action. Although adhering to the old slogans and paying lip service to the willingness to die in battle, few were going to sacrifice their lives for the nation.[76] Patrick, however, had a tendency to personify abstractions such as Ireland and wanted to make her happy: 'Yes I would give much – my all – just to know that Dark Haired Rosaleen was at long last at peace.'[77] The logic of his own argument that God was on the side of the few drove Patrick also to the idea that one man's action could be enough to obtain an ideal. Already in his story *The King* dating from 1912 he argued that sacrifice of the pure, the innocent in the quest for freedom would bring victory which should be celebrated not mourned.

There is also an unspoken connection made between Christ's sacrifice on Calvary and the heroic self-sacrifice of Ireland's epic heroes, which he makes explicit in relation to Cúchulainn: 'the story of Cuchulain symbolises the redemption of man by a sinless God. … It is like retelling (or is it foretelling?) of the story of Calvary.'[78] In *The Singer* written in 1915 he makes this more explicit when such a Christ-like individual sacrifices himself to compensate for the sins of the populace and the incompetence of its leaders. When the main character wants to go into battle against a superior force of Englishmen he is opposed by the people who argue it is foolish. 'Do you want us to be wise? … One man can free a people as one man redeemed the world. I will take no pike, I will go into battle with bare hands. I will stand up before the Gael as Christ hung naked before men on the tree.'[79] After the 1916 Rising Yeats used this as a way to explain Patrick's actions: 'Pearse I have long looked upon as a man made dangerous by the Vertigo of Self Sacrifice.'[80] According to Patrick's French biographer people spoke freely of an insurrection to redeem Ireland at the end of 1915.[81] The expectation of redemption was also current in socialist thinking at that time, where through the revolution salvation could be reached.

Although it is claimed that the play *The Singer* was dropped from being staged in the Abbey early in 1916 'because it was felt it revealed too much of the plans for the coming Rising',[82] these stories mainly function as an allegory to illustrate that to serve an ideal is admirable. Patrick was convinced something needed to be done to save the nation, not just on a cultural or political level but now also in a military sense. This could be a mass rising of the people, an elite rising or even the action of an individual. He was certainly taken by the then widespread ideal of sacrifice and what it could do. To him sacrifice was not an object in itself but was done with a very clear objective in mind. 'A man's life for a nation's happiness! What a magnificent exchange that would be!'[83] The symbolism of the act of rebellion would be enough to keep the ideal alive in the people and thereby ensure the ultimate resurrection of the nation. 'We may have to devote ourselves to our own destruction so that Ireland can be free.' Therefore sacrifice was victory in itself.[84] Nevertheless, although he certainly anticipated being killed in the Rising it is impossible to identify a single-minded desire to die for Ireland during the preparations.

It was extremely important to Patrick to have the systematic exposé of his thinking in these pamphlets published before the Rising. *Ghosts* had come out early in January and *The Separatist Idea* was on sale around the beginning of March. On 31 March he pressed the bookseller Whelan to rush through the last two pamphlets with the printers and make sure they were out by 17 April. 'I ask you to do this for me and you will later appreciate the reason and regard it as sufficient.' On 12 April he sent the final proofs back to the printers, ironically a 'loyal' firm based in Belfast, and insisted they would be printed off at once and delivered at Whelan's by the seventeenth. Whelan recalls how Patrick called by and asked him to send him 200 copies the moment the issue appeared, adding that 'if they are after Good Friday, they will be too late'. He clearly saw this as his last words on the subject of Irish nationality. The introduction to the last pamphlet *The Sovereign People* ended with the words: 'For my part, I have no more to say', clearly indicating it was time for action.[85]

Preparations

After the initial target date of September 1915 for an insurrection had not been met, Easter 1916 was set as the new date. From the end of 1915 onwards the IRB increased its efforts to prepare effectively. Recruiting for the Volunteers continued, an arms delivery from Germany was organised and an overall campaign plan was formulated mostly by Clarke, MacDermott and Joseph Plunkett.[86] During the last general council of all Volunteers officers before Easter the question of a rising was discussed. The officers were not aware of the plans of the Military Council, and the general feeling was that they would be beaten militarily if there was a rising. The best estimates were that there were about 1400 Volunteers in Dublin and 4500 in the provinces of which only 1817 were armed.[87]

To counter the defeatist attitude Sean MacDermott had jumped up at this meeting and asked whether Robert Emmet was a failure. This seemed to have turned the mood. 'The feeling of those present at these meetings was that we should not let the war end without our generation making a gesture or a protest against the British rule and occupation of the country.'[88] In January 1916 a mobilisation order for a three-day march and field manoeuvre starting on Easter Sunday was published in *The Irish Volunteer*. Patrick sent people down the country to convey orally to various units the positions which were to be occupied at these manoeuvres, but did not make clear these instructions were for a rising.[89] In preparation for the event large-scale manoeuvres were held in Dublin during St Patrick's Day and on Palm Sunday to test the Volunteers and defy the authorities.[90]

Patrick did not excel in practical organisational work, but was instrumental in propagating their message right up to the outbreak of the Rising. Apart from his written work and visits down the country this also involved lectures in various places. On 1 March he gave an Emmet Commemoration lecture in Enniscorthy and the next day one in Belfast.[91] The area in which he was most practically involved was the effort to arm the Volunteers. He bought two signalling lamps for communications with the German ship and a marquee to give shelter while landing the arms. On 12 February he wrote to McGarrity instructing him to pass on the message to the Germans that arms needed to arrive between Good Friday and Easter Sunday.[92] It took until 9 March before the Clann could inform him that the Germans were sending 20,000 rifles and ten machine guns to a place near Tralee, between 23 and 25 April.[93]

The young students and some of the pupils who resided at St Enda's were involved in setting up a grenade factory in the basement of the school with their chemistry teachers. The grenades made from tin cans were ultimately brought to Dublin by car and seemed to have functioned quite well.[94] A general order also went out to collect all kinds of implements needed for the Rising such as shovels, picks, crowbars, wire cutters, sandbags, paraffin oil, food, particularly oxo cubes, medical supplies and even haircutting instruments.[95]

Patrick also busied himself with the symbolic elements. All Volunteers officers were to wear uniforms and yellow tabs to make them recognisable, and as a member of the Uniform Committee Patrick also discussed the type and shape of the flag, cap badge, belt buckles, etc. Finding suitable headgear appeared to be a particular problem. Many wanted a soft hat modelled on the Boer slouch hat 'but it was found impossible to get a suitable hat of Irish manufacture'. At a very late stage in March 1916 Patrick approached a Dublin hatter looking for samples of different style military hats, including South African, Australian and Canadian. He wanted to know the price if he ordered less than a hundred and inquired about delivery times.[96] During the Rising Patrick wore a type of Boer hat and the tricolour was flown over the positions of the Volunteers. At the GPO a green flag with 'Irish Republic' in golden letters was also raised.[97]

The plans for a rising at Easter came under threat from various quarters. The most immediate worry was the impatience of James Connolly, who was convinced that the country would rise as soon as a vanguard, like his ICA, attacked. His calls for a rebellion in the Labour paper were an open invitation to the authorities to intervene and thereby could frustrate the IRB plans. Although Patrick had moved closer to Connolly's thinking, he distrusted his intentions. 'He will never be satisfied until he goads us into action and then he will think most of us too moderate, and want to guillotine half of us.'[98] Neither did Patrick understand Connolly's recent criticism of his call for blood sacrifice.[99] The threat of unilateral action by the ICA forced the Military Council to speed up their plans, and Patrick more openly discussed their intentions at the end of 1915 probably to induce the ICA to wait.[100] Early in 1916 it nevertheless became clear that Connolly was ready to strike, and the IRB was forced to forestall his plans. Initially this was done by the Volunteers Executive who did not countenance any rising but MacNeill and Hobson failed in their mission. Seamas O'Conor claims that Patrick and probably

MacDermott then tried to persuade Connolly on 19 January to call off his attempt and join the planned rising at Easter instead.[101]

It was difficult to reach agreement and Connolly was held for three days by the IRB. Although this was almost certainly not done against Connolly's will, it gave some of his supporters the idea he had been kidnapped. One of his associates, Michael Mallin, went to the Military Council demanding Connolly's return and threatening action. Ceannt did not take this threat by the few ICA men very seriously but Mallin replied: 'We can fight & die if necessary & it will be to our eternal glory & your eternal shame.' This apparently brought in Patrick who thumped the table saying dramatically 'Yes, by God, you are right, and here is one who will be with you.'[102] Finally, after a long struggle, Connolly agreed to postpone his actions. Patrick recounted to Desmond Ryan how Connolly with tears in his eyes grasped his hand and said: 'God grant, Pearse, that you are right.' After which Patrick told Ryan 'Perhaps Connolly is right. He is a very great man.' Connolly was then sworn into the IRB and made a member of the Military Council.[103] Patrick subsequently informed the Volunteers Executive that he had been successful in persuading Connolly not to rise.[104] This episode also initiated a series of discussions with MacNeill which led the latter to accept the idea of a pre-emptive strike providing Casement would be able to secure German arms.[105]

The attitude of the more moderate Volunteers leaders was another serious worry to the insurrectionists. MacNeill had made clear he would only countenance the use of force in certain very subscribed circumstances, but the relatively small IRB organisation needed the Volunteers as manpower. MacNeill was not very involved in the day-to-day running of the movement but Hobson was very aware of the scheming which went on behind their backs and tried to force MacNeill to confront Patrick and his fellow conspirators. In September 1915 Patrick had been able to allay the fears of MacNeill, and was able to continue to do so almost to the end, partly due to the fact MacNeill rarely attended Executive meetings and Patrick then took his place in the chair.

In mid-February, however, MacNeill wrote a letter to the Executive challenging the insurrectionists. In this he argued that the use of force could only be justified if the survival of the nation was on the line. The desire of the insurrectionists to use action to produce an effect on the national mind was in his eyes an attempt to try to escape a difficult and complex situation and satisfy their own emotions, impelled by a sense of feebleness, despondency or fatalism.[106] In the absence of a deep and widespread discontent action would be equal to murder of the men led into it and of those to be shot. However, MacNeill did not show up for the meeting, and in his absence Patrick simply read out the letter without allowing discussion on it. MacNeill subsequently prepared a memo on Volunteers policy to which he demanded unanimous assent. However, at the meeting where the memo was to be discussed Patrick and MacDermott pre-empted MacNeill by immediately denying that they were planning an insurrection and the memo disappeared in a drawer.[107] Another attempt by MacNeill on 5 April to assert his authority failed to delay the plans of the insurrectionists, although they agreed not to issue any more orders without MacNeill's consent.[108]

Although even most Volunteers were unaware of the exact plans, it had been clear to many, including the authorities, that something big was afoot. Already on 8 January 1915 the Dublin Castle Intelligence Officer had warned of dangerous developments in the Volunteers:

> It may without exaggeration be said that in the personnel of its Committee, in its Declaration of Policy, in the utterances of its leading representatives, in its opposition to the efforts of Mr Redmond to bring Ireland into line at the present National Crisis, and in its crusade against enlistment in the Army, the Irish Volunteer organization has shown itself to be disloyal and seditious, and revolutionary if the means and opportunity were at hand.[109]

The growing defiance of the authorities early in 1916 caused serious alarm. Two weeks before the Rising Major Price submitted a report claiming the 'Sinn Fein Volunteers now totalled about 10,000 men with 4,800 rifles revolvers and shotguns and with large caches of home made bayonets and grenades recently found'. He believed they were 'working up for rebellion and revolution if ever they got a good opportunity'.[110]

Patrick was nevertheless not a prime suspect. From the end of 1915 he was fearful of being arrested, and believed to be under surveillance. He sent his letters to McGarrity through a Ms McKenna, a mutual friend in the United States, to avoid detection, but in reality Patrick's mail was never censored.[111] Although featuring on a list of violent men who needed careful monitoring, the authorities apparently still regarded his calls for the use of force as harmless remarks from a cultural nationalist.[112] As shown Patrick was always deliberately ambiguous in his speeches to avoid giving the authorities cause for action, while at the same time preparing for a rising. In this vein he forbade the public display of extremism by Volunteers by banning the use of the tricolour and replacing it with a more traditional nationalist flag.[113] On 10 March 1915 he instructed every company to provide itself with a flag to be carried on recruiting marches, church parades and other such occasions. The flag should be green with a plain gold harp. No other flags were to be carried, and the companies needed to be exercised in saluting the flag.[114]

The secrecy which surrounded the planning was of course vital to the success of the Rising, but also meant that many of those who were supposed to fight were practically unaware of what was going on. Nevertheless several hints were dropped in the weeks leading up to the Rising. Members of the Volunteers 'were warned to be at hand for Easter Sunday. We were told there would be extensive manoeuvres and that the absence of any Volunteer would be regarded as a serious breach of discipline.' They did not all know what to make of these instructions. Some expected a rising, others believed it was meant as a show of strength to ensure they were not to be disarmed and the remainder thought it was just an ordinary parade.[115] Those in Patrick's immediate environment who were going to be involved and even some who opposed it were made aware the Rising was near, while some of his pupils surmised as much.

There were various signs, some more obvious than others. Maurice Collins drew his conclusions when early in 1916 the Volunteers were instructed to procure all arms possible. Patrick's own Volunteers Company in Rathfarnham realised what was going on when they were told to go to confession. The Dublin Brigade officers who were appointed and sounded out by Patrick were more openly involved. Frank Henderson remembers receiving instructions from Ceannt and MacDonagh at a meeting of officers about three weeks before the Rising. During this Patrick came in: 'after a dramatic silence of a few moments while he stood with his head down, he raised his head quickly and said, "Is every man here prepared to meet his God?" He said it not loudly but with the force of tremendous seriousness.' He then gave those who were not in earnest time to get out, but only one or two men failed to turn up afterwards. On 15 April he told a meeting of the Dublin Brigade council that anybody who was afraid of losing his job should not come out at Easter Sunday.[116]

From late 1915 it was clear in Patrick's mind what had to be done. He acted increasingly militarily and started to wear his Volunteers uniform at public occasions.[117] He also considered his own future, as anyone intending to lead an uprising must contemplate the possibilities of being killed in action, defeat or success. All these three outcomes went through Patrick's mind in the months leading up to the Rising and even during it. At his darker moments he was despondent, doubted the Rising's rationale and felt defeat was inevitable. At a social gathering in St Enda's on New Year's Day 1916 he expressed disillusionment with old Gaelic League friends like Mary Hayden who supported Britain in the war. 'It's for people like her that we want to save Ireland.' He also claimed the well-intentioned efforts of people like John Devoy, who had done all he could for a free Ireland for sixty years, were not appreciated, and that this could also happen to them.

In his story *The Fool*, written at this time, he questions whether living for an ideal was worth squandering one's youth for. In it the main character is criticised for believing in his dream and for being willing to give his life for it. Against this he argued that Christ had told people to scatter and not to hoard, and asks them what if it came true and millions would live in this dream. The same questioning of the choices he had made in his life came to the fore in other poems. In 'Renunciation', written in 1915, this became a positive choice. It describes someone who has forsaken physical beauty, music, lust and desire for the 'deed that I see And the death I shall die'. He speaks in similar words about Wolfe Tone which he seemed to emulate:

> Such is the high and sorrowful destiny of the heroes: to turn their backs to the pleasant paths and their faces to the hard paths, to blind their eyes to the fair things of life, to stifle all sweet music in the heart, the low voice of women and the laughter of little children, and to follow only the far, faint call that leads them into battle or to the harder death at the foot of a gibbet.[118]

The need for a blood-sacrifice to awaken the nation and safeguard its honour became ever more prominent in his thinking: 'Blood will flow. Maybe it is the best way out.'[119]

A martyr's death could also have its benefits. In answer to a request early in 1916 from the organisers of the Emmet commemoration in Wexford for Patrick's portrait for the booklet they wanted to publish he half jokingly wrote: 'I think a portrait of Emmet would be better (as well as handsomer) on the cover. After I am hanged my portrait will be interesting, but not before.'[120] In the poem 'A Rann I made' he describes someone at peace with death through salvation. On a more practical level he realised he might die during the Rising. Shortly before the Rising he told his mother 'It would be better to be killed than imprisoned.'[121] To cover for this eventuality he had made arrangements for what should be done in case of his death in November 1914 and again in the spring of 1915: 'in view of the probability of my being arrested or losing my life ... [in] the call of action for my country'.[122] A couple of nights before the Rising he mentally said goodbye to his life by visiting scenes of his childhood with Willie including all the houses they had ever lived in.[123]

The possibility of success was certainly on most of the participants' minds including occasionally on Patrick's. In his 1915 story *The Fool* the main character answers the wise men's criticism that he squandered the splendid years of his youth attempting impossible things, by arguing he only follows Christ's word and what if dreams come true.[124] In his poem 'The Rebel' he warns those who keep the people in bondage to beware of the risen people: 'Who shall take what ye would not give.' MacDonagh believed that if MacNeill could be separated from the 'evil genius' of Bulmer Hobson all would be well. Colm O Loughlin stated that Patrick believed that if the Volunteers could hold Dublin for a week the British would be forced to make terms. A number of close associates remember how the ministerial posts of a free Irish government were allocated in the weeks before the Rising. Patrick suggested Plunkett as Minister of Fine Arts, and was himself suggested as Minister of Education. When someone suggested Clarke for the job of President Patrick seemed to have been very disappointed.[125] In one of these final meetings concerns were expressed about a fight in the city, to which Patrick answered that he believed 'something spectacular should be done, otherwise the rest of the country would not rise'.[126]

There has long been an intensive discussion on the actual objectives of the insurrectionists. It is clear that ordinary members always believed they had a chance of success. For the leaders the issue is more complicated.[127] The initial plans were centred on Dublin in the vein of a nineteenth century revolution similar to the Paris Commune of 1871, but the plans had been extended to encompass the Volunteers in the entire country. Whether this constituted a serious attempt at a government takeover or simply another platform for a blood sacrifice is unclear. However, apart from Patrick none of the leaders really seemed to believe in a bloody sacrifice, their rhetoric simply being a pose.[128] Despite the strong theme of sacrifice for the nation in Patrick's thinking and writings, even he displayed behaviour and expressed concerns which indicated a hope for success. To some extent the military failure of the Rising has made it attractive both to supporters and detractors of Patrick to emphasise the sacrificial aspect of his thinking thereby neglecting those elements indicating the hope of success and misreading those accounting for the obvious possibility of dying in action.[129]

The purpose of the Rising in case of failure was something that nevertheless played on the leaders' minds. To Patrick the chance to redeem what he called Dublin's shame for their failure to come to Robert Emmet's aid had been a motivating force for some time. The possibility of putting Dublin up there with other cities which had staged memorable revolts also appealed to him. In the GPO during the Rising he said with 'deep feeling and passion': 'Dublin's name will be glorious for ever … Men will speak of her as one of the splendid cities as they speak now of Paris. Dublin! Paris!'[130] The erection of barricades, which had very little military use except for safely crossing streets, seems to have been an imitation of the Paris Commune, while the issuing of pikes to the rebels had more of a historic resonance with 1798 than any practical military value. The fear that Irish nationality would disappear if the generation of Irishmen he belonged to did not attempt to assert their independence was something that brought together a number of his ideas. Patrick's mother is said to have told Mrs Rahilly on the day before Easter: 'Pat is going to die for Ireland. He will die like Wolfe Tone.'[131]

All these motivational ideas can be seen as part of a heroic sacrifice for a good cause, a concept widely seen as admirable in western society at that time. Already in the 1860s sacrifice was put forward in Ireland as a way to redeem the nation's soul.[132] International socialist movements had been inspired by the Paris Commune of 1871 in particular to view heroic sacrifice as an admirable deed and as a transformative power. Revenge for past wrongs inflicted by an oppressor, a celebration of martyrs for the cause and a general militarisation in socialist thinking of all types from social democrats to anarchists had taken place in the late nineteenth and early twentieth centuries. The sacrifice of the leader and his redemption in the future revolution was also a standard trope of socialist literature.[133] At the same time there developed among militarists and especially among military officers in Europe a growing cult of self-sacrifice; this was part of the ethos of the army but was also legitimised by calling upon the ideal of service to the nation. In Germany the army circulated myths of dead officers who showed 'boundless initiative, inordinate capacity for suffering, and blind self-sacrifice'.[134] Although the violence and sacrifice of soldiers was seen by socialists as meaningless and wrong, they saw their own fight as historically meaningful and their sacrifice as productive in the revolutionary upheaval. The romantic ideal of a short but heroic life became particularly popular in this period from among the *Futurists* in Italy in the 1890s to Dutch social democrats in the 1930s.

Although there were thus various motivational ideas going around, by Easter 1916 the Irish conspirators had boxed themselves into a corner which they could only get out of by pursuing a rising which was, through various mishaps, by then doomed to fail. They therefore emphasised the sacrificial element in their motivation. By Saturday there was no way to back out without losing face. 'After all our marchings and speeches what else can we do? Would any one ever listen to our oratory again if we let this chance pass?'[135] A very similar sudden emphasis on the virtue of sacrifice was shown by Karl Liebknecht, the leader of the January 1919 revolution of Spartakists in Germany, when it became clear that their revolution was failing. In his last words published on the day of his execution he stated: 'es gibt niederlagen, die Siege sind; und Siege, verhängnisvoller als Niederlage' [There are defeats which are victories; and victories which are more disastrous than defeats.] He continued to say that the workers had acted honourably, that they had fought for the most honourable goal of the spiritual and material relief of the suffering masses, that they had shed holy blood, which was thus sanctified. From each drop of this blood the fallen avenger would rise up. Only from the experience of defeat could the art of succeeding be learned. The life of the individual was not important as long as the programme continued to live. The

Golgotha road of the workers had ended. If in all this the workers are replaced by Irishmen it could have been said by Patrick.[136]

The Rising

Events became very hectic in the final week before the planned rising. On Monday a Provisional Revolutionary Government was constituted with Pearse as President and the Proclamation of the Republic was discussed by its seven members. It had been drafted by Patrick with some amendments by Connolly and possibly MacDonagh.[137] The main obstacle to setting the Rising in motion was the attitude of the leaders of the Volunteers who were not in the know. During the week MacNeill became more and more suspicious, but the exposure on Wednesday of the so-called 'Castle Documents', which seemed to indicate that the authorities were ready to suppress the Volunteers, convinced him an act of resistance was necessary. The documents were apparently based on a leaked government plan of action to deal with opposition in case of the introduction of conscription. They were in reality not a plan of immediate action, but had been embellished by Joseph Plunkett in such a way to generate widespread opposition. In response MacNeill ordered a mobilisation and resistance if necessary by all units on Thursday morning.[138]

However, by Thursday evening it became inescapable to the moderates that a rising was planned for Easter Sunday when they discovered mobilisation orders being issued for Sunday with a starting time of 4.00 p.m.[139] Late that night MacNeill, Hobson and J.J. O'Connell went to St Enda's to confront Pearse who confirmed a rising was indeed on. MacNeill protested and stated he would make every effort to prevent it short of informing the authorities. Patrick apparently made clear to him it would not stop them, and that the Volunteers were now under IRB control. MacNeill, nevertheless, refused to call out men with bare hands to face the guns, and went home to issue orders countermanding Patrick's mobilisation and taking control of the Volunteers by sending out senior officers down the country.[140]

On Friday morning the conspirators, MacDermott, Pearse and MacDonagh, visited MacNeill and made an effort to get him on board by informing him of the imminent arrival of German arms, which

MacNeill had earlier defined as a condition for a pre-emptive strike. In combination with the apparent threat of disarmament from the Castle MacNeill now decided to go along with them in a defensive action, sending orders down the country retracting the previous ones. In the meantime Patrick oversaw the transfer of the grenades and bombs made in St Enda's to the city and was in touch with several country officers who visited him during Friday and Saturday concerning final arrangements. Happy with the progress, all Military Council members slept away from home on Friday night to avoid possible action by the authorities. Patrick did not sleep in Rathfarnham from Thursday, but returned home during the day.[141]

That morning MacNeill changed his mind for a third time. When he heard that the German arms were lost, the Castle Documents were a forgery and Hobson was arrested by the IRB he went over to St Enda's again with O'Rahilly and some others to try to dissuade the rebels from action. When they arrived they found Patrick in a very excited and belligerent state. 'We have used your name and influence for what they were worth, but we have done with you now.' When MacNeill threatened to forbid the Sunday mobilisation Patrick added: 'It does not matter what U do. Our men won't obey U.' The delegation then went home to consider further action. Patrick subsequently wrote to Sean T. O'Kelly to ask him to put him and Willie up for the night as they were worried they would not be able to get into Dublin on Sunday, announcing the arrival of some traps with material in the early evening with them following on bicycles.[142]

Those in the know reacted in different ways to the news the Military Council would press on with a rising regardless of the changed circumstances. Most remained passive and nobody went to the authorities. Some like The O'Rahilly and Arthur Griffith, who told his wife he did not expect to come back, eventually joined the fighting. O'Rahilly justified this by arguing: 'I have helped wind up the clock, and must be there to hear it strike.'[143] MacNeill refused to either go to the police or join in the rising. He argued that he 'could shoot the men who are coming to arrest me but what good would it do?'[144] However, he did actively try to prevent the Rising. By midnight on Saturday he decided to issue a formal countermanding order. Loyal officers were sent to Munster on Sunday morning to deliver the order which also appeared in the *Sunday Independent*.[145] This had a huge effect on the Volunteers and also on the members of the Military Council who had assembled for an emergency meeting when it appeared on Sunday morning. Tom Clarke in particular regarded MacNeill's action as 'of the blackest and greatest treachery' and now saw his real hopes of success dashed. 'I found Tom Clarke afterwards and for the first time since I knew him he seemed crushed. He was very weary and seemed crestfallen.'[146]

The belief in success had now virtually disappeared among the leaders, but Clarke who quickly recovered from the shock insisted on pressing ahead with the Rising that day. The others felt there was too much confusion and on Patrick's insistence decided to postpone it by one day and commence at noon on Easter Monday.[147] They made sure they had the active cooperation of the Dublin Brigade. After assuring Michael Staines as representative of the brigade that everything had been done to try to get MacNeill's consent, he agreed with Patrick's argument that they were 'all going to be arrested anyhow, and on behalf of this generation we will have to make a gesture'.[148]

That afternoon before returning home Patrick signed an order cancelling the Sunday operations thereby confirming MacNeill's order, but in the evening he sent a second one by courier ordering a Monday mobilisation. Neither of them were dated or timed which caused further confusion and a lack of response to the mobilisation order for Monday.[149] Only on Monday morning did MacDonagh as Commander of the Dublin Brigade order all battalions to parade for 'inspection and route march' at 10.00 a.m. with full arms and one day's rations.[150] The constant arguments among the leadership and the conflicting orders had confused most Volunteers; some of those who turned up anxiously inquired whether MacNeill supported the Rising.[151] A great many Volunteers, some of whom had mobilised in vain on Sunday, were unaware they were to mobilise again for the actual insurrection on Monday. Most slept in, many of them being awoken after the established mobilisation time. As a result the actual numbers of men involved, less than 1000, were probably much lower than they would have been on Sunday.[152]

On Monday morning the leadership and headquarters staff met for some final arrangements at Liberty Hall from where they marched to O'Connell Street at about 11.50 a.m. with a motley crew of about 150 men. The leadership was weary about the prospects of the Rising, but felt it could not be stopped. This led Connolly to his famous assertion to William O'Brien that they were 'going out to be slaughtered'. When they left, Patrick was implored by his sister Mary Brighid, who had so far been unaware of the actual plans, to: 'Come home, Pat, and leave all the foolishness.' The sister of The O'Rahilly, who had joined the Rising at the last minute, laid responsibility for what was about to happen at Patrick's feet, but he did not react to her accusation that: 'This is all your fault.'[153]

The secrecy and confusion surrounding the organisation of the Rising had left the Volunteers in disarray, but also meant the action was a great surprise to most ordinary people and the authorities. The sight of marching Volunteers at weekends was not uncommon, but when a group of them suddenly stormed the GPO on Easter Monday this was reacted to with mixed emotions. Inside the GPO customers seemed not to have shown any fear at this stage and some could only be forced out by a threat and sometimes actual use of force.[154] After the building was secured by the Volunteers, Patrick read out the Proclamation of the Republic apparently standing on the edge of the footpath in front of the closed doors of the GPO to a rather bewildered audience of a few hundred onlookers.

He declared an independent and sovereign republic with a Provisional Government at its head, and called upon the people to give their allegiance and support to it. It was apparently perceived to be necessary to convince everyone of the right of the Irish people to independence by claiming that each historic generation in Ireland had expressed their desire for it, often in arms. Similarly it tried to encompass all the Irish including Protestants and the poor by the promise to cherish 'all the children of the nation equally' and institute a fully representative democratic government. The less than lukewarm response to the Proclamation and the rebellion itself seems to have worried Patrick.

During the morning he appeared again & again under the portico of the Post Office & on O'Connell St; very pale he was, very cold of face as he scanned the crowd, the indifferent seeming crowd that at times & in places warmed only to show positive hostility. I saw him at about noon, I think, read the Proclamation of the Irish Republic; but for once his magnetism had left him; the response was chilling; a few thin perfunctory cheers; no direct hostility just then; but no enthusiasm whatever; the people were evidently quite unprepared, quite unwilling to see in the uniformed figure, whose burning words had thrilled them again & again elsewhere, a person of significance to the country. A chill must have gone to his heart; no doubt whatever but that his will held staunch and stalwart, but this dismal reception of the astonishing Order of the Day was not what he had dreamed of when in many an hour of fevered passion & many a careful weaving of plan he had rehearsed the Act.[155]

When a former pupil of St Enda's and nephew of The O'Rahilly joined the Volunteers in the GPO and told them the printed version of the Proclamation attracted attention and caused excitement in the streets, Patrick's mood lifted.[156]

The response of the people and the Volunteers throughout the country remained very muted. The initial plan for a nationwide rising failed to materialise. The Dublin Brigade came out in force led by their officers, many of whom had been appointed by the conspirators, but most of the country units were confused by the conflicting orders they had received from Pearse and MacNeill. Sympathetic officers like the adjutant of Patrick's Rathfarnham Company thought MacNeill's countermanding order was a 'British dodge to cause confusion', but most were less sure.[157] The lack of a clear indication of time on the quick succession of orders sent down made many officers even more uncertain. Some units met and came out, like those from Belfast who went out to a rendezvous point in mid-Ulster where they met other mobilised units. However, the lack of arms and men, and the confusion over the responsibility for the Rising caused them to return home. Some of the Volunteers in Tyrone and Cork believed the Rising was really staged by the ICA and not backed by the IRB. 'When we heard of the rising it was said that Connolly and his crowd had forced it, the scum of Dublin had forced it.'[158] In the end only Volunteers in Galway, Wexford and north County Dublin actually fought.

Even many of the Dublin Volunteers were unaware of the fact that a rebellion was staged until the morning of Easter Monday. Pearse was well supported by the Volunteers of his own Rathfarnham Company, most of whom were loyal to him personally and had been with him from the start and through the split of 1914. More than thirty past pupils of St Enda's, many of whom boarded in St Enda's, also joined in the Rising despite attempts by MacNeill to induce their acting captain to go home. The majority of them served in the GPO with the Rathfarnham men. Although St Enda's was closed about a fortnight before Easter, a few current pupils also participated in Dublin as well as in Galway. Eunan McGinley, the youngest of them, was sixteen, while Gerald Keogh was the only one killed while running messages for the rebels.[159]

During the Rising the leadership in Dublin was barely aware of the events outside the capital, although their activities did play a central role in the official plans for the Rising. Alec McCabe, the IRB centre in Sligo, remembers how during a walk to Liberty Hall some time before Easter Connolly and Patrick discussed the mobilisation:

> the terrible odds they would be up against and how, when the Rising started in the city, they would be out of touch with areas in the country. I ascertained from their discussion that Pearse was for taking to the country, while Connolly was for fighting in the city from house to house. Eventually Connolly agreed that they might be able to retreat into the country from the city. Pearse told me to do my best and said that as they retreated they would be gathering strength by being joined by the country centres of the I.R.B. and some of the Volunteers.[160]

The confusion in the last days had scuppered any serious implementation of an overall strategy. The operations in Dublin, however, went quite smoothly. All targeted buildings were occupied and fortified except for Dublin Castle, the seat of government. The thirty men strong ICA party successfully overwhelmed the very small guard but were repelled by the lone attack by Major Price who confronted them in the courtyard firing his revolver. They apparently anticipated strong resistance after having been discovered but there were actually not any other guards present. The sheer size of the buildings to be occupied may also have prevented the small attacking party from pressing on with their action. However, their failure to push on may well be ranked among the greatest missed opportunities of the Rising.[161]

The absence of a serious defence force in the Castle showed the lack of preparedness on the side of the authorities. Through their intelligence services they were well aware of the restlessness of the Volunteers and they had received several warnings that a rebellion with German aid was being planned. But they did not seriously believe a rebellion by the poorly armed Volunteers had any hope of success without a German intervention and therefore did not anticipate one unless they provoked one themselves by suppressing the Volunteers or introducing conscription. The events in Holy Week did heighten their fear but the interception of the German arms shipment, the arrest of Roger Casement and the countermanding order by MacNeill took away any sense of urgency. Although a list of those to be arrested was drawn up in the weekend, this was postponed until after Easter partly due to legal requirements. There are indications that troops were indeed mobilised in Dublin on Saturday but these were put at ease by Sunday morning. The fact that the majority of army officers went to the races in Fairyhouse on Monday morning indicated the authorities were caught completely by surprise.[162]

Initially their reaction was very muted. Only about 400 soldiers were available for action, and after a party of lancers sent down to the GPO on Monday afternoon were repelled at the cost of three deaths no further action was taken until reinforcements arrived.[163] In most areas serious fighting only started on Wednesday, reaching the GPO in the evening when some machine-gun fire was directed at guards on the roof. During the week Patrick displayed the same mixed emotions associated with possible death, failure or success as before Easter. Despite all the setbacks he still considered victory possible. In particular an uprising by the people and the arrival of German aid fired the insurrectionists on. In a four-page newssheet *Irish War News*, printed on confiscated printers and published on Tuesday, Patrick referred to the support of the populace of Dublin for the Republic, and claimed that although communication with the country was cut, reports indicated it was rising.[164] In a one-page manifesto to the citizens of Dublin read out by Patrick from a table in Sackville Street on Tuesday, he announced that 'the final achievement of Ireland's freedom is now, with God's help, only a matter of days'. He called upon the Dubliners to come to their aid by building barricades and to 'preserve order and self-restraint'.[165] In a speech held on Thursday morning he claimed that a large body of Volunteers was marching on Dublin from Dundalk and would soon be from Wexford.[166]

Both contemporaries and historians have claimed that before and during the Rising the participants including Patrick believed in a German landing. This idea was based on the statement the Germans had issued on 20 November 1915 expressing the wish that Ireland would attain national welfare and liberty, and also on their willingness to provide practical support. However, the Germans had clearly indicated to Casement and Plunkett that it would be impossible to send troops or submarines due to the strength of the British Navy.[167]

A rumour nevertheless went around the Volunteers of the landing of thousands of German troops. There are some indications that Patrick himself believed this. He does refer to his conviction that a German expedition had actually set sail but was defeated by the British in a letter to his mother after the surrender. And during his court-martial Patrick is also said to have mentioned that the German Navy was to have landed but had been waylaid.[168]

However, one of those present in the GPO recounts how Patrick asked him to spread the rumour that 15,000 Germans had landed in Galway to buoy up spirits. Although he refused to spread the rumour it was nevertheless going around the troops. Patrick himself apparently told the men to listen for German gunfire from Dublin bay. Such deliberate manipulation by Patrick is supported by his threat to have J.J. Walsh shot when he told the GPO regiment that he had reliable information that Cork and Kerry had not risen.[169] There are other indications that Patrick had already accepted the inevitability of defeat. By Monday afternoon he declared that the Rising was a success and that 'Ireland's honour had already been redeemed' because they had lasted longer that Emmet's revolt of 1803. Adding later that as they had held out for three days they would under international law now be entitled to send a delegation to the peace conference at the end of the war.[170]

During the fighting Patrick remained optimistic. He sent a note to his mother to put her mind at ease. Assuring her he, Willie and the students of St Enda's who participated were in good spirits, ate well and each had mattresses and some of them even had sheets, blankets, pillows and quilts.[171] He also made sure his men felt at ease by requesting Marlboro Street Church to send a priest to the GPO to hear confessions. Fr John Flanagan came over on Monday evening and on Thursday and Friday.[172] Most participants in the Rising reported that Patrick was very calm and spoke little during Easter week, sometimes even retreating in an apparent trance, but not showing any fear. There are no reports he actually participated in the fighting but as the commander that is not unusual.[173]

In general, Patrick did not lack bravery and cared little about his own comforts and safety. There are signs of bravery and exultation while fighting small fires in the years before the Rising. His sister recalls his excitement extinguishing a small fire at home, while the actress Maire Nic Shiubhlaigh remembered how Patrick reacted to a fire during the fundraising fete at Jones' Road in 1913:

> One of the stands was full of boys who were not taking part in the pageant. The stand caught fire. Pearse was off the field in a moment and had flung himself into the midst of the flames almost before anyone knew what was happening. He was shaking all over, not from fear, but from anxiety for the safety of the boys who were trapped yet he climbed to the top of the flaming structure handing the smaller children to safety and calling for an orderly withdrawal. The boys heard his voice, lined up, and walked quietly to the ground through the flames. When it was all over he leaned against a nearby railing, the grease-paint smeared down his face from the heat, his head bowed. In a moment he was back with the boys on the field, clapping his hands for order, calling names, making jokes. That was the Pearse his pupils knew.[174]

The less sympathetic Sean O'Casey does not mention any such heroics at this occasion. He simply recalled Patrick asking the firemen who were busy putting out the fire whether the pageant could go on while trying to avoid getting his polished shoes dirty.[175]

Militarily Patrick's role seemed to have been somewhat peripheral. He left the command to Connolly, and occupied himself more with encouraging the men and public perception than with strategy. Greg Murphy recalls how he was asked on Tuesday to get some Volunteers with pikes to take down recruiting posters which were stuck on the fluted columns of the GPO. They did so until Connolly came along and asked them what on earth they were doing.[176]

When the fighting intensified he became more active in motivating the men. By Tuesday night all present began to take 'it for granted we would finally be crushed'. They expected to be rushed by a superior force followed by a fight to a finish with enormous losses on their side. This caused 'no feeling of despondency but subdued excitement and determination – desperation maybe'.[177] One night when the men were feeling the strain he went around with some Cumann na mBan girls pinning holy medals on them, shaking hands and giving them 'a few words of cheer'. After that some of the girls kissed the Volunteers.[178] Frank Henderson remembered how Patrick gave a speech from a table in the central hall of the GPO congratulating them on what they had done, and preparing them for what was to come. 'We were all deeply moved by his address.'[179] In other speeches Patrick told the men that if nothing else they had redeemed Dublin's name, and that ultimately they would find victory even it may be found in death. In a speech held on Thursday morning he turned to the claim that the country was rising, and to his insistence that the Germans could land at any moment.

He also tried to ensure that the general public saw the insurrectionists as high-minded men, in line with the chivalric ethos of Victorian thinking which he had grown up with. In the Proclamation he called upon Volunteers not to dishonour their actions 'by cowardice, inhumanity or rapine'. He refused to allow shots to be fired at soldiers in Amiens St station tower because he believed that since they belonged to an Irish regiment they might be friendly. After he heard an unarmed soldier had been shot in Mount Street he ordered that nobody unarmed should be shot in or out of uniform, and insisted commandeered supplies should be paid for. During his court-martial he only cross-examined one witness with the sole purpose of establishing that a soldier who was kept prisoner by the Volunteers was treated well, which the soldier indeed acknowledged.[180]

He was appalled by the looting which took place in the early days of the Rising. Although the Volunteers had prepared for this by having police batons made they were unable to stop it. At one point the bails of cloths the Volunteers were using to build a barricade in Moore Street or Henry Street were taken away quicker than that they could place them. Firing shots over the heads of the looters did not help but a baton charge at least allowed the Volunteers to finish the barricade. Looting also caused some fires in shops around the GPO which had to be quelled by the Volunteers. Although orders to shoot looters were issued, Patrick was soft-hearted in his dealings with them. When one was brought before him he refused to condemn him: 'Ah, poor man. Put him with the others.' Eventually the looting stopped when the fighting became more intense on Wednesday.[181]

In the official statements of the insurgents Patrick condemned the looting and called upon the people to stop. At the same time he claimed it had been done by hangers-on of the British Army. He also condemned the alleged firing by British soldiers on Red Cross workers and nurses with stretchers. In the War Bulletin it was stated he had informed the commander of the British forces that 'British prisoners held by the Republican forces will be treated as hostages for the observance on the part of the British of the laws of warfare and humanity, especially as regards the Red Cross.'[182]

Inside the GPO Patrick frequently discussed the moral justification for the Rising and the ethics of armed insurrection with Plunkett and others. There were also moments of doubt. Desmond Ryan recalls how Patrick in a contemplative mood suddenly asked him a most unexpected question on Wednesday night when most men were sleeping.

> 'It was the right thing to do, was it not?'
> 'Yes,' I replied
> 'And if we fail it means the end of everything, Volunteers, Ireland, all?'
> 'I suppose so,' I replied.

He continued more defiantly expressing his belief that in the end they would be vindicated: 'When we are all wiped out, people will blame us for everything, condemn us. But for this protest, the war would have ended & nothing would have been done. After a few years they will see the meaning of what we tried to do.' He then returned to the shame Dublin should feel for failing to come to Robert Emmet's aid, and the glory of their deed.[183] The themes of having redeemed Dublin's name and saved Ireland's honour are also present in the various statements the rebels issued during the week. However, each of them also expressed the belief that the country had risen with them and that they would succeed in establishing a free Ireland.

During Wednesday and Thursday slowly all the Volunteers outposts were overwhelmed and many retreated to the GPO. The fight now approached the GPO where the Volunteers were somewhat despondent after the long wait. On Thursday afternoon the shelling of Sackville Street started. The fires spread from Abbey Street to Sackville Street and by evening the opposite side of the street was ablaze. 'It was a truly magnificent spectacle and for a while I continued to watch and admire it, fascinated by its awfulness.'[184] The highlight was the explosion of some oil works in Abbey Street which caused a huge flame springing hundreds of feet into the air forcing the Volunteers to close their eyes. In the very subdued atmosphere this caused Patrick to read out his final memorandum. The men did not cheer due to the solemnity of the situation 'that hushed every voice. Nor had Mr. Pearse any doubt of us. For a moment he stood fronting us, serene and confident, his countenance untroubled by any shade. He looked down to us and we looked back up to him – each of us praying in his heart. Then with grave deliberation he folded up his papers and walked away.'[185]

The last manifesto issued by Patrick on Friday morning was the first to acknowledge defeat was likely, but asserted that ultimate victory would still be their share, although maybe winning it in death. He also claimed that had the original plan been allowed to go through on Easter Sunday more would have been achieved. 'I am satisfied that we should have accomplished more, that we should have accomplished the task of enthroning, as well as proclaiming, the Irish Republic as a Sovereign State.' Even at this stage he was magnanimous enough to claim that MacNeill who had issued the fatal countermanding order had 'acted in the best interest of Ireland'. He reported they were attacked with shrapnel and machine-gun fire but still held all their posts, and were determined to hold the GPO while the buildings lasted.[186]

The fighting itself had not inspired Patrick, but when they were forced to evacuate the post office on Friday evening, after bombing with incendiary shells had put the building on fire, he came into his own. Participants recall an agitated MacDermott who gave a final speech from the top of a barrel and how Patrick calmly led the move from the GPO. Patrick told the men they would try to retreat to the Williams and Woods jam factory in Parnell Street. At noon the thirty or so women in the GPO, mostly Cumann na mBan members, had been ordered against their will to take away the wounded escorted by Fr Flanagan. Before leaving Patrick had assured them that 'when the history of the week would be written, the highest honour and credit should be given to the women whose bravery, heroism and devotion in the face of danger surpassed that of the women of Limerick in the days of Sarsfield'.[187]

The men followed in the evening in good spirits, with a wounded Connolly on a stretcher.[188] Patrick was the last to leave after a final check of the burning building to make sure nobody had been left behind. This was not done very thoroughly as he apparently overlooked Harry Boland and Diarmuid Lynch who were safeguarding some explosives. The main group went via Henry Place on to Moore Street, but there was no clear plan of action and nobody seems to have taken charge. When they came under machine-gun fire the men panicked and as none of the leaders took action Sean McLoughlin took it upon himself to steady the men. They subsequently took refuge in one of the houses in Moore Street. In the meantime The O'Rahilly, who had been sent out with a party of men as an advance guard to secure possession of the Williams and Woods factory, was killed by fire from the same machine-gun.[189]

On Saturday morning the men burrowed from one house to another ending up in 16 Moore Street. Plans were then made to storm the barricade from there with bayonets fixed, but before this could take place the Provisional Government decided after an emotional meeting by majority vote to surrender. It is said Tom Clarke in particular opposed it, and wanted a glorious stand, while Patrick wanted to make a dash for the Four Courts. The final decision was influenced by the killing of three elderly men who were shot by soldiers when they left their houses opposite the rebels to escape the approaching fires. This seems to have convinced the majority to surrender 'to avoid further casualties'. In a letter to his mother after his arrest Patrick claims he had been in favour of 'one more desperate sally before opening negotiations'. Apparently the men felt deflated by the decision, some burst out crying after they were told their cause was 'postponed to a future generation'. They were then given the option to escape instead of surrender which some did.[190]

Elizabeth O'Farrell who had acted as a nurse during the fighting went to Brigadier-General Lowe under a white flag to inform him Patrick wished to negotiate terms of surrender. Lowe gave her a written reply: 'A woman has come in and tells me you wish to negotiate with me. I am prepared to receive you in BRITAIN ST. at the North end of MOORE ST. provided that you surrender unconditionally. You will proceed up MOORE ST. accompanied only by the woman who brought you this note, under a white flag.'[191] They were given half an hour to surrender unconditionally, which was accepted. Before Patrick actually went over to make the surrender he and the wounded Connolly made sure they were clean shaven by borrowing a safety razor from one of the men.[192] Patrick then walked over to the corner of Moore Street and Parnell Street and handed over his sword, automatic pistol in its holder, his ammunition and a canteen. He was taken to the Army Headquarters in the Royal Hospital at Parkgate, and on Saturday evening to Arbour Hill Detention Barracks. Contrary to some reports Patrick went with them in a calm and controlled manner.[193]

The leaders seemed to be under the illusion that they would be executed but that the lives of their followers would be spared. Patrick had told them 'the survivors could work on when the conscience of the people had been aroused'. Although officially there was an unconditional surrender, General Maxwell seems to have indicated in an interview with Patrick after the surrender that he had no doubt that the British Government would exercise clemency for the rank and file.[194] In the letter to his mother from prison Patrick wrote 'Our hope and belief is that the Government will spare the lives of all our followers but we do not expect that they will spare the lives of the leaders. We are ready to die and we shall die cheerfully and proudly.'[195] In the men he included his brother Willie who had no official status in the Volunteers.

In the same vein Patrick signed surrender orders for all the other units fighting in the city, north Co. Dublin and Wexford. Various representatives of units who refused to accept a surrender came to Patrick in prison on Saturday to verify the genuineness of the orders. Richard Mulcahy who had fought successfully under Thomas Ashe around Fingal, Co. Dublin, was brought to Arbour Hill where he saw Patrick who was lying on a bed-board in a cell with a table, a glass of water and some biscuits. After Patrick was ordered to get up a short conversation took place: 'I asked (1) was order bona fide. He said "yes" (2) Did it refer to the whole of Ireland or only Dublin. He said the whole of Ireland. (3) Would any good be done by a small band holding out … longer. He said no.' During the conversation Patrick seemed quite detached, but showed no sign of mental stress.[196]

Despite the explicit orders the fighting continued for some time. Most Volunteers eventually surrendered and were arrested. When they were led away the response of the people was rather negative. The damage and deaths caused a general revulsion which was expressed by booing and throwing mud and garbage at the Volunteers, while some of the British soldiers received chocolate and tea. One exception was the cheers from a number of prisoners who had managed to escape during the Rising.[197] Patrick anticipated the feelings of dejection which were no doubt rife among the defeated rebels and made clear in the original surrender order that the rebellion was more than just a symbolic sacrifice. He argued it had practical benefits for Ireland, 'the glorious stand which had been made by the soldiers of Irish freedom during the last five days in Dublin has been sufficient to gain recognition of Ireland's claim at an international peace conference'.[198]

During his court-martial on Tuesday 2 May, which was presided over by Brigadier-General C.G. Blackader, Patrick refused to have anything said in his defence. The only time he spoke was to read out a prepared statement. By all accounts he was calm and collected before and during the proceedings. Some remarked he was silent and broody 'but he was always that way'.[199] In the statement he admitted being President of the Provisional Government and Commandant General of the forces of the Irish Republic. 'I stand over all my acts and words done or spoken in those capacities.' He expressed no regret for their actions, and again claimed victory in defeat by having kept the fire of Irish nationalism burning: 'We seem to have lost. We have not lost. To refuse to fight would have been to lose; to fight is to win. We have kept faith with the past, and handed on a tradition to the future.' He further denied the charge of aiding and abetting England's enemy, stating: 'Germany is no more to me than England is.' Acknowledging German aid he denied having been a paid agent of theirs. The rebels had fought for freedom which was the all encompassing motive behind their actions which would eventually succeed. 'To us it is more desirable than anything in the world. If you strike us down now, we shall rise again and renew the fight. You cannot conquer Ireland. You cannot extinguish the Irish passion for freedom. If our deed has not been sufficient to win freedom, then our children will win it by a better deed.'[200] He ended with a plea to spare his men:

> I fully understand now, as then, that my own life is forfeit to British law, and I shall die very cheerfully if I can think that the British Government, as it has already shown itself strong, will now show itself magnanimous enough to accept my single life in forfeiture and give a general amnesty to the brave men and boys who have fought at my bidding.

Blackader was very impressed with the way Patrick conducted himself. The Countess of Fingall famously recalled how Blackader said afterwards: 'I have just done one of the hardest things I have ever had to do. I have had to condemn to death one of the finest characters I have ever come across. There must be something very wrong in the state of things that makes a man like that a rebel.'[201] Patrick retained this peaceful acceptance of his fate and calmly prepared for his execution. After his court-martial he wrote a number of letters and poems which expressed his state of mind. In a very practical manner he wrote statements dealing with the settlement of his business and his literary affairs, and asked Sir John Maxwell the commanding officer to make sure the seven pounds and some loose change he had on him would be handed over to his mother. While maintaining his poise and reserve he became more expressive of his feelings in his final hours. In the poem 'To My Brother' he emphasised how important Willie had been to him. 'Of all the men that I have known on earth, You only have been my familiar friend.' He expressed the same sentiment in a letter in which he thanked Willie for his support in their endeavours.[202]

He was even more expressive of his feelings to his mother. In the poem 'To My Mother' he thanked her for all the things she gave him, life, love, pity, sanity and faith. He is sorry for the great reserve they maintained towards each other. How he was unable to express his love or sorrow to her, but trust that she knew it was there:

> You must have known, when I was silent,
> That some strange thing within me kept me dumb,
> Some strange deep thing, when I should shout my love?
> I have sobbed in secret
> For that reserve which yet I could not master

In the accompanying letter he told her he was happy to die 'except for the great grief of parting from you'. He finished the letter with a declaration of his love: 'I have not words to tell my love of you and how my heart yearns to you all. I will call to you in my heart at the last moment.' He called upon her not to grieve for him but to 'think of it as a sacrifice which God asked of me and of you'. In the poem 'A Mother Speaks' which accompanied the letter he compared his mother's feelings to those of Mary and his act to that of Jesus: 'Receive my first-born into thy arms, Who also hath gone out to die for men.'[203] This theme had become more prominent in his writings towards the end of 1915. In his little poem 'Christmas' he called upon Jesus to help the Gael in the coming battle, while in two of his four English poems, 'The Rebel' and 'The Fool', he used symbols of Christian sacrifice to intimate a connection between the speaker and the Messiah. Such expressions of messianic nationalism were, however, quite common in Irish, English and European poetry.[204]

He claimed to be happy to die 'a soldier's death for Ireland and for freedom', a death he would have chosen if he had had the choice. He was satisfied with the role he had played, and although the rebels might not be appreciated now, history would vindicate their actions. He repeated his assertion in the letter he had written on Monday: 'We have preserved Ireland's honour and our own. Our deeds of last week are the most splendid in Ireland's history. People will say hard things of us now, but we shall be remembered by posterity and blessed by unborn generations.'[205] In his final poem 'The Wayfarer' he expressed his sadness over the passing of youth and beauty, and how he leaves sorrowfully.

In his final hours Patrick was initially denied any visits. Fr Aloysius, who was fetched by military car to cater for the prisoners, had to approach the Irish Party leaders Dillon and Nugent to get access to Patrick to administer the last sacraments. Dillon had been alarmed by the actions of the rebels but also admired them and reacted positively to this request. Patrick was very calm and prayed with the priest. He expressed particularly pleasure and relief when Fr Aloysius told him even the atheistic James Connolly had taken Holy Communion: 'I can't forget the fervour with which, looking up to heaven, he said "Thank God. It is the one thing I was anxious about".' Fr Aloysius stayed with Patrick almost to the time of his execution on Wednesday morning 3.30 a.m.[206]

6 Legacy: The failure in triumph

I shouldn't, if I were you, waste my time on Pearse. He wasn't worth anybody's attention.[1]

Early responses

Despite this damning judgement, a great many people have given Patrick Pearse a great deal of attention ever since his execution. In death Patrick quickly achieved a status he never had had during his life. Ruth Dudley Edwards has most famously attested to this, to some extent self-predicted success, in the title of her influential biography *The Triumph of Failure*. Indeed even before his execution Patrick had already become something of a celebrity as indicated by a letter he received from an American cashier who congratulated him on his 'appointment as the first President of Ireland' and requested an autograph.[2] Obviously answering a widespread demand, a whole range of handbills were printed immediately after the Rising circulating Patrick's last letters, some of his poems and his oration for O'Donovan Rossa. A great many pictures of the executed leaders of the Rising, in which Patrick always was the central figure, were also produced.[3] Over time his image became revered in Irish households, only rivalled by Jesus Christ and from 1963 on by John F. Kennedy as the first Irish-American president. The admiration for Pearse and his comrades generated a range of unlikely stories about their actions and pedigree including the ridiculous proposition that Patrick had nearly been appointed provost of the Unionist bulwark of Trinity College, Dublin.[4]

The Rising and its immediate aftermath also sparked off a spree of other publications. The first three books on the events appeared in 1916. These came from the hands of some admiring Irish-American acquaintances, a British and a Canadian journalist, who all attempted to explain why the Rising occurred to a flabbergasted public outside Ireland.[5] The title of F. MacKenzie's book *The Irish Rebellion What Happened and Why* typifies this approach. The Irish-Americans were unreservedly admiring about his abilities claiming he could have been 'a great lawyer, a great writer, or a great scholar' and that he was the 'finest orator I have ever heard'. Some realism nevertheless shone through regarding Patrick's lack of charisma in personal relations: 'his greatness was rarely apparent at first acquaintance'.[6] In the latter works the authors more objectively identified most of Patrick's strengths and weakness, but although they had a unionist sentiment they ultimately were also admiring. John F. Boyle described Patrick as a visionary leader: 'Gifted with eloquence of a kind that powerfully appealed to the Celtic temperament.'[7] While MacKenzie saw him as 'a man of letters, of delicate and fine sensibilities, a barrister, an Irish scholar, and above all profoundly religious'.[8]

The need to explain 1916 seemed to dissipate after 1916. The attention of interested outsiders was taken away by the political and later military conflict which developed in Ireland at that time. An exception was a short booklet by the Irish writer S. MacGiollanate, which sought 'to bring people to understand why he [Patrick] went into so terrible an enterprise' but at the same time argued that it was not yet possible to judge whether it had been justified or should be condemned.[9] All other publications before the Anglo-Irish Treaty of 1921 eulogised the lives of the leaders of the Easter Rising and in particular that of Patrick, with titles such as *Memories of the Dead* and *Golden Moments with P.H. Pearse*. In it his stature was aggrandised by comparing Patrick to President Wilson and describing him as 'the Gael incarnate'.[10] The most influential biography *The Man Called Pearse*, which did attempt to show Patrick as a human being with his faults, came from the hands of his former secretary and onetime pupil Desmond Ryan.[11]

More attention was also paid to specific aspects of Patrick's life. In 1917 a booklet appeared describing his work at St Enda's, while his writings in Irish and English were dealt with by James Hayes in 1920.[12] Most indicative of his new status as national hero were the numerous reprints of his literary writings, his plays and poems, his educational and political thoughts and his writings on St Enda's. Most of these were first published in 1917. Significantly there were a number of different publishers engaged in this, often bringing out competing compilations of similar work.[13] In the United States one such compilation of writings from a number of the rebels was published in 1921 still with the intention of explaining the Rising.[14] All these works certainly had their effect on public perception. In 1920 a twelve-year-old girl wrote a poem in which Patrick was portrayed as one who gave his life for freedom, stood for justice and had no fear. This was also noticeable abroad. The first foreign language compilation appeared in 1922 in Germany which had long had strong academic ties with Ireland in the area of linguistics.[15]

The idealisation of Patrick and his life became most apparent in the United States. It reached an unrivalled height in a booklet published in 1920 by the writer M.J. Hannan. In it Patrick was positioned as a model for almost everyone:

> in person and life of P.H. Pearse, the novelist will find the most fertile field for his pen. … The soldier will find in him the most disinterested patriotism … the statesmen may well learn from him what goes to make for real democracy and true contentment … the countrymen will see in him Irish thought, culture and nationality developed to their highest.[16]

The first comprehensive treatment of his life also came from abroad. In 1925 the Fleming Steven Debroey published a Dutch language biography in which the many virtues of Patrick were celebrated without restraint. 'He was a noble man, conscientious, principled, pious, magnanimous, hard on himself and mild on others, simultaneously strong-willed and tender, wise and tolerant, talented and modest, passionate yet controlled, honest and incorruptible, inspired by high ideals and able to communicate these to others.'[17] Debroey believed that Pearse lived on in the heart of the Irish.[18] In 1932 the Frenchman Louis N. Le Roux published his *La vie de Patrice Pearse* which became the standard work for most Irish nationalists upon its translation into English by Desmond Ryan in 1932. To him Patrick was more than human: 'He possessed all the qualities which go to the making of a saint to a degree that it is hardly within my province to analyse.'[19] The idea Patrick had saint-like qualities was supported by Irish writers such as Aodh de Blacam, Brennan Whitmore, Desmond Ryan and a reviewer in *Studies* of 1922 who claimed Patrick's writings were like St John of the Cross or Thomas a Kempis.[20]

Contested independence

The new Irish state instituted in 1922 had more difficulties with Patrick's legacy. On the one hand, he was celebrated as one of its founding fathers and streets were renamed after him in many towns and cities. Great Brunswick Street in Dublin, where Patrick was born, was renamed Pearse Street in 1926, while other places like Nenagh and Clonakilty had done the same even before that. The outbreak of the civil war in 1922 had made Patrick a more controversial figure. His celebration of anti-state violence became a problem to the new Cumann na nGaedheal Government in the face of republican opposition. RTE's first director of broadcasting, Seamus Clandillon, refused to broadcast an item on a speech by Patrick in 1926: 'Owing to various circumstances which I need not particularise, I think that your suggested talk re Pearse's speech might not be quite suitable, as we have a very mixed audience indeed. We have to be very careful about broadcasting anything of a political character.'[21]

Once the losing side in the civil war under Eamon de Valera came to power in 1932 they began to claim Patrick as their own and tried to control his legacy. The Rising was commemorated annually without trepidation, culminating in a big 'victory' parade in 1941 at its 25th anniversary. This appropriation by Fianna Fáil culminated in a row over the unveiling of the sculpture 'Death of Cúchulainn' in the GPO. A large number of IRA veterans refused to attend because of the partisan approach taken. In many ways 1916 and its commemoration always remained a party political issue thereafter.[22]

The uncritical admiration that characterised the writings on Patrick can also be detected in the way politicians referred to him in Dáil Eireann from 1919 well into the 1970s. Already during the debates over the Anglo-Irish Treaty of December 1921 both sides occasionally called upon him to support their position. The anti-Treaty side mentioned him ten times, generally emphasising that he gave his life for freedom, thereby saving the soul of Ireland which was now allegedly given away by the pro-Treaty party. The latter retorted four times mostly recalling Patrick's support for the Irish Council Bill in 1907 and thereby implying he would have been in favour of compromise and thus of the Treaty.[23]

In the absence of republicans in the Dáil from the outbreak of the civil war in June 1922 until 1927 only eleven references were made to Patrick or his thinking after the Treaty debates, of which six were by the opposition. When his name was used this was usually in passing and to add weight to some point made regarding language policy, respectability, or by opposition deputies against the executions of republicans. Several TDs including Kevin O'Higgins tried to boost their statements by peppering them with short references like 'what Pearse called', 'as Pearse said' or 'Pearse was right when he said'.[24] A more instrumental use of Patrick's thinking was made by Labour leader Thomas Johnson in September 1922 when he quoted from Patrick's writings on social policy to attract support for an amendment to the Free State constitution which would bring it in line with the Democratic Programme, which had set out the social objectives of the Dáil in 1919.[25]

After Fianna Fáil entered the parliament in August 1927 the debate on Pearse became more strident. In October 1928 Fianna Fáil TD Patrick Little, for instance, accused Minister Hogan of preferring pornography over the ideals of Padraic Pearse.[26] Although his name was now invoked at least five times each year, the essence did not change. He was generally called upon to support a criticism or to undermine someone's position by arguing that Patrick would have disagreed with it, but there was no real attempt to implement his ideas. This was pointed out by another Fianna Fáil TD, Eamonn Cooney, in December 1931 during a debate on poverty in Dublin: 'Pearse – the man to whose memory we all pay lip service.'[27] A few months earlier Little had complained that the parliamentary library did not contain any of Patrick's works and he claimed that children in Dublin did not know who he was.[28] In 1929 he had attempted to deal more seriously with Patrick's ideas in a debate on the jury's Protection Bill, but he was prevented by the Leas-Cheann Comhairle from quoting him, after which he meekly called for progress on fulfilling his ideals.[29]

After Fianna Fáil came to power in 1932 the frequency with which Patrick or his ideas were referred to went down dramatically. He had been mentioned by them twenty-three times between August 1927 and March 1932, his name was brought up just seventeen times during their sixteen years in office which ended in February 1948. Ever since Patrick's death, opposition parties, irrespective of their origin, seemed to have been more comfortable with the implication of his thinking on policy than those in government, and anti-treatyites more so than pro-treatyites. This was particularly apparent during the politically charged period from 1927 until the late 1940s. Cumann na nGaedheal had been quiet regarding Patrick's thinking while in government but became quite vocal after 1932. During their initial ten years in office they referred to him eight times, but this went up to thirty during the following sixteen years in opposition, while another thirteen references were made by other opposition parties.

Looking at the development of the Irish Free State and later the Republic of Ireland it could well be argued that despite the triumph which lay in the successful institution of a separate Irish state it failed from the start to become the type of society Patrick had dreamed of. Consequently he was used mostly to criticise those in power irrespective of their party affiliation. From the end of the Treaty debates in 1922 until the summer of 2008 Patrick was called upon almost twice as often by opposition than by government parties, 179 versus 106 times. This applied in particular to Fine Gael and its predecessor Cumann na nGaedheal. They mentioned his ideas fifty-nine times in opposition but only twenty-one times in their admittedly fewer years in office. In general it is clear that all parties referred to him irrespective of their political colour, from Cumann na nGaedheal to die-hard republicans like Clan na Poblachta, and from Labour to the farmers' party, Clan na Talmham. As a result of this cross-party acceptance his ideas did not become part of a specific party programme. Between 1919 and the summer of 2008 Patrick or his thinking was mentioned in the Dáil 295 times, just more than three times per year on average. Fianna Fáil had a slight edge over Fine Gael and its immediate predecessors. They used him 125 times in debates, while he was mentioned eighty-four times by Fine Gael deputies, fifty-two times by Labour and thirty-four times by deputies of other parties and independents. These figures are roughly in line with the electoral strength of these parties and groupings.

The change of government in 1932 had no real impact on the manner in which Patrick's name was used. His writings were called upon to attack particular policies. Cuts in the salaries of primary school teachers were, for instance, criticised by citing an editorial written by Patrick in 1907 that teachers should be paid properly.[30] There was also a certain amount of selective quoting by all parties to support their ideas on education and language policy. In a debate on the amount of money the poor had to live on in 1941 Minister Sean Lemass showed himself to be exasperated with this: 'It is possible to quote from documents written by Padraig Pearse and others as to the inadequacy of £1 a week for the purpose of maintaining and educating a family. All these things get us nowhere.'[31] It was not just the government parties who felt the use of Patrick's writings could obscure the real issues. In 1935 Frank MacDermot from the National Centre Party attacked the Old IRA Association of veterans for intolerance, and stated: 'They are fond of quoting Pearse to the effect that those who love good must hate evil, but before you apply a motto of that sort it is very necessary that you should understand what evil consists in.'[32]

Most parties nevertheless continued in the now well-established way of strengthening their argument by referring to something Pearse said. The reaction of the Labour TD James Hickey to Lemass's statement cited above indicated Patrick's almost oracle-type status at that time: 'What comes before the family if you say that what Patrick Pearse said does not matter?'[33] He was given a similar position by another Labour TD in a debate on free education in 1948. 'That does not conform to the ideas for which Pearse and Connolly strove and laid down their lives.'[34] Of course the interpretation of the various parties of the essence of his thinking varied. Where Fianna Fáil stressed his republicanism, Fine Gael concentrated on his cultural agenda and Labour on his association with the ideas of Connolly.[35] All the more remarkable is that Patrick was not even mentioned in the debates on the new constitution in 1937. Apparently all parties felt it represented his ideas, even on social policy and the position of women.

During this period there were some more sustained attempts by opposition members to use Patrick to attack Fianna Fáil. Leading Fine Gael deputy Richard Mulcahy who had fought in 1916 and had known Patrick personally was particularly prominent in this. He returned repeatedly to the contention that Pearse was never a doctrinaire republican, but that he had always supported a compromise like the Irish Council Bill or the Home Rule Bill of 1912. Without such willingness to compromise, which had been displayed by people like Michael Collins and Arthur Griffith in 1922, he argued the state would never have been as free as it was now. 1916, he said, would never have been successful 'if we had not a Clarke and a Pearse and a Connolly to beat down the judgments of some people who sit on the Front Bench of Fianna Fáil now'.[36] In 1939 he blamed the lack of progress on implementing Patrick's ideas on what he called the obsession of Fianna Fáil and by implication the IRA with the type of state to be established instead of the creation of what he called real freedom:

> what Pearse did immolate himself in 1916 for was the very same thing that he self-dedicated himself to in 1908 and 1912. And, instead of the minds of the people of this country being allowed to dwell on what are the real things for which our people struggled in the past and the real things that in their hearts and minds were their national traditions, their minds have been concentrated on the State and on the particular type of State labelled in the particular circumstances of 1916.

Minister Frank Aiken countered with the argument that the people could only develop their own culture and their own resources if there was no 'interference or any coercion by an outside Power'.[37]

In its educational policy Fianna Fáil indeed showed itself to be particularly concerned with the portrayal of Patrick. In the *Notes for Teachers* issued by the Department of Education in 1933 the importance of his role was underlined. It stipulated that '[t]he continuity of the separatist idea from Tone to Pearse should be stressed', and that the teacher should be 'imbuing the minds of his pupils with the ideals and aspirations of men such as Thomas Davis and Patrick Pearse'.[38] This was an addition to the emphasis on national identity and Irish history in schools which had been instigated by the Cumann na nGaedheal governments after independence.[39] All history textbooks issued until the mid-1960s, except the one for Protestant schools, indeed focused mainly on Patrick's contribution when dealing with the Easter Rising. One of the first books written for use in primary teaching described him as 'the greatest of these leaders and one of the noblest characters in Irish history'.[40] The tone of the various history textbooks remained the same until the mid-1960s.[41] In 1963 children were still taught that after 1916 'Pearse and his comrades took their place with Emmet and Tone in the hearts of the people.'[42] Some of Patrick's actions were also idealised over time. His role in the court case on the carrying of a name in Irish on a cart was greatly embellished by the famous lawyer Tim Healy between 1905 and 1942.[43]

The long 1950s

No fundamental change in the references to Patrick can be detected in the Dáil discussions up to the mid-1960s either. Although Deputy Donnellan of Clan na Talmham claimed in 1953 that some young people had almost forgotten Patrick's name despite the emphasis on his role in schools, these decades saw the most frequent mention of his name in the Dáil, with a peak of fifty-four times in the 1950s.[44] The more serious examples concerned an attack by the former Clan na Poblachta TD McQuillan on the government for its willingness to give up financial control over the country by spending money abroad and invite foreign investors to buy up Irish industry.[45] He claimed this was not what Pearse and the other men of 1916 made the supreme sacrifice for. His former party colleague Dr Browne objected to the reforms of the education system in 1958 as they would only perpetuate the existing class-tiered system in society which Patrick had objected to.[46] The Irish language was as always the most frequently mentioned aspect. Bringing the Fine Gale TD Thaddeus Lynch to the lament:

> It is not right to come in here, talk about Republicanism and to bring the memory of poor Pádraig Pearse into all this. Another thing that has done the Irish language revival movement an immense amount of harm is the bringing of Pádraig Pearse's name and memory, and the bones, relics and records of fine people to the hustings, debasing their memory for political gun-powder purposes.[47]

In the course of the 1960s the references became much more matter of fact but generally remained admiring. Referring simply to what 'the late Commandant General Pearse wished'.[48] Some were able to be somewhat irreverent, using him to make opponents look silly: 'May I take the opportunity of quoting from that wonderful man, P.H. Pearse: "If one man redeemed the world, one man can free a people"? It seems to me that Deputy Sherwin now believes that he can free or save a Government.'[49] A more concrete reference was made to the restoration with government funds of what was called Pearse Memorial Cottage at Ros Muc, Co. Galway, in 1964.[50]

A similar stasis can be detected in the literature on Pearse. No biography was published between 1938 and 1966, when the fiftieth anniversary of the Rising took place.[51] Neither was there much attention paid to his writings. After the abundance of reproductions including several issues of his complete works, which started shortly after his execution, virtually nothing appeared after 1924 apart from three minor publications of some of his stories. Patrick had clearly become a fixture in the nationalist canon, which apparently did not need any serious attention. One 1916 veteran claimed later that even in their 1916 Club Patrick was ignored: 'they will talk of Tom Clarke, Sean McDermott and Jim Connolly (his name always gets a hand) but P[earse] is never mentioned'.[52]

The experiment in education Patrick initiated in St Enda's also came to an early end. Having been run by some of its former pupils since 1917 the school was closed in 1935 due to financial considerations, despite large donations which had enabled his family to buy the building in 1920 and keep the school running in 1924.[53] After the school's demise Patrick's sister Margaret continued to live in the building till her death in 1968. The property was then handed over to the state and eventually turned into the Pearse Museum. Patrick's life and work also continued to be remembered actively in the history curriculum and Irish language teaching in the schools. There were of course annual commemorations of the Rising in Ireland and in the United States, and Patrick was frequently mentioned in various publications in glowing terms.[54]

Before the late 1960s this universal praise and the occasional lamenting of the misuse of his name was only broken on a very odd occasion. Some of his former fellow students at Trinity College were critical, but the most damning attack came from one of Patrick's former star pupils, Denis Gwynn. He was the son of a Redmondite MP and had joined the British Army in 1914. In 1923 he published a scathing article in the *Dublin Review* in which he accused Patrick of having used St Enda's 'to provide himself with the nucleus of a band of young politicians who would follow him to the scaffold as the political successor of Wolfe Tone and Robert Emmet'.[55] This accusation may well have something to do with the difficult position Irish veterans of the British Army found themselves in after the war, when Patrick's revolutionary brand of nationalism had become dominant and ex-soldiers were widely seen as traitors. Gwynn's claim that 'Colossal egoism was perhaps the leading feature of Pearse's otherwise attractive personality' also fits in with this argument as Gwynn had been particularly close to Patrick in his years at St Enda's.[56]

1966 and thereafter

A more in-depth revaluation of Patrick's life and works only came with the fiftieth anniversary of the Rising in 1966. There was of course a great deal of hagiographical pomp and ceremony surrounding this event. The state celebrated on a large scale with a military parade through O'Connell Street and other public proceedings. Privately various events were also organised. The Christian Brothers School where Patrick went to school and taught staged a play on his life and organised a wreath laying at his grave.[57] There were nevertheless some signs of a more critical attitude starting to develop. The official *Guide to the Historical Exhibition Commemorative of the Rising of 1916* dealt with Patrick's life in a very matter of fact manner. In the lead-up to the commemoration Tom Clarke's widow Kathleen objected to a reference to Patrick as President of the Irish Republic. A title she claimed belonged to her late husband. In letters to the Taoiseach Sean Lemass she was particularly irreverent about Patrick's role in the rising and his ability to lead: 'he knew as much about commanding as my dog'. Lemass did apparently not see the need to defend Patrick against her allegations.[58]

Written accounts of his life also slowly became more critical. In 1948 J.J. Horgan had already published a book on Irish nationalism in which he called the Rising unjustified and had started to take a more dispassionate look at Patrick.[59] Hedley McCay's biography from 1966, although generally admiring, was critical of Patrick's more extreme statements and his support for violence. She also rejected his unquestioned celebration of the merits of the ancient Gaelic civilisation and culture. His belief that its myths and education system were the best in the world she saw as 'presumptuous to say the least' and as 'a very eccentric and wild conclusion that could only be arrived at through the use of a not very critical faculty'.[60] She even compared this to the attitude of fascists and communists.[61] Although she nevertheless positioned herself as an Irish nationalist who celebrated Patrick's legacy, his brand of nationalism was certainly too extreme for her.[62]

Thus it is in the nature of things that the GL [Gaelic League] will produce hundreds and hundreds of harmless devotees of Gaelic culture and at the same time will cast up the few rare hotheads, bombasts and that most dangerous of all threats to the ordered Establishment – the intellectual gunman who fondles the weapon probably while reciting the Rosary in Gaelic. Sean Sabhat and Padraic Pearse are not freaks thrown up by a harmless literary movement, but the epitome of frustrated men of action who seek to set nations ablaze with their own faith.[63]

She blamed this on his 'obsessive love for wronged Ireland' which had come to cloud his scholarly outlook. If it had not been for his commonsense this blindness would have come close to madness she argued.[64] She was also the first to address the issue of his sexuality. The lack of activity in this regard she blamed on a mother complex and a tendency to excessive religiosity which accounted for the unnatural treatment of women and religion in his writing that could 'be morbid and bordering on the neurotic'.[65]

In an essay written at the same time but published only posthumously in 1972 Fr Francis Shaw took a similar line. He portrayed the men of 1916 as brave but argued their work should be approached critically. He challenged Patrick's image of the ancient Gaelic world as largely a product of his imagination and as a sanitised version of reality where sexual activity, incestuous relations and violent behaviour were excised. Although appreciating Patrick's incisive mind and particularly his thinking on education, Shaw claimed Patrick was out of step with most Irishmen of his time in a political sense. His thinking in this regard was neither profound nor original. Shaw took issue with Patrick's equation of the patriot with Christ, which was against Christian teaching, and his glorification of violence, of which 'it is hard to imagine anyone reading those words today without a shudder'. Shaw tried to rehabilitate Douglas Hyde and Eoin MacNeill, and claimed that 1916 was largely responsible for partition and the civil war.[66]

The eccentricity of the rebels thinking in Irish society prior to 1916 is also a major element in the work of William Irwin Thompson published in 1967, which focused on Patrick's obsession with violence and growing identification with Christ. He argued that radicals in Ireland including Patrick slowly started to believe in their own violent slogans as a result of the ridicule and indifference they encountered in society which ultimately led them to martyrdom. That Patrick's voice had become more and more desperate and violent was almost inevitable. If he had not taken up arms his whole life would have been meaningless and absurd, even failed violence became a relief.[67] In his death Patrick sought to become a martyr and mirrored himself in this on the life of Christ. His ascetic lifestyle was another example of this identification.[68] Describing Patrick's actions as stemming from personal gratification did not sit well with the sacrificial notion of Patrick's motives that had been propagated up to then.

The critical revaluation of Patrick's life and work reached its height in Ruth Dudley Edwards' biography of 1977. Like the largely descriptive work of R.J. Porter published in 1973 she based her book on what Patrick really said but combined it with information from other sources. Although not adding much to the analysis in the works mentioned above, including Porter's emphasis on Patrick's open-mindedness,[69] she constructed a systematic critique and placed the development of his thinking in a social and personal context. The direct combination of ideas and experience made this book the standard work on Patrick. Popularising the critical assessments and for the first time openly suggesting Patrick was homosexual has certainly also made this a controversial book. Surprisingly considering the level of psychological interpretation she relied primarily on his public utterances and dismissed his numerous private letters as disappointing.[70]

The development of a critical treatment of Pearse and in particular his thinking on the use of force at the end of the 1960s is of course not surprising in light of the outbreak of the troubles in Northern Ireland. A general fear that his words might inspire people to fight for a free Ireland was certainly present. Xavier Carty's 1978 biography was most explicit about this. Although admiring Patrick's courage, bravery and strength of character, he had great difficulties with Patrick's portrayal of himself as a Messiah, whose death could save Ireland.[71] Carty made a very passionate condemnation of Patrick's celebration of the use of violence, and even argued that his writings 'indicate a narrow fanaticism as well as an obsession with racial purity and the pre-eminence of a mythical Gaelic race suggesting that if he had not died at Kilmainham he might have been an Irish Hitler'.[72] The outbreak of violence in the North was directly linked by him to the actions of the 1916 men. He declared that he had written his 'book to expose the myth of 1916 and the false interpretation of Irish history which created it'. In a direct reference to Ruth Dudley Edwards he argued that Patrick's life was 'a lesson in the errors to be avoided', and that 'His was not the triumph of failure, but a terrible mistake.'[73]

The development of a critical attitude was slower to reach the Dáil. In the late 1960s his name was still used to support various policies, and Fianna Fáil still openly claimed to be the inheritor of his aims and thinking.[74] In 1968 the Fine Gaeler Patrick Lindsay even defended what he termed agitators by calling upon the fact that Pearse, Collins and Connolly were seen as such in their days.[75] Not surprisingly it was Conor Cruise O'Brien, who had just left the Labour Party at that time, who was the first to remark on the dangers associated with the veneration of Patrick in the Dáil in 1971. Although he still argued that the use of force in 1916 had been 'retrospectively and posthumously upheld by a majority of the Irish people, excluding the northeast corner', he very carefully warned of the potential consequences: 'The fact that the 1916 tradition is the central venerated one in our society and is essentially not one of Parliamentary democracy introduces an ambiguity in the relation of the Irish people to Parliament and to democracy, an ambiguity which it is very dangerous to upset.'[76] This lesson was soon drawn by many southern politicians. In 1971 the parade to commemorate 1916 was abandoned, and his name was now rarely mentioned in the Dáil.[77] In 1972 the Labour TD and Pearse supporter Dr David Thornley could justifiably lament that 'it is not fashionable to quote Pearse now in some places in this House'.[78]

It is clear that all TDs wrestled with the close association between Patrick and the use of physical force in light of the fast escalating IRA bombing campaign in the North in the early 1970s. The unanimous support for Patrick in the recent past made this a difficult process. The more outspoken supporters of Patrick attempted to draw a distinction between him and the members of the provisional IRA just like Conor Cruise O'Brien had done. Ruairí Brugha, Fianna Fáil TD and son of the former IRA Chief of Staff Cathal Brugha, claimed that control of the situation in the North was drifting into the hands of immature children and posed a rhetorical question: 'Do you think James Connolly or Patrick Pearse would send teenagers into the market place carrying bombs set to detonate?'[79] Even Dr Thornley was fully aware of the danger of being associated with the IRA, but accused others of tactical repudiation of violence: 'I am not ashamed of what I did. I would do it again in the morning but I wonder how those people who sit on the back benches over there and who were preaching republicanism as recently as three years ago, feel when they look in their shaving mirrors.' He also warned for the creation of new martyrs for the cause by the harsh policies towards the Provisional IRA.[80]

There was some criticism of the position of people like Thornley, but he felt it was necessary to acknowledge their past: 'We have to face the fact that this State was born in violence, that the tradition of violence runs right through it and runs right through its history books and runs right through its newspaper articles until very recently.'[81] Labour, he said, was founded by 'a gunman', Fine Gael by 'perhaps the most sophisticated assassin of his generation', and the Fianna Fáil Minister for Justice 'would not be sitting where he is sitting at this moment if Pearse had not stood aside and Tom Clarke had shot down the door of the General Post Office in 1916.'[82] He admired these men and politicians had to deal with the tradition they all had inherited.

One of the few TDs who actually attempted to do so was the Fine Gaeler Richard Burke, who tackled the central role of Patrick's writings in the Irish education system. He gave the example of the discussion of Patrick's graveside oration at O'Donovan Rossa's funeral in the English course for the intermediate: 'The emphasis on the military is there right through this man's writing. We must be very careful, I suggest, in dealing with these matters to give the pupils a sound philosophical basis for their judgment in relation to these matters.' Paraphrasing the words of William Yeats in reference to the 1916 Rising he wondered: 'have those who had in their hands the malleable mind of the Irish youth, ever lain awake at night and asked: "Did any words of mine send out certain men"' – turning the original phrase slightly – 'who shot the English?' He felt there was a special responsibility for politicians in this regard.[83] Teachers seem to have accepted this lead during the 1970s. In interviews they claimed not to have taught much about Patrick, because he was considered an ultra-nationalist and associated with the ideology of the Provisional IRA.[84] The rejection by the Abbey in 1979 of the play they commissioned for the centenary of Patrick's birth also fits in with this new outlook.[85]

Although reference to Patrick's political thinking thus became increasingly difficult in the Dáil,[86] he was still called upon to support less controversial policies such as nature conservation: 'if we are genuinely anxious to pursue the ideas of Pearse we can best do so through the national parks which the nation controls, the wildlife, the flora and fauna'.[87] Dr Thornley even paraphrased him in support of the legalisation of contraception.[88] The Dáil also remained willing to associate itself with his name. In 1975 money was allocated for the restoration of Patrick's old home, and in honour of the centenary IR£50,000 was reserved for bursaries and scholarship. In 1973 Sean Lemass proudly reported that a study of the Pearse family papers revealed to him that Patrick was a good businessman as well as a patriot.[89]

Modern times

In the academic community almost complete silence followed the critical biographies of Edwards and Carty of the late 1970s. The only works that appeared around the time of his centenary were a number of often short Irish language biographies which were only accessible to a small audience. Although somewhat innocent in their portrayal they based themselves on a thorough revaluation of the sources, in particular of his writings in *An Claidheamh Soluis*.[90] The sole English language book was a traditional assessment of Patrick's connection with Scotland, where a cross was erected to his memory in 1979 in the midst of the troubles in Northern Ireland.[91] A more influential contribution in the long run was made at this time by Seamus Ó Buachalla, who was responsible for the publication of Patrick's letters, literary and educational writings, emphasising in particular Patrick's contribution to educational thought.[92]

   A more sophisticated treatment of Patrick emerged in the 1990s. The decade began, however, with the publication of Brian P. Murphy's belated defence of Patrick against what Murphy termed attacks on the undemocratic and unnecessary nature of the Rising contained in recent historiography. He claimed that Edwards in particular had impugned not only Patrick's motives, but also his methods and principles, and that considering the actions of Unionists and Conservatives he had been fully justified in his use of force. Although making some good points about the influences of political developments on Patrick's thinking, the fundamental premise that Patrick converted from a harmless adept of the language movement and a home ruler to a revolutionary does not concur with the evidence presented here.[93]

Murphy's book did herald the start of a growing assertiveness of nationalists against what many of them saw as a revisionist plot.

Subsequently the emphasis in historiography moved from general biography to the study of aspects of Patrick's life and works based on a thorough revaluation of the sources. A number of specialised studies appeared dealing with his prose and poetry, his educational writings and his role as a teacher. In these more positive assessments it was emphasised that Patrick was in many ways a progressive whose thinking fitted in with European-wide developments. The first of these was Philip O'Leary's analysis of Patrick's Irish language writings, in which he was portrayed as a multi-faceted personality and a modernist author. With this O'Leary meant a writer who attempted to break away from the conventions of old Gaelic prose and develop a modern literature in line with international literature.[94] This theme of Patrick as a modernist concurred with Ó Buachalla's treatment of Patrick's educational writings in which it had been shown he had tapped into an international debate on new educational methods.[95] Declan Kiberd later developed this further, by emphasising that Patrick was not only a modernist in his thinking on education but also on the position of women and social relations. Patrick had hidden this because he realised it was wise to present such ideas as a restoration of something ancient.[96] This linking of Irish developments and Patrick's ideas with those in Europe was done most explicitly by Eva Roe White who identified great similarities in the development of cultural nationalism in Ireland and Galicia.[97]

The psychological analysis of Patrick's involvement in the 1916 rising by Sean Farrell Moran dating from 1994 also fits into this attempt to show Patrick as a representative of his time. It positions the 1916 Rising in the context of what he terms a revolt against reason in Europe, as witnessed in the First World War and in other nationalist movements where the use of force was presented as a spiritual and moral force and even as a necessity. Moran did, however, not see this as a progressive but rather as a conservative and even racialist ideology.[98] For his analysis he based himself entirely on existing material, mostly the biographies of Edwards and McCay, but tried to make sense of Patrick by applying psychological theory to it. The lack of material available on his personal development and family background inevitably led to a certain amount of unfounded speculation.[99]

The main contribution of these books, however, was that they showed Patrick as a child of the time he was living in, instead of measuring his actions against the political and moral standards of the present. Apart from portraying Patrick's thinking in the context of contemporary thinking in the area of literature and education recent historiography has wrestled with the connection he made between violence and religion. Although most of his ideas in this area also fit in with contemporary ideas, an uncertainty can be detected in the reading of Patrick's willingness to sacrifice himself for the freedom of the nation. This sense of messianic duty associated with youth, rebirth and political violence seemed to come close to fascism to some.[100]

The discussions in the Dáil mirrored these historiographical developments. In the late 1970s Patrick was still called upon to criticise the government's social policy but in the 1980s Pearse became almost non-existent.[101] As the historian Vincent Comerford argued in 2003: 'Twenty or thirty years ago, a citation from Wolfe Tone, or Thomas Davis, or Patrick Pearse, or some other giant of the nationalist pantheon, was the most effective weapon for routing an opponent in public debate; now, such invocation is seldom heard.'[102] In the 1990s attitudes indeed clearly changed. Many TDs now argued that Patrick's thinking was irrelevant for the problems of today. In response to Tony Gregory, calling upon Patrick in his efforts to stop hare coursing in June 1993, the Fine Gaeler Browne stated: 'Is it not time we let the dead rest in peace? How do we know what he would think.'[103] Even Fianna Fáil colleagues expressed such sentiments: 'When I hear reference being made to Seán Lemass, Pádraig Pearse or Wolfe Tone in the Dáil or anywhere else I get goose pimples. People always talk about what these people would do now. We should let the dead generation rest in peace.'[104]

In the 1990s it became widely acceptable to be critical of Patrick. Fianna Fáil TD Mary Hanafin even made fun of his statement that he 'Squandered the splendid years that the Lord God gave to my youth in attempting impossible things' to criticise the people's obsession with the Lotto.[105] Unequivocal condemnations of his association with physical force were also now made more freely. 'Pearse's slogan that "Ireland unfree will never be at peace" has left us with more than 3,000 graves but without peace the people of Northern Ireland can never be free.'[106] Pronsias de Rossa turned the slogan around stating that as far as he was concerned 'the Irish people will never be free until we have peace'.[107]

This open criticism of Patrick's support for the use of force did, however, not prevent other TDs continuing to call upon him to support their policies. His description of the education system as a murder machine, his call to cherish all children equally, and his argument that a free Ireland should be Gaelic was widely used to put forward changes in educational, social and Irish language policy. Even the attempt to remake Ireland into a pluralist republic that would unite Catholic, Protestant and dissenter by allowing divorce and remarriage was connected to his thinking.[108] It apparently remained important to all parties to maintain an association with Patrick. The peace process in the North made this again even more attractive politically. In 2005 the military parade to commemorate the 1916 Rising which had been abandoned in 1972 was reinstated by the Fianna Fáil Government, which was portrayed by them as taking back Patrick's legacy from Sinn Féin.[109] Such partisan treatment was, however, unacceptable to all other parties including the Greens who also claimed a part of this:

> Because Fianna Fáil has decided the ceremonies are an Ard-Fheis device to rally its troops and try to out-do the Sinn Féin Party. People will see it for what it is. If Fianna Fáil was serious about the 1916 commemoration, rather than turning it into a political football it would have established a cross-party forum to establish a consensus on how all parties and Independents in the House, and civic society, would wish to commemorate the 1916 Rising centenary.[110]

Fianna Fáil in a sense reignited the controversy that had started in the 1930s over the ownership of Patrick. The controversy over this showed that right up to today he continues to be accepted by all as the central reference point for their conception of what Ireland should be.

Patrick Henry Pearse

Where does this leave us with this biography? The new evidence presented here has hopefully corrected a good many factual mistakes in the existing biographies, particularly regarding his early life and family background where one has had to rely largely on Patrick's own autobiographical account and the unreferenced older biographies which had the benefit of some personal acquaintance. Many aspects of my analysis of his personal development have been mentioned by different authors. It has been shown here that Patrick's thinking can indeed best be understood in the context of his time. There is in fact little extraordinary about his ideas which were primarily a personal interpretation of currents in Irish and international thought.

Where Patrick was unusual is in the, at times, fanatical application of these ideas. In explaining this we are inevitably drawn to his personality. Crucial in his personal development has been his family surroundings. The social aspirations of the family combined with the overanxious attitude of his father meant that the Pearse children socialised mostly within the extended family. The primary focus of Patrick always remained there throughout his life. This in some ways accounted for a stunted emotional development which manifested itself in a number of physical impediments and possibly his sexual ambivalence. Within the family Patrick obtained a central role from early on probably due to a combination of a strong personality and a creative mind. The fact that none of the siblings married and in many ways all became increasingly engrossed in Patrick's endeavours after his father's death indicates none of the family managed to develop an independent life beyond their childhood relationships.

Patrick's lack of social skills caused him to focus on self-development. He found a suitable subject in the Irish language and culture. The extreme devotion he showed to his studies as well as to his work was thus largely rooted in his personal circumstances. Looking for acceptance he soon discovered that working with others for a common purpose was a way of overcoming his social isolation. The Gaelic League provided a suitable environment where he could mix with higher social circles – something attractive to a member of the Catholic lower middle-class family with aspirations. During his time at university he also discovered that he did not fit in with legal circles. He subsequently gave up on a career in law which could have channelled these aspirations in a more innocuous direction. It could be argued that the concept of blocked mobility introduced by Benedict Anderson can at least partly explain Patrick's move to extreme politics.

In the focus on Irish language and culture his mixed background certainly played a role. Having an English father and an Irish mother made him acutely aware of his own identity. In the polarised public debate of the period he was forced to take sides. This made his choice for an Irish identity a much more deeply felt one than for those who were born on either side of the divide. To justify himself he was forced to argue that his mother's culture was superior to his father's. Being a man of extremes he went the whole way in this. To Patrick something was either black or white and nothing in between. In his outlook he constantly veered from optimism to pessimism and from the positive to the negative. He was also unable to do anything by half and where others just spoke he took his ideas seriously and felt compelled to act. The growing conviction that he had a higher calling was a way to justify his self-defined strangeness. All this made him more open to the widely propagated idea of the time that a respectable life was not worth living but that one needed to live a heroic one.

In his ideas Patrick was always strongly influenced by his environment and his readings. In his early years he often followed the lead taken by prominent figures in the League. In choosing models he was certainly led by an increasingly modernist tendency. This is most clearly shown in his attitude towards women's rights, social relations, educational thinking, Church–state relations and also as a writer. The questioning and independent attitude he seemed to have inherited from his father predisposed him to taking an independent position in the debates that were played out ever more stridently in the early twentieth century.

Within his thinking there are consistent lines of noticeable development, for instance in relation to Irish mythology. He first heard about them as a child, then began to act them out with his siblings, subsequently studied and wrote about them, republished them and wrote some himself and finally he emulated them in his own rebellion. A similar change can be traced in relation to the use of force for political purposes in which he mirrored the growing militarisation of western society at that time. Initially he rejected it as both impossible and irrelevant in the Irish case. Then he reinterpreted it in his early career and stories as metaphorical in the sense of struggle and dedication to a cause. Under the influence of the politically charged circumstances around 1912 he began to see it as something that was possibly needed to obtain a goal, and by 1915 it became a goal in itself. It could thus be argued that he initially tried to induce the Irish to change voluntarily through acquiring the language by his work in the Gaelic League. He subsequently tried to actively force that change by raising a new generation of children in an Irish environment in St Enda's and finally by forcing that change upon the nation through the Volunteers.

Contrary to the image of a somewhat hysterical persona which I encountered when first starting to hear and read about him, Patrick Pearse always wrote in a sane and rational manner and expressed many progressive ideas. His total dedication to the regeneration of the Irish nation accounts for the content of his writings as well as for his actions. The extremist form this took in the lead-up to the 1916 Rising was still couched in terms of the public debate of the period, but has largely informed our image of him. Although it can be argued that the adherents of his thinking triumphed when they became the new leaders of an independent southern Ireland, his social and cultural ideas were read but never implemented. The failure to act upon these can, as Martin Daly already claimed in 1917, mainly be attributed to a backward country not to the irrelevance of his ideas.[111]

Appendix

Brady family

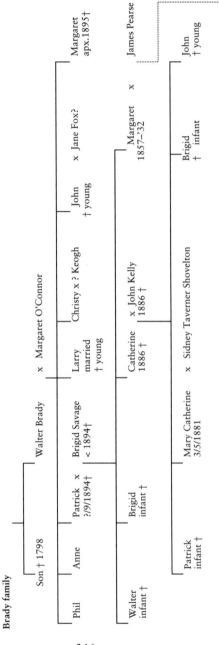

Pearse family

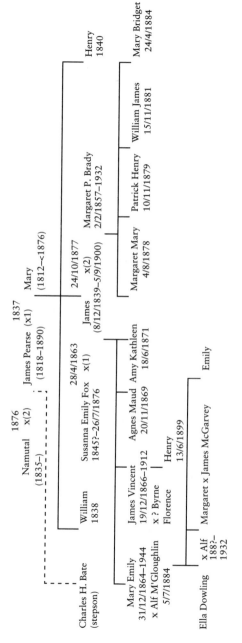

Notes

Introduction

1. Letter Jimmy Whelan dated 30 Oct. 1945, LP (Lennon Papers, in author's possession).

2. Miroslav Hroch, *Social Preconditions of National Revival in Europe: A Comparative Analysis of the Social Composition of Patriotic Groups among the Smaller European Nations* (New York 2000), pp. 22–3 and 129–31; Joep Leerssen, *National Thought in Europe. A Cultural History* (Amsterdam 2006), pp. 159 and 164–5; Joep Leerssen, 'Nationalism and the Cultivation of Culture', in *Nations and Nationalism* 12/4 (2006), pp. 559–78.

3. Leerssen, *National Thought*, p. 102; Anne-Marie Thiesse, *La Création des Identitiés Nationales. Europe XVIIIe–XXe siècle* (Paris 1999), pp. 67–72; Hroch, *Social Preconditions*, pp. 8–13.

4. Oliver Zimmer, *Nationalism in Europe, 1890–1940* (Houndmills 2003), pp. 27–43; A.D. Smith, 'The Formation of Nationalist Movements', in Anthony D. Smith (ed.), *Nationalist Movements* (London and Basingstoke 1976), p. 2; John Hutchinson, *Nations as Zones of Conflict* (London 2005), p. 45; Hagen Schulze, *States, Nations and Nationalism. From the Middle Ages to the Present* (Oxford 1998), pp. 212–29; Leerssen, *National Thought*, pp. 185–9; Thiesse, *La Création*, pp. 185–231 and 237–8 and 256–60; Leerssen, 'Nationalism and the Cultivation', pp. 559–78.

5. Bill Kissane, *The Politics of the Irish Civil War* (Oxford 2005), pp. 24–5. There are clear parallels with Galicia in Spain; Eva Roa White, *A Case Study of Ireland and Galicia's Parallel Paths to Nationhood* (Lewiston 2004), pp. 53–60.

6. Kevin Collins, *Catholic Churchmen and the Celtic Revival in Ireland 1848–1916* (Dublin 2002), pp. 100–1; Leerssen, *National Thought*, pp. 193–4; Hutchinson, *Nations as Zones*, p. 115; Manfred Beller, Joep Leerssen (eds), *Imagology. The Cultural Construction and Literary Representation of National Characters. A Critical Survey* (Amsterdam, New York 2007), p. 193.

7. Hroch, *Social Preconditions*, pp. xv and 178–90; Smith, 'Formation of', pp. 9 and 21–4; Eric Storm, 'Regionalism in History, 1890–1945: The Cultural Approach', in *European History Quarterly* 33/2 (2003), pp. 253–6.

8. Kissane, *The Politics*, p. 27; Len Scales, Oliver Zimmer (eds), *Power and the Nation in European History* (Cambridge 2005), pp. 20–1; Hroch, *Social Preconditions*, pp. 178 and 184–6; William Irwin Thompson,

348

The Imagination of an Insurrection: Dublin Easter 1916. A Study of an Ideological Movement (New York 1967), pp. 25–7 and 32 and 42 and 55.

9. Ibid., pp. 14–22.
10. Ibid., pp. 24 and 39–45 and 57–8 and 64.
11. Schulze, States, Nations, pp. 212–29; Leerssen, National Thought, pp. 185–9; Zimmer, Nationalism in Europe, pp. 27–43; Thiesse, La Création, pp. 185–231 and 237–8 and 256–60; Leerssen, 'Nationalism and the Cultivation', pp. 559–78.
12. Ibid., pp. 559–78.

Chapter 1: Person

1. 'Fragment of Autobiography by Patrick Pearse', Pearse Museum, Dublin.
2. Kate Elizabeth Field (daughter of Henry Pearse, the brother of James), LP.
3. 'Autobiography by Patrick Pearse'.
4. NLI (National Library of Ireland), P7642.
5. Kate Elizabeth Field, LP; 'Autobiography by Patrick Pearse'; Census records 1851, 1861, 1871, 1881, http://www.ancestry.co.uk/; England and Wales, Civil Registration Index: 1837–1983, http://www.ancestry.co.uk/; White's Directory 1855, quoted in Letter Robert J. Hetherington dated 21 Aug. 1947, LP. James did not get on with his stepmother, Letter Margaret Pearse dated 19 July 1947, LP.
6. 'Autobiography by Patrick Pearse'; Letter Margaret Pearse dated 19 July 1947, LP.
7. Letter J.J. O'Looney dated 15 Nov. 1947, LP.
8. Kate Elizabeth Field, LP.
9. Census records 1851 and 1861, http://www.ancestry.co.uk/.
10. 'Autobiography by Patrick Pearse'.
11. Lennon's father, LP; 'Autobiography by Patrick Pearse'.
12. Letter J.J. O'Looney dated 15 Nov. 1947, LP.
13. Lennon, LP.
14. Letter John Early dated 8 May 1947, LP.
15. Brian Crowley, '"His Father's Son": James and Patrick Pearse', in Folk Life. Journal of Ethnological Studies Vol. 43 2004–2005, p. 75.
16. Crowley, 'His Father's', p. 78.
17. Letter J.C. Harrison dated 5 Sept. 1947, LP; Lennon Snr, LP; Letter Mr Harrison dated 25 Sept. 1947, LP.
18. Letter J.J. O'Looney dated 15 Nov. 1947, LP.
19. The Dublin Builder 15 Aug. 1861, LP.
20. Census records 1861, http://www.ancestry.co.uk/.
21. Letter John Early dated 8 May 1947, LP; Margaret Pearse, LP; Letter Eily McLoughlin dated 8 Apr. 1947, LP; Letter Mrs McLoughlin dated 19 Oct. 1947; Thom's Irish Almanac and Official Directory, 1850–1870.
22. England and Wales, Civil Registration Index: 1837–1983, http://www.ancestry.co.uk/.

23. Copy of Marriage Certificate, LP. Kate Elizabeth Field, LP.

24. Letter K.E. Field dated 9 Mar. 1948, LP; Margaret M. Pearse, LP.

25. Census records 1851, 1861 and 1871; Birth Records of England and Wales, http://www.ancestry.co.uk/.

26. *Thom's Irish Almanac and Official Directory*, 1850–1880. Margaret Pearse, LP; Lennon Snr, LP; Letter J.J. O'Looney dated 15 Nov. 1947, LP; Letter Eily McLoughlin dated 8 Apr. 1947, LP; Letter J.C. Harrison dated 5 Sep. 1947, LP; Letter W. Brennan dated 11 June 1947, LP; Michael Cummins, LP; Letter Mrs McLoughlin dated 19 Oct. 1947, LP; Letter John Early dated 8 May 1947, LP; Edwards, *Triumph*, p. 9; Crowley, 'His Father's', p. 75.

27. Birth certificates of the Pearse children, Oifig An Ard-Chláraitheora (General Register Office) Dublin.

28. Letter W. Brennan dated 11 June 1947, LP.

29. *Thom's Irish Almanac and Official Directory*, 1880–1890; 'Autobiography by Patrick Pearse'.

30. NLI, ms. 21,078.

31. Letter Lennon Snr dated 14 Sep. 1946, LP; Miss Pearse, LP.

32. Margaret Pearse, LP; Michael Cummins, LP; Letter John Early dated 8 May 1947, LP; Letter W. Brennan dated 11 June 1947, LP.

33. *Thom's Official Directory*, 1916.

34. Letter W. Brennan dated 11 June 1947, LP; Letter John Early dated 8 May 1947, LP; Statement by an 'Ex-rel. father', LP.

35. Xavier Carty, *In Bloody Protest. The Tragedy of Patrick Pearse* (Dublin 1978), p. 16.

36. Letter J.J. O'Looney dated 15 Nov. 1947, LP; Letter J.A. Duffy dated 30 Sep. 1947, LP; Letter J.C. Harrison dated 5 Sep. 1947, LP; Letter W. Brennan dated 11 June 1947, LP; Letter John Early dated 8 May 1947, LP.

37. Letter J.J. O'Looney dated 15 Nov. 1947, LP.

38. Lennon, LP; Letter Lennon Snr dated 14 Sep. 1946, LP; Letter J.A. Duffy dated 30 Sep. 1947, LP.

39. These were Henry's sons, statement by 'Mrs Pearse of 116 Nigel Avenue', LP.

40. Letter J.A. Duffy dated 30 Sep. 1947, LP.

41. Margaret Pearse, LP, 'Autobiography by Patrick Pearse'.

42. Letter J.J. O'Looney dated 15 Nov. 1947, LP; Lennon, LP; Letter W. Brennan dated 11 June 1947, LP; Letter J.A. Duffy dated 30 Sep. 1947, LP.

43. Letter Mrs McLoughlin dated 19 Oct. 1947, LP.

44. Letter J.C. Harrison dated 5 Sep. 1947, LP; Letter W. Brennan dated 11 June 1947, LP; Letter John Early dated 8 May 1947, LP; Lennon, LP; Letter J.J. O'Looney dated 15 Nov. 1947, LP; Letter J.A. Duffy dated 30 Sep. 1947, LP.

45. Crowley, 'His Father's', pp. 73–4; Pat Cooke, *Sceal Sgoil Eanna*, The story of an educational adventure (Dublin 1986), p. 7.

46. Brian Crowley, '"I am the son of a good father": James and Patrick Pearse', in Roisín Higgins and Regina Uí Chollatáin (eds), *The Life and After Life*

   of P.H. Pearse. Pádraic Mac Piarais Saol agus Oidhreacht (Dublin 2009),
   p. 22; Kate Elizabeth Field, LP; Michael Cummins, LP.

47. Charles Bradlaugh, *Oxford Dictionary of National Biography*, http://www.
    oxforddnb.com/view/article/3183?docPos=3

48. Letter Mrs McLoughlin dated 19 Oct. 1947, LP.

49. Michael Cummins, LP; John J. Horgan, *From Parnell to Pearse: Some
    Recollections and Reflections* (Dublin 1948), p. 242.

50. Kate Elizabeth Field, LP.

51. Crowley, 'His Father's', p. 83.

52. Edwards, *Triumph*, p. 10.

53. Thomas Maguire, *England's Duty to Ireland, as Plain to a Loyal Irish
    Roman Catholic* (Dublin, London 1886).

54. NLI, ms. 21,079. The total cost for 1000 copies was £10/13/0.

55. Draft contained in NLI, ms. 21,079.

56. Ibid.

57. Letter J.J. O'Looney dated 15 Nov. 1947, LP.

58. Crowley, 'His Father's', pp. 80–2.

59. Ruth Dudley Edwards' claim that this pamphlet was published in 1888
    is probably responsible for Crowley's denial, because he could not find
    an advertisement in the *Agnostic Journal* or *The Freethinker* in that year.
    However, the entry in James Pearse's Papers clearly mentions the title of
    the pamphlet *Will Socialism Benefit the English People* and is dated not
    in 1888 but on 11 September 1885. An advertisement for it is placed not
    explicitly with the *Agnostic Journal* but with Annie Besant, Bradlaugh's
    partner, NLI, ms. 21,080; Edwards, *Triumph*, pp. 10–11; Crowley, 'His
    Father's', p. 81.

60. NLI, ms. 21,081.

61. Michael Cummins, LP. See also Hedley McCay, *Pádraic Pearse; A New
    Biography* (Cork 1966), p. 6.

62. Michael Cummins, LP; W. Brennan, LP.

63. Sean Farrell Moran, *Patrick Pearse and the Politics of Redemption: The
    Mind of the Easter Rising, 1916* (Washington DC 1994), p. 25.

64. Letter Mrs Bradley dated 22 Feb. 1947, LP.

65. Louis N. Le Roux, *Patrick H. Pearse* (Dublin 1932), p. 225.

66. 'Autobiography by Patrick Pearse'.

67. Marriage certificate, LP; 'Autobiography by Patrick Pearse'.

68. Letter J.J. O'Looney dated 15 Nov. 1947. Consider James' alleged statement
    mentioned under footnote 7. The grand secretary of the Freemasons in
    Ireland declared in a letter to Michael Lennon that on the basis of a search
    in their archives he was 'inclined to think that he [James] did not desire to
    join this order', LP.

69. Lennon, LP; J.J. O'Looney, LP.

70. Margaret Brady, LP.

71. Quoted in Edwards, *Triumph*, p. 2.

72. 'Autobiography by Patrick Pearse'.

73. Michael Cummins, LP.

74. NLI, P7642.
75. Marriage certificate, LP; Letter W. Brennan dated 11 June 1947. The marriage certificate identifies James's friend John M'Gloughlin and Margaret's sister Catherine as witnesses.
76. Letter J.J. O'Looney dated 15 Nov. 1947, LP.
77. NLI, ms. 21,076(2).
78. Kate Elizabeth Field, LP; Death certificate James Pearse.
79. Crowley, 'His Father's', p. 83.
80. 'Autobiography by Patrick Pearse'; Michael Cummins, LP.
81. 'Autobiography by Patrick Pearse'; Miss Pearse, LP.
82. Letter Bulmer Hobson dated 27 Mar. 1947, LP. See also Lennon Snr, LP.
83. Kate Elizabeth Field, LP. All members of the Pearse family at that time were serious drinkers, including the son and daughter from this marriage; Letter W. Brennan dated 11 June 1947, LP.
84. Death certificate of Emily Pearse, LP.
85. The Lennon Papers contain a birth certificate of a Margaret Brady born 8 Jan. 1869 whose parents were John Brady and Jane Fox. Patrick's grandfather had a brother named John Brady and the fact the birth certificate indicates John was a dairyman living at 4 King's Lane ties in with the family business. Another certificate shows this Jane Fox, the child of John Fox and Eliza Cole, to have been baptised as a Catholic on 24 Nov. 1829 in Rockfortbridge in Co. Westmeath.
86. Letter dated 22 Dec. 1874, NLI, ms. 21,082.
87. Letter dated around Dec. 1876, NLI, P7642.
88. Letter Mrs McLoughlin dated 19 Oct. 1947, LP; Edwards, *Triumph*, p. 3.
89. Pat Cooke, 'Patrick Pearse: The Victorian Gael', in Higgins and Uí Chollatáin, *Life and After-Life*, p. 46.
90. Coilin, *Patrick H. Pearse. A Sketch of His Life* (Dublin n.d.), p. 3.
91. Letter Mrs McLoughlin dated 19 Oct. 1947, LP.
92. 'Autobiography by Patrick Pearse'.
93. Edwards, *Triumph*, p. 45.
94. Letter dated 30 Mar. 1912, Seamus Ó Buachalla (ed.), *The Letters of P.H. Pearse* (Gerrards Cross, Bucks. 1980), pp. 258–9.
95. Letter Michael Kavanagh dated 16 Sep. 1947, LP; Letter Frank Fahey dated 15 Mar. 1948, LP.
96. 'Autobiography by Patrick Pearse'.
97. NLI, P7642.
98. Letter J.J. O'Looney dated 15 Nov. 1947, LP.
99. NLI, P7642 and ms. 21,082.
100. NLI, P7642.
101. Ibid.
102. Ibid.
103. Letter W. Brennan dated 11 Jun. 1947, LP.
104. Ibid.; Michael Cummins, LP; Crowley, 'His Father's', p. 83. There are some unconvincing references in the Lennon Papers about a suicide of James Pearse Jnr, Letter Frank Fahey, dated 15 Mar. 1948, LP.

105. Letter W. Brennan 11 Jun. 1947, LP.

106. Birth certificate Patrick Pierce; Baptismal certificate out of Baptismal Register of the united parishes of St Andrew, St Mark, St Peter and St Anne, Allen Library, Box 187; Letter Margaret Pearse dated 19 July 1947, LP; 'Autobiography by Patrick Pearse'.

107. Letter Mrs McLoughlin dated 19 Oct. 1947, LP; Letter J.J. O'Looney dated 15 Nov. 1947, LP.

108. Letter W. Brennan dated 11 June 1947, LP.

109. 'Autobiography by Patrick Pearse'.

110. M.B. Pearse (ed.), *The Home Life of Pádraig Pearse as told by himself, his family and friends* (1934, 1979), pp. 33 and 86.

111. Letter to Miss C. Doyle dated 24 Oct. 1909, NLI, ms. 5049.

112. Moran, *Patrick Pearse*, p. 47.

113. Pearse (ed.), *Home Life*, p. 98.

114. Desmond Ryan, *Remembering Sion: A Chronical of Storm and Quiet* (London 1934), p. 129.

115. Margaret Pearse, LP. These poems are in the possession of the Pearse Museum.

116. Letter to mother dated 3 May 1916, Ó Buachalla (ed.), *Letters*, pp. 381–2.

117. 'Autobiography by Patrick Pearse'. See also, Letter Margaret Pearse dated 19 July 1947, LP.

118. Ibid.

119. 'Autobiography by Patrick Pearse'; NLI, P7642 and ms. 21,082; Pearse (ed.), *Home Life*, p. 54.

120. Edwards, *Triumph*, p. 12; Crowley, 'His Father's', p. 77; Pearse (ed.), *Home Life* , pp. 45, 50–3, 62, 64–84; L. Ua Gallchobhair, 'The Children of Patrick Pearse', in *The Irish Monthly* 1922, pp. 125–6. A similar enacting of mass was still commonplace even in the Netherlands around 1960 among future socialistic TV presenters, *De Volkskrant* 15 Mar. 2008, 'Volkskrant Magazine', p. 40.

121. Edwards, *Triumph*, p. 12; Crowley, 'His Father's', p. 77; Pearse (ed.), *Home Life*, pp. 45, 50–3, 62 and 64–84.

122. Jerome F. Cronin, *Irish Independent* 27 Mar. 1957.

123. Ryan, *Remembering Sion*, p. 126.

124. Pearse (ed.), *Home Life*, pp. 54, 61 and 98.

125. Michael Dowling, LP; Mrs Tom Pearse (daughter-in-law of Henry Pearse), LP; Osborn Bergin, LP; Edwards, *Triumph*, p. 120; Sighle Bairead, LP.

126. Eamonn O'Neill, LP.

127. Letter J.C. Harrison dated 5 Sep. 1947, LP. See also Letter W. Brennan dated 11 June 1947, LP; Letter Dan Maher dated 10 Aug. 1944, LP.

128. Letter Hamill dated 26 Aug. 1946, LP. See also Letter J.J. O'Looney dated 15 Nov. 1947, LP; Letter W. Brennan dated 11 June 1947, LP; Letter Seamus Mullivan, dated 28 Feb. 1947, LP; Letter J.A. Duffy dated 30 Sep. 1947, LP; Eamonn O'Neill(?) Conan & Sceilg(?), LP.

129. Edwards, *Triumph*, pp. 46–8.

130. Pearse (ed.), *Home Life*, p. 106.

131. Sean T., LP. See also Jerome F. Cronin, *Irish Independent* 27 Mar. 1957.

132. Michael Dowling, LP. See also Letter W. Brennan dated 11 June 1947, LP; Lennon, LP, D61 and C1.

133. Letter Seamus Mullivan dated 28 Feb. 1947, LP. See also Letter W. Brennan dated 11 June 1947, LP; Letter Dan Maher dated 10 Aug. 1944, LP; Letter John Early dated 8 May 1947, LP; Edwards, *Triumph*, pp. 112 and 149.

134. Quoted in Edwards, *Triumph*, p. 136.

135. Letter John Early dated 8 May 1947, LP.

136. Máire nic Shiubhlaigh, *The Splendid Years* (Dublin 1955), p. 150.

137. Letter John Early dated 8 May 1947, LP; Letter J.A. Duffy dated 30 Sep. 1947, LP; Lennon, LP, D61.

138. Nic Shiubhlaigh, *Splendid*, p. 151; Joseph Holloway, quoted in Edwards, *Triumph*, p. 166.

139. Desmond Ryan, *The Man called Pearse*, in *Collected Works of Padraic H. Pearse* (Dublin etc. n.d.), pp. 190–1 and 202; Edwards, *Triumph*, pp. 46–8.

140. Quoted in ibid., p. 114.

141. Pearse (ed.), *Home Life*, pp. 39–40 and 55.

142. 'Autobiography by Patrick Pearse'.

143. Moran, *Patrick Pearse*, p. 34; Letter W. Brennan dated 11 June 1947, LP.

144. NLI, P7642.

145. NLI, P7642; Pearse (ed.), *Home Life*, pp. 36–7.

146. Moran, *Patrick Pearse*, pp. 32–3.

147. NLI, P7642.

148. 'Autobiography by Patrick Pearse'.

149. Ibid.

150. NLI, P7642.

151. NLI, ms. 21,082.

152. Ryan, *Man called Pearse*, p. 157.

153. Edwards, *Triumph*, pp. 46–7; Letter dated 24 Sep. 1900, Ó Buachalla (ed.), *Letters*, pp. 20–1.

154. Donnchadh Ó Súilleabháin, *An Piarsach agus Conradh na Gaeilge* (Dublin 1981), p. 1.

155. Ryan, *Remembering Sion*, pp. 102 and 130; 'Recollections by Patrick Shovelton', Pearse Museum.

156. Letter dated 11 May 1912, Ó Buachalla (ed.), *Letters*, pp. 264–5.

157. 'Autobiography by Patrick Pearse'.

158. Pearse (ed.), *Home Life*, pp. 25, 42, 44–7 and 87–8; 'Recollections by Patrick Shovelton'.

159. 'Autobiography by Patrick Pearse'.

160. Ibid.; Margaret Pearse, LP; Mrs Tom Pearse, LP.

161. Kate Elizabeth Field, LP.

162. NLI, ms. 21,076(1–2).

163. NLI, ms. 21,076(1); Kate Elizabeth Field, LP.

164. Ibid.; 'Autobiography by Patrick Pearse'; Margaret Pearse, LP; Letter J.J. O'Looney dated 15 Nov. 1947, LP; Mrs Tom Pearse, LP.

165. Kate Elizabeth Field, LP; Margaret Pearse, LP.

166. Margaret Pearse, LP.
167. Letter Eily McLoughlin dated 8 Apr. 1947, LP.
168. Liam O'Donnell, LP; Carty, *Bloody Protest*, p. 33.
169. *Thom's Irish Almanac and Official Directory*, 1880–1890; 'Autobiography by Patrick Pearse'. Edwards, *Triumph*, p. 9 claims this was in 1884, while Pat Cooke argues in *Scéal Scoil Éanna* that they attended private school for three years before going into the CBS in 1891, p. 8.
170. 'Autobiography by Patrick Pearse'; Michael Cummins, LP; Miss Pearse, LP.
171. 'Autobiography by Patrick Pearse'.
172. *Thom's Irish Almanac and Official Directory*, 1888–1893; Letter Dan Maher dated 10 Aug. 1944, LP; Eamonn O'Neill(?) Conan & Sceilg(?), LP; Carty, *Bloody Protest*, p. 16; 'They were Schoolboys! The Pearse Brothers at the "Row"', in Christian Brothers Westland Row, *Centenary Record 1864–1964*, p. 43.
173. Veale, LP; Letter J.A. Duffy, dated 30 Sep. 1947, LP; Lennon Snr, LP; Eamonn O'Neill(?) Conan & Sceilg(?), LP; Pearse (ed.), *Home Life*, p. 54.
174. Letter J.A. Duffy dated 30 Sep. 1947, LP.
175. Ibid.
176. Letter Hamill dated 26 Aug. 1946, LP.
177. Kate Elizabeth Field, LP.
178. 'The Scholastic Story of Padraic Pearse', Allen Library, Box 187; 'They were Schoolboys', p. 43.
179. Moran, *Patrick Pearse*, pp. 35–43; McCay, *Pádraic Pearse*, p. 14.
180. Ibid., p. 11.
181. O'Neill, quoted in Edwards, *Triumph*, p. 14.
182. Letter J.A. Duffy dated 30 Sep. 1947, LP. See also Letter Jimmy Whelan dated 30 Oct. 1945, LP.
183. Veale, LP; Letter J.A. Duffy dated 30 Sep. 1947, LP.
184. Carty, *Bloody Protest*, p. 21; McCay, *Pádraic Pearse*, p. 11.
185. Veale, LP; Letter Dan Maher dated 10 Aug. 1944, LP.
186. Pearse (ed.), *Home Life*, pp. 92–3.
187. Letter Jimmy Whelan dated 30 Oct 1945, LP. See also Letter J.A. Duffy dated 30 Sep. 1947, LP.
188. 'They were Schoolboys', pp. 43–5.
189. Pearse (ed.), *Home Life,* pp. 34, 51 and 62.
190. Ibid., p. 93.
191. Ryan, *Remembering Sion*, p. 106; McCay, *Pádraic Pearse*, p. 12.
192. Letter Wm. Val. Jackson dated 19 [...] 1947, LP.
193. Veale, LP.
194. Ibid.; Ó Buachalla (ed.), *Letters*, p. 172; 'Memories of Pearse', article by M.H. in the *London Herald*, no date, in scrapbook of Frank Martin, NLI, ms. 32,695/1; Pearse (ed.), *Home Life*, pp. 92–3.
195. Ryan, *Remembering Sion*, p. 188.
196. Omar Crowley, LP.
197. Eamonn O'Neill(?), Conan & Sceilg(?), LP; Eamonn O'Neill, LP.

198. Letter Dan Maher dated 10 Aug. 1944, LP; Letter E. O Danluan[?] dated 19 [...] 1947, LP; Veale, LP.

199. Letter J.A. Duffy dated 30 Sep. 1947, LP.

200. Ibid.; Veale, LP.

201. Letter Hamill dated 26 Aug. 1946, LP; Letter Frank Fahey dated 15 Mar. 1948, LP.

202. Letter J.A. Duffy dated 30 Sep. 1947, LP.

203. Ibid.

204. Pearse (ed.), *Home Life*, p. 103.

205. 'They were Schoolboys', 45.

206. Eamonn O'Neill(?) Conan & Sceilg(?), LP; Veale, LP; Edwards, *Triumph*, p. 10.

207. Sean O'Casey, *Drums under the Windows* (London 1945), pp. 127–8.

208. Liam O Donhnaill, LP. See also, James Mullin, *The Story of a Toiler's Life* (Dublin 2000), pp. 202–3. In his mind his empathy was better developed, 'Autobiography by Patrick Pearse'.

209. Letter J.J. O'Looney dated 15 Nov. 1947, LP; Larry Kettle, LP; Letter Liam de Roiste dated 10 Oct. 1947, LP; P.J. McGill, 'Padraig Pearse in Donegal', *Donegal Annual* Vol. VII No. 1 1966, p. 74.

210. 'Autobiography by Patrick Pearse'.

211. Letter Sean O Huadhaigh dated 15 July 1948, LP; Letter Frank Fahey dated 15 Mar. 1948, LP; Letter Seamus Mullivan dated 28 Feb. 1947, LP; Liam O Donhnaill, LP; Liam O Donnell, LP; Letter Torna (O Donehada) dated 26 Nov. 1946, LP; Letter Justice Wm S. Black dated 6 Dec. 1946, LP; Letter Sean D. MacGaunair[?], Allen Library, Box 187.

212. Letter dated 11 May 1912, Ó Buachalla (ed.), *Letters*, pp. 264–5.

213. Ryan, *Remembering Sion*, pp. 93–4.

214. 'Memories of Pearse', article by M.H. in the *London Herald*, no date, in scrapbook of Frank Martin, NLI, ms. 32,695/1. See also Letter Mrs Bradley dated 22 Feb. 1947, LP.

215. Sean T. O'Kelly, LP; Nic Shiubhlaigh, *Splendid*, pp. 147–8.

216. Ibid., p. 147; Michael Dowling, LP.

217. 'Autobiography by Patrick Pearse'.

218. Ryan, *Remembering Sion*, p. 159.

219. Mary Brigid Pearse in *Irish Press* 3 May 1940.

220. Letter Colm O Loughlin dated 13 May 1947, LP. See also Letter Hamill dated 26 Aug. 1946, LP.

221. Letter Seamus Mullivan dated 28 Feb. 1947, LP; Rd Foley, LP; Seamas O'Conor, LP.

222. 'Autobiography by Patrick Pearse'.

223. Interview with Joe McSweeney conducted by Séan Ó hÉalaí of RTE (in private possession).

224. Jerome F. Cronin in *Irish Independent* 27 Mar. 1957.

225. Letter Colm O Loughlin dated 13 May 1947; Letter Frank Fahey dated 15 Mar. 1948, LP; Rd Foley, LP; Bulmer Hobson, LP; Jerome F. Cronin in

Irish Independent 27 Mar. 1957; C.P. Curran and Sidney Czira, quoted in Carty, *Bloody Protest*, p. 14; Interview with Joe McSweeney.

226. Liam O Donnell, LP; 'Memories of Pearse', NLI, ms. 32,695/1; 'Autobiography by Patrick Pearse'.
227. Letter Frank Fahey dated 15 Mar. 1948, LP.
228. Letter Seamus Mullivan dated 28 Feb. 1947, LP. See also Michael Dowling, LP.
229. O'Hickey to Eoin MacNeill, quoted in Edwards, *Triumph*, p. 49.
230. Lennon, LP. See also Osborn Bergin, LP.
231. Letter Colm O Loughlin dated 13 May 1947, LP; Rd Foley, LP; Letter Mrs Bradley dated 22 Feb. 1947, LP.
232. Letter Colm O Loughlin dated 13 May 1947, LP. See also Letter Sean O Huadhaigh dated 15 July 1948, LP.
233. Letter E. O Danluan[?] dated 19 [...] 1947, LP.
234. Michael Dowling, LP.
235. Kate Elizabeth Field, LP.
236. Osborn Bergin, LP; Liam O Donnell, LP.
237. Joseph Holloway diaries, quoted in Edwards, *Triumph*, p. 28.
238. Letter James J. Doyle dated 1 Dec. 1946, LP. See also Letter Michael Christie dated 12 Dec. 1946, LP.
239. McCay, *Pádraic Pearse*, pp. 50–1.
240. Quoted in Carty, *Bloody Protest*, p. 14. See also Liam O Donnell, LP.
241. Osborn Bergin, LP; See also McCay, *Pádraic Pearse*, pp. 50–1.
242. Ryan, *Man called Pearse*, p. 185.
243. Pearse (ed.), *Home Life*, p. 84.
244. Jerome F. Cronin in *Irish Independent* 2 Apr. 1957; Staunton (Crown solr), LP; Letter Colm O Loughlin dated 13 May 1947, LP; Edwards, *Triumph*, pp. 16 and 47; Pearse (ed.), *Home Life*, pp. 103–4.
245. Letter dated Feb. 1900, Ó Buachalla (ed.), *Letters*, p. 12.
246. Bulmer Hobson, LP.
247. Veale, LP; Osborn Bergin, LP.
248. Jerome F. Cronin in *Irish Independent* 2 Apr. 1957. See also Pearse (ed.), *Home Life*, pp. 44–7.
249. Letter Owen Hynes dated 17 May 1947, LP; Ryan, *Remembering Sion*, pp. 91–2. His predecessor as editor of the Gaelic League newspaper claimed he was the best speaker in the land; Letter Eoghan ÓNeachtain dated 28 Sep. 1947, LP.
250. Carty, *Bloody Protest*, p. 91.
251. Letter dated 11 May 1912, Ó Buachalla (ed.), *Letters*, pp. 264–5.
252. Ryan, *Remembering Sion*, p. 126.
253. Letter St John Ervine dated 19 Feb. 1947, LP.
254. Letter dated 11 May 1912, Ó Buachalla (ed.), *Letters*, pp. 264–5.
255. Liam O Donnell, LP; Michael Dowling, LP; Sir Arnold Bax, LP, C27.
256. Ryan, *Man called Pearse*, p. 196; Jerome F. Cronin in *Irish Independent* 27 Mar. 1957, LP; Stephen McKenna in *Irish Press* 29 Mar. 1937; Letter Frank Fahey dated 15 Mar. 1948, LP; Letter Justice Forde dated 4 Aug. 1948.

257. Jerome F. Cronin in *Irish Independent* 2 Apr. 1957. See also his contribution in *Irish Independent* 27 Mar. 1957; 'Memories of Pearse', NLI, ms. 32,695/1.

258. Letter Hickey to MacNeill dated 23 Oct. 1901, quoted in Edwards, *Triumph*, p. 49.

259. Mary Hayden, quoted in Edwards, *Triumph*, p. 56.

260. 'From a Hermitage' published in *Irish Freedom* in *Collected works of P.H. Pearse. Political Writings and Speeches*, p. 143.

261. Letter to John Kilgallon, Kilmainham Jail, 23LR IP14/13.

262. Letter to Miss McKenna dated 21 May 1914, Pearse Museum.

263. 'Memories of Pearse', NLI, ms. 32,695/1; Letter Colm O Loughlin dated 13 May 1947, LP.

264. Pearse (ed.), *Home Life*, p. 48. See also Ryan, *Remembering Sion*, p. 117.

265. Letter Maire ní Cinneide dated 23 Oct. 1947, LP; Letter Ian Bloomer pupil of St Enda's 1910–1912 dated 16 Dec. 1968, LP; Letter Mrs Bradley dated 22 Feb. 1947, LP; Interview with Joe McSweeney.

266. Michael Dowling, LP.

267. Staunton, Crown Solicitor, LP.

268. 'Memories of Pearse', NLI, ms. 32,695/1.

269. Liam O Donnell, LP; 'Memories of Pearse', NLI, ms. 32,695/1.

270. Pearse (ed.), *Home Life*, pp. 51 and 57–8.

271. Letter J.J. Hutchinson dated 9 June 1948, LP.

272. Liam O Donnell, LP.

273. Ryan, *Remembering Sion*, pp. 91–2; P.S. O'Hegarty, 'P.H. Pearse' in *Irish Commonwealth* March 1919, p. 29.

274. Carty, *Bloody Protest*, p. 14.

275. Mullin, *Toiler's Life*, pp. 202–3.

276. LP.

277. Ryan, *Man called Pearse*, p. 179. Ryan, *Remembering Sion*, p. 160.

278. Larry Kettle, LP; Jerome F. Cronin in *Irish Independent* 2 Apr. 1957 and 27 Mar. 1957; Veale, LP; Letter Colm O Loughlin dated 13 May 1947, LP; Eamonn O'Neill, LP; Sean O Briain, LP; Margaret Pearse, LP; Carty, *Bloody Protest*, p. 57; Rev. Bernard J. Canning, *Patrick H. Pearse and Schotland* (Glasgow 1979), p. 14.

279. Letter J.E. Hackett dated 20 Nov. 1947, LP; Margaret Pearse, LP; Eamonn O'Neill, LP; Jerome F. Cronin, *Irish Independent* 2 Apr. 1957.

280. Letter Margaret Pearse dated 19 July 1947; Edwards, *Triumph*, p. 106.

281. *Eoineen of the Birds* (1905), in *Collected Works. Plays, Stories, Poems*, pp. 287–308.

282. Letter dated 11 May 1912, Ó Buachalla (ed.), *Letters*, pp. 264–5.

283. Peter Merkl, 'Conclusion', in P.H. Merkl (ed.), *Political Violence and Terror: Motifs and Motivations* (Berkeley 1986), pp. 375–6.

284. Pearse (ed.), *Home Life*, pp. 87–8.

285. Ibid., pp. 44–7 and 64.

286. Jerome F. Cronin in *Irish Independent* 27 Mar. 1957.

287. Michael Dowling, LP.

288. Joyce Padbury, ' "A Young Schoolmaster of Great Literary Talent': Mary Hayden's friend, Patrick Pearse', in Higgins and Uí Chollatáin, *Life and After-Life*, pp. 35 and 39.

289. Mary Hayden, quoted in Edwards, *Triumph*, p. 56.

290. 'Memories of Pearse', article by M.H. in the *London Herald*, no date, in scrapbook of Frank Martin, NLI, ms. 32,695/1.

291. Padbury, 'A Young Schoolmaster', p. 40.

292. Patrick Pearse, *Three Lectures on Gaelic Topics* (Dublin 1898), in *Collected Works of Pádraic H. Pearse* (Dublin etc. n.d.), p. 211.

293. *The Singer* (1915), *The Mother* (1915), in *Collected Works. Plays, Stories, Poems*, pp. 1–44 and 125–36.

294. Elaine Sisson, *Pearse's Patriots: St Enda's and the Cult of Boyhood* (Cork 2004), p. 151.

295. 'Rebel Pearse was no gay blade but had autistic temperament', *Sunday Independent* 9 Apr. 2006; http://www.nieuws.leidenuniv.nl/index. php3?m=&c=1672; Antoinette Walker and Michael Fitzgerald, *Unstoppable Brilliance: Irish Geniuses and Asperger's Syndrome* (Dublin 2006), pp. 12 and 24–5.

296. Letter Seamus Cooling dated 11 Nov. 1947, LP; Le Roux, *Patrick H. Pearse*, p. 39.

297. LP; Letter Mrs Bradley dated 22 Feb. 1947, LP.

298. Jerome F. Cronin in *Irish Independent* 27 Mar. 1957.

299. Quoted in Edwards, *Triumph*, p. 125; *ACS* 21 Aug. 1909.

300. Mary Brigid Pearse in *Irish Press* 3 May 1940.

301. Letter Seamus Cooling dated 11 Nov. 1947, LP.

302. 'O Lovely Head', in *Collected Works. Plays, Stories, Poems*, p. 318.

303. Moran, *Patrick Pearse*, p. 123.

304. Edwards, *Triumph*, p. 126; Sisson, *Pearse's Patriots*, pp. 137–41.

305. Quoted in Edwards, *Triumph*, p. 121.

306. Letter dated 29 Dec. 1913, Ó Buachalla (ed.), *Letters*, p. 297.

307. *ACS* 7 Nov. 1908.

308. See, for instance, *The Priest* (1905–1906) and *Eoineen of the Birds* (1905–1906), in *Collected Works. Plays, Stories, Poems*, pp. 245–58 and 287–308.

309. *The Master*, in *Collected Works. Plays, Stories, Poems*, pp. 72–3.

310. Sisson, *Pearse's Patriots*, p. 141.

311. 'O Lovely Head', in *Collected Works. Plays, Stories, Poems*, p. 318.

312. 'Little Lad of the Tricks, in *Collected Works. Plays, Stories, Poems*, p. 316. The same compulsion to kiss a young boy on the lips can be found in his story *The Priest* (1905–1906), in *Collected Works*, pp. 245–58.

313. Sisson, *Pearse's Patriots*, pp. 142–4.

314. Letter J.A. Duffy dated 30 Sep. 1947, LP.

315. See, for instance, *The Singer* (1915); *The Priest* (1905–1906); 'Lullaby of a Woman of the Mountain'; 'A Woman of the Mountain Keens her Son'; 'To a Beloved Child', in *Collected Works. Plays, Stories, Poems*, passim.

316. Sisson, *Pearse's Patriots*, pp. 132–3.

317. Ibid., p. 133.
318. Ibid., pp. 136–7.
319. Ibid., p. 64; *ACS* 5 Jan. 1907.
320. Ua Gallchobhair, 'Children of Patrick Pearse', pp. 120–1.
321. *An Macaomh* 1909.
322. 'Memories of Pearse', article by M.H. in the *London Herald,* no date, in scrapbook of Frank Martin, NLI, ms. 32,695/1; Sisson, *Pearse's Patriots,* p. 151.
323. See *Íosagán* (1905), *Eoineen of the Birds* (1905–1906) and *Barbara* (1905–1906), *Collected Works. Plays, Stories, Poems*, pp. 227–308.
324. Letter dated 31 July 1907, Ó Buachalla (ed.), *Letters*, p. 111.
325. Moran, *Patrick Pearse*, pp. 121–2.
326. Osborn Bergin, LP.
327. Letter dated 20 Oct. 1913, Ó Buachalla (ed.), *Letters*, p. 294; Le Roux, *Patrick H. Pearse*, p. 155.
328. Jerome F. Cronin in *Irish Independent* 2 Apr. 1957.
329. Letter Sears dated 2 Dec. 1946, LP.
330. Sisson, *Pearse's Patriots*, pp. 123–6 and 155; Hobson, LP.
331. Seamus O'Sullivan, LP; Letter J.A. Duffy dated 30 Sep. 1947, LP.
332. Letter Seamus Mullivan dated 28 Feb. 1947, LP.
333. Letter Colm O Loughlin dated 13 May 1947, LP.
334. Sisson, *Pearse's Patriots*, p. 152.
335. Ibid., p. 140.
336. Moran, *Patrick Pearse*, p. 124.
337. Sisson, *Pearse's Patriots*, p. 32.
338. Margaret Pearse, LP; Michael Dowling, LP.
339. Letter Sean D. MacGaunair[?], Allen Library, Box 187; 'They were Schoolboys', p. 43; Crowley, 'His Father's', p. 78.
340. Kate Elizabeth Field, LP.
341. Michael Dowling, LP.
342. Pearse (ed.), *Home Life*, pp. 118–20.
343. Tobias, LP.
344. Minutes of the Law Students Debating Society at King's Inns, LP.
345. F. MacKenzie, *The Irish Rebellion What Happened and Why* (London 1916), p. 12.
346. Letter Justice Wm S. Black dated 6 Dec. 1946, LP; Letter J. Campion dated 24 Dec. 1947, LP.
347. Letter W. Fallon dated 10 Apr. 1947, LP.
348. Letter J. Campion dated 24 Dec. 1947, LP.
349. R.J. Porter, *P.H. Pearse* (New York 1973), p. 143; Edwards, *Triumph*, p. 47.
350. Letter of recommendation by Douglas Hyde dated 2 Oct. 1905, Kilmainham Jail, 23LR1P15 3.
351. Edwards, *Triumph*, p. 48.
352. Letter Justice Wm S. Black dated 6 Dec. 1946, LP.
353. Kate Elizabeth Field, LP; Edwards, *Triumph*, p. 48. See also Michael Dowling, LP.

354. Margaret Pearse, LP; Michael Dowling, LP.
355. 'Memories of Pearse', NLI, ms. 32,695/1; Ryan, *Remembering Sion*, p. 125; Colm O'Loch, LP.
356. Letter, W. Fallon dated 10 Apr. 1947, LP.
357. Letters from Civil Service Commission, India Office, and Colonial Office, LP; Eamonn O'Neill(?) Conan & Sceilg(?), LP.
358. McCay, *Pádraic Pearse*, p. 44.
359. Carty, *Bloody Protest*, p. 22; Ryan, *Man called Pearse*, p. 161.
360. Margaret's father, Patrick Brady, died in September 1894 leaving an estate of £216.14.6d (including three cottages in Aldborough Street, a house in North Clarence Street, various cattle, horses, cars and carts). He left his sister Margaret a life interest in these houses, but the rest went to Patrick's mother. As Aunt Margaret died soon afterwards all, except £10 each for the children of his deceased daughter Catherine Kelly, Mary Kate and John, went to Margaret Pearse; Edwards, *Triumph*, p. 45.
361. Edwards, *Triumph*, pp. 48–9.
362. Policy dated 16 Jan. 1901, NLI, ms. 21,406.
363. Letter Mrs McLoughlin dated 19 Oct. 1947, LP; private conversation with later relatives of the M'Cloughlin family; 'Pearse Association with Donegal' in *Donegal Annual* Vol.VII No. 1 1966, p. 86.
364. Sighle Barrett, LP; Letter dated 1 May 1916, Ó Buachalla (ed.), *Letters*, p. 377.
365. Letter W. Brennan dated 11 June 1947, LP; Michael Dowling, LP.
366. *The Derry People* 10 Oct. 1942.
367. Ibid., 20 May 1905.
368. Edwards, *Triumph*, pp. 79–81; Janet Egleson Dunleavy and Gareth W. Dunleavy, *Douglas Hyde. A Maker of Modern History* (Berkeley etc. 1991), p. 243.
369. Letter Seamus Cooling dated 11 Nov. 1947, LP.
370. Wolfe Tone memorial lecture at Bodenstown 22 June 1913, *Collected Works. Political Writings and Speeches*.

Chapter 2: Cultural nationalist

1. *ACS*, 24 Dec. 1904, quoted in Higgins and Uí Chollatáin, *Life and After-Life*, p. 81.
2. 'Autobiography by Patrick Pearse'.
3. Ó Súilleabháin, *An Piarsach*, p. 7; 'They were Schoolboys', pp. 44–6; Letter Margaret Pearse dated 19 July 1947, LP; Porter, *P.H. Pearse*, p. 26.
4. 'They were Schoolboys', p. 44.
5. Letter Eoghan ÓNeachtain dated 28 Aug. 1947, LP.
6. Ryan, *Man called Pearse*, p. 160; Ryan, *Remembering Sion*, pp. 104–5; Ó Súilleabháin, *An Piarsach*, p. 7; Le Roux, *Patrick H. Pearse*, p. 7.
7. Porter, *P.H. Pearse*, p. 26.
8. Veale, LP.

9. Michael Dowling, LP.

10. *Fáinna an Lae* 22 Eanair 1898, quoted in Frank O'Brien, *An Piarsach Óg agus Conradh na Gaeilge* (Dublin 1974).

11. Porter, *P.H. Pearse*, p. 17; S.P. Breathnach (S.P. Walsh), *Free and Gaelic. Pearse's Idea of a National Culture* (n.p. 1979), p. 6.

12. Quoted in Edwards, *Triumph*, pp. 16–7. Pearse (ed.), *Home Life*, p. 104; Porter, *P.H. Pearse*, p. 27.

13. Pearse, *Three Lectures*, p. 223.

14. Eamonn O'Neill, LP.

15. Letter Omar Crowley dated 19 Apr. 1947, LP. See also Pearse (ed.), *Home Life*, p. 88.

16. Ó Buachalla (ed.), *Letters*, pp. 3–4.

17. Pearse, *Three Lectures*, pp. 161–3; Ó Súilleabháin, *An Piarsach*, pp. 11–12.

18. Letter dated 7 Feb. 1902, Ó Buachalla (ed.), *Letters*, p. 51.

19. Edwards, *Triumph*, p. 168; Ó Súilleabháin, *An Piarsach*, pp. 26–7.

20. Ryan, *Remembering Sion*, p. 184.

21. J.J. O'Looney, LP; Letter Torna (O Donehada) dated 26 Nov. 1946, LP; Letter Wm. Val. Jackson dated 19 [?] 1947, LP; Porter, *P.H. Pearse*, p. 26.

22. Ó Súilleabháin, *An Piarsach*, p. 25.

23. *Freeman's Journal* 2 Nov. 1899, quoted in O'Brien, *An Piarsach*.

24. Philip O'Leary, *The Prose Literature of the Gaelic Revival, 1881–1921: Ideology and Innovation* (Pennsylvania, 1994), pp. 5–7.

25. 'Irish or Anglo-Irish', Eagarfhocal, *ACS* 10 Jan. 1903; Kissane, *Politics*, p. 25.

26. O'Leary, *Prose Literature*, pp. 19–21, 28–30; Kissane, *Politics*, p. 25; *ACS* 24 Apr. 1909; Moran, *Patrick Pearse*, pp. 53–60.

27. 'Up with the Town Halls', Eagarfhocal, *ACS* 15 Apr. 1899.

28. Schulze, *States, Nations*, pp. 237–8.

29. Collins, *Catholic Churchmen*, pp. 148–50; O'Leary, *Prose Literature*, pp. 32–8.

30. 'Notes', *ACS* 16 June 1900.

31. Ryan, *Remembering Sion*, p. 161.

32. 'Irish Industries', Eagarfhocal, *ACS* 18 Mar. 1899.

33. 'Irish in the Schools', Eagarfhocal, *ACS* 11 Nov. 1899. Patrick felt the same way, P.S. O'Hegarty, 'P.H. Pearse', in *Irish Commonwealth* March 1919, p. 29.

34. 'A Few Words in Season', Eagarfhocal, *ACS* 18 Nov. 1899.

35. 'A too Late Regret for Cornish', *ACS* 6 Jan. 1900.

36. This refers to William O'Brien, a somewhat eccentric representative of the Irish Party.

37. 'Mr William O Brien's Criticisms', *ACS* 24 Nov. 1900.

38. 'The Gaelic and the Other Movement', *ACS* 8 July 1899.

39. 'Do chum ar muinntir féin. The Gaelic League's Public Policy', *ACS* 16 Nov. 1901.

40. 'The Blind Pelting the Blind', Eagarfhocal, *ACS* 31 Mar. 1900.

41. Mullin, *Toiler's Life*, pp. 202–3.

Notes 363

42. O'Leary, *Prose Literature*, p. 32.
43. Edwards, *Triumph*, p. 21.
44. Ibid., pp. 20 and 23.
45. See, 'Notes', *ACS* 19 Jan. and 14 Dec. 1901 and 25 Jan. and 22 Nov. 1902.
46. 'Notes', *ACS* 14 Feb. 1903.
47. 'Notes', *ACS* 28 Sep. 1901.
48. *ACS* 27 June 1905, quoted in McGill, 'Pearse in Donegal', p. 85.
49. Porter, *P.H. Pearse*, pp. 27 and 143.
50. Edwards, *Triumph*, p. 26; Eamonn O'Neill, LP; Letter Torna (O Donehada) dated 26 Nov. 1946, LP; Eoin MacNeill's memoirs, NLI, ms. 10,883. The last meeting of the society had been held on 5 April 1898, Porter, *P.H. Pearse*, p. 142. According to O Ó Súilleabháin, *An Piarsach*, p. 21 the last session was reported in *Fáinne an Lae* 4 June 1898.
51. Ó Buachalla (ed.), *Letters*, p. 3.
52. McCay, *Pádraic Pearse*, p. 34.
53. *ACS* 23 July 1904.
54. Letter Mrs Bradley dated 22 Feb. 1947, LP.
55. Letter dated 12 Jan. 1901, Ó Buachalla (ed.), *Letters*, p. 31; Fr Joy, LP.
56. Witness statement of Harry Phibbs for the Bureau of Military History, NA (National Archive of Ireland), WS848.
57. Porter, *P.H. Pearse*, p. 28.
58. Pearse, *Three Lectures*, p. 215.
59. Ibid., p. 221, see also pp. 196, 206, 215 and 218–36.
60. *ACS* 14 Mar. 1903 and 28 Jan. 1905.
61. Letter dated 13 May 1899, Ó Buachalla (ed.), *Letters*, p. 9.
62. Ibid.
63. 'Notes', *ACS* 6 May 1899.
64. 'What is Irish National Literature II', *ACS* 8 July 1899. See also 'The Gaelic and the Other Movement', *ACS* 8 July 1899; 'Glimmerings of the Dawn', Eagarfhocal, *ACS* 3 Mar. 1900.
65. Holloway Diaries 5 Jan. 1899, quoted in Edwards, *Triumph*, pp. 28–9.
66. Frank Budgen, *Further Recollections of James Joyce* (London 1955), quoted in Edwards, *Triumph*, p. 29; Porter, *P.H. Pearse*, pp. 28 and 143.
67. O'Leary, *Prose Literature*, pp. 28–40 and 52–6 and 109–10.
68. *ACS* 19 May 1906, quoted in O'Leary, *Prose Literature*, pp. 114–15.
69. Edwards, *Triumph*, p. 33.
70. Ibid., p. 32; O'Leary, *Prose Literature*, pp. 19–24.
71. 'The Pan-Celtic Congress', Eagarfhocal, *ACS* 27 May 1899.
72. Letter Sean O Huadhaigh dated 15 July 1948, LP; Letter Ml Foley dated 17 June 1947, LP Eamonn O'Neill(?) Conan & Sceilg(?), LP.
73. Quoted in Edwards, *Triumph*, p. 33; copy of speech delivered by Pearse at 'public reception given on the Pavilion platform to the Celtic Deputations' on Tuesday 18 July 1899, *Weekly Mail* 22 July 1899.
74. 'Irish Hospitality', Eagarfhocal, *ACS* 12 Aug. 1899.
75. *Fáinne an Lae* 19 Aug. 1899, quoted in Edwards, *Triumph*, pp. 33–4.

76. Minutes of the Coiste Gnotha of the Gaelic League 15 Aug. 1899, NLI, mss 9799–800, quoted in Regina Uí Chollatáin, *An Claidheamh Soluis agus Fáinne an Lae 1899–1932* (Dublin 2004).

77. Ibid.

78. 'The Pan-Celtic Congress', *ACS* 19 Aug. 1899.

79. Minutes of the Coiste Gnotha of the Gaelic League 22 Aug. 1899, NLI, mss 9799–800; 'The Gaelic League and the Pan-Celtic Movement' *ACS* 2 Sep. 1899.

80. Edwards, *Triumph*, pp. 34–5; Photograph 'Representative Congress in Paris 1900', Pearse Museum (04.0081); Subscription of 10 shillings to Pan Celtic-Congress, NLI, ms. 21,047(6).

81. Borthwick to Hyde, quoted in Edwards, *Triumph*, p. 35; See also Letter Ml Kavanagh dated 16 Sep. 1947, LP; Edwards, *Triumph*, p. 42.

82. 'A Pitched Battle', Eagarfhocal, *ACS* 18 Mar. 1899; Seamus Ó Buachalla, *A Significant Irish Educationalist: The Educational Writings of P.H. Pearse* (Dublin 1980), p. xi; Rev. Bernard J. Canning, *Patrick H. Pearse and Scotland* (Glasgow 1979), p. 5; Tomas Ó Fiach, 'The Great Controversy', in Sean Ó Tuama (ed.), *The Gaelic League Idea* (Dublin 1972), p. 67.

83. Letter dated 31 Aug. 1901, Ó Buachalla (ed.), *Letters*, p. 46.

84. Ó Súilleabháin, *An Piarsach*, pp. 2–5.

85. *ACS* 23 Mar. 1907.

86. Ó Buachalla, *Irish Educationalist*, pp. 311–13; *ACS* 8 Oct. 1904.

87. *ACS* 2 Jan. 1904.

88. Although the Lord Lieutenant convinced Walsh to reconsider his resignation, he ultimately left in protest in 1901, Ó Buachalla (ed.), *Letters*, pp. 17 and 21.

89. Letter dated 10 July 1903, Ó Buachalla (ed.), *Letters*, p. 76; 'The Language Question at Westminster', *ACS* 28 July 1900; *ACS* 9 May 1903.

90. 'Irish in the Intermediate', *ACS* 6 July 1901.

91. 'More Intrigue', Eagarfhocal, *ACS* 25 Jan. 1902.

92. *ACS* 5 Dec. 1903 and 15 Mar. 1905.

93. *ACS* 18 Nov. 1905; Brendan Walsh, 'Radicalising the Classroom: Pearse, Pedagogy of Progressivism', in Higgins and Uí Chollatáin, *Life and After-Life*, p. 223.

94. Reg Hindley, *The Death of the Irish Language; A Qualified Obituary* (London 1990), p. 24; Moran, *Patrick Pearse*, p. 57.

95. *ACS* 23 Apr. 1904; Ó Buachalla, *Irish Educationalist*, p. xxiii.

96. *ACS* 7 May 1904. See also *ACS* 30 Apr. 1904.

97. Letter Ml Kavanagh dated 16 Sep. 1947, LP.

98. Edwards, *Triumph*, pp. 49–50 and 54; NLI, ms. 21,047(4).

99. Ó Buachalla (ed.), *Letters*, passim.

100. Letter to the *Irish Press* 27 July 1948; Geo Irvine, LP.

101. Letter dated 12 Jan. 1901, Ó Buachalla (ed.), *Letters*, p. 31; NLI, ms. 21,047; Kilmainham Jail, 23LRIP15/5 and 6.

102. Moran, *Patrick Pearse*, pp. 112–13.

103. Ó Buachalla (ed.), *Letters*, p. 15.

104. 'Notes', *ACS* 15 Apr. 1899; Ó Súilleabháin, *An Piarsach*, p. 16.

105. Ó Buachalla (ed.), *Letters*, pp. 15–18.

106. Porter, *P.H. Pearse*, p. 28.

107. Ibid., pp. 46–52 and 66–8; O'Leary, *Prose Literature*, pp. 9–12; Leerssen, *National Thought*, pp. 200–1.

108. Porter, *P.H. Pearse*, pp. 112–14.

109. 'Is Irish a Living Language?', Eagarfhocal, *ACS* 21 Nov. 1908.

110. Eoghan ÓNeachtain lauds Patrick's achievements in this field; Letter dated 28 Sep. 1947, LP.

111. Edwards, *Triumph*, pp. 44 and 48.

112. 'About Literature', Eagarfhocal, *ACS* 26 May 1906.

113. Lecture to the National Literary Society published as 'Some Aspects of Irish Literature', in *Studies* March 1913, quoted in Edwards, *Triumph*, p. 168.

114. Sisson, *Pearse's Patriots*, p. 99.

115. *ACS* 7 Mar. 1908 and 24 Apr. 1909.

116. This included: Edward Martyn, *Ireland's Battle for the Language* (1900); *Irish in the Schools*; *Parliament and the Teaching of Irish*; Mary E.L. Butler, *Irishwomen and the Home Language*; Ten pamphlets with evidence presented to the Commission on Intermediate Education; Archbishop Dr Walsh, *Bilingual Education*; *Bilingual Instruction on National Schools*; Fr O'Reilly, *The Threatening Metempsychosis of a Nation* (1901).

117. Letters dated 19 Dec. 1900, 19 Jan. and 27 July 1901, Ó Buachalla (ed.), *Letters*, pp. 26–7, 32 and 40–1.

118. O'Leary, *Prose Literature*, pp. 96–7; Letter dated 21 Jan 1901, Ó Buachalla (ed.), *Letters*, p. 32.

119. Ibid.

120. Letter dated 19 July 1901, Ó Buachalla (ed.), *Letters*, p. 39. See also Letter Wm. Val. Jackson dated 19 [?] 1947, LP.

121. Letter dated 23 Apr. 1902, Ó Buachalla (ed.), *Letters*, p. 54.

122. O'Leary, *Prose Literature*, pp. 12–13.

123. Letters dated 9 Dec. 1902, 2 Feb. 1903 and 4 Feb. 1903, Ó Buachalla (ed.), *Letters*, pp. 59–60 and 63–4.

124. NLI, ms. 21,047(6).

125. Letter dated 26 Oct. 1900, Ó Buachalla (ed.), *Letters*, pp. 22–3. These trews can still be seen in the National Museum of Ireland in Kildare Street, Dublin.

126. Letter dated 8 Aug. 1901, Ó Buachalla (ed.), *Letters*, p. 43.

127. Letter dated 24 Feb. 1903, Ó Buachalla (ed.), *Letters*, pp. 65–6. Some Munstermen agreed; Letter Liam de Roiste dated 10 Oct. 1947, LP.

128. Letter dated 9 Jan. 1901, Ó Buachalla (ed.), *Letters*, p. 30.

129. Kate Elizabeth Field, LP.

130. Jerome F. Cronin in *Irish Independent* 27 Mar. 1957.

131. Pearse (ed.), *Home Life*, p. 42.

132. Undated, Sisson, *Pearse's Patriots*, p. 64.

133. Joseph O'Neill, LP.

134. Eric Storm, 'Region-Building in Stone. Nationalism, Regionalism and Architecture in Germany, France and Spain (1900–1920)', paper presented 11 Apr. 2007 to the Graduate Seminar, Institute for History, Leiden University.

135. Ó Buachalla (ed.), *Letters*, pp. 141–3. The cottage is now a museum dedicated to Pearse.

136. Pearse (ed.), *Home Life*, pp. 110–12.

137. Angela Bourke, 'The Imagined Community of Pearse's Short Stories', in Higgins and Uí Chollatáin, *Life and After-Life*, pp. 142–7.

138. 'Education in the West of Ireland', Ó Buachalla, *Irish Educationalist*, p. 314; Edwards, *Triumph*, pp. 50–4.

139. *ACS* 18 July 1903, see also 25 Apr. 1903.

140. *ACS* 27 Aug. 1904 and 7 Dec. 1907.

141. Letter Justice Forde dated 4 Aug. 1948, LP.

142. P.S. O'Hegarty, 'P.H. Pearse' in *Irish Commonwealth* March 1919, p. 29.

143. Letter Justice Forde dated 4 Aug. 1948, LP.

144. 'Fear Faire' in *The Irish Educational Review* 1910 Vol. III No. 7, pp. 410–12.

145. Pearse McLoughlin (son of Alf and Mary Emily Pearse), LP.

146. Letter J.A. Duffy dated 30 Sep. 1947, LP.

147. Eamonn O'Neill, LP.

148. Letter Liam de Roiste dated 10 Oct. 1947, LP; Brian P. Murphy, *Patrick Pearse and the Lost Republican Ideal* (Dublin 1991), pp. 19–27.

149. Minutes of the Coiste Gnotha of the Gaelic League 17 Dec. 1898, NLI, ms. 9799; Osborn Bergin, LP.

150. 'Strengthen the Weak Points', Eagarfhocal, *ACS* 11 Aug. 1900.

151. Minutes of the Coiste Gnotha of the Gaelic League 14 Feb. 1899, NLI, ms. 9800.

152. Ibid., 8 and 17 May 1900.

153. Edwards, *Triumph*, pp. 42–3; Porter, *P.H. Pearse*, p. 142.

154. Liam O Donnell, LP.

155. J.J. O'Looney, LP; Eamonn O'Neill, LP; Pearse (ed.), *Home Life*, p. 106; Ó Súilleabháin, *An Piarsach*, p. 65; Letter Maire ní Cinneide dated 23 Oct. 1947, LP.

156. Letter Ml Foley dated 17 June 1947, LP.

157. Seamus Fenton, LP.

158. Letter Eoghan ÓNeachtain dated 14 Oct. 1947, LP; Letter Ml Kavanagh dated 16 Sep. 1947, LP; Letter Mrs Bradley dated 22 Feb. 1947, LP; Edwards, *Triumph*, pp. 58–9.

159. Quoted in ibid., p. 57.

160. Ó Buachalla (ed.), *Letters*, p. 65; Letter Sean O Brian dated 7 Oct. 1947, LP.

161. Letters dated 24 Feb. and 25 Mar. 1903, Ó Buachalla (ed.), *Letters*, pp. 65–6 and 73; Letter Mrs Bradley dated 22 Feb. 1947, LP.

162. Letters dated 24 and 25 Feb. 1903, Ó Buachalla (ed.), *Letters*, pp. 65–8. See also Letter Omar Crowley dated 19 Apr. 1947, LP.

163. Letter Stephen Barrett to Eoin MacNeill dated 27 Feb. 1903 on Gaelic League notepaper in Noel Kissane, *Pádraic Mac Piarais: Pearse from Documents* (Dublin 1979).

164. Including those who were canvassed were the writers Doyle and Morris who Patrick had supported many times as secretary of the Publication Committee, and the London members Dr MacEnrí and T.P. Mac Fhionlaoigh, Ó Buachalla (ed.), *Letters*, p. 66. Letters in support of Patrick quoted in Edwards, *Triumph*, p. 62.

165. Letter Omar Crowley dated 19 Apr. 1947, LP.

166. Letter Maire ní Cinneide dated 23 Oct. 1947, LP; Edwards, *Triumph*, pp. 59–63.

167. Letter Mrs Bradley dated 22 Feb. 1947, LP.

168. Ibid.

169. Liam O Donnell, LP; Letter Ml. Kavanagh dated 16 Sep. 1947, LP.

170. *Annual Report of the Gaelic League 1902*; *Proceedings of Ard-Fheis 1903*, p. 12; Eamonn O'Neill(?) Conan & Sceilg(?), LP.

171. *Banba Abran* 1903, p. 180.

172. Letter Mrs Bradley 22 Feb. 1947, LP.

173. Appendix to letter dated 28 Feb. 1903, Ó Buachalla (ed.), *Letters*, pp. 69–72.

174. Quoted in Edwards, *Triumph*, p. 66.

175. 'Gleo na gCath', *ACS* 6 June 1903.

176. *Proceedings of Árd Fheis 1904*.

177. 'Sinn Féin', 'Gleo na gCath', *ACS* 5 Mar. 1904.

178. 'Gleo na gCath', *ACS* 4 July 1903.

179. Letter dated 17 Oct. 1903, Ó Buachalla (ed.), *Letters*, p. 78.

180. Letter dated 17 May 1907, ibid., p. 108.

181. Letter Mrs Bradley dated 22 Feb. 1947, LP.

182. Letter to Sean T. O'Kelly, quoted in Edwards, *Triumph*, pp. 66–7; Letter dated 31 Dec. 1903, Ó Buachalla (ed.), *Letters*, pp. 80–1.

183. Ml. Kavanagh, LP; Edwards, *Triumph*, pp. 68–9.

184. Circular, quoted in Edwards, *Triumph*, pp. 67–8.

185. *Proceedings of Ard Fheis 1905–1909*; Uí Chollatáin, *Claidheamh Soluis*, p. 260; Edwards, *Triumph*, p. 68.

186. Edwards, *Triumph*, p. 89

187. Letters dated 10 Feb. 1902 and 17 Oct. 1903, Ó Buachalla (ed.), *Letters*, pp. 51–2 and 78.

188. 'The Irish Stage', Eagarfhocal, *ACS* 16 June 1906.

189. Letter Mrs Margaret Hutton dated 9 Sep. 1903, NLI, ms. 8617. See also Letter to Lady Gregory dated 29 Apr. 1905, NLI, ms. 27,828.

190. 'About Literature', 'Gleo na gCath', *ACS* 29 Apr. 1905. See also 'A Movement of Defeat', 'Gleo na gCath', *ACS* 6 Feb. 1904.

191. R.F. Foster, *W.B, Yeats: A Life. 1, The Apprentice Mage: 1865–1914* (Oxford 1997), p. 220.

192. Stephen McKenna, *Irish Press* 29 Mar 1937, LP; Letter Seamus Cooling dated 11 Nov. 1947, LP; 'From a Hermitage', p. 145; Ryan, *Remembering Sion*, p. 41; Edwards, *Triumph*, p. 169.

193. Porter, *P.H. Pearse*, p. 54.

194. Letter to Lady Gregory dated 29 Apr. 1905, NLI, ms. 27,828.

195. Porter, *P.H. Pearse*, p. 53.

196. Foster, *Yeats*, p. 399.

197. 'About Literature', 'Gleo na gCath', *ACS* 29 Apr. 1905; 'Drama', 'Gleo na gCath', *ACS* 21 Nov. 1908.

198. *ACS* 6 Feb. 1904; Letter to Lady Gregory dated 29 Apr. 1905, NLI, ms. 27,828. See also 'Mr Yeats on his failure', 'Gleo na gCath', *ACS* 5 Mar. 1907; 'A Movement of Defeat', 'Gleo na gCath', *ACS* 6 Feb. 1904.

199. 'Drama', 'Gleo na gCath', *ACS* 21 Nov. 1908.

200. 'A Movement of Defeat', 'Gleo na gCath', *ACS* 6 Feb. 1904.

201. Sisson, *Pearse's Patriots*, pp. 10–13; Thompson, *Imagination*, p. 64.

202. *ACS* 27 Aug. 1904.

203. Article on display in Pearse Museum in 2008.

204. Ó Buachalla, *Irish Educationalist*, p. x; Porter, *P.H. Pearse*, pp. 30 and 93; Sisson, *Pearse's Patriots*, p. 34.

205. *ACS* 12 Dec. 1903 and 10 Feb. 1906; Murphy, *Lost Republican Ideal*, p. 36.

206. *ACS* 12 Dec. 1903.

207. Ryan, *Man called Pearse*, pp. 151–2.

208. McGill, 'Pearse in Donegal', p. 69.

209. McGill, 'Pearse in Donegal', p. 70.

210. Ibid., pp. 68–75; Ryan, *Remembering Sion*, p. 188.

211. Letter dated 31 July 1907, Ó Buachalla (ed.), *Letters*, p. 111.

212. Letter dated 30 Sep. 1905, Ó Buachalla (ed.), *Letters*, p. 98. See also Letter Sean O Brian dated 7 Oct. 1947, LP.

213. Ibid.

214. Letter of recommendation by Douglas Hyde dated 2 Oct. 1905, Kilmainham Jail, 23LRIP15/3. See also Letter Edmund Hogan, Kilmainham Jail, 23LRIP15/4.

215. Letter dated 15 May 1909, Ó Buachalla (ed.), *Letters*, p. 143.

216. Edwards, *Triumph*, pp. 69 and 89–96.

217. Letter Sean O Brian dated 7 Oct. 1947, LP.

218. Porter, *P.H. Pearse*, p. 70.

219. Review in *The Leader* 30 Jan. 1909, quoted in O'Leary, *Prose Literature*, p. 91.

220. Porter, *P.H. Pearse*, pp. 66–71 and 144. See also Eamonn O'Neill(?) Conan & Sceilg(?), LP; D65, LP; John Dowling, LP.

221. D65, LP; Rd Foley, LP; Letter Torna (O Donehada) dated 26 Nov. 1946, LP; Eamonn O'Neill(?) Conan & Sceilg(?), LP; Liam O Donnell, LP; Osborn Bergin, LP.

222. *An Macaomh* Dec. 1909, quoted in O'Leary, *Prose Literature*, p. 91.

223. O'Leary, *Prose Literature*, pp. 124–7.

224. See Declan Kiberd, 'Patrick Pearse: Irish Modernist', in Higgins and Uí Chollatáin, *Life and After-Life*, p. 67.

225. Letters dated 10 June 1903, 8 and 29 July 1903, Ó Buachalla (ed.), *Letters*, pp. 74–6; Edwards, *Triumph*, p. 90.

226. Letter dated 9 Sep. 1903, Ó Buachalla (ed.), *Letters*, pp. 77–8.
227. Letter to W.J. Ryan editor of *Irish Independent* 1 Feb. 1905, NLI, ms. 13,098; Letter dated 1 Feb. 1905, Ó Buachalla (ed.), *Letters*, p. 92.
228. Letters dated 25 and 26 Nov. 1903, 24 Dec. 1906 and 2 Jan. 1908, Ó Buachalla (ed.), *Letters*, pp. 79–80, 104 and 116.
229. Edwards, *Triumph*, pp. 106–7.
230. Letter dated 19 Nov. 1904, Ó Buachalla (ed.), *Letters*, pp. 85–6; *ACS* 9 May 1903.
231. Ó Buachalla (ed.), *Letters*, p. 114.
232. Conan & Sceilg, LP.
233. Dunleavy, *Douglas Hyde*, p. 303.
234. *ACS* 10 and 17 June 1905.
235. Letter dated 4 July 1905, Ó Buachalla (ed.), *Letters*, p. 96.
236. 'Gleo na gCath', *ACS* 22 July 1905; Edwards, *Triumph*, pp. 105–7. Ó Buachalla (ed.), *Letters*, p. 95.
237. P.S. O'Hegarty, quoted in Edwards, *Triumph*, p. 105.
238. *ACS* 28 Jan. 1905; Senia Paseta, 'The Catholic Hierarchy and the Irish University Question, 1880–1908', in *History* Vol. 85 No. 278, pp. 268–84.
239. 'Notes', *ACS* 4 Oct. 1902.
240. *ACS* 28 Jan. 1905. See also *ACS* 9 Feb. 1907.
241. *ACS* 28 Mar. 1903. See also *ACS* 30 Jan. 1904.
242. Dr Con Murphy Papers on Catholic Graduates Association minutes, 1st meeting held 31 Oct. 1903, LP.
243. Meeting of 2 June 1905, Catholic Graduates Association minutes, LP. See also *ACS* 17 Dec. 1904.
244. Meeting of 16 Nov. 1905, Catholic Graduates Association minutes, LP.
245. Letter Omar Crowley dated 19 Apr. 1947, LP; Pearse (ed.), *Home Life*, pp. 108–9.
246. Moran, *Patrick Pearse*, pp. 156–9 and 171.
247. Sister Francesca, NA, WS717.
248. Letter dated 23 Nov. 1905, Ó Buachalla (ed.), *Letters*, p. 99.
249. *ACS* 7 Jan. 1905, quoted in Edwards, *Triumph*, p. 76.
250. Submission of Bishops to Royal Commission dated 25 July 1906, LP.
251. *ACS* 1 Feb. 1908.
252. *ACS* 11 Apr. 1908.
253. *ACS* 25 Apr. 1908. See also *ACS* 16 May 1908; NLI, P7216. He displayed a similar concern for female representation concerning the Board of Education in 1906, *ACS* 8 Dec. 1906.
254. *ACS* 16 May 1908.
255. *ACS* 5 Dec. 1908. See also *ACS* 5 June 1909.
256. *ACS* 12 Dec. 1908.
257. *ACS* 30 Jan. 1909.
258. *ACS* 6 Mar. 1909. See also *ACS* 30 Jan. 1909.
259. Ibid.
260. *ACS* 5 June 1909.
261. *ACS* 1 May 1909.

262. Edwards, *Triumph*, p. 77.
263. 'Manifesto for the Coiste Gnótha on the Question of Irish in the National University', *ACS* 6 Feb. 1909.
264. *ACS* 3 July 1909.
265. *ACS* 26 June 1909. See also *ACS* 3 July 1909.
266. Murphy, *Lost Republican Ideal*, p. 29.
267. *ACS* 7 Aug. 1909, quoted in Edwards, *Triumph*, pp. 77–8.
268. Ibid.
269. *ACS* 18 May 1907.
270. *ACS* 6 Oct. 1906; Hannay, quoted in Edwards, *Triumph*, p. 93.
271. See the case of Fr White, 'Letter Father White', *ACS* 14 Dec. 1901; 'Comhairle', *ACS* 25 Oct. 1902; 'Father Farragher, The Gaelic League and Ourselves', *ACS* 1 Nov. 1902; 'Comhairle', *ACS* 15 Nov. 1902.
272. Porter, *P.H. Pearse*, p. 40; O'Leary, *Prose Literature*, pp. 24–8.
273. Letters dated 22 Nov. and 22 Dec. 1900, Ó Buachalla (ed.), *Letters*, pp. 24–5 and 28.
274. Letter Omar Crowley dated 19 Apr. 1947, LP.
275. Letter Greg Murphy dated 8 May 1947, LP.
276. Letter Omar Crowley dated 19 Apr. 1947, LP.
277. Letter to Séamus Ó Ceallaigh dated 26 Dec. 1904, NLI, ms. 5049.
278. Edwards, *Triumph*, p. 19; *Fáinne an Lae* 28 May 1898.
279. *ACS* 19 Dec. 1903.
280. *ACS* 12 Nov. 1904 and 9 and 16 Nov. 1907.
281. *ACS* 30 Nov. 1907.
282. *ACS* 28 Dec. 1907.
283. Ibid. See also *ACS* 9 and 16 Nov. 1907.
284. Sisson, *Pearse's Patriots*, p. 33.
285. LP.
286. See letters dated 19 Nov. 1904 and 25 Apr. 1907, Ó Buachalla (ed.), *Letters*, pp. 86 and 107.
287. Eamonn O'Neill(?) Conan & Sceilg(?), LP.
288. *ACS* 15 Mar. and 22 Apr. 1905 and 23 Mar. 1907.
289. *ACS* 9 Sep. 1905.
290. *ACS* 22 Apr. and 16 Sep. 1905.
291. *ACS* 16 Sep. 1905.
292. *ACS* 23 June 1906.
293. *ACS* 23 Mar. 1907.
294. *ACS* 23 Mar. 1907.
295. *ACS* 5 Oct. 1907.
296. *ACS* 13 Apr. and 12 Oct. 1907.
297. *ACS* 28 Mar. 1908.
298. *ACS* 7 Mar. 1908 and 24 Apr. 1909.
299. Letter Béaslai to MacNeill dated 4 Apr. 1908, quoted in Edwards, *Triumph*, p. 110; *ACS* 4 Apr. 1908.
300. Ibid.
301. Ibid.

302. *ACS* 4 Apr. 1908; 'The Fees Question', Eagarfhocal, *ACS* 18 Apr. 1908.
303. *ACS* 4 Apr. 1908.
304. *ACS* 25 Apr. and 30 May 1908.
305. *ACS* 4 Apr. 1908.
306. *ACS* 24 Sep. 1904.
307. *ACS* 22 Oct. 1904.
308. *ACS* 26 Dec. 1903, 9 Dec. 1905 and 6 Jan. 1906.
309. Hindley, *Death of*, p. 24.
310. 'The Language Question at Westminster', *ACS* 28 July 1900.
311. 'A National Insult', Eagarfhocal, *ACS* 22 Feb. 1902.
312. *ACS* 15 July 1905.
313. *ACS* 26 Aug. 1905. See also *ACS* 9 Sep. 1905 and 23 June 1906.
314. *ACS* 25 Feb. 1905.
315. Dunleavy, *Douglas Hyde*, p. 251.
316. *ACS* 24 Nov. 1906.
317. *ACS* 7 Sep. 1907.
318. *ACS* 4 Dec. 1909.
319. *ACS* 11 Jan. 1908.
320. *ACS* 29 July 1907. See also *ACS* 13 Apr. 1907.
321. *ACS* 7 and 14 May 1904.
322. *ACS* 29 July 1907. See also *ACS* 13 Apr. 1907.
323. *ACS* 8 and 22 Apr. 1905 and 2 Feb. 1907.
324. *ACS* 25 Feb. 1905.
325. *ACS* 2 Feb. 1907.
326. *ACS* 22 Oct. 1904.
327. *ACS* 29 July 1907. See also 'The Schools', Eagarfhocal, *ACS* 11 Jan. 1908.
328. *ACS* 1 Oct. 1904.
329. *ACS* 2 Jan. and 9 May and 7 Nov. and 26 Dec. 1903.
330. Séamus Ó Buachalla, *An Piarsach sa Bheilg = P.H. Pearse in Belgium = P.H. Pearse in België* (Dublin 1998), p. 114.
331. *ACS* 18 May 1907.
332. *ACS* 20 June 1908.
333. *ACS* 29 Feb. 1908.
334. *ACS* 15 Feb. 1908.
335. *ACS* 20 June 1908.
336. Coilin, *Patrick H. Pearse*, p. 7.
337. Letters dated 26 Oct. 1904 and 14 Mar. and 16 May 1907, Ó Buachalla (ed.), *Letters*, pp. 85, 106 and 108.
338. Letter to Col. Maurice Moore dated 18 Aug. 1909, NLI, ms. 5049.
339. Letter dated 24 Dec. 1907, Ó Buachalla (ed.), *Letters*, p. 115.
340. Letters dated 20 June 1907, 11 Apr. 1908, 10 Apr. and 12 Dec. 1909 and 23 Feb. 1910, Ó Buachalla (ed.), *Letters*, pp. 109, 131, 142 and 148–50.
341. Letter to Lady Gregory dated 29 Apr. 1905, NLI, ms. 27,828.
342. Letter dated 16 Sep. 1905, Ó Buachalla (ed.), *Letters*, p. 97.
343. Undated letter probably from 10 Aug. 1907 to Sean T. O'Kelly, Ó Buachalla (ed.), *Letters*, p. 112.

344. Letter dated 31 Dec. 1903, Ó Buachalla (ed.), *Letters*, pp. 80–1.

345. Letter Wm. Val. Jackson dated 19 [?] 1947, LP.

346. Letter dated 20 June 1907, Ó Buachalla (ed.), *Letters*, p. 109.

347. Letter dated 19 Oct. 1904, Ó Buachalla (ed.), *Letters*, p. 84.

348. Letter dated 3 Jan. 1907, Ó Buachalla (ed.), *Letters*, p. 104.

349. Letters dated 24 Dec. 1907 and 11 Apr. 1908, Ó Buachalla (ed.), *Letters*, pp. 115 and 131.

350. Letter dated 13 Jan. 1905, Ó Buachalla (ed.), *Letters*, p. 90.

351. See Letter Fr Peadar Ó Laoghaire (1839–1920) dated 2 July 1903, in uncatalogued material Kilmainham Jail collection; Letter Maire ní Cinneide dated 23 Oct. 1947, LP; Letter dated 20 Jan. 1905, Ó Buachalla (ed.), *Letters*, pp. 90–1.

352. Letter dated 1 Feb. 1905, Ó Buachalla (ed.), *Letters*, pp. 91–2.

353. Ibid.; Letter dated 1 Feb. 1905 to W.J. Ryan, NLI, ms. 13,098.

354. O'Hegarty, 'P.H. Pearse', quoted in Edwards, *Triumph*, p. 83.

355. For an example of all these feelings towards Patrick, Rd Foley, LP. See also Lennon, LP; Letter Mrs Bradley dated 22 Feb. 1947, LP.

356. Letter Mrs Bradley dated 22 Feb. 1947, LP.

357. Letter Torna (O Donehada) dated 26 Nov. 1946, LP.

358. Letter Maire ní Cinneide dated 23 Oct. 1947, LP.

359. Ryan, *Man called Pearse*, p. 175.

360. Sisson, *Pearse's Patriots*, p. 66.

361. Letter Frank Fahey dated 15 Mar. 1948, LP.

362. Letter Wm. Val. Jackson dated 19 [?] 1947, LP.

363. Letter dated 20 Feb. 1905, Ó Buachalla (ed.), *Letters*, p. 93.

364. Rd Foley, LP; Letter Ml Kavanagh dated 16 Sep. 1947, LP; Michael Foley, LP.

365. Margaret Pearse, LP.

366. Liam O Donnell, LP.

367. Rd Foley, LP.

368. Maire Ni Cillin, LP. See also Letter Mrs Bradley dated 22 Feb. 1947, LP.

369. *ACS* 15 and 18 Mar. and 22 Apr. 1905; Letter Mrs Bradley dated 22 Feb. 1947, LP; Letter Justice Forde dated 4 Aug. 1948, LP.

370. Letter Mrs Bradley dated 22 Feb. 1947, LP. In his letter Justice Sean Forde disagreed, but refers to others who do state this was a contributing factor, letter dated 4 Aug. 1948, LP.

371. *ACS* 27 Aug. 1904, quoted in Edwards, *Triumph*, p. 83.

372. *ACS* 28 July 1906, quoted in Edwards, *Triumph*, pp. 84–5.

373. *Leader* 22 Feb. 1908, quoted in Edwards, *Triumph*, p. 85.

374. *ACS* 23 May 1908, quoted in Edwards, *Triumph*, p. 87; Murphy, *Lost Republican Ideal*, p. 35.

375. *ACS* 23 May 1908, quoted in Edwards, *Triumph*, p. 87.

376. Letter dated 11 Apr. 1908, Ó Buachalla (ed.), *Letters*, p. 131. See also Ryan, *Remembering Sion*, p. 106; Letter Mrs Bradley dated 22 Feb. 1947, LP.

377. 'Father Dineen, The Coiste Gnótha, and the Policy of Bilingualism', Eagarfhocal, *ACS* 6 June 1908; Murphy, *Lost Republican Ideal*, p. 32.

378. *ACS* 30 May 1908, quoted in Edwards, *Triumph*, p. 88.

379. Edwards, *Triumph*, p. 89. See also Lennon, LP.

380. Letter dated 19 June 1908, Ó Buachalla (ed.), *Letters*, pp. 132–3.

381. Quoted in Edwards, *Triumph*, p. 73.

382. Ibid.

383. Uí Chollatáin, *Claidheamh Soluis*, p. 260.

384. *Proceedings of Ard Fheis, 1904–09.*

385. Letter dated 19 June 1908, Ó Buachalla (ed.), *Letters*, pp. 132–3; Edwards, *Triumph*, p. 117.

386. Letter dated 4 July 1905, Ó Buachalla (ed.), *Letters*, pp. 95–6.

387. *ACS* Oct. 1908, quoted in Edwards, *Triumph*, p. 121.

388. Letters dated 22 and 26 Oct. 1908, Ó Buachalla (ed.), *Letters*, pp. 136–7.

389. Sean Forde, LP.

390. Letter dated 12 Dec. 1909, Ó Buachalla (ed.), *Letters*, pp. 148–9.

391. Ryan, *Man called Pearse*, pp. 151–2.

392. Edwards, *Triumph*, p. 130.

393. *An Macaomh* Dec. 1909, quoted in Edwards, *Triumph*, p. 129.

394. O'Leary, *Prose Literature*, p. 458.

395. Open letter to Douglas Hyde dated 4 May 1912, Ó Buachalla (ed.), *Letters*, pp. 262–4.

396. 'The Psychology of a Volunteer' in *ACS* 3 Jan. 1914; Ryan, *Man called Pearse*, pp. 231–2.

397. 'The Coming Revolution', *ACS* 8 Nov. 1913.

Chapter 3: Educationalist

1. *ACS* 12 Nov. 1904. See also Edwards, *Triumph*, p. 109; *ACS* 26 Jan. 1907.

2. Pearse, *Three Lectures*, p. 206.

3. Letter to *The Press* Feb. 1900, Ó Buachalla (ed.), *Letters*, p. 13.

4. Ó Buachalla (ed.), *Letters*, p. 17.

5. *ACS* 18 Apr. 1904, quoted in Ó Buachalla, *Irish Educationalist*, p. ix.

6. *ACS* 2 Jan. 1903.

7. *ACS* 16 Jan. 1903.

8. *ACS* 7 Nov. 1903.

9. 'Gleo na gCath', *ACS* 15 Aug. 1903.

10. *ACS* 7 Nov. and 26 Dec. 1903.

11. 'The School Atmosphere', 'Gleo na gCath', *ACS* 3 Dec. 1904.

12. Sisson, *Pearse's Patriots*, pp. 27–8.

13. *ACS* 7 Jan. 1905.

14. *ACS* 12 Nov. 1904. See also Edwards, *Triumph*, p. 109; *ACS* 26 Jan. 1907.

15. *ACS* 16 Apr. 1904 and 7 Mar. 1908.

16. *ACS* 25 Nov. 1905.

17. *ACS* 12 Nov. and 16 Apr. 1904.

18. *ACS* 16 Apr. 1904.

19. *ACS* 12 Nov. 1904. A similar sensitivity over the death of a bird can be found in his poem 'O Little Bird', in *Collected Works. Plays, Stories, Poems*, p. 314.

20. 'The Language Question in Belgium', *ACS* 2 Dec. 1899; Monsieur A. Sluys, 'Bi-lingual Belgium. How the Flemish have Stood by their Language', *ACS* 24 Mar. and 7 Apr. 1900.

21. T.R. Dawes, *Bilingual Teaching in Belgian Schools being the Report on a Visit to Belgian Schools as Gillchrist Travelling Student* (Cambridge 1902).

22. Ó Buachalla, *Irish Educationalist*, p. xi; Ó Buachalla, *Pearse in Belgium*, p. 117.

23. Ibid., p. 106.

24. Eamonn O Donehada, LP

25. Ó Buachalla (ed.), *Letters*, p. 95.

26. Ó Buachalla, *Pearse in Belgium*, pp. 109–10.

27. Letter dated 4 July 1905, Ó Buachalla (ed.), *Letters*, pp. 95–6.

28. Ó Buachalla, *Pearse in Belgium*, p. 110.

29. Ibid., p. 109, Ó Buachalla, *Irish Educationalist*, p. xi.

30. Sisson, *Pearse's Patriots*, p. 30.

31. Ó Buachalla, *Pearse in Belgium*, p. 114.

32. Sisson, *Pearse's Patriots*, p. 28; Ó Buachalla, *Irish Educationalist*, p. xiv.

33. *ACS* 7 Mar. 1908 and 24 Apr. 1909.

34. Ó Buachalla, *Pearse in Belgium*, p. 105. This link with modern reformism was already recognised in 1916, MacKenzie, *Irish Rebellion*, pp. 11–12.

35. Edwards, *Triumph*, p. 72; *ACS* 16 Jan. 1903 and 16 Apr. 1904.

36. Ó Buachalla, *Pearse in Belgium*, p. 116; Ó Buachalla (ed.), *Letters*, p. 304; Kilmainham Jail, 23LR1P14 24; Ryan, *Man called Pearse*, pp. 217–18; Pearse (ed.), *Home Life*, p. 108.

37. Ibid.

38. Seán Oliver, 'Irish Revolutionary Nationalism: Tone to Pearse', in Maurice O'Connell, *People Power: Proceedings of the Third Annual Daniel O'Connell Workshop* (Dublin 1993), p. 110; Thompson, *Imagination*, pp. 26–7.

39. Entry 23 Oct. 1909, Scribbling diary for 1909, Pearse Museum; Sisson, *Pearse's Patriots*, pp. 38, 70–4 and 88–90; Ó Buachalla, *Pearse in Belgium*, pp. 107 and 116; Ó Buachalla, *Irish Educationalist*, pp. xi and xxiv; Edwards, *Triumph*, p. 72; Le Roux, *Patrick H. Pearse*, p. 159.

40. Ó Buachalla, *Irish Educationalist*, pp. xiv–xv.

41. Ibid., p. xxii.

42. *ACS* 5 Nov. 1904.

43. Letter dated 3 Mar. 1906, quoted in Ó Buachalla, *Pearse in Belgium*, pp. 113–14.

44. Ibid., p. 113.

45. *ACS* 20 Jan. 1906.

46. Letter Seamus Cooling dated 11 Nov. 1947, LP; Edwards, *Triumph*, p. 107.

47. *ACS* 7 Sep. 1907.

48. *ACS* 7 Mar. 1908.

49. Sisson, *Pearse's Patriots*, p. 31.

50. *ACS* 18 Nov. 1905.

51. *ACS* 18 Jan. 1908.

52. *ACS* 7 Sep. 1907.

53. Sisson, *Pearse's Patriots*, pp. 25 and 32; Ó Buachalla, *Irish Educationalist*, p. xxi; *ACS* 13 Jan. 1906.

54. *ACS* 1 May 1909.

55. Eamonn O Donehada, LP.

56. Edwards, *Triumph*, pp. 111–12; Ó Buachalla (ed.), *Letters*, p. 126.

57. Sisson, *Pearse's Patriots*, p. 31.

58. Letter dated 29 Feb. 1908, Ó Buachalla (ed.), *Letters*, pp. 124–5.

59. Letter dated 24 Feb. 1908, Ó Buachalla (ed.), *Letters*, p. 120, see also pp. 121–30.

60. Edwards, *Triumph*, pp. 111–12; Ó Buachalla (ed.), *Letters*, p. 126.

61. Letter dated 4 Mar. 1908, ibid, p. 127; Sisson, *Pearse's Patriots*, pp. 34–5.

62. Sisson, *Pearse's Patriots*, p. 36; Letter dated 4 Mar. 1908; Undated draft of the 'Object and Scope of Sgoil Lopcán (St Lorcan's School): An Irish School for Catholic Boys', NLI, ms. 18,578.

63. Sisson, *Pearse's Patriots*, p. 15; Cooke, *Scéal Scoil Éanna*, pp. 21–2.

64. Ruth Dudley Edwards claims that Patrick put in either £100 or £150, Edwards, *Triumph*, pp. 113 and 144.

65. Letter dated 27 Feb. 1908, Ó Buachalla (ed.), *Letters*, pp. 122–3.

66. Michael Dowling, LP.

67. Letter dated 29 Feb. 1908, Ó Buachalla (ed.), *Letters*, p. 124.

68. Ibid.

69. Letters dated 4 Mar. 1908 and 13 Mar. 1908; Edwards, *Triumph*, p. 114.

70. Eoin MacNeill, quoted in Edwards, *Triumph*, p. 114.

71. Letter to Conn Murphy dated 13 Mar. 1908, LP.

72. Letter Ml Kavanagh dated 16 Sep. 1947 and Letter Ml Foley dated 17 June 1947, LP.

73. Ó Buachalla, *Pearse in Belgium*, p. 107; Sisson, *Pearse's Patriots*, p. 135.

74. Edwards, *Triumph*, p. 115; Letter dated 27 Feb. 1908, Ó Buachalla (ed.), *Letters*, pp. 122–3.

75. Sisson, *Pearse's Patriots*, p. 20.

76. Ibid., p. 37.

77. Crowley, 'His Father's', p. 83.

78. Ibid.; *An Macaomh* Dec. 1909.

79. Edwards, *Triumph*, p. 115.

80. *An Macaomh* Summer 1909; Letters dated 17 Nov. 1908 and 1 Feb. 1909, Ó Buachalla (ed.), *Letters*, pp. 138–9 and 141; Circular dated 10 May 1910, Kilmainham Jail, 23LP 1P14.

81. NLI, ms. 35,262/28; Horgan, *From Parnell*, p. 245.

82. St Enda's prospectus 1908; Edwards, *Triumph*, p. 129; Circular dated 10 May 1910, Kilmainham Jail, 23LP 1P14.

83. Ó Buachalla, *Pearse in Belgium*, p. 107.

84. Sisson, *Pearse's Patriots*, pp. 7–8; Edwards, *Triumph*, p. 118.

85. *An Macaomh* Summer 1909; Edwards, *Triumph*, p. 128.

86. Edwards, *Triumph*, p. 129.

87. School prospectus 1910/11; *An Macaomh* 1910.

88. Letter MacNeill dated 4 Mar. 1908, NLI, ms. 10,883.

89. Letter dated 4 Mar. 1908, Ó Buachalla (ed.), *Letters*, pp. 127–30.

90. Letter dated 15 July 1908, ibid., pp. 134–5.

91. Letter dated 17 Nov. 1908, ibid., pp. 138–9.

92. Letters dated 16 Dec. 1908 and 15 May 1910, ibid., pp. 140 and 159–60.

93. Letter dated 16 July 1910, ibid., pp. 171–2; Sisson, *Pearse's Patriots*, pp. 33–4 and 68 note 36.

94. Letter dated 17 Nov. 1908, Ó Buachalla (ed.), *Letters*, pp. 138–9; Carty, *Bloody Protest*, p. 35.

95. Letters dated 16 July and 23 Aug. 1910, Ó Buachalla (ed.), *Letters*, pp. 171–2 and 177.

96. Letter dated Sep. 1911, ibid., pp. 217–18; Entry dated 27 May 1909, Scribbling diary for 1909, Pearse Museum.

97. Joseph Sweeney, 'Donegal and the Easter Rising', in *Donegal Annual* Vol. VII No. 1, 1966, p. 5.

98. Le Roux, *Patrick H. Pearse*, p. 138.

99. Letter dated 13 May 1911, Ó Buachalla (ed.), *Letters*, pp. 191–2.

100. Letters dated 29 June and 7 July 1911, ibid., pp. 197–8.

101. Letters dated 9 and 18 Mar. 1915, ibid. pp. 339–41.

102. Letter dated 3 Mar. 1914, NLI, ms. 40,454/2.

103. Letter dated 4 Mar. 1908, Ó Buachalla (ed.), *Letters*, p. 129.

104. Brendan J. Walsh, 'The Progressive Credentials of Patrick Henry Pearse: A Response to David Limond', *History of Education Review* 2006 Vol. 35 No. 2.

105. K. Manton, 'Establishing the Fellowship: Harry Lowerison and Ruskin School Home, a Turn-of-the-Century Socialist and His Educational Experiment', *History of Education* Vol. 26 (1997), pp. 53–70. For the experiences of a young Irish Catholic teacher at Ruskin see Joost Augusteijn (ed.), *The Memoirs of John M. Regan, a Catholic Officer in the RIC and RUC, 1909–1948* (Dublin 2007), Chapter 2.

106. *An Macaomh* 1909. See also 'Education under Home Rule', in Ó Buachalla, *Irish Educationalist*, pp. 348–56.

107. Ryan, *Man called Pearse*, p. 231; Carty, *Bloody Protest*, p. 36; Interview with Joe McSweeney; Sweeney, 'Donegal', p. 4.

108. Sisson, *Pearse's Patriots*, p. 21.

109. The love of Irish nature is exposed in many of his stories. See *Eoineen of the Birds* (1905–1906), *Barbara* (1905–1906), *The Keening Woman* (1915) and *Brigid of the Songs* (1906), see also his poems: 'The Rann of the Little Playmate' and 'On the Strand of Howth', in *Collected Works. Plays, Stories, Poems*, pp. 169–78, 193–226, 259–308, 326 and 329–31.

110. Sweeney, 'Donegal', p. 4.

111. Sisson, *Pearse's Patriots*, p. 38.

112. Sisson, *Pearse's Patriots*, p. 129.

113. Ibid, p. 120.
114. Ibid, pp. 123–6 and 155; Hobson, LP; *An Macaomh* 1913.
115. Ibid., p. 122.
116. Ibid., p. 135.
117. 'Education under Home Rule' 1912–1914, in Ó Buachalla, *Irish Educationalist*, pp. 348–56; Sisson, *Pearse's Patriots*, pp. 17–19 and 34.
118. Ibid.
119. 'Education under Home Rule' 1912–1914, in Ó Buachalla, *Irish Educationalist*, pp. 348–56.
120. *An Macaomh* 1913; Ryan, *Man called Pearse*, p. 164.
121. *An Macaomh* 1913.
122. *An Macaomh* Dec. 1909.
123. Breathnach, *Free and Gaelic*, pp. 7–8; Pearse, *Three Lectures*.
124. Leerssen, *National Thought*, pp. 201–3.
125. Sisson, *Pearse's Patriots*, pp. 49–50.
126. Oliver, 'Irish Revolutionary Nationalism', p. 106.
127. Sisson, *Pearse's Patriots*, pp. 80–3 and 95–6.
128. Quoted in ibid., p. 79.
129. Caoimhín Breatnach, 'Exploiting the Past: Pearse as Editor and Interpreter of *Fiannaíocht* Literature', in Higgins and Uí Chollatáin, *Life and After-Life*, p. 199; Edwards, *Triumph*, pp. 90–110; Moran, *Patrick Pearse*, p. 117.
130. *An Macaomh* Dec. 1909.
131. Sisson, *Pearse's Patriots*, p. 80.
132. Ibid., pp. 85–6.
133. Ibid., p. 17.
134. Ibid., p. 14.
135. Ibid., pp. 46–8 and 80–1 and 85–6.
136. Ryan, *Remembering Sion*, p. 95; Ryan, *Man called Pearse*, p. 176.
137. Carty, *Bloody Protest*, p. 58.
138. C26, LP.
139. Sisson, *Pearse's Patriots*, pp. 79 and 127.
140. *An Macaomh* Dec. 1909.
141. Edwards, *Triumph*, p. 130.
142. Ibid., pp. 122–3. Patrick does not mention O'Grady's presence in *An Macaomh*.
143. Quoted in Edwards, *Triumph*, p. 124. See also Sisson, *Pearse's Patriots*, p. 96.
144. Porter, *P.H. Pearse*, pp. 31 and 94–7. Ryan, *Man called Pearse*, pp. 195–6; *An Macaomh* 1913; Carty, *Bloody Protest*, pp. 46–7.
145. *An Macaomh* Summer 1909.
146. *An Macaomh* Dec. 1909. There are many other examples of the popularity of pageants among all classes in this period. See, for instance, www.oldukphotos.com/walesgeneral.htm, accessed 9 May 2008.
147. Sisson, *Pearse's Patriots*, pp. 83 and 110.
148. Stephen McKenna in *Irish Press* 29 Mar. 1937; Martin Daly (Stephen McKenna), *Memories of the Dead: Some Impressions* (Dublin n.d. (1917?)), p. 18.

149. Sisson, *Pearse's Patriots*, pp. 45 and 83; Porter, *P.H. Pearse*, p. 95; Carty, *Bloody Protest*, pp. 46–7.

150. Nic Shiubhlaigh, *Splendid*, pp. 145–6.

151. Sisson, *Pearse's Patriots*, pp. 40–6.

152. Letter Lady Gleneary dated 3 Apr. 1947, LP. See also Carty, *Bloody Protest*, p. 33.

153. Letter dated 4 Mar. 1908, Ó Buachalla (ed.), *Letters*, p. 127.

154. 'They were Schoolboys', p. 45; Ó Buachalla, *Irish Educationalist*, p. x.

155. Letter Hamill dated 26 Aug. 1946, LP.

156. Letter Sean D. MacGaunair[?], Allen Library, Box 187; Letter Greg Murphy dated 8 May 1947, LP; Veale, LP.

157. 'They were Schoolboys', p. 45; Ó Buachalla, *Irish Educationalist*, p. x.

158. Letter James Doyle dated 1 Dec. 1946, LP. See also Letter Michael Christie dated 12 Dec. 1946, LP.

159. Letter Maire ní Cinneide dated 23 Oct. 1947, LP. The novel *My Lord Conceit* is actually written by Eliza Humphreys under the penname Rita. Other examples of the less than inspiring teacher Pearse was then, Edwards, *Triumph*, pp. 28–9.

160. Letter Michael Christie dated 12 Dec. 1946, LP. See also Seamus Fenton, LP.

161. Ibid.

162. 'Gleo na gCath', *ACS* 22 July 1905.

163. Ó Buachalla, *Pearse in Belgium*, p. 115.

164. Michael Dowling, LP. See also Interview with Joe McSweeney; Sweeney, 'Donegal', p. 5.

165. LP.

166. Joseph O'Neill, LP.

167. Ansor, LP.

168. Interview with Joe McSweeney.

169. Letter dated 17 Nov. 1908, Ó Buachalla (ed.), *Letters*, pp. 138–9.

170. Letter Ian Bloomer dated 16 Dec. 1968, LP. See also Interview with Joe McSweeney; Letter Willie, NLI, ms. 40,454/2.

171. Jerome F. Cronin in *Irish Independent* 27 Mar. 1957.

172. McCay, *Pádraic Pearse*, p. 64.

173. *ACS* 5 Jan. 1907.

174. Especially in his early stories like *Íosagán* (1905), *Eoineen of the Birds* (1905–1906) and *Barbara* (1905–1906), but can also be found in *The King* written in 1912, in *Collected Works. Plays, Stories, Poems*, passim.

175. Nic Shiubhlaigh, *Splendid*, p. 148; *An Macaomh* 1910 and 1913. See also Porter, *P.H. Pearse*, pp. 72 and 121; Letter dated 11 Nov. 1915, Ó Buachalla (ed.), *Letters*, p. 351; Ua Gallchobhair, 'Children of Patrick Pearse', pp. 121–6; Carty, *Bloody Protest*, p. 11.

176. Edwards, *Triumph*, p. 108; Sisson, *Pearse's Patriots*, p. 104.

177. *ACS* 13 Jan. 1906.

178. Edwards, *Triumph*, p. 108; *ACS* 6 Jan. 1906.

179. Ryan, *Remembering Sion*, p. 125; Ryan, *Man called Pearse*, pp. 177 and 215; Sweeney, 'Donegal', p. 5.

180. Keith Jeffery, *The GPO and the Easter Rising* (Dublin 2006), pp. 142–3.

181. Osborn Bergin, LP.

182. Letter dated 20 May 1911, Ó Buachalla (ed.), *Letters*, p. 193.

183. Jerome F. Cronin in *Irish Independent* 2 Apr. 1957; Osborn Bergin, LP.

184. Edwards, *Triumph*, p. 132; Sisson, *Pearse's Patriots*, p. 104.

185. Letter to Michael Cronin dated 22 June 1914, Kilmainham Jail, 23LR IP1304.

186. *ACS* 26 Jan. 1907.

187. Edwards, *Triumph*, p. 132.

188. Letter Ian Bloomer dated 16 Dec. 1968, LP; Osborn Bergin, LP; Letter Colm O Loughlin dated 13 May 1947, LP; Jerome F. Cronin in *Irish Independent* 27 Mar. 1957; Pearse (ed.), *Home Life*, pp. 118–20.

189. Reddin, 'A Man Called Pearse', quoted in Edwards, *Triumph*, pp. 131–2. See also Interview with Joe McSweeney; Sisson, *Pearse's Patriots*, pp. 104–5.

190. 'Memories of Pearse', article by M.H. in the *London Herald,* no date, in scrapbook of Frank Martin, NLI, ms. 32,695/1.

191. Letter Ian Bloomer dated 16 Dec. 1968, LP; Sisson, *Pearse's Patriots*, pp. 104–5; Interview with Joe McSweeney. Patrick acknowledged such behaviour in a general sense, *An Macaomh* 1913.

192. 'Memories of Pearse', article by M.H. in the *London Herald,* no date, in scrapbook of Frank Martin, NLI, ms. 32,695/1.

193. Letter R.J. McKeenan dated 8 Mar. 1910, NLI ms. 7216.

194. Alf White, LP.

195. Sisson, *Pearse's Patriots*, p. 105.

196. Sisson, *Pearse's Patriots*, p. 37.

197. Nic Shiubhlaigh, *Splendid*, p. 148.

198. Letter Maire ní Cinneide dated 23 Oct. 1947, LP; Rd Foley, LP. Interview with Joe McSweeney.

199. In November 1911 this happened to J. Donnellan and previously to a boy called O'Connor, Entry dated 4 Sep. 1909, Scribbling diary for 1909, Pearse Museum; Letter dated November 1911, Ó Buachalla (ed.), *Letters*, p. 237.

200. Osborn Bergin, LP.

201. Joseph O'Neill, LP.

202. Letter Joseph O'Neill dated 6 Apr. 1946, LP.

203. Letter Maire ní Cinneide dated 23 Oct. 1947, LP; Sisson, *Pearse's Patriots*, p. 162.

204. Letter dated 17 Nov. 1908, Ó Buachalla (ed.), *Letters*, p. 139.

205. *An Macaomh* 1913.

206. Osborn Bergin, LP.

207. Edwards, *Triumph*, p. 130.

208. Entry dated Dec. 1909, Scribbling diary for 1909, Pearse Museum; Ó Buachalla (ed.), *Letters*, passim.

209. Letter to Mr Cronin dated 1 May 1914, Pearse Museum.

210. Letters dated 14 May, 23 May and 22 June 1914, Kilmainham Jail, 23LR IP1302 and 1303 and 1304.

211. *An Macaomh* 1909; St Enda's prospectus 1908.

212. Letter dated September 1911, Ó Buachalla (ed.), *Letters*, p. 209; Entry dated 19 Mar. 1909, Scribbling diary for 1909, Pearse Museum.

213. Entry dated 23 Feb. 1909, Scribbling diary for 1909, Pearse Museum.

214. *An Macaomh* Dec. 1909.

215. Letters dated 17 Oct. and 15 Nov. 1910, Ó Buachalla (ed.), *Letters*, pp. 471–3.

216. NLI, ms. 10,723/9. See also Letter dated 17 Aug. 1910, Ó Buachalla (ed.), *Letters*, pp. 174–5.

217. Letters to Board of Education dated 16 and 30 Aug. 1910, Kilmainham Jail, 23 LR 1P15 13; Letters dated 16, 17 and 20 Aug. and 17 Sep. 1910, Ó Buachalla (ed.), *Letters*, pp. 174–5, 178 and 483–4.

218. Letter dated 30 Aug. 1913, ibid., p. 293.

219. *An Macaomh* 1913; Entry dated 11 Jan. 1909, Scribbling diary for 1909, Pearse Museum.

220. Memo with Letter dated 23 June 1912, Ó Buachalla (ed.), *Letters*, pp. 272–5; *An Macaomh* 1913.

221. Quote, Alf White, LP. Ryan, *Man called Pearse*, pp. 241–3; McCay, *Pádraic Pearse*, p. 63.

222. Letter dated 27 Feb. 1908, Ó Buachalla (ed.), *Letters*, pp. 121–3; *ACS* 23 Nov. 1907.

223. Edwards, *Triumph*, p. 116.

224. Letter dated 17 Nov. 1908, Ó Buachalla (ed.), *Letters*, p. 138.

225. *ACS* 27 Mar. 1909.

226. *An Macaomh* Dec. 1909. See also LP.

227. Letter dated 14 Sep. 1909, Ó Buachalla (ed.), *Letters*, pp. 246–7.

228. *An Macaomh* 1910.

229. *An Macaomh* 1913.

230. Circular sent 10 May 1910, Ó Buachalla (ed.), *Letters*, p. 155.

231. Edwards, *Triumph*, p. 13; Ó Buachalla, *Irish Educationalist*, pp. 371–90.

232. *An Macaomh* 1910. See also fundraising circular, dated 10 May 1910, Kilmainham Jail, 23LP 1p14.

233. Letter dated 10 May 1910, Ó Buachalla (ed.), *Letters*, pp. 152–8.

234. Letter dated 18 Aug. 1909, NLI, ms. 5049.

235. Letter dated 29 June 1910, Ó Buachalla (ed.), *Letters*, p. 169.

236. Ó Buachalla (ed.), *Letters*, pp. 158–9; *An Macaomh* 1910.

237. Letter dated 29 June 1910, Ó Buachalla (ed.), *Letters*, p. 169.

238. Circular, Kilmainham Jail, 23LP 1p14.

239. Ibid.

240. Letter dated 2 May 1910, Ó Buachalla (ed.), *Letters*, pp. 478–9; Letter McCartan dated 27 May 1910, quoted in Edwards, *Triumph*, p. 154.

241. *An Macaomh* 1910.

242. Edwards, *Triumph*, p. 145.

243. Quoted in Edwards, *Triumph*, p. 139.

244. Letter dated 1 Feb. 1909, Ó Buachalla (ed.), *Letters*, pp. 140–1.

245. Edwards, *Triumph*, p. 145.
246. Letters to Pearse, NLI P7216.
247. *An Macaomh* 1909.
248. Letter to Board of Education dated 25 Jan. 1910, Kilmainham Jail, 23 LR
     1P15 11; Letters dated 25 Jan. and 16 Apr. 1910, Ó Buachalla (ed.), *Letters*,
     pp. 480–2; Edwards, *Triumph*, p. 145.
249. Circular, Kilmainham Jail, 23LP 1p14; Letters Apr. and May 1910, NLI,
     ms. 35,262/28.
250. NLI, P7216.
251. Letter dated 9 June 1910, Ó Buachalla (ed.), *Letters*, p. 164.
252. Letters dated 22 and 29 June 1910, ibid., pp. 167–9.
253. Another £100 came in from the United States over the next six months.
     Edwards, *Triumph*, p. 146.
254. Letter dated 18 May 1910, Ó Buachalla (ed.), *Letters*, p. 161.
255. Letter to Wow Wow dated 18 July 1910, Kilmainham Jail, 23 LR 1P15 8.
256. Ibid., 23 LR 1P23 24.
257. Letter dated 15 May 1910, Ó Buachalla (ed.), *Letters*, pp. 159–60.
258. Letter dated 29 June 1910, ibid., p.169.
259. Letter dated 16 July 1910, ibid., p. 171.
260. Letters dated 15 May and 9, 13 and 16 June 1910, Ó Buachalla (ed.),
     Letters, pp. 159–60 and 164–6.
261. NLI, ms. 35,262/28.
262. Letter to George F.H. Berkeley dated 23 Nov. 1910, NLI, ms. 7879.
263. Circular dated 21 Jan. 1911, Ó Buachalla (ed.), *Letters*, pp. 185–6; NLI,
     ms. 8617.
264. Letter dated 16 Dec. 1910, Ó Buachalla (ed.), *Letters*, pp. 182–3.
265. Ibid. See also letters to Bolger & Doyle Ltd dated Jan. 1910, ibid., pp. 183–4.
266. Letter dated 29 June 1911, ibid., pp. 196–7.
267. Letter to Mrs Hutton dated 12 June 1911, NLI, ms. 8617.
268. Letter dated 29 June 1911, Ó Buachalla (ed.), *Letters*, pp. 197–8.
269. Letter Frank Fahey dated 15 Mar. 1948, LP. See also Letter Jimmy Whelan
     dated 30 Oct. 1945, LP.
270. Letter dated 11 Feb. 1911, Ó Buachalla (ed.), *Letters*, pp. 187–8.
271. Letter to F.J. Bigger dated 3 July 1911, NLI, ms. 35,456/3.
272. Letter dated Sep. 1911, Ó Buachalla (ed.), *Letters*, p. 210; Entry for 11 Jan.
     1909, Scribbling diary for 1909, Pearse Museum.
273. Letters dated Sep. and 1 Dec. 1911, Ó Buachalla (ed.), *Letters*, pp. 210–11
     and 241.
274. Desmond Ryan, quoted in Edwards, *Triumph*, p. 166.
275. Jerome F. Cronin in *Irish Independent* 27 Mar. and 2 Apr. 1957.
276. Letter Sígle Cenpead[?] dated 30 Apr. 1958, LP.
277. LP.
278. Porter, *P.H. Pearse*, p. 45.
279. Eamonn O'Neill(?) Conan & Sceilg(?), LP.
280. Frank Sweeney, LP.
281. L2, LP.

282. Alf White, LP; Margaret Pearse, LP; C1, LP.

283. Letter Jimmy Whelan dated 30 Oct. 1945, LP.

284. Edwards, *Triumph*, p. 165.

285. Letter dated 23 Feb. 1910, Ó Buachalla (ed.), *Letters*, p. 149; Edwards, *Triumph*, pp. 112–13.

286. LP.

287. Circular sent 10 May 1910, Ó Buachalla (ed.), *Letters*, p. 155; Sisson, *Pearse's Patriots*, pp. 45 and 129; *An Macaomh* 1910 and 1913.

288. Ó Buachalla (ed.), *Letters*, p. 236.

289. *An Macaomh* 1913.

290. Memo with Letter dated 23 June 1912, Ó Buachalla (ed.), *Letters*, pp. 272–5.

291. Letter to Pearse, NLI, ms. 7216.

292. Allen Library, Box 186; Letters dated 21 and 27 July 1910, Ó Buachalla (ed.), *Letters*, pp. 476–7.

293. See, for instance, his stories *The Singer* (1915), *The Roads* (1915?) and *The Mother* (1915?), *Collected Works. Plays, Stories, Poems*, pp. 1–44, 125–36 and 147–68.

294. Quoted in Edwards, *Triumph*, p. 140.

295. Ibid., *Triumph*, pp. 138–9.

296. Letter Colm O Loughlin dated 13 May 1947, LP; Osborn Bergin, LP. This may also explain the fact why F.P. Nolan, the classics teacher engaged in 1910, left after little more than a year's service; Letter dated December 1911, Ó Buachalla (ed.), *Letters*, pp. 245–6.

297. Ibid.; Letters dated 20 May 1911, ibid., p. 193.

298. Quoted in Edwards, *Triumph*, p. 139.

299. Ibid., pp. 46–8; Sisson, *Pearse's Patriots*, p. 38.

300. Ryan, *Remembering Sion*, p. 114.

301. Edwards, *Triumph*, pp. 112–13.

302. Letters dated 7 Feb. and 17 July 1914, Ó Buachalla (ed.), *Letters*, pp. 297–8 and 320–1; Edwards, *Triumph*, pp. 112–13 and 167.

303. Ibid., pp. 137–8; Letter dated 21 Jan. 1911, Ó Buachalla (ed.), *Letters*, pp. 185–6. An official statement mentioned there were fifty-four boarders in 1910/11 and sixty in 1911/12. The additional sixteen claimed for the year 1910/11 might be girls from St Ita's.

304. NLI, ms. 8617.

305. Letter dated 12 Oct. 1911, Ó Buachalla (ed.), *Letters*, pp. 227–8.

306. Letter to Mrs Green dated 28 July 1912, NLI, ms. 46,553/1; Scribbling diary for 1911, Pearse Museum; Letters dated Nov. 1911, Ó Buachalla (ed.), *Letters*, p. 238.

307. Letter dated 13 Oct. 1911, NLI, ms. 8617; Letters dated 13 Oct. 1911 and 22 Jan 1912, Ó Buachalla (ed.), *Letters*, pp. 229–30 and 248.

308. Letter dated 12 Oct. 1911, ibid., pp. 227–9.

309. Letter dated October 1911, ibid., pp. 220–1 and 227.

310. Letter dated 13 Oct. 1911, NLI, ms. 8617.

311. Letter dated 28 Jan. 1912, Ó Buachalla (ed.), *Letters*, p. 250.

312. Letter dated 28 Jan. 1912, ibid., p. 251.

313. Liam O Donhnaill, LP.
314. Letter dated 12 Oct. 1911, Ó Buachalla (ed.), *Letters*, pp. 227–8.
315. Letters dated Oct. 1911 and 15 July 1912 ibid., pp. 225 and 276.
316. Allen Library, Box 186; Edwards, *Triumph*, p. 148.
317. Kilmainham Jail, loose item; Account book, NLI, ms. 835; Letter dated 15 July 1912, NLI, ms. 7879.
318. Letter dated 7 June 1912, Ó Buachalla (ed.), *Letters*, p. 270.
319. Letter dated 13 June 1912, Ó Buachalla (ed.), *Letters*, p. 270.
320. Letters dated 13 and 23 June and 1 Aug. 1912, Ó Buachalla (ed.), *Letters*, pp. 270–5 and 279.
321. Letter dated 15 July 1912, NLI, ms. 7879; Letter dated 23 July 1912, NLI, ms. 46,553/1.
322. Letter dated 6 July 1912, NLI, ms. 46,553/2.
323. Quoted in Edwards, *Triumph*, p. 149.
324. Letter to George Berkeley dated 15 July 1912, NLI, ms. 7879; Letter dated 30 July 1912, Ó Buachalla (ed.), *Letters*, pp. 277–8; Letter to Mrs Green dated 4 Aug. 1912, NLI, ms. 46,553/1.
325. Letter Sígle Cenpead[?] dated 30 Apr. 1958, LP; Lennon, LP.
326. Letter dated 6 July 1912, NLI, ms. 46,553/2.
327. Letter dated 1 Aug. 1912, Ó Buachalla (ed.), *Letters*, p. 279.
328. Letter dated 4 Dec. 1914, ibid., pp. 337–8; Ryan, *Remembering Sion*, pp. 116 and 160; Letter dated 23 July 1912, NLI, ms. 46,553/1.
329. Letters dated 4 Dec. 1914 and 12 Apr. 1915, Ó Buachalla (ed.), *Letters*, pp. 337–8 and 341.
330. The rent they paid for Glanmire was £22.10.0d p.a., while they had sublet it to Mr F.F. Armstrong for £50.2.0d p.a., LP.
331. The deeds show that on 13 July 1911 Joseph P. O'Dolan of Ardee, Co. Louth, was the grantee for the mortgage and Patrick the grantor; Hand search in the Registry of Deeds Office 1 Jan. 1910–31 Dec. 1914, LP.
332. Letter dated 3 Sep. 1912, Ó Buachalla (ed.), *Letters*, pp. 283–4.
333. Quoted in Edwards, *Triumph*, p. 150.
334. NLI, ms. 10,192. Letter dated 24 Aug. 1912, Ó Buachalla (ed.), *Letters*, pp. 281–2.
335. Letter dated 23 Aug. 1912, ibid., p. 280.
336. Letter Douglas Hyde dated 3 Sep. 1912, NLI, ms. 18,578.
337. Only Lord Ashbourne and Edward Martyn had been added to the original committee.
338. Letter dated 19 Sep. 1912, Ó Buachalla (ed.), *Letters*, p. 285. He was also engaging new staff; Letter dated 28 Sep. 1912, ibid., p. 286.
339. Letter Edward Martyn dated 2 Sep. 1912, quoted in Edwards, *Triumph*, p. 150.
340. Desmond Ryan (ed.), 'The Story of a Success', in *Collected Works of Padraic H. Pearse* (Dublin etc. n.d.), p. 73; Allen Library, Box 186.
341. Letter dated 26 June 1913, Ó Buachalla (ed.), *Letters*, p. 291. See also St Enda's Circular dated 3 Sep. 1912; Letters dated 1 Aug. and 3 Sep. 1912,

ibid., pp. 279 and 283–4; NLI, ms. 24,554; Letter dated 15 July 1912, NLI, ms. 7879.

342. See letters Aug. 1912 onwards, Ó Buachalla (ed.), *Letters*, passim.

343. *An Macaohm* 1913.

344. Letters dated 25 Apr. and 19 May 1913, Ó Buachalla (ed.), *Letters*, pp. 288–9. The raffle was held on 21 June 1913.

345. Porter, *P.H. Pearse*, p. 150; *ACS* 28 Aug. 1915.

346. *ACS* 12 Apr. 1913; Edwards, *Triumph*, p. 172; O'Casey, *Drums*, p. 278; *An Macaomh* 1913, 46; Porter, *P.H. Pearse*, p. 96.

347. Sisson, *Pearse's Patriots*, pp. 111–12; O'Casey, *Drums*, p. 280.

348. Letters dated 26 June, 31 Oct. and 8 Nov. 1913 and 7 Feb. and 20 Mar. 1914, Ó Buachalla (ed.), *Letters*, pp. 290–1, 295, 297–8 and 300.

349. Letter dated 15 Oct. 1913, ibid., p. 487.

350. Ibid.

351. L2, LP.

352. Letter dated 7 Feb. 1914, Ó Buachalla (ed.), *Letters*, p. 298.

353. Letter dated 2 Mar. 1914, ibid., pp. 299–300.

354. NLI, ms. 17,633.

355. Letter dated 5 Mar. 1914, Kilmainham Jail, 23 LR IP14/19.

356. Letters dated 20, 24 and 27 Apr. and 4 May 1914, Ó Buachalla (ed.), *Letters*, pp. 306–10.

357. Letter dated 5 Mar. 1914, Kilmainham Jail, 23LR1P14/19.

358. Letters dated 13 Apr. and 19 June 1914, Ó Buachalla (ed.), *Letters*, pp. 304–5 and 314–15; Letter Colm O Loughlin dated 13 May 1947, LP. A list of all contributors in the United States appeared in the *Gaelic American*.

359. Letters dated 13 Apr. and 14 June and 6 July 1914, Ó Buachalla (ed.), *Letters*, pp. 304–5 and 313–17.

360. Letter dated 18 May 1914, Kilmainham Jail, 23LP1P19.

361. Appeal dated 9 Oct. 1914, Kilmainham Jail, 23LP1P19; Letters dated autumn and 30 Oct. 1914, Ó Buachalla (ed.), *Letters*, pp. 328 and 334; Letter Willie dated 3 Mar. 1914, NLI, ms. 40,454/2.

362. Letter dated 25 Nov. 1914, Ó Buachalla (ed.), *Letters*, pp. 335–7.

363. Sisson, *Pearse's Patriots*, p. 154; Edwards, *Triumph*, p. 138; Letters 1915–1916, Ó Buachalla (ed.), *Letters*, passim.

364. Account book, NLI, ms. 835.

365. Letter to McGarrity dated 24 Sep. 1914, NLI, ms. 17,477.

366. Letter dated 2 Sep. 1915, NLI, ms. 17,477. See also Letter to McGarrity dated 12 Aug. 1915, NLI, ms 17,477; Letter dated 12 Apr. 1915, Ó Buachalla (ed.), *Letters*, p. 341.

367. Letter dated 15 Oct. 1915, NLI, ms. 17,477.

368. NLI, ms. 17,633.

369. Letters dated 4 Dec. 1914 and 7 Oct. and 1 Dec. 1915, Ó Buachalla (ed.), *Letters*, pp. 337–8, 349–50 and 353; NLI ms.33,460G/3; Letter dated 7 Oct. 1915, Allen Library, Box 186; Letter to McGarrity dated 12 Aug. 1915, NLI, ms. 17,477.

370. Letter to Mrs Bloomer dated 3 Dec. 1915, Allen Library, Box 187.
371. Letter dated 23 Apr. 1916, Ó Buachalla (ed.), *Letters*, p. 364.
372. Brian Barton, *From Behind a Closed Door. Secret Court Martial Records of the 1916 Easter Rising* (Belfast 2002), p. 107.
373. Osborn Bergin, LP; Interview with Joe McSweeney.
374. Edwards, *Triumph*, pp. 137 and 168; Sisson, *Pearse's Patriots*, pp. 153 and 161; Ryan, *Remembering Sion*, p. 118; *An Macaomh* 1913; *An Macaomh* Summer 1909.
375. Michael Dowling, LP.
376. Sisson, *Pearse's Patriots*, p. 162.
377. Letter dated 17 Nov. 1908, Ó Buachalla (ed.), *Letters*, pp. 138–9.
378. Letter 7, NLI, ms. 40,454/1.
379. Letter dated 17 Feb. 1912, Ó Buachalla (ed.), *Letters*, p. 254.
380. Yeats, quoted in Edwards, *Triumph*, p. 137.
381. Sisson, *Pearse's Patriots*, p. 153.
382. *An Macaomh* 1910, quoted in Edwards, *Triumph*, p. 135; Ryan, *Remembering Sion*, p. 118. See also Daly, *Memories*, p. 17.
383. Letter dated 11 May 1912, Ó Buachalla (ed.), *Letters*, p. 265.
384. Letter dated 18 Mar. 1915, ibid., pp. 490–1.
385. Desmond Ryan, quoted in Edwards, *Triumph*, p. 135.
386. Alf White, LP.
387. Ryan, *Remembering Sion*, p. 96.
388. *An Macaomh* 1913. Yeats referred to this dream in a letter to Lady Gregory in November 1914, Foster, *Yeats*, p. 525. See also Jerome F. Cronin in *Irish Independent* 27 Mar. and 2 Apr. 1957; David Cairns and Shaun Richards, *Writing Ireland* (Manchester 1988), pp. 110–11.
389. Sisson, *Pearse's Patriots*, pp. 155–6.
390. Letter from Bro Cullen O'Connell dated 4 Feb. 1958, LP.
391. Letter to Michael Cronin dated 22 June 1914, Kilmainham Jail, 23LR IP1305; Sweeney, 'Donegal', p. 5.
392. Sisson, *Pearse's Patriots*, pp. 123–6 and 155; Hobson, LP; *An Macaomh* 1913.
393. LP.
394. Lennon, LP.

Chapter 4: Politician

1. *ACS* 28 Mar. 1908.
2. 'Autobiography by Patrick Pearse'.
3. *Oxford Dictionary of National Biography*, http://www.oxforddnb.com/view/article/37840?docPos=5.
4. 1914 speech, NLI, ms. 33,702.
5. Letter dated 27 Jan. 1901, NLI, P7638 and ms. 21,406.
6. Ryan, *Remembering Sion,* p. 103; Le Roux, *Patrick H. Pearse*, p. 8.
7. Letter dated 30 Mar. 1912, Ó Buachalla (ed.), *Letters*, p. 259.

8. Brigid Pearse, LP.

9. Veale, LP.

10. Liam O'Donnell, LP.

11. Eamonn O'Neill, LP.

12. C27, LP; Sir Arnold Bax, LP.

13. 1914 speech, NLI, ms. 33,702.

14. Veale, LP. See also Letter by Sean D MacGaunair[?], Allen Library, Box 187.

15. Ryan, *Remembering Sion,* p. 106. Le Roux probably mistakingly places this at the time of the first Home Rule Bill in 1886, Le Roux, *Patrick H. Pearse*, p. 8.

16. Veale, LP.

17. Quoted in Edwards, *Triumph*, p. 16.

18. Pearse (ed.), *Home Life*, pp. 85–6.

19. Letter dated 15 Feb. 1901, NLI, ms. 10,833.

20. O'Leary, *Prose Literature*, p. 26.

21. *ACS* 2 Feb. 1907.

22. Pearse, *Three Lectures*, pp. 200 and 215.

23. Ibid., pp. 200 and 215–21.

24. Edwards, *Triumph*, pp. 35–6; Senia Pašeta, 'Nationalist responses to two royal visits to Ireland, 1900 and 1903', in *Irish Historical Studies* Vol. XXXI No. 124, pp. 488–504; Veale, LP.

25. Lord Salisbury was then prime minister.

26. Letter dated 13 May 1899, Ó Buchalla, *Letters of P.H. Pearse*, pp. 8–9.

27. *ACS* 19 Nov. 1904, quoted in Edwards, *Triumph*, p. 72.

28. Ibid., pp. 70–1.

29. *ACS* 26 Nov. 1904, quoted in Edwards, *Patrick Pearse*, p. 72; Ó Buachalla, *Pearse in Belgium*, pp. 111–12.

30. Ibid., pp. 111–12.

31. *ACS* 4 Feb. 1905.

32. *ACS* 28 Mar. 1903.

33. *ACS* 12 Nov. 1904 and 12 Oct. 1907.

34. *ACS* 24 Apr. 1909.

35. Edwards, *Triumph*, p. 178.

36. 'The Language Question at Westminster', *ACS* 28 July 1900. See also *ACS* 17 Dec. 1904.

37. 'The Campaign of the Irish Parliamentary Party against the Irish Language', Eagarfhocal, *ACS* 28 Sep. 1901.

38. 'Glenmalure', Eagarfhocal, *ACS* 19 Oct. 1901.

39. Letter to Séamus Ó Ceallaigh dated 26 Dec. 1904, NLI, ms. 5049.

40. Letter A. Griffith 2 Feb. 1902, Kilmainham Jail, 23LRIP15/6.

41. Edwards, *Patrick Pearse*, p. 152.

42. Mrs Bradley, LP.

43. Mrs Bradley, LP; Veale, LP; Letter Justice Wm S. Black dated 6 Dec. 1946, LP; Hobson, LP; Pearse (ed.), *Home Life*, pp. 113–16.

44. *ACS* 18 May 1907.

45. *ACS* 16 Dec. 1905.
46. Ibid.
47. *ACS* 24 Nov. 1906.
48. *ACS* 11 May 1907.
49. 'The Dead Bill and Ourselves', *ACS* 25 May 1907.
50. 'Memories of Pearse', article by M.H. in the *London Herald*, no date, in scrapbook of Frank Martin, NLI, ms. 32,695/1; Letter Omar Crowley dated 19 Apr. 1947, LP; Liam O Donnell, LP; Letter Seamus Cooling dated 11 Nov. 1947, LP.
51. 'The Dead Bill and Ourselves', *ACS* 25 May 1907.
52. Edwards, *Triumph*, p. 73.
53. *ACS* 23 May 1908, quoted in Edwards, *Triumph*, p. 86, see also pp. 86–9.
54. *ACS* 1 Feb. 1908.
55. *ACS* 24 July 1909.
56. *ACS* 13 Nov. 1909.
57. *ACS* 27 Nov. 1909; Joseph Lee, *The Modernisation of Irish Society 1848–1918* (Dublin 1973), p. 145.
58. Quoted in Charles Townshend, *Easter 1916. The Irish Rebellion* (London 2005), pp. 114–15.
59. Edwards, *Triumph*, p. 153; Moran, *Patrick Pearse*, p. 153.
60. McCay, *Pádraic Pearse*, pp. 68 and 74; Le Roux, *Patrick H. Pearse*, pp. 161–2; Ryan, *Remembering Sion*, p. 109.
61. *An Macaomh* 1910.
62. Ryan, *Man called Pearse*, p. 176.
63. *An Macaomh* 1910.
64. 'Fornocht do Chonnach', in *Collected Works. Plays, Stories, Poems*, pp. 322 and 324.
65. *The Fool* and *The Master*, in *Collected Works. Plays, Stories, Poems*, pp. 96–100 and 334–6; Porter, *P.H. Pearse*, pp. 134–5.
66. Ibid.; Edwards, *Triumph*, pp. 154–5; Townshend, *Easter 1916*, p. 22.
67. Letter Mrs Bradley dated 22 Feb. 1947, LP.
68. Letter dated Jan. 1912, Ó Buachalla (ed.), *Letters,* p. 246.
69. Letter dated 17 Feb. 1912, ibid., p. 253.
70. Hobson, quoted in Edwards, *Triumph*, p. 157.
71. Desmond Ryan, quoted in ibid., p. 164.
72. Sweeney, 'Donegal', p. 5.
73. Letter dated 18 Feb. 1912, Ó Buachalla (ed.), *Letters*, p. 255.
74. Staunton, LP; Letter Ml Kavanagh dated 16 Sep. 1947, LP.
75. Ryan, *Remembering Sion,* pp. 160 and 164.
76. F.X. Martin, 'MacNeill and the Irish Volunteers', in F.X. Martin and F.J. Byrne (eds), *The Scholar Revolutionary: Eoin MacNeill 1867–1945, and the Making of a New Ireland* (Shannon 1973), p. 108; Carty, *Bloody Protest*, p. 81.
77. Ryan, *Remembering Sion*, p. 112.
78. Letter dated 17 Feb. 1912, Ó Buachalla (ed.), *Letters*, p. 253. See also Letter dated 30 Mar. 1912, pp. 258–9.

79. Dunleavy, *Douglas Hyde*, p. 321.

80. 'Home Rule and Nationality', Eagarfhocal, *ACS* 20 Apr. 1912.

81. Letter dated 23 Mar. 1912, Ó Buachalla (ed.), *Letters*, p. 257.

82. Widow of Eamonn Ceannt, NA, WS264; Ó Buachalla (ed.), *Letters*, p. 259; Martin, 'MacNeill and the Irish Volunteers', p. 107.

83. *An Barr Buadh* 5 Apr. 1912, quoted in Edwards, *Patrick Pearse*, p. 159. See also Dorothy MacArdle, *The Irish Republic* (London 1968), pp. 77–8; Letters W.S. Fallon dated 19 Nov. 1946 and 10 Apr. 1947, LP; Veale, LP.

84. *Freeman's Journal* 1 Apr. 1912.

85. *An Barr Buadh* 27 Apr. 1912, quoted in Edwards, *Patrick Pearse*, p. 160.

86. Letter dated 5 Apr. 1912, Ó Buachalla (ed.), *Letters*, p. 260.

87. Quoted in Edwards, *Patrick Pearse*, p. 164. First meeting was 2 Apr. 1912, Letters dated 28 Mar. 1912, Ó Buachalla (ed.), *Letters*, pp. 252–3 and 257–8; Carty, *Bloody Protest*, pp. 82–3; Martin, 'MacNeill and the Irish Volunteers', p. 113.

88. *Irish Freedom* March 1912, quoted in Edwards, *Triumph*, pp. 157–8.

89. Townshend, *Easter 1916*, pp. 36–7; Joan Montgomery Byles, 'Women's Experience of World War One: Suffragists, Pacifists and Poets', in *Women's Studies International Forum* Vol. 8 No. 5 (1985), p. 476; Eamonn O'Neill, LP; Owen McGee, *The I.R.B.: The Irish Republican Brotherhood from the Land League to Sinn Féin* (Dublin 2005), passim.

90. J. O'Leary, *Recollections of Fenians and Fenianism* Vol. II (London 1896); McGee, *The I.R.B.*, pp. 29–31.

91. McGill, 'Pearse in Donegal', pp. 79–81.

92. McGee, *The I.R.B.*, pp. 18–19.

93. Letter dated 12 Apr. 1912, Ó Buachalla (ed.), *Letters*, pp. 260–1.

94. Quoted in Porter, *P.H. Pearse*, p. 58.

95. Newspaper clipping dated 7 Dec. 1912, LP.

96. 'Education under Home Rule', in Ó Buachalla, *Irish Educationalist*, pp. 348–56.

97. Letter dated 4 May 1912, Ó Buachalla (ed.), *Letters*, pp. 262–4.

98. 'Education under Home Rule', in Ó Buachalla, *Irish Educationalist*, pp. 348–56. See also 'The Murder Machine', ibid., p. 371.

99. Letter dated 16 Mar. 1912, Ó Buachalla (ed.), *Letters*, p. 256. See also Undated letter probably from 10 Aug. 1907, Ó Buachalla (ed.), *Letters*, p. 112.

100. Letter dated 18 May 1912, Ó Buachalla (ed.), *Letters*, pp. 266–7; Widow of Eamonn Ceannt, NA, WS264; Ryan, *Remembering Sion*, pp. 96 and 111.

101. *ACS* 12 July 1913.

102. 'An Craoibhín and his Critics', Gleo na gCath, *ACS* 19 July 1913; 'An Craoibhín's reply to "Sinn Féin"', Eagarfhocal, *ACS* 26 July 1913.

103. Letter dated 11 May 1912, Ó Buachalla (ed.), *Letters*, pp. 264–5.

104. Letter dated 31 May 1912, Ó Buachalla (ed.), *Letters*, p. 269.

105. Letter Greg Murphy dated 8 May 1947, LP; Edwards, *Triumph*, p. 158.

106. Address by Patrick to Gaelic League in Carrick-on-Suir, dated 27 Nov. 1912, LP.

107. *An Macaomh* 1913. See also *The Singer* (1915), *Collected Works. Plays, Stories, Poems*, pp. 1–3.

108. Letters dated 20 Apr. and 23 May 1913, Ó Buachalla (ed.), *Letters*, pp. 288 and 290.

109. 'From a Hermitage'.

110. June article, ibid.

111. July article, ibid.

112. Wolfe Tone memorial lecture at Bodenstown 22 June 1913, *Collected Works. Political Writings and Speeches*.

113. Sep. and Oct. articles in 'From a Hermitage'.

114. Pearse (ed.), *Home Life*, pp. 41 and 55.

115. *ACS* 11 Apr. 1903, quoted in O'Leary, *Prose Literature*, p. 143.

116. Edwards, *Triumph*, p. 163.

117. Ryan, *Remembering Sion,* pp. 178–9; O'Casey, 223. See also *The Singer* (1915), *Collected Works. Plays, Stories, Poem* , pp. 1–3.

118. Ryan, *Man called Pearse*, p. 243; Ryan, *Remembering Sion*, p. 123.

119. Letter Frank Fahey dated 15 Mar. 1948, LP.

120. Sep. and Oct. articles in 'From a Hermitage'.

121. Ryan, *Remembering Sion*, p. 160.

122. Sep. and Oct. articles in 'From a Hermitage'.

123. Pearse (ed.), *Home Life*, pp. 48–9 and 56.

124. Pearse (ed.), *Home Life*, pp. 44–7.

125. Sep. and Oct. articles in 'From a Hermitage'.

126. Letter dated 29 Oct. 1913, Ó Buachalla (ed.), *Letters*, pp. 488–9.

127. Quoted in Townshend, *Political Violence in Ireland. Government and Resistance since 1848* (Oxford 1983), p. 259.

128. Speech in Enniscorthy dated 26 Sep. 1915, NLI, ms. 15,556.

129. Isabel V. Hull, *Absolute Destruction: Military Culture and the Practices of War in Imperial Germany* (Ithaca 2005), p. 101.

130. Cairns and Richards, *Writing Ireland*, p. 91.

131. Michael Dowling, LP.

132. Edwards, *Triumph*, p. 142.

133. Sir Arnold Bax recalled how Molly Maquire, the sister of Patrick Colm, introduced Patrick in 1913 as someone with an ambition to die for Ireland, LP, C27.

134. Letter dated 29 Oct. 1913, Ó Buachalla (ed.), *Letters*, pp. 488–9.

135. Joseph Gleeson, NA, WS367. Fr T. O'Donoghue claimed that an organisation called 'The Irish National Guard' was formed for young men in 1912. It had three branches in Dublin, three in Galway and one in Cork. Some of them participated in the lockout and joined the ICA before ending up in the Irish Volunteers, Fr T. O'Donoghue, NA, WS1666.

136. Martin, 'MacNeill and the Irish Volunteers', p. 135.

137. 'The Coming Revolution', *ACS* 8 Nov. 1913. See also Dec. article in 'From a Hermitage'.

138. John Gray, *Black Mass. Apocalyptic Religion and the Death of Utopia* (2007), passim.

139. Richard Connolly, NA, WS523.

140. Martin, 'MacNeill and the Volunteers', p. 135.

141. Hobson memoirs NLI, ms. 12,177, p. 29; Sean Fitzgibbon, NA, WS130; P.S. O'Hegarty, NA, WS26; Eoin MacNeill, 'How the Volunteers Began', in F.X. Martin (ed.), *The Irish Volunteers 1913–1915. Recollections and Documents* (Dublin 1963), pp. 71–2; The O'Rahilly, 'The Irish Prepare to Arm', in Martin (ed.), *The Irish Volunteers*, pp. 76–7; Piaras Béaslai, 'The National Army is Founded', in Martin (ed.), *The Irish* Volunteers, pp. 79–81. According to Sean McGarry it was Tom Clarke, McDermott and Pearse who contacted people representing different elements of national life, Sean McGarry, NA, WS368.

142. 'From a Hermitage'.

143. F.X. Martin, 'The Provisional Committee of the Irish Volunteers', in Martin (ed.), *The Irish Volunteers*, pp. 95–7.

144. Kissane, *Politics*, p. 34; Carty, *Bloody Protest*, p. 88.

145. Edwards, *Triumph*, p. 210.

146. Widow of Eamonn Ceannt, NA, WS264.

147. Frank Henderson, NA, WS249.

148. Letter dated 30 Nov. 1913, Ó Buachalla (ed.), *Letters*, p. 296.

149. McGill, 'Pearse in Donegal', p. 79.

150. Ibid., p. 79; Edwards, *Triumph*, pp. 180–1.

151. A. Kinsella, 'Medical Aspects of the 1916 Rising', in *Dublin Historical Record* Vol. L, No. 2, Autumn 1997, p. 137.

152. Jan. article in 'From a Hermitage'.

153. Ibid., p. 209; McGill, 'Pearse in Donegal', pp. 81–2; Martin, 'MacNeill and the Irish Volunteers', p. 169.

154. Quoted in Carty, *Bloody Protest*, p. 91.

155. 'The Psychology of a Volunteer' Jan. 1914, *Collected Works. Political Writings and Speeches*.

156. Porter, *P.H. Pearse*, p. 132.

157. Edwards, *Triumph*, pp. 203 and 229–230.

158. 'To the Boys of Ireland' Feb. 1914, *Collected Works. Political Writings and Speeches*.

159. Seamus Pounds, NA, WS267; Patrick Ward, NA, WS1140; Gearoid Uah-Uallachain, NA, WS328.

160. Ibid.

161. Letter dated 27 May 1910, quoted in Edwards, *Triumph*, p. 154.

162. Edwards, *Triumph*, pp. 184–6.

163. Rd Foley, LP. See also Letter Omar Crowley dated 19 Apr. 1947, LP.

164. Edwards, *Triumph*, pp. 189–190.

165. Copy of article in *New York Evening Journal* St Patrick's Day 1914, LP; NLI, ms. 33,702 and ms. 17,634.

166. 'How Does She Stand?', *Collected Works. Political Writings and Speeches*, pp. 64–75; NLI, ms. 33,702.

167. Speech held in the United States, NLI, ms. 33,702 and ms. 17,634; 2 Mar. 1914 Emmet Commemoration Brooklyn; 9 Mar. Emmet Commemoration New York, *Collected Works. Political Writings and Speeches*.

168. Ibid.; Copy of article in *New York Evening Journal* St Patrick's Day 1914, LP.

169. Ibid.

170. NLI, ms. 17,633.

171. Letters dated 20, 24 and 27 Apr. and 4 May 1914, Ó Buachalla (ed.), *Letters*, pp. 306–10.

172. Edwards, *Triumph*, pp. 188–9 and 197; Carty, *Bloody Protest*, p. 92.

173. Eamonn Bulfin, NA, WS497; Gearoid Uah-Uallachain, NA, WS328; Sisson, *Pearse's Patriots*, p. 155.

174. Letter Colm O Loughlin dated 13 May 1947, LP. See also Osborn Bergin, LP; Ryan, *Remembering Sion*, p. 121.

175. C.P. Curran, *Under the Receding Wave* (Dublin 1970), p. 83.

176. Pearse (ed.), *Home Life*, p. 30; Sisson, *Pearse's Patriots*, pp. 155–6; Le Roux, *Patrick H. Pearse*, p. 48; Padraic Colum a.o., *The Irish Rebellion of 1916 and its Martyrs* (New York 1916), pp. 283–5.

177. Edwards, *Triumph*, p. 203.

178. Letter to Miss McKenna dated 21 May 1914, Pearse Museum.

179. Letter dated 14 June 1914, Ó Buachalla (ed.), *Letters*, p. 313. On membership, Townshend, *Easter 1916*, p. 52.

180. Liam S. Gogan, NA, WS799; Redmond, *Irish Volunteer* 31 Oct. 1914, quoted in Martin (ed.), *The Irish Volunteers*, p. 166.

181. Hobson, quoted in Edwards, *Triumph*, p. 212.

182. Quoted in Martin (ed.), *The Irish Volunteers*, p. 144.

183. Letter dated 19 June 1914, Ó Buachalla (ed.), *Letters*, pp. 314–15. See also Letter dated 14 June 1914, ibid., pp. 312–3; Sean Fitzgibbon, NA, WS130.

184. Letter dated 6 July 1914, Ó Buachalla (ed.), *Letters*, p. 316.

185. *The Irish Volunteer* 4 July 1914, quoted in Martin (ed.), *The Irish Volunteers*, pp. 136–8.

186. Letter to McGarrity dated 17 July 1914, NLI, ms. 17,477.

187. Ibid.

188. Sean McGarry, NA, WS368; Hobson, LP; Edwards, *Triumph*, p. 179.

189. Hobson, LP.

190. Letter to McGarrity dated 17 July 1914, NLI, ms. 17,477.

191. Letter dated 19 Oct. 1914, Ó Buachalla (ed.), *Letters*, pp. 331–3.

192. Ó Buachalla (ed.), *Letters*, p. 321; Edwards, *Triumph*, p. 215. Jimmy Whelan claimed Figgis's presence on board the *Asgard* was unintentional, Letter Jimmy Whelan dated 30 Oct. 1945, LP.

193. Le Roux, *Patrick H. Pearse*, p. 289.

194. Letter Frank Fahey dated 15 Mar. 1948, LP.

195. Robert Holland, NA, WS280. See also Seamus Pounds, NA, WS267; Gearoid Uah-Uallachain, NA, WS328; Kinsella, 'Medical Aspects', p. 141.

196. Letter to McGarrity dated 28 July 1914, NLI, ms. 17,477.

197. Letter dated 3 Aug. 1914, Ó Buachalla (ed.), *Letters*, pp. 324–5.

198. Letter to McGarrity dated 28 July 1914, NLI, ms. 17,477.
199. Ó Buachalla (ed.), *Letters*, p. 325.
200. McGarrity in Edwards, *Triumph*, p. 194.
201. Letter dated 3 Aug. 1914, Ó Buachalla (ed.), *Letters*, pp. 324–5.
202. Addendum of Aug. 1914 to 'How Does She Stand?', p. 87.
203. Pearse speech on home rule dated 19 Aug. 1914, *Retrospect* Vol. 1, LP.
204. Letter dated 12 Aug. 1914, Ó Buachalla (ed.), *Letters*, pp. 325–7.
205. Ryan, *Remembering Sion*, p. 182; Edwards, *Triumph*, pp. 220–1.
206. Liam S. Gogan, NA, WS799.
207. Letter dated 12 Aug. 1914, Ó Buachalla (ed.), *Letters*, pp. 325–7.
208. Ibid.
209. Letter Greg Murphy dated 8 May 1947, LP.
210. Ó Buachalla (ed.), *Letters*, p. 329.
211. Martin (ed.), *The Irish Volunteers*, pp. 152–5; Edwards, *Triumph*, p. 221; Le Roux, *Patrick H. Pearse*, pp. 294–7.
212. Letter dated 26 Sep. 1914, Ó Buachalla (ed.), *Letters*, pp. 329–30; Ml Cremlin, LP.
213. Letter to McGarrity dated 19 Oct. 1914, NLI, ms. 17,477.
214. Ibid.
215. Michael Staines, NA, WS284; Edwards, *Triumph*, p. 226.
216. Letter dated 30 Oct. 1914, Ó Buachalla (ed.), *Letters*, pp. 333–4.
217. Frank Henderson, NA, WS249; Letter dated 30 Nov. 1913, Ó Buachalla (ed.), *Letters*, p. 296; Edwards, *Triumph*, p. 178. Townshend, *Easter 1916*, p. 41; *Freeman's Journal* and *Irish Independent* 26 Nov. 1913, quoted in Martin (ed.), *The Irish Volunteers*, pp. 105–9.
218. Quoted in Edwards, *Triumph*, p. 207.
219. Ibid., p. 208.
220. Ibid., p. 226.
221. Letters to McGarrity 1915–1916, Ó Buachalla (ed.), *Letters*, passim.
222. Edwards, *Triumph*, pp. 226–7.
223. Foster, *Yeats*, p. 524.
224. Letter dated 25 Nov. 1914, Ó Buachalla (ed.), *Letters*, pp. 335–7.
225. Edwards, *Triumph*, p. 228.
226. Scheme of Military Organisation, quoted in Martin (ed.), *The Irish Volunteers*, pp. 170–83; Edwards, *Triumph*, p. 228.
227. Letters to Ms McKenna dated 12 Dec. 1914, Kilmainham Jail, 23LR1P14 14.
228. Letter dated 18 Mar. 1915, Ó Buachalla (ed.), *Letters*, pp. 490–1.
229. Edwards, *Triumph*, pp. 228–9; Letter dated 11 Mar. 1915, Ó Buachalla (ed.), *Letters*, p. 340.
230. Edwards, *Triumph*, p. 244.
231. Battle plan and after battle reports, Allen Library, Box 186.
232. 'Why We Want Recruits' May 1915, *Collected Works. Political Writings and Speeches*.
233. Edwards, *Triumph*, pp. 234–5.
234. NLI, ms. 17,477.

235. Rosemary Cullen Owens, *Louie Bennett* (Cork 2001), p. 34. Bennett did not reject Patrick. In 1916 she asked Sheey-Skeffington for a copy of his pamphlets *Ghosts* and *The Sovereign People*, ibid., p. 24.
236. Byles, 'Women's Experience', pp. 474–5.
237. Letter dated 9 Dec. 1915, Ó Buachalla (ed.), *Letters*, pp. 354–5.
238. Liam O Donnell, LP; Letter J.A. Duffy dated 30 Sep. 1947, LP; Sean T, LP.
239. Osborn Bergin, LP; Letter Torna (O Donehada) dated 26 Nov. 1946, LP; Sean Forde, LP. See also 'Letter Professor Kettle', *ACS* 7 Nov. 1914; Letter Michael P. O'Hedly (Maynooth College) dated 10 May 1901, NLI, P7638.
240. 'The Position of the Gaelic League – An Craoibhín's Address in Cork', Eagarfhocal, *ACS* 26 Dec. 1914. See also Michael Tierney, *Eoin MacNeill: Scholar and Man of Action 1867–1945* (Oxford 1980), p. 178; Diarmuid Lynch, *The I.R.B. and the 1916 Insurrection* (Cork 1957), pp. 26–8; Dunleavy, *Douglas Hyde*, p. 328; Murphy, *Lost Republican Ideal*, p. 46.
241. Edwards, *Triumph*, p. 231; 'From a Hermitage'.
242. Letter Omar Crowley dated 19 Apr. 1947, LP; Murphy, *Lost Republican Ideal*, p. 47.
243. Letter Seamus Cooling dated 11 Nov. 1947, LP.
244. Lee, *Modernisation*, p. 146.
245. Carty, *Bloody Protest*, p. 104.
246. NLI, ms. 17,477; Ryan, *Remembering Sion*, pp. 178–9.
247. Edwards, *Triumph*, p. 244; Ryan, *Man called Pearse*, pp. 238–9 and 247.
248. Christopher Bailey in Wiles Lectures, hosted by the School of History at Queens University, Belfast, in 2007.
249. Ibid., pp. 241–5 and 253–8.
250. Quoted in Carty, *Bloody Protest*, p. 85.
251. Edwards, *Triumph*, p. 231.
252. Connolly in February 1916, quoted in Charles Townshend, *Ireland. The Twentieth Century* (London 1998), p. 73.
253. Edwards, *Triumph*, pp. 235–6.
254. Letter dated 6 Aug.[?] 1915, Kilmainham Jail, 23LR1P13 07.
255. Letter Owen Hynes dated 17 May 1947, LP.
256. Richard Walsh, NA, WS400.
257. Moran, *Patrick Pearse*, p. 147.
258. Letter dated 2 Sep. 1915, Ó Buachalla (ed.), *Letters*, pp. 343–5.
259. Letter dated 2 Sep. 1915, NLI, ms. 17,477.
260. Letter dated 15 Oct. 1915, Ó Buachalla (ed.), *Letters*, pp. 350–1.
261. Edwards, *Triumph*, pp. 242–3.
262. Letter dated 5 Mar. 1915, Ó Buachalla (ed.), *Letters*, p. 490.
263. Ibid.
264. Letter dated 15 Nov. 1915, Ó Buachalla (ed.), *Letters*, p. 352.
265. 26 Sep. 1915, Breandan Mac Giolla Choille (ed.), *Intelligence Notes 1910–16* (Dublin 1966); Letters dated 29 Sep. 1915 and 17 and 19 Feb. 1916, Ó Buachalla (ed.), *Letters*, pp. 348–9 and 356–7; Letter dated 4 Mar. 1916, Pearse Museum.

Chapter 5: Revolutionary

1. Copy of Court Martial and Execution of Pearse taken from National Archives, London, WO71/345, Allen Library, Box 187. Other more embellished versions, Le Roux, *Patrick H. Pearse*, p. 15; *The Sinn Fein Leaders of 1916* (Dublin 1917), p. 6.

2. Ryan, *Remembering Sion*, pp. 103–4.

3. Mullin, *Toiler's Life*, pp. 202–3.

4. Quoted in Donal Lowry, 'The Play of Forces World-Wide. The South African War as an International Event', *South African Historical Journal*, 1999, Vol. 41, p. 99.

5. *Fianna an Lea* 26 May 1900, quoted in O'Leary, *Prose Literature*, p. 33.

6. Quoted in Moran, *Patrick Pearse*, p. 52.

7. Lowry, 'Play of Forces', p. 98; Edwards, *Triumph*, p. 152; Kate Elizabeth Field, LP.

8. Letter Dan Maher dated 10 Aug. 1944, LP.

9. Ryan, *Remembering Sion*, pp. 109–11; Le Roux, *Patrick H. Pearse*, pp. 161–2; McCay, *Pádraic Pearse*, pp. 68 and 74.

10. Edwards, *Triumph*, p. 116.

11. Eamonn Bulfin, NA, WS497.

12. Edwards, *Triumph*, p. 154.

13. Dan Lugding, LP; Thomas Barry, NA, WS1; Sean McGarry, NA, WS368; Moran, *Patrick Pearse*, p. 128.

14. Sean McGarry, NA, WS368; Edwards, *Triumph*, p. 155, Townshend, *Easter 1916*, p. 22.

15. Letter Sean O Huadhaigh dated 15 July 1948, LP; Townshend, *Easter 1916*, p. 22.

16. Sean McGarry, NA, WS368.

17. Letter Omar Crowley dated 19 Apr. 1947, LP; Moran, *Patrick Pearse*, pp. 82–3.

18. Letter Ml Foley dated 17 June 1947, LP; Letter Frank Fahey dated 15 Mar. 1948, LP; Sean O Briain, LP; Eamonn Bulfin, NA, WS497; Townshend, *Easter 1916*, pp. 39–40; Edwards, *Triumph*, p. 204.

19. Ibid., p. 173.

20. Ryan, *Remembering Sion,* p. 162.

21. *Collected Works.*

22. Moran, *Patrick Pearse*, p. 78.

23. Hobson, LP; Kissane, *Pearse from Documents.* According to Le Roux Sean T. O'Kelly enrolled Patrick not MacDermott or Hobson, Le Roux, *Patrick H. Pearse*, pp. 22–3.

24. L2, LP; Seamus O'Connor, LP.

25. Lynch, *The I.R.B.*, p. 23; Diarmuid Lynch, NA, WS4; Letter Greg Murphy dated 8 May 1947, LP.

26. Letter Frank Fahey dated 15 Mar. 1948, LP.

27. Townshend, *Easter 1916*, p. 39; Thompson, *Imagination*, p. 91.

28. McGarrity quoted in Edwards, *Triumph*, p. 194.

29. Edwards, *Triumph*, p. 197; Moran, *Patrick Pearse*, pp. 141–3.
30. Letter Willie dated 26 Feb. 1914, NLI, ms. 40,454/2.
31. *The Irish Volunteer* 4 July 1914 quoted in Martin (ed.), *The Irish Volunteers*, pp. 136–8.
32. Letter Joe Murroy dated 28 Apr. 1947, LP; Richard Connolly, NA, WS523.
33. Letter to Joe McGarrity dated 17 July 1914, NLI, ms. 17,477. See also Lynch, *The I.R.B.*, p. 25.
34. Joseph Gleeson, NA, WS367.
35. Edwards, *Triumph*, pp. 217–18.
36. Richard Connolly, NA, WS523; Ó Buachalla (ed.), *Letters*, p. 328; Townshend, *Easter 1916*, p. 93.
37. Edwards, *Triumph*, pp. 227–8.
38. Richard Connolly, NA, WS523; Edwards, *Triumph*, p. 224; Ó Buachalla (ed.), *Letters*, p. 330.
39. Letter to Joe McGarrity dated 19 Oct. 1914, NLI, ms. 17,477.
40. Ibid.
41. Edwards, *Triumph*, pp. 224–5.
42. Edwards, *Triumph*, pp. 223–4; Barton, *From Behind*, p. 6.
43. Letter to Joe McGarrity dated 19 Oct. 1914, NLI, ms. 17,477.
44. Frank Henderson, NA, WS249; Piaras Béaslai, NA, WS261.
45. Liam S. Gogan, NA, WS799.
46. Letters dated 15 Nov. 1915, Ó Buachalla (ed.), *Letters*, p. 352; Edwards, *Triumph*, pp. 232–3 and 240.
47. Michael Staines, NA, WS284.
48. Piaras Béaslai, NA, WS261.
49. Michael Staines, NA, WS284.
50. Report of speech, NLI, ms. 15,556.
51. Edwards, *Triumph*, p. 240; Letter Liam de Roiste dated 10 Oct. 1947, LP.
52. Lynch, *The I.R.B.*, p. 25.
53. Mac Giolla Choille (ed.), *Intelligence Notes*, p. 222.
54. Diarmuid Lynch, NA, WS4; Alec McCabe, NA, WS277; Richard Connolly, NA, WS523; Patrick McCormack, NA, WS339; Townshend, *Easter 1916*, pp. 94–5; Edwards, *Triumph*, pp. 241–2.
55. Edwards. *Triumph*, pp. 241–2; Patrick McCormack, NA, WS339; Sean McGarry, NA, WS368; Le Roux, *Patrick H. Pearse*, p. 291.
56. Joseph Gleeson, NA, WS367; Diarmuid Lynch, NA, WS4; Alec McCabe, NA, WS277; Richard Connolly, NA, WS523; Patrick McCormack, NA, WS339; Widow of Eamonn Ceannt, NA, WS264; Townshend, *Easter 1916*, pp. 94–5; Edwards, *Triumph*, pp. 241–2; Carty, *Bloody Protest*, p. 99; Lynch, *The I.R.B.*, p. 28.
57. Edwards, *Triumph*, pp. 241–2 and 246; Carty, *Bloody Protest*, p. 102, Lynch, *The I.R.B.*, pp. 29–30.
58. Ibid., p. 28.
59. P.S. O'Hegarty, NA, WS 26; Edwards, *Triumph*, p. 244.
60. Townshend, *Easter 1916*, p. 48.
61. P.S. O'Hegarty, NA, WS26; Townshend, *Easter 1916*, p. 117.

62. Edwards, *Triumph*, pp. 241–2 and 246; Le Roux, *Patrick H. Pearse*, pp. 338–9.

63. Hobson quoted in Edwards, *Triumph*, pp. 250 and 240–1.

64. Porter, *P.H. Pearse*, pp. 104 and 108.

65. Desmond FitzGerald and Alfred Cotton, quoted in Townshend, *Easter 1916*, pp. 98–99. Murphy, *Lost Republican Ideal*, pp. 47–8.

66. Oliver, 'Irish Revolutionary Nationalism', p. 107.

67. Edwards, *Triumph*, pp. 226–7.

68. Ibid., p. 245; *Workers Republic* 25 Dec. 1915.

69. Moran, *Patrick Pearse*, pp. 190 and 177–90. See also Oliver, 'Irish Revolutionary Nationalism', p. 105.

70. War Sonnets I and III, Geoffrey Keynes, *The Poetical Works of Rupert Brooke* (London 1963), pp. 19 and 21; Moran, *Patrick Pearse*, pp. 185–7.

71. James Joyce, 'The Dead', in *The Dubliners* (London 1914), p. 205.

72. Gail Braybon, 'Women and the War', in Stephen Constantine, Maurice W. Kirby and Mary B. Rose (eds), *The First World War in British History* (London, New York 1995), p. 163; Lee, *Modernisation*, pp. 26–7.

73. Carty, *Bloody Protest*, p. 62.

74. Quoted in Townshend, *Easter 1916*, p. 114. See also Collins, *Catholic Churchmen*, pp. 148–50.

75. Moran, *Patrick Pearse*, pp. 86–100.

76. Townshend, *Easter 1916*, p. 115; Collins, *Catholic Churchmen*, pp. 110–11. This is also prominent in many English novels about the Great War. See, for instance, E. Raymond, *Tell England: A Study in a Generation* (London 1922), pp. 379–80.

77. Jerome F. Cronin in *Irish Independent* 27 Mar. 1957.

78. Quoted in Oliver, 'Irish Revolutionary Nationalism', p. 106. See also Thompson, *Imagination*, p. 71.

79. *The Singer* (1915), *The King* (1912), *Collected Works. Plays, Stories, Poems*, pp. 1–5. See also Daniel J. O'Neill, *The Irish Revolution and the Cult of the Leader: Observations on Griffith, Moran, Pearse and Connolly* (Boston 1988), p. 13; Porter, *P.H. Pearse*, p. 98.

80. R.F. Foster, *W.B. Yeats: A Life. 2, The Arch-poet, 1915–1939* (Oxford 2005), p. 46.

81. Le Roux, *Patrick H. Pearse*, p. 326.

82. 'The Abbey Theatre 1916 Plaque', in *Dublin Historical Record*, Vol. L No. 1, Spring 1997.

83. Jerome F. Cronin in *Irish Independent* 27 Mar. 1957.

84. O'Neill, *The Irish Revolution*, pp. 13–15; Murray G.H. Pittock, *Celtic Identity and the British Image* (Manchester 1999), pp. 81–2; Coilin, *Patrick H. Pearse*, pp. 2 and 15–16.

85. Letters dated 31 Mar. and 12 Apr. 1916, Ó Buachalla (ed.), *Letters*, pp. 359 and 361; Letter Jimmy Whelan dated 30 Oct. 1945, LP.

86. Motion in a January 1916 meeting of the IRB Supreme Council stated that a rising should be staged 'at the earliest date possible', Lynch, *The I.R.B.*, p. 31; Edwards, *Triumph*, pp. 246–7; Townshend, *Easter 1916*, p. 122.

87. Townshend, *Easter 1916*, pp. 123–5 and 148.

88. Michael Staines, NA, WS284.

89. Diarmuid Lynch, NA, WS4; Carty, *Bloody Protest*, p. 102.

90. Townshend, *Easter 1916*, pp. 123–5 and 148.

91. Letter dated 17 Feb. 1916, Ó Buachalla (ed.), *Letters*, pp. 356–7.

92. Michael Staines, NA, WS284; Townshend, *Easter 1916*, p. 129.

93. Edwards, *Triumph*, p. 247.

94. Letter Frank Fahey dated 15 Mar. 1948, LP; Seamus Pounds, NA, WS267; Eamonn Bulfin, NA, WS497; Frank Burke, LP; Interview with Joe McSweeney; Sisson, *Pearse's Patriots*, p. 156.

95. Michael Staines, NA, WS284; Townshend, *Easter 1916*, p. 129.

96. Ibid., pp. 45–6; Letter dated 4 Mar. 1916, Ó Buachalla (ed.), *Letters*, p. 358; Hobson, LP; Letter Frank Fahey dated 15 Mar. 1948, LP.

97. Kinsella, 'Medical Aspects', p. 150. Some assert that the green flag had a golden harp on it, Townshend, *Easter 1916*, p. 159. However, the actual flag returned by the British Government in 1966 shows a simple green flag with 'Irish Republic' written in golden lettering on both sides, Michael Kenny, *The Road to Freedom. Photographs and Memorabilia from the 1916 Rising and Afterwards* (Dublin 1993), p. 23.

98. Carty, *Bloody Protest*, p. 104.

99. Ryan, *Remembering Sion*, p. 122.

100. Townshend, *Easter 1916*, p. 113.

101. Seamas O'Conor, LP.

102. Frank Robbins, *Irish Press* 1 Feb. 1937, LP. See also Le Roux, *Patrick H. Pearse*, p. 333.

103. Diarmuid Lynch, NA, WS4; Edwards, *Triumph*, pp. 246–7; Townshend, *Easter 1916*, p. 119.

104. Seamas O'Conor, LP.

105. Townshend, *Ireland*, p. 75.

106. Thompson, *Imagination*, p. 94; Townshend, *Easter 1916*, pp. 120–1.

107. Ibid., pp. 119–21; Edwards, *Triumph*, pp. 248–9; Seamas O'Conor, LP; Eamonn O'Neill(?) Conan & Sceilg(?), LP.

108. Le Roux, *Patrick H. Pearse*, pp. 342–3; Townshend, *Easter 1916*, p. 134.

109. Quoted in Townshend, *Easter 1916*, p. 85. See also MacKenzie, *Irish Rebellion*, pp. 28–30.

110. Quoted in Townshend, *Easter 1916*, pp. 143–4.

111. Ibid., p. 86; Ben Novick, 'Postal Censorship in Ireland 1914–16', in *Irish Historical Studies* Vol. XXXI No. 123, pp. 346 and 356; Letters to Ms McKenna dated 18 and 28 July 1914, Kilmainham Jail, 23LR1P14 14; Letters dated 2 Sep. 1915, Ó Buachalla (ed.), *Letters*, pp. 343–6.

112. Barton, *From Behind*, p. 98; A.J. Jordan, *Major John McBride: 1865–1916: 'MacDonagh and MacBride and Connolly and Pearse'* (Westport 1991), p. 106.

113. Michael Staines, NA, WS284; Barton, *From Behind*, p. 98.

114. Carty, *Bloody Protest*, p. 97.

115. Dr James Ryan, TD, 'My Easter Week in the G.P.O.', in *Easter Fires. Pages from Personal Records of 1916* (Waterford 1943), p. 21.

116. Frank Henderson, NA, WS249; Maurice J. Collins, NA, WS550; Frank Burke, LP; Eamonn Bulfin, NA, WS497; Frank Burke, LP; Letter W.S. Fallon dated 19 Nov. 1946, LP; Townshend, *Easter 1916*, pp. 124–5; Sweeney, 'Donegal', pp. 5–6.

117. John F. Boyle, *The Irish Rebellion of 1916: A Brief History of the Revolt and its Suppression* (London 1916), p. 191.

118. Carty, *Bloody Protest*, p. 64.

119. Eamonn O'Neill(?) Conan & Sceilg(?), LP.

120. Letter dated 17 Feb. 1916, Ó Buachalla (ed.), *Letters*, pp. 356–7.

121. Pearse (ed.), *Home Life*, p. 37.

122. Barton, *From Behind*, p. 97.

123. Letter from Seamus Cooling dated 11 Nov. 1947, LP; Pearse (ed.), *Home Life*, p. 9.

124. Porter, *P.H. Pearse*, pp. 134–5.

125. Dr Dick Hayes, LP; Letter Colm O Loughlin dated 13 May 1947, LP; Widow of Eamonn Ceannt, NA, WS264.

126. Gregory Murphy, NA, WS150.

127. F.X. Martin, 'The 1916 Rising: A Coup d'Etat or a Bloody Protest', *Studia Hibernica* 8 (1968), pp. 108–37; Dan MacCarthy, NA, WS722.

128. Townshend, *Easter 1916*, p. 115; Letter Colm O Loughlin dated 13 May 1947, LP; Barton, *From Behind*, pp. 5–6; Lee, *Modernisation*, p. 25.

129. Bulmer Hobson in particular emphasised this element in Patrick's thinking after the Rising, Kissane, *Pearse from Documents*.

130. Ryan, *Man called Pearse*, p. 188.

131. Sean T. O'Kelly, LP.

132. From Roy Foster, *The Irish Story: Telling Tales and Making it up in Ireland* (Oxford 2002), p. 7; Cairns and Richards, *Writing Ireland*, pp. 104–6.

133. Dennis Bos, ' "Liever den eeredood sterven." De Parijse Commune en de militarisering van de socialistische partijcultuur', *Leidschrift. Historisch Tijdschrift* Vol. 22 No. 2, 2007. Todd Weir, 'Colonial Violence and Socialist Imagination: The Conversions of Ernst Däumig', http://www.ghi-dc.org/index.php?option=com_content&view=article&id=589:german-imperial-biographies&catid=80:conferences-2006&Itemid=342.

134. Hull, *Absolute Destruction*, p. 145.

135. Ryan, *Remembering Sion*, p. 165. See also Ryan, *Man called Pearse*, p. 203; Edwards, *Triumph*, p. 250.

136. *Rote Fahne* 15 Jan. 1919. Thanks for this reference to Dennis Bos.

137. Ó Buachalla (ed.), *Letters*, pp. 362 and 365.

138. Townshend, *Easter 1916*, pp. 132–3.

139. Mobilisation Order, Letter dated Holy Thursday and 20 Apr. 1916, Ó Buachalla (ed.), *Letters*, pp. 362 and 475.

140. Townshend, *Easter 1916*, pp. 134–7.

141. Barton, *From Behind*, p. 161; Sweeney, 'Donegal', p. 6.

142. Letter dated 22 Apr. 1916, Ó Buachalla (ed.), *Letters*, p. 363; Carty, *Bloody Protest*, p. 108; Townshend, *Easter 1916*, p. 137.

143. Quoted in Jeffery, *The GPO*, p. 140.

144. Letter Mrs Bradley dated 22 Feb. 1947, LP; Stephen McKenna in *Irish Press* 29 Mar. 1937.

145. Richard Balfe, NA, WS251; Carty, *Bloody Protest*, p. 111; Letter Colm O Loughlin dated 13 May 1947, LP; Townshend, *Easter 1916*, pp. 136–8; Ryan, 'My Easter Week', pp. 22–3.

146. Sean McGarry, NA, WS368.

147. Townshend, *Easter 1916*, p. 138.

148. Michael Staines, NA, WS284.

149. Letter dated 23 Apr. 1916, Ó Buachalla (ed.), *Letters*, p. 364; Nancy Wyse-Power, NA, WS541; Townshend, *Easter 1916*, p. 139; Lynch, *The I.R.B.*, p. 154.

150. Letter dated 24 Apr. 1916, Ó Buachalla (ed.), *Letters*, p. 364.

151. Handwritten notes, A5-20, LP.

152. Townshend, *Easter 1916*, pp. 138–41 and 158; Kinsella, 'Medical Aspects', p. 140; John Joseph Scallan[?], NA, WS318.

153. Barton, *From Behind*, p. 99; Pearse (ed.), *Home Life*, p. 94; Townshend, *Easter 1916*, p. 157.

154. Ibid., p. 158.

155. Stephen McKenna in *Irish Press* 29 Mar. 1937. See also Michael Staines, NA, WS284; Townshend, *Easter 1916*, pp. 160–1.

156. Jeffery, *The GPO*, p. 143.

157. Ml Cremin, LP.

158. Letter Liam de Roiste dated 10 Oct. 1947, LP; McCullough, LP; Joost Augusteijn, 'Radical Nationalist Activities in County Derry 1900–1921', in Gerard O'Brien, *Derry and Londonderry. History and Society* (Dublin 1999), pp. 576–7.

159. Frank Burke, LP; Sisson, *Pearse's Patriots*, p. 156; Carty, *Bloody Protest*, p. 49; Sweeney, 'Donegal', p. 6; Le Roux, *Patrick H. Pearse*, pp. 371–2.

160. Alec McCabe, NA, WS277.

161. Michael Staines, NA, WS284; Townshend, *Easter 1916*, pp. 162–4; Seamus Pounds, NA, WS267; Gregory Murphy, NA, WS150.

162. Barton, *From Behind*, pp. 8–9; Augusteijn, *Memoirs of John M. Regan*, pp. 87–96; Townshend, *Easter 1916*, pp. 143–51 and 181; McCay, *Pádraic Pearse*, p. 87; Moran, *Patrick Pearse*, p. 164.

163. Lynch, *The I.R.B.*, p. 160; Townshend, *Easter 1916*, pp. 183–4.

164. *Irish War News* in Ó Buachalla (ed.), *Letters*, p. 367. Printing facilities, Charlie Walker, NA, WS214; Lynch, *The I.R.B.*, p. 164.

165. *Manifesto to the Citizens of Dublin* 25 Apr. 1916, copy in Ó Buachalla (ed.), *Letters*, pp. 368–9. Similar statements were made in *War Bulletin* 28 Apr. 1916 but actually issued on Thursday 27 Apr. 1916 and written on Wednesday night, Ó Buachalla (ed.), *Letters*, pp. 369–71. For a draft of this bulletin, NLI, ms. 15,556.

166.   Barton, *From Behind*, pp. 102–3; Townshend, *Easter 1916*, p. 214; Jeffrey, *The GPO*, 147–8 and 159; Lynch, *The I.R.B.*, p. 169.

167.   Letter Ml Kavanagh dated 16 Sep. 1947, LP; Townshend, *Easter 1916*, pp. 105–8; Barton, *From Behind*, pp. 6–7, 97 and 100.

168.   Letter J. Wylie dated 4 Dec. 1947, LP.

169.   Ibid.; Letter Mrs Bradley dated 22 Feb. 1947, LP; Letter Charley Steinmeyer dated 18 July 1947, LP; Letter Joe Murroy dated 28 Apr. 1947, LP; M.W. O'Reilly, LP; Michael Staines, NA, WS284; Seamus Pounds, NA, WS267; Carty, *Bloody Protest*, p. 122; Barton, *From Behind*, pp. 97 and 100; Letter dated 1 May 1916, Ó Buachalla (ed.), *Letters*, pp. 375–7. Some doubt over the genuineness of this letter or at least its treasonous remark on German aid might be justified as the location of the original letter is not known. Only a typed copy of the letter has been located in the Asquith Papers.

170.   Carty, *Bloody Protest*, p. 118; *Manifesto to the Citizens of Dublin* 25 Apr. 1916, Ó Buachalla (ed.), *Letters*, pp. 368–9; Barton, *From Behind*, pp. 102–3; Townshend, *Easter 1916*, p. 214; Jeffrey, *The GPO*, pp. 147–8 and 159; Lynch, *The I.R.B.*, p. 169.

171.   Letter dated 26 Apr. 1916, Ó Buachalla (ed.), *Letters*, p. 369.

172.   Letter headed 'Army of the Irish Republic' directed to 'Rev. Administrator or other priest Marlboro Street' dated 24 Apr. 1916, signed P.H. Pearse Commandant-General, NLI, ms. 15,002; Carty, *Bloody Protest*, p. 118. Confessions were heard, Sean MacEntee, 'Pages from a Record of Easter Week 1916', in *Easter Fires*, p. 12. Flanagan's recollections, Jeffery, *The GPO*, pp. 157–61.

173.   Thompson, *Imagination*, p. 99; Moran, *Patrick Pearse*, p. 168.

174.   Nic Shiubhlaigh, *Splendid*, pp. 148–9. See also Pearse (ed.), *Home Life*, p. 59; Letter Joe Murroy dated 28 Apr. 1947, LP; Letter Greg Murphy dated 8 May 1947, LP; M.W. O'Reilly, LP; Ml Cremin, LP.

175.   O'Casey, *Drums*, p. 279.

176.   Letter Greg Murphy dated 8 May 1947, LP.

177.   Ryan, 'My Easter Week', p. 24.

178.   Letter Charley Steinmeyer dated 18 July 1947, LP.

179.   Frank Henderson, NA, WS249.

180.   Original in Barton, *From Behind*, pp. 116–17; Oliver, 'Irish Revolutionary Nationalism', p. 110; Sweeney, 'Donegal', p. 7; Eamonn Bulfin, NA, WS417; Frank Henderson, NA, WS249; Jeffery, *The GPO*, pp. 143–5; Lynch, *The I.R.B.*, p. 165; Carty, *Bloody Protest*, p. 118.

181.   Claire Hourihan, 'A Series of Accidents' in *The Dublin Review* 23, http://www.thedublinreview.com/archive/twentythree/hourihane. html; Townshend, *Easter 1916*, pp. 263–4; Oliver, 'Irish Revolutionary Nationalism', p. 110; Sweeney, 'Donegal', p. 7; Eamonn Bulfin, NA, WS417; Frank Henderson, NA, WS249; Jeffery, *The GPO*, pp. 143–5; Lynch, *The I.R.B.*, p. 165; Carty, *Bloody Protest*, p. 118.

182.   Barton, *From Behind*, p. 100; *War News*, Ó Buachalla (ed.), *Letters*, pp. 368–71.

183. Oliver, 'Irish Revolutionary Nationalism', p. 110; Written notes, LP. See also Stephen McKenna in *Irish Press* 29 Mar. 1937; Manifesto issued by the 'Army of the Republic' on Friday 28 Apr. 1916, Ó Buachalla (ed.), *Letters*, pp. 371–3; Barton, *From Behind*, pp. 101–2.

184. MacEntee, 'Pages from', p. 10.

185. Ibid., p. 13.

186. Ó Buachalla (ed.), *Letters*, pp. 367–73; NLI, ms. 33,460 G/3.

187. Lynch, *The I.R.B.*, p. 176.

188. Ibid., 169; Barton, *From Behind*, pp. 102–3; Townshend, *Easter 1916*, p. 212; Jeffrey, *The GPO*, pp. 147–8 and 159.

189. Letter Charley Steinmeyer dated 18 July 1947, LP; M.W. O'Reilly, LP; Michael Staines, NA, WS284; Ml Cremin, LP; Eamonn Bulfin, NA, WS497; Frank Henderson, NA, WS249; Barton, *From Behind*, pp. 104–5; Elizabeth O'Farrell, *Catholic Bulletin*, Vol. VIII No. 4, April 1917, p. 266, in NLI, ms. 33,460 G/2; MacEntee, 'Pages from', p. 15; Ryan, 'My Easter Week', pp. 26–7; Jeffrey, *The GPO*, pp. 12–14 Townshend, *Easter 1916*, pp. 211–12, Lynch, *The I.R.B.*, p. 179.

190. Robert Holland, NA, WS280. See also Letter Charley Steinmeyer dated 18 July 1947, LP; M.W. O'Reilly, LP; Ml Cremin, LP; Eamonn Bulfin, NA, WS497; Frank Henderson, NA, WS249; Sean McGarry, NA, WS368; Barton, *From Behind*, pp. 104–5; O'Farrell, *Catholic Bulletin*, Vol. VIII No. 4, April 1917, p. 266; Sweeney, 'Donegal', p. 8; Ryan, 'My Easter Week', pp. 29–30; Copy of surrender order, Ó Buachalla (ed.), *Letters*, p. 373; Townshend, *Easter 1916*, p. 245. In the surrender order it is stated that 'the members of the Provisional Government here present have agreed by a majority to open negotiations with the British Commander'. Patrick opposed this, Letter dated 1 May 1916, Ó Buachalla (ed.), *Letters*, p. 376.

191. Letter to P.H. Pearse dated 29 Apr. 1.40 p.m., Allen Library, Box 187; Letter Major de Courcy Wheeler dated 12 Apr. 1947, LP.

192. M.W. O'Reilly, LP.

193. Letters Major de Courcy Wheeler dated 10 Dec. 1945 and 12 Apr. 1947, LP; NA, WS920. Apparently accusations were made by St John Ervine and Sean O'Casey on the basis of statements by Lord Basil Blackwood that Patrick had acted like 'a stricken animal, his great head lolling on its neck as if it were about to fall off', Letter St John Irvine dated 19 Feb. 1947, LP.

194. Townshend, *Easter 1916*, p. 246; Ryan, 'My Easter Week', pp. 29–30; MacEntee, 'Pages from', p. 18; Sweeney, 'Donegal', pp. 9–10.

195. Letter dated 1 May 1916, Ó Buachalla (ed.), *Letters*, pp. 376–7.

196. Letter Richard Mulcahy dated 17 Sep. 1947, LP; Rev. Fr Aloysius, NA, WS200; Ó Buachalla (ed.), *Letters*, pp. 374–5; Surrender note written by James Connolly and Thomas McDonagh and countersigned, http:// irelandsown.net/tempo.html.

197. M.W. O'Reilly, LP; Letter Charley Steinmeyer dated 18 July 1947, LP; Joseph Gleeson, NA, WS367; Michael Staines, NA, WS284; John Joseph Scallan[?], NA, WS318; Ryan, 'My Easter Week', p. 31; Fr Aloysius, LP; Rev. Fr Aloysius, NA, WS200.

198. Copy of surrender order, Ó Buachalla (ed.), *Letters*, p. 373; Rev. Fr Aloysius, NA, WS200.

199. Beasley, LP; Letter J. Wylie dated 4 Dec. 1947, LP; Court Martial Statement, Ó Buachalla (ed.), *Letters*, pp. 378–380; Barton, *From Behind*, p. 109; Le Roux, *Patrick H. Pearse*, p. 409. See also 'Life of General Blackader' by Robin Jenkins in *Transactions* 80 (2006).

200. Court Martial Statement, Ó Buachalla (ed.), *Letters*, pp. 378–80; Original in Barton, *From Behind*, pp. 116–17.

201. Ibid., pp. 109–10.

202. Letters dated 2 and 3 May 1916, Ó Buachalla (ed.), *Letters*, pp. 378–80.

203. Letter dated 3 May 1916, ibid., pp. 381–2.

204. Patrick Crotty, 'The Irish Renaissance, 1890–1940: Poetry in English', in Margaret Kelleher and Philip O'Leary, *The Cambridge History of Irish Literature* (Cambridge 2006), p. 93; Cairns and Richards, *Writing Ireland*, pp. 104–11. Philip O'Leary, 'The Irish Renaissance, 1890–1940: Poetry in Irish', in Kelleher and O'Leary, *Cambridge History*, p. 232.

205. Letters dated 1 and 3 May 1916, Ó Buachalla (ed.), *Letters*, pp. 376–7 and 381–2.

206. Fr Aloysius, LP; Rev. Fr Aloysius, NA, WS200; Le Roux, *Patrick H. Pearse*, p. 418.

Chapter 6: Legacy: The failure in triumph

1. Letter St John Ervine dated 19 Feb. 1947, LP.

2. Letter dated 29 Apr. 1916, Kilmainham Jail, 23LR1P15/20.

3. A large sample of these can be found in the National Library of Ireland.

4. *The Sinn Fein Leaders of 1916 with Numerous Illustrations and Complete Lists of Deportees, Casualties, etc.; with Appendix on New Parliamentary Party, Count Plunkett, Joseph MacGuinness, De Valera, Cosgrave* (Dublin 1917), p. 6.

5. Boyle, *The Irish rebellion*, p. 5; MacKenzie, *Irish rebellion*, Preface.

6. Padraic and Mary Colum, *The Irish Rebellion of 1916 and its Martyrs* (New York 1916), pp. 269 and 281. See also Martin Daly (Stephen MacKenna), *Memories of the Dead: Some Impressions* (Dublin 1917[?]), p. 18.

7. Boyle, *The Irish Rebellion*, pp. 189–91.

8. MacKenzie, *Irish Rebellion*, pp. 9–10.

9. Coilin (S. MacGiollanate), *Patrick H. Pearse*, pp. 3 and 17.

10. *The Sinn Fein Leaders*, p. 6; Daly, *Memories*, p. 17. See also C.F. Connolly, *Pádraic H. Pearse* (n.p. n.d. (1920)); M.J. Hannan, *Irish Leaders of 1916 – Who are They?* (Butte Montana, n.d. (1920)).

11. Ryan, *Man called Pearse*.

12. Mary Maguire Colum, *St. Enda's School, Rathfarnham, Dublin. Founded by Pádraic H. Pearse* (New York 1917); James Hayes, *Padraic MacPiarais, Sgéaluidhe; Patrick H. Pearse, Storyteller* (Dublin 1920).

13. For a list of works found in the libraries of Trinity College, Dublin, the National Library of Ireland and Queens University Belfast see the bibliography.

14. John X. Regan (ed.), *What made Ireland Sinn Fein* (Boston 1921).

15. Julius Pokorny, *Die Seele Irlands: Novellen und Gedichte aus dem Irisch-Galischen des Patrick Henry Pearse und Anderer zum ersten Male ins Deutsche übertragen* (Halle a.S. 1922).

16. Hannan, *Irish Leaders*, p. 1.

17. 'Hij was een edel man, gewetensvol, beginselvast, vroom, streng voor zichzelf en mild voor anderen, wilskrachtig en teder tegelijk, wijs en verdraagzaam, begaafd en bescheiden, vurig en toch beheerst, oprecht en onomkoopbaar, bezield met hoge idealen en in staat zijn bezieling aan anderen mede te delen.' Steven Debroey, *Rebel uit roeping: het leven van de Ierse vrijheidsheld Patrick Pearse* (n.p. 1925 and 1953), p. 11.

18. Ibid., p. 202.

19. Louis N. Le Roux, *La vie de Patrice Pearse* (Rennes 1932). Translated into English by Desmond Ryan (Dublin 1932), p. x.

20. Carty, *In Bloody Protest*, p. 134.

21. Letter by Seamus de Clandillon dated 28 Oct. 1926, LP.

22. D. Ferriter, 'Commemorating the Rising, 1922–65: "A Figurative Scramble for the Bones of the Patriot Dead"?', in Mary E. Daly and Margaret O'Callaghan (eds), *1916 in 1966: Commemorating the Easter Rising* (Dublin 2007), pp. 201–15; Claire Hourihan, 'A Series of Accidents', in *The Dublin Review* 23 (Autumn 2006), http://www.thedublinreview.com/archive/twentythree/hourihane.html.

23. Treaty Debates, http://historical-debates.oireachtas.ie/.

24. Kevin O'Higgins, Debate 29 Sep. 1922, Dáil Éireann Vol. 1.

25. Thomas Johnson, Debate 20 Aug. 1922, Dáil Éireann Vol. 1.

26. Patrick Little, Debate 25 Oct. 1928, Dáil Éireann Vol. 26.

27. Mr Cooney, Debate 3 Dec. 1931, Dáil Éireann Vol. 40. See also Mr Little, Debate 9 May 1929, Dáil Éireann Vol. 29; Mr O'Neill, Debate 28 Aug. 1930, Seanad Éireann, Vol. 13.

28. Mr Little, Debate 27 May 1931, Dáil Éireann Vol. 38.

29. Eamonn Cooney, Debate 9 May 1929, Dáil Éireann Vol. 29.

30. Mr Hurley, Debate 24 Mar. 1938, Dáil Éireann Vol. 70.

31. Sean Lemass, Debate 11 Mar. 1941, Dáil Éireann Vol. 82.

32. Frank MacDermot, Debate 13 Nov. 1941, Dáil Éireann Vol. 59.

33. James Hickey, Debate 11 Mar. 1941, Dáil Éireann Vol. 82.

34. Mr Dunne, Debate 26 May 1945, Dáil Éireann Vol. 110.

35. See D. Ua Braoin, *Pearse and the Workers' Republic* (n.p., n.d.).

36. Richard Mulcahy, Debate 11 May 1933, Dáil Éireann Vol. 47.

37. Frank Aiken, Debate 3 Mar. 1939, Dáil Éireann Vol. 74.

38. *Notes for Teachers: History, Department of Education, National Education* (The Stationary Office, Dublin, 1933), pp. 27–8.

39. David Fitzpatrick, 'The Futility of History: A Failed Experiment in Irish Education', in C. Brady (ed.), *Ideology and the Historians* (Dublin 1991), p. 176; Jack Magee, *The Teaching of Irish History in Schools* (Belfast 1971),

p. 2; Gabriel Doherty, 'The Irish History Textbook, 1900–1960. Problems and Development', *Oideas*, No. 42 (Dublin 1994), p. 16. All cited in Tessa van Keeken, 'Telling a National Story. History Teaching and the Formation of National Identity. A Case Study of Primary School History Teaching in Ireland, 1922–71' (unpublished MA thesis, Utrecht University 2007).

40. Carty, James, *A Class-Book of Irish History. Book IV: From the Act of Union* (London 1943), p. 111.

41. van Keeken, 'Telling a National Story', pp. 114–16.

42. Máiréad Ní Ghráda, *A Primary History of Ireland. Book 2: From 1691 to 1949* (Dublin, 1963[?]), p. 113.

43. Compare the reporting in *The Derry People* on 20 May 1905 with 10 Oct. 1942.

44. Mr Donnellan, Debate 5 Feb. 1953, Dáil Éireann Vol. 136.

45. Mr McQuillan, Debate 23 May 1956, Dáil Éireann Vol. 157.

46. Dr Browne, Debate 29 May 1958, Dáil Éireann Vol. 168.

47. Thaddeus Lynch, Debate 4 June 1958, Dáil Éireann Vol. 168.

48. Mr Davern, Debate 8 May 1962, Dáil Éireann Vol. 195.

49. Mr Carroll, Debate 30 Oct. 1963, Dáil Éireann Vol. 205.

50. Debate on Pearse Memorial Cottage 8 May 1962, Dáil Éireann Vol. 214.

51. Séamus Ó Searcaigh, *Pádraig Mac Piarais* (Dublin 1938); McCay, *Pádraic Pearse*.

52. Rd Foley, LP.

53. Sisson, *Pearse's Patriots*, pp. 157–8.

54. *Irish Press* 26 Apr. 1943.

55. Quoted in Sisson, *Pearse's Patriots*, p. 161.

56. Gwynn quoted in Le Roux, *Patrick H. Pearse*, p. 144.

57. Christian Brothers Westland Row, *Centenary Record*, p. 97.

58. Letters dated 11 May 1965 and 29 Mar. 1965, Ferriter, 'Commemorating the Rising', pp. 214–15.

59. J.J. Horgan, *From Parnell to Pearse* (Dublin 1948), p. 243.

60. McCay, *Pádraic Pearse*, pp. 13, 27, 31 and 49.

61. Ibid., pp. 13 and 30.

62. Ibid., pp. 94–5.

63. Ibid., p. 36.

64. Ibid., p. 16.

65. Ibid., pp. 67–8.

66. Rev. Francis Shaw, 'The Canon of Irish History – A Challenge', in *Studies* Vol. LXI, Summer 1972, No. 242, pp. 117–50.

67. Thompson, *Imagination*, pp. 67, 74–7.

68. Ibid., pp. 119–25.

69. Porter, *P.H. Pearse*, pp. 54–8.

70. Edwards, *Triumph*, p. 129.

71. Carty, *Bloody Protest*, pp. 134–8.

72. Ibid., p. 29, see also p. 136.

73. Ibid., pp. 29, 134–40.

74. P.J. Lenihan, Debate 1 Mar. 1967, Dáil Éireann Vol. 226. See also Mr Meaney, Debate 13 Dec. 1967; Mr Lindsay, Debate 7 Feb. 1968, Dáil Éireann Vol. 232.

75. Mr Lindsay, Debate 2 May 1968, Dáil Éireann Vol. 234; Mr Moore, Debate 9 July 1970, Dáil Éireann Vol. 248. He even argued Pearse would have supported entry into Europe to put a stop to the wars that had plagued Europe for so long.

76. Dr Cruise-O'Brien, Debate 16 July 1971, Dáil Éireann Vol. 255.

77. Hourihan, 'A Series of Accidents'.

78. Dr Thornley, Debate 25 Jan. 1972, Dáil Éireann Vol. 258. See also R.V. Comerford, *Inventing the Nation. Ireland* (London 2003), p. 2.

79. Ruari Brugha, Debate 26 June 1974, Dáil Éireann Vol. 273.

80. Dr Thornley, Debate 30 Nov. 1972, Dáil Éireann Vol. 264.

81. Dr Thornley, Debate 3 Dec. 1975, Dáil Éireann Vol. 286.

82. Ibid.

83. R. Burke, Debate 2 Mar. 1972, Dáil Éireann Vol. 259. For the role of Patrick's writing in the curriculum, Sisson, *Pearse's Patriots*, pp. 159–60.

84. van Keeken, 'Telling a National Story', Ch. 5.

85. Criostoir O'Flynn, *A Man Called Pearse: A Play in Three Acts* (Dublin 1980), pp. 13–14.

86. On 23 Oct. 1988 Jonathan Bowman stated in the *Sunday Times* that the critique had meant that 'Pearse's imprimatur is no longer holy writ for all the South's politicians'. Quoted in Murphy, *Lost Republican Ideal*, p. 185.

87. Sean Lemass, Debate 28 May 1974, Dáil Éireann Vol. 273.

88. Dr Thornley, Debate 11 July 1974, Dáil Éireann Vol. 274.

89. Sean Lemass, Debate 7 June 1973, Dáil Éireann Vol. 266.

90. Padraig De Barra, *Pádraig Mac Piarais: cuntas gairid ar a bheatha* (Dublin 1979); Tomás Ó Laoi, *Pádraig Mac Piarais* (Dublin, 1979); Séamas Ó Buachalla, *Pádraig Mac Piarais agus Éire lena linn* (Dublin 1979); Donnchadh Ó Súilleabháin, *An Piarsach agus Conradh na Gaeilge* (Dublin 1981).

91. Canning, *Pearse and Schotland*, p. 20.

92. Ó Buachalla, *Irish Educationalist*; Ó Buachalla (ed.), *Letters*; Seamus Ó Buachalla (ed.), *The Literary Writings of Patrick Pearse: Writings in English* (Dublin 1979); Seamus Ó Buachalla (ed.), *The Literary Writings of Patrick Pearse: Writings in Irish* (Dublin 1979).

93. Murphy, *Lost Republican Ideal*, pp. 18, 35–9, 42, 58–60 and 185. The same mistake is repeated in the recent history of the IRB, McGee, *The I.R.B.*, pp. 356–8.

94. O'Leary, *Prose Literature*.

95. Recent versions of this modernist theme can be found in Sisson, *Pearse's Patriots*, and B. Walsh, *The Pedagogy of Protest: The Educational Thought and Work of Patrick H. Pearse* (Bern, Oxford 2007).

96. Declan Kiberd, 'Literature and Politics', in Kelleher and O'Leary, *Cambridge History of Irish Literature*, pp. 26–9.

97. White, *A Case Study*, pp. 41–60.

98. Moran, *Patrick Pearse*, pp. 54 and 175–7.

99. His claim that Patrick was forced by his father to study law is, for instance, not based on any known facts, and the conclusions he draws from Patrick's childhood tendency to dress up like an old woman are taken to an extreme, ibid., pp. 40–51.

100. Pittock, *Celtic Identity*, pp. 81–2; Collins, *Catholic Churchmen*, pp. 110–11; Foster, *Yeats 2*, p. 44.

101. See, for instance, Patrick Harte, Debate 15 May 1979, Dáil Éireann Vol. 314.

102. Comerford, *Inventing the Nation*, p. 2.

103. Mr Browne and Mr Gregory, Debate 23 June 1993, Dáil Éireann Vol. 432.

104. John Browne, Debate 21 Feb. 1991, Dáil Éireann Vol. 405. See also Mr Kelly, Debate 24 Oct. 1979, Dáil Éireann Vol. 316; Proinsias De Rossa, Debate 1 Apr. 1993, Dáil Éireann Vol. 429.

105. Mary Hanafin, Debate 9 Oct. 1997, Dáil Éireann Vol. 481.

106. Eamon Gilmore, Debate 27 Oct. 1993, Dáil Éireann Vol. 435.

107. Proinsias De Rossa, Debate 1 Apr. 1993, Dáil Éireann Vol. 429.

108. Declan Bree, Debate 27 June 1996, Dáil Éireann Vol. 467.

109. Hourihan, 'A Series of Accidents'.

110. Trevor Sargent, Debate 21 Feb. 1991, Dáil Éireann Vol. 609.

111. Daly, *Memories of the Dead*, p. 18.

Bibliography

Works by Patrick Pearse arranged in order of first publication date:

Patrick Pearse, *Three Lectures on Gaelic Topics* (Dublin 1898)

Pádraic Pearse and Tadhg O Donnchadha (eds), *An t-aithriseoir* (leabhairinn Gaedhilge Irish Language Reader, 1900)

Pádraic Pearse and Tadhg O Donnchadha (eds), *An t-aithriseoir cuid 2* (leabhairinn Gaedhilge Irish Language Reader, 1902)

P. Pearse, *The Seven Hundred Years War* (1901–1902)

Pádraig Mac Piarais, Poll an Phíobaire (Dublin 1906 reprinted from *An Claidheamh Soluis* ó Mhárta 11 go Márta 25, 1905)

Pádraic Mac Piarais (ed.), *Bodach an chóta lachtna*: ar n-a chur i n-eagar do Phádraic Mac Piarais (Baile Átha Cliath 1906)

Pearse, Pádraic H., Íosagán, agus scéalta eile (Dublin 1907)

Pádraic Pearse (ed.), *Bruidhean Chaortainn: Sgeal Fiannaidheachta* (Dublin 1908)

An Macaoṁ, edited by P.H. Pearse and written by the masters and pupils of St Enda's School, vol. 1, no. 1 (Midsummer 1909); vol. 1, no. 2 (Christmas 1909); vol. 2, no. 3 (Christmas 1910); vol. 2, no. 4 (May 1913)

Pádraic Pearse, *Songs of the Irish Rebels and Specimens from an Irish Anthology: Some Aspects of Irish Literature: Three Lectures on Gaelic Topics* (Collected works of Pádraic H. Pearse) (Dublin 1910)

Pádraic Mac Piarais, *Bruidhean chaorthainn: sgéal Fiannaídheachta* (Baile Átha Cliath 1912)

P.H. Pearse, *An sgoil: A Direct Method Course in Irish* (Dublin 1913)

P.H. Pearse, Suantraidhe agus goltraidhe (Dublin 1914)

Pádraic H. Pearse, *An ṁátair agus sgéalta eile (The Mother and other stories)* (Dundalk 1915)

P.H. Pearse, *How Does She Stand?: Three Addresses* (The Bodenstown series no. 1) (Dublin 1914)

P.H. Pearse, *From a Hermitage* (The Bodenstown series no. 2) (Dublin 1915)

P.H. Pearse, *The Murder Machine* (The Bodenstown series no. 3) (Dublin 1916)

P.H. Pearse, *Ghosts* (Tracts for the Times) (Dublin 1916)

P.H. Pearse, *The Spiritual Nation* (Tracts for the Times) (Dublin 1916)

P.H. Pearse, *The Sovereign People* (Tracts for the Times) (Dublin 1916)

P.H. Pearse, *The Separatist Idea* (Tracts for the Times) (Dublin: Whelan, 1916)

Pearse, Pádraic H., *An ṁátair agus sgéalta eile (The Mother and other stories)* (Dundalk 1916)

Pearse, Pádraic H*., The Mother, and other tales*/by Padraig H. Pearse. English edition by T.A. Fitzgerald (Dundalk 1916)

Pádraic Colum, E.J. Harrington O'Brien (ed.), *Poems of the Irish Revolutionary Brotherhood, Thomas MacDonagh, P.H. Pearse (Pádraic MacPiarais), Joseph Mary Plunkett, Sir Roger Casement* (Boston 1916)

Pádraic Pearse, *Songs of the Irish Rebels* (Collected works of Pádraic H. Pearse) (Dublin 1917)

Pádraic Pearse, *Plays Stories Poems* (Collected works of Pádraic H. Pearse) (Dublin, London 1917)

Pádraic Pearse, *The Story of a Success* (The complete works of P.H. Pearse) (Dublin 1917)

Pádraic Pearse, *Scríbinní* (The complete works of P.H. Pearse) (Dublin 1917)

Pádraic Pearse, *Íosagán and Other Stories* (London, Dublin 1918)

Pádraic Pearse, *Poems* (Dublin, London 1918)

Pádraic Pearse, *The Singer and Other Plays* (Dublin 1918)

Pádraic Pearse, *Collected Works of Pádraic H. Pearse* (Dublin 1910–1919). 4 vols: 1. Political writings and speeches. 2. Plays, stories, poems. 3. Songs of the Irish rebels and specimens from an Irish anthology. Some aspects of Irish literature. Three lectures on Gaelic topics. 4. The story of a success, edited by Desmond Ryan, and The man called Pearse, by Desmond Ryan

Pádraic Pearse, *Collected Works of Pádraic H. Pearse* (Dublin; Belfast 1916–1917). 5 vols: 5 *Scríbinní*

Padraic Henry Pearse, *Connemara Stories* (Sydney 1921) Translated from Irish

Julius Pokorny, *Die Seele Irlands: Novellen und Gedichte aus dem Irisch-Galischen des Patrick Henry Pearse und Anderer zum ersten Male ins Deutsche übertragen* (Halle a.S. 1922)

P.S. O'Hegarty, *A Bibliography of Books Written by P. H. Pearse* (n.p. 1931)

Mary Brigid Pearse (ed.), *The Home-life of Padraig Pearse as Told by Himself, His Family and Friends* (Dublin 1934, 1979)

Michael Henry Gaffney, *The Stories of Pádraic Pearse* (Dublin 1935)

Padraic Pearse, *In First Century Ireland* (Dublin 1935)

Pádraig Mac Piarais, *Maingín Scéeal:* nuasach de scéaltaibh i gcomhair an aosa óig ar n-a n-aith-déanamh i nGaedhilg (Dublin 1936)

Pádraic Pearse, *The Singer and Other Plays* (Dublin 1960)

Proinsias Mac Aonghusa, Liam Ó Reagain (ed), *The Best of Pearse* (1967)

Pádraic Pearse, *Short Stories of Pádraic Pearse* (Cork 1968)

Mac Lochlainn, Piaras, *Last Words. Letters and Statements of Leaders Executed after the Rising at Easter 1916* (Dublin 1971)

Pádraic Pearse, *The Murder Machine and Other Essays* (Dublin 1976)

Seamus Ó Buachalla (ed), *The Literary Writings of Patrick Pearse: Writings in English* (Dublin 1979)

Seamus Ó Buachalla (ed), *The Literary Writings of Patrick Pearse: Writings in Irish* (Dublin 1979)

Noel Kissane, *Pádraic Mac Piarais: Pearse from Documents* (Dublin 1979)

Proinsias Mac Aonghusa, *Quotations from P.H. Pearse* (Dublin 1979)

Cathal Ó hAinle (ed), *Gearrscéalta an Phiarsaigh* (Dublin 1979)

Tom Cullivan, *The Pearse Songs: Voice and Piano 3* (Greystones 1979)

Pádraic H. Pearse, *Litreacha oscailte le Pádraic Mac Piarais* (edited by P. Ó Snodaigh)

Seamus Ó Buachalla, *A Significant Irish Educationalist: The Educational Writings of P.H. Pearse* (Dublin 1980)

Seamus Ó Buachalla (ed.), *The Letters of P. H. Pearse* (Gerrards Cross, Bucks 1980)

Storiau byrion Padraig Pearse (stories translated into Welsh) (Bala 1980)

Ciarán Ó Coigligh (ed.), *Filíocht Ghaeilge: Phádraig Mhic Phiarais* (Baile Átha Cliath 1981)

Pádraig Mac Piarais, et al., *Une île et d'autres îles: poèmes gaeliques XXeme siècle* (Quimper 1984)

Pronsias MacAonghusa, *Quotations from P.H. Pearse* (Dublin, Cork 1979)

Pádraic Pearse, *Selected Poems = Rogha Danta* (Dublin 2001)

Pádraig H. Pearse, *Vijf Korte Verhalen* (Nijmegen, Münster 2002)

Works used:

'The Abbey Theatre 1916 Plaque', *Dublin Historical Record*, Vol. L No. 1, Spring 1997

Joost Augusteijn, 'Radical Nationalist Activities in County Derry 1900–1921', in Gerard O'Brien, *Derry and Londonderry. History and Society* (Dublin 1999)

Joost Augusteijn (ed.), *The Memoirs of John M. Regan, a Catholic Officer in the RIC and RUC, 1909–1948* (Dublin 2007)

Padraig De Barra, *Pádraig Mac Piarais: cuntas gairid ar a bheatha* (Dublin 1979)

Brian Barton, *From Behind a Closed Door. Secret Court Martial Records of the 1916 Easter Rising* (Belfast 2002)

Piaras Béaslai, 'The National Army is Founded', in F.X. Martin (ed.), *The Irish Volunteers 1913–1915. Recollections and Documents* (Dublin 1963)

Manfred Beller, Joep Leerssen (eds), *Imagology. The Cultural Construction and Literary Representation of National Characters. A Critical Survey* (Amsterdam, New York 2007)

Dennis Bos, ' "Liever den eeredood sterven." De Parijse Commune en de militarisering van de socialistische partijcultuur', *Leidschrift. Historisch Tijdschrift* Vol. 22 No. 2, 2007

Angela Bourke, 'The Imagined Community of Pearse's Short Stories', in Roisín Higgins and Regina Uí Chollatáin (eds), *The Life and After-Life of P.H. Pearse. Pádraic Mac Piarais Saol agus Oidhreacht* (Dublin 2009)

John F. Boyle, *The Irish Rebellion of 1916: A Brief History of the Revolt and its Suppression* (London 1916)

Gail Braybon, 'Women and the War', in Stephen Constantine, Maurice W. Kirby and Mary B. Rose (eds), *The First World War in British History* (London, New York 1995)

Caoimhín Breatnach, 'Exploiting the Past: Pearse as Editor and Interpreter of *Fiannaíocht* Literature', in Roisín Higgins and Regina Uí Chollatáin (eds), *The Life and After-Life of P.H. Pearse. Pádraic Mac Piarais Saol agus Oidhreacht* (Dublin 2009)

S.P. Breathnach (S.P. Walsh), *Free and Gaelic. Pearse's Idea of a National Culture* (n.p. 1979)

T. Brown (ed.), *Celticism* (Amsterdam 1996)

Frank Budgen, *Further Recollections of James Joyce* (London 1955)

Joan Montgomery Byles, 'Women's Experience of World War One: Suffragists, Pacifists and Poets', *Women's Studies International Forum* Vol. 8 No. 5 (1985)

Katriona Byrne, *Pearse Street* (Dublin 2001)

David Cairns and Shaun Richards, *Writing Ireland* (Manchester 1988)

Rev. Bernard J. Canning, *Patrick H. Pearse and Scotland* (Glasgow 1979)

James Carty, *A Class-book of Irish History. Book IV: From the Act of Union* (London 1943)

Xavier Carty, *In Bloody Protest. The Tragedy of Patrick Pearse* (Dublin 1978)

Regina Uí Chollatáin, *An Claidheamh Soluis agus Fainne an Lae 1899–1932* (Dublin 2004)

Kathleen Clarke, *Revolutionary Woman: Kathleen Clarke 1878–1972* (Dublin 1991)

Coilin (S. MacGiollanate), *Patrick H. Pearse. A Sketch of His Life* (Dublin 1917)

Barry Coldrey, *Faith and Fatherland: The Christian Brothers and the Development of Irish Nationalism 1838–1921* (Dublin 1988)

Kevin Collins, *Catholic Churchmen and the Celtic Revival in Ireland, 1848–1916* (Dublin 2002)

Padraic and Mary Colum, *The Irish Rebellion of 1916 and its Martyrs* (New York 1916)

Mary Maguire Colum, *St. Enda's School, Rathfarnham, Dublin. Founded by Pádraic H. Pearse* (New York 1917)

Mary Colum, *Life and the Dream* (New York 1947)

Phadraic Comhartha-Chuimhne, *Pearse Memorial: An Appeal to the Irish Race* [for funds to keep St Enda's School at the Hermitage, Rathfarnham] (Dublin [1918])

Anthony Comerford, *The Easter Rising, Dublin 1916* (London 1969)

R.V. Comerford, *Inventing the Nation. Ireland* (London 2003)

C.F. Connolly, *Pádraic H. Pearse* (n.p. 1920)

Pat Cooke, *Sceal Sgoil Eanna, The Story of an Educational Adventure* (Dublin 1986)

Pat Cooke, 'Patrick Pearse: The Victorian Gael', in Roisín Higgins and Regina Uí Chollatáin (eds), *The Life and After-Life of P.H. Pearse. Pádraic Mac Piarais Saol agus Oidhreacht* (Dublin 2009)

Patrick Crotty, 'The Irish Renaissance, 1890–1940: Poetry in English', in Margaret Kelleher and Philip O'Leary, *The Cambridge History of Irish Literature* (Cambridge 2006)

Brian Crowley, '"His Father's Son": James and Patrick Pearse', *Folk Life. Journal of Ethnological Studies* Vol. 43, 2004–2005

Brian Crowley, '"I am the Son of a Good Father": James and Patrick Pearse', in Roisín Higgins and Regina Uí Chollatáin (eds), *The Life and After-Life of P.H. Pearse. Pádraic Mac Piarais Saol agus Oidhreacht* (Dublin 2009)

C.P. Curran, *Under the Receding Wave* (Dublin 1970)

Mary E. Daly and Margaret O'Callaghan, *1916 in 1966: Commemorating the Easter Rising* (Dublin 2007)

Martin Daly (Stephen MacKenna), *Memories of the Dead: Some Impressions* (Dublin 1917[?])

T.R. Dawes, *Bilingual Teaching in Belgian Schools being the Report on a Visit to Belgian Schools as Gillchrist Travelling Student* (Cambridge 1902)

Steven Debroey, *Rebel uit roeping: het leven van de Ierse vrijheidsheld Patrick Pearse* (n.p. 1925)

Gabriel Doherty, 'The Irish History Textbook, 1900–1960. Problems and Development', *Oideas*, No. 42 (Dublin 1994)

Theo Dorgan and Máirín Ní Dhonnchadha (eds), *Revising the Rising* (Derry 1991)

Janet Egleson Dunleavy and Gareth W. Dunleavy, *Douglas Hyde. A Maker of Modern History* (Berkeley etc. 1991)

Ruth Dudley Edwards, *Patrick Pearse: The Triumph of Failure* (London 1977)

Ruth Dudley Edwards, *Patrick Pearse: The Triumph of Failure* (Dublin Portland, repr. 2006)

'Fear Faire', *The Irish Educational Review* 1910 Vol. III No. 7

D. Ferriter, 'Commemorating the Rising, 1922–65: "A Figurative Scramble for the Bones of the Patriot Dead"?', in Mary E. Daly and Margaret O'Callaghan (eds), *1916 in 1966: Commemorating the Easter Rising* (Dublin 2007)

David Fitzpatrick, 'The Futility of History: A Failed Experiment in Irish Education', in C. Brady (ed.), *Ideology and the Historians* (Dublin 1991)

John Wilson Foster, *Fictions of the Irish Literary Revival: A Changeling Art* (Syracuse 1987)

Roy Foster, *The Irish Story: Telling Tales and Making it up in Ireland* (Oxford 2002)

R.F. Foster, *W.B, Yeats: A Life. 1, The Apprentice Mage: 1865–1914* (Oxford 1997)

R.F. Foster, *W.B. Yeats: A Life. 2, The Arch-poet, 1915–1939* (Oxford 2005)

L. Ua Gallchobhair, 'The Children of Patrick Pearse', *The Irish Monthly* 1922

Máiréad Ní Ghráda, *A Primary History of Ireland. Book 2: From 1691 to 1949* (Dublin, 1963[?])

John Gray, *Black Mass. Apocalyptic Religion and the Death of Utopia* (London 2007)

Guide to the Historical Exhibition Commemorative of the Rising of 1916 (Dublin 1966)

Denis Gwynn, 'Patrick Pearse', *Dublin Review* Jan.–Mar. 1923, 92–105

M.J. Hannan, *Irish Leaders of 1916 – Who are They?* (Butte Montana 1920)

James Hayes, *Padraic MacPiarais, Sgéaluidhe; Patrick H. Pearse, Storyteller* (Dublin 1920)

Roisín Higgins and Regina Uí Chollatáin (eds), *The Life and After-Life of P.H. Pearse. Pádraic Mac Piarais Saol agus Oidhreacht* (Dublin 2009)

Reg Hindley, *The Death of the Irish Language; A Qualified Obituary* (London 1990)

John J. Horgan, *From Parnell to Pearse: Some Recollections and Reflections* (Dublin 1948)

Claire Hourihan, 'A Series of Accidents', *The Dublin Review* 23 (Autumn 2006)

Miroslav Hroch, *Social Preconditions of National Revival in Europe: A Comparative Analysis of the Social Composition of Patriotic Groups among the Smaller European Nations* (New York 2000)

Isabel V. Hull, *Absolute Destruction: Military Culture and the Practices of War in Imperial Germany* (Ithaca 2005)

John Hutchinson, *The Dynamics of Cultural Nationalism: The Gaelic Revival and the Creation of the Irish Nation State* (London 1987)

John Hutchinson, *Nations as Zones of Conflict* (London 2005)

Keith Jeffery, *The GPO and the Easter Rising* (Dublin 2006)

Robin Jenkins, 'Life of General Blackader', *Transactions* 80 (2006)

A.J. Jordan, *Major John McBride: 1865–1916: 'MacDonagh and MacBride and Connolly and Pearse'* (Westport 1991)

Maurice Joy (ed.), *The Irish Rebellion of 1916 and its Martyrs: Erin's Tragic Easter* (New York 1916)

James Joyce, 'The Dead', in James Joyce, *The Dubliners* (London 1914)

Tessa van Keeken, 'Telling a National Story. History Teaching and the Formation of National Identity. A Case Study of Primary School History Teaching in Ireland, 1922–71' (unpublished MA thesis, Utrecht University 2007)

Michael Kenny, *The Road to Freedom. Photographs and Memorabilia from the 1916 Rising and Afterwards* (Dublin 1993)

Geoffrey Keynes, *The Poetical Works of Rupert Brooke* (London 1963)

Declan Kiberd, 'Patrick Pearse: Irish Modernist', in Roisín Higgins and Regina Uí Chollatáin (eds), *The Life and After-Life of P.H. Pearse. Pádraic Mac Piarais Saol agus Oidhreacht* (Dublin 2009)

A. Kinsella, 'Medical Aspects of the 1916 Rising', *Dublin Historical Record* Vol. L No. 2, Autumn 1997

Bill Kissane, *The Politics of the Irish Civil War* (Oxford 2005)

B. Lacey, *'Terrible Queer Creatures': A History of Homosexuality in Ireland* (Bray 2008)

Joseph Lee, *The Modernisation of Irish Society 1848–1918* (Dublin 1973)

Joep Leerssen, *National Thought in Europe. A Cultural History* (Amsterdam 2006)

Joep Leerssen, 'Nationalism and the Cultivation of Culture', *Nations and Nationalism* Vol. 12 No. 4 (2006)

Donal Lowry, 'The Play of Forces World-Wide. The South African War as an International Event', *South African Historical Journal*, 1999, Vol. 41

Diarmuid Lynch, *The I.R.B. and the 1916 Insurrection* (Cork 1957)

Dorothy MacArdle, *The Irish Republic* (London 1968)

Sean MacEntee, 'Pages from a Record of Easter Week 1916', in Sean MacEntee and Dr James Ryan, *Easter Fires: Personal Records of 1916* (Waterford 1943)

F. MacKenzie, *The Irish Rebellion: What Happened And Why* (London 1916)

Lian Mac Uistín, *An ród seo romhain: saol agus saothar: Phádraic Mhic Phiarais* (Dublin 2006)

Jack Magee, *The Teaching of Irish History in Schools* (Belfast 1971)

Thomas Maguire, *England's Duty to Ireland, as Plain to a Loyal Irish Roman Catholic* (Dublin, London 1886)

K. Manton, 'Establishing the Fellowship: Harry Lowerison and Ruskin School Home, a Turn-of-the-Century Socialist and His Educational Experiment', *History of Education* Vol. 26 (1997)

F.X. Martin, 'The Provisional Committee of the Irish Volunteers', in F.X. Martin, *The Irish Volunteers 1913–1915 Recollections and Documents* (Dublin 1963)

F.X. Martin, 'The 1916 Rising: A Coup d'Etat or a Bloody Protest', *Studia Hibernica* 8 (1968)

F.X. Martin, 'MacNeill and the Irish Volunteers', in F.X. Martin and F.J. Byrne (eds), *The Scholar Revolutionary: Eoin MacNeill 1867–1945, and the Making of a New Ireland* (Shannon 1973)

Hedley McCay, *Pádraic Pearse; A New Biography* (Cork 1966)

Owen McGee, *The I.R.B.: The Irish Republican Brotherhood from the Land League to Sinn Féin* (Dublin 2005)

P.J. McGill, 'Padraig Pearse in Donegal', *Donegal Annual* Vol. VII No. 1, 1966

P.H. Merkl (ed.), *Political Violence and Terror: Motifs and Motivations* (Berkeley 1986)

Seán Farrell Moran, 'Patrick Pearse and the European Revolt against Reason', *Journal of the History of Ideas*, 50 (1989)

Sean Farrell Moran, *Patrick Pearse and the Politics of Redemption: The Mind of the Easter Rising, 1916* (Washington, DC 1994)

Thomas J. Morrissey SJ, *William J. Walsh, Archbishop of Dublin, 1841–1921. No Uncertain Voice* (Dublin, Portland 2000)

Sean Moynihan, *Memories of Prof. Sam Fahy, Muiris Breathnach, Pádraig Ó Conaire, Thomas Shaw, Bro. Fitzpatrick, Pádraig Pearse, Terence McSwiney: Poems and Sketches* (Dublin n.d.)

James Mullin, *The Story of a Toiler's Life* (Dublin 2000)

Brian P. Murphy, *Patrick Pearse and the Lost Republican Ideal* (Dublin 1991)

Notes for Teachers: History, Department of Education, National Education (Dublin 1933)

Ben Novick, 'Postal Censorship in Ireland 1914–16', *Irish Historical Studies* Vol. XXXI No. 123, 1999

Kevin Nowlan (ed.), *The Making of 1916: Studies in the History of the Rising* (Dublin 1969)

Nioclás Ó hAodha, *Foclóir, nótaí agus achoimre do ó pheann an phiarsaigh* (Dublin 1970)

C.C. O'Brien (ed.), *The Shaping of Modern Ireland* (New York 1960)

Frank O'Brien, *An Piarsach Óg agus Conradh na Gaeilge* (Dublin 1974)

Séamas Ó Buachalla, *Pádraig Mac Piarais agus Éire lena linn* (Dublin 1979)

Séamas Ó Buachalla, *Pádraig Mac Piarais agus Éire lena linn* (Dublin 1979)

Séamas Ó Buachalla, *An Piarsach sa Bheilg = P.H. Pearse in Belgium = P.H. Pearse in België* (Dublin 1998)

Sean O'Casey, *Drums under the Windows* (London 1945)

Ruan O'Donnell (ed.), *The Impact of the 1916 Rising: Among the Nations* (Dublin 2008)

Ciáran Ó Duibhir, *Sinn Fein. The First Election 1908* (Nure, Manorhamilton, Co. Leitrim 1993)

O'Farrell, *Catholic Bulletin*, Vol. VIII No. 4, Apr. 1917

Tomas Ó Fiach, 'The Great Controversy', in Sean Ó Tuama (ed.), *The Gaelic League Idea* (Dublin 1972)

Criostoir O'Flynn, *A Man called Pearse: A Play in Three Acts* (Dublin 1980)

P.S. O'Hegarty, 'P.H. Pearse', *Irish Commonwealth* Mar. 1919

Tomás Ó Laoi, *Pádraig Mac Piarais* (Dublin 1979)

J. O'Leary, *Recollections of Fenians and Fenianism* Vol. II (London 1896)

Philip O'Leary, 'What Stalked through the Post Office?: Pearse's Cú Chulainn.' *Proceedings of the Harvard Celtic Colloquium*, 3 (1983), 21–38

Philip O'Leary, *The Prose Literature of the Gaelic Revival , 1881–1921: Ideology and Innovation* (Pennsylvania 1994)

Philip O'Leary, 'The Irish Renaissance, 1890–1940: Poetry in Irish', in Margaret Kelleher and Philip O'Leary, *The Cambridge History of Irish Literature* (Cambridge 2006)

Seán Oliver, 'Irish Revolutionary Nationalism: Tone to Pearse', in Maurice O'Connell, *People Power: Proceedings of the Third Annual Daniel O'Connell Workshop* (Dublin 1993)

Daniel J. O'Neill, *The Irish Revolution and the Cult of the Leader: Observations on Griffith, Moran, Pearse and Connolly* (Boston 1988)

The O'Rahilly, 'The Irish Prepare to Arm', in F.X. Martin (ed.), *The Irish Volunteers 1913–1915. Recollections and Documents* (Dublin 1963)

Séamus Ó Searcaigh, *Pádraig Mac Piarais* (Dublin 1938)

Donnchadh Ó Súilleabháin, *An Piarsach agus Conradh na Gaeilge* (Dublin 1981)

Rosemary Cullen Owens, *Louie Bennett* (Cork 2001)

Joyce Padbury, '"A Young Schoolmaster of Great Literary Talent": Mary Hayden's friend, Patrick Pearse', in Roisín Higgins and Regina Uí Chollatáin (eds), *The Life and After-Life of P.H. Pearse. Pádraic Mac Piarais Saol agus Oidhreacht* (Dublin 2009)

Senia Pašeta, 'The Catholic Hierarchy and the Irish University Question, 1880–1908', *History* Vol. 85 No. 278

Senia Pašeta, 'Nationalist Responses to Two Royal Visits to Ireland, 1900 and 1903', *Irish Historical Studies* Vol. XXXI No. 124

James Pearse, *A Reply to Professor Maguire's Pamphlet 'England's Duty to Ireland' as it Appears to an Englishman* (Dublin 1886)

Cuimhi na bPiarsach: *Memories of the Brothers Pearse* (1966)

Murray G.H. Pittock, *Celtic Identity and the British Image* (Manchester 1999)

R.J. Porter, *P.H. Pearse* (1973)

E. Raymond, *Tell England: A Study in a Generation* (London 1922)

John X. Regan (ed.), *What Made Ireland Sinn Fein* (Boston 1921)

Louis N. Le Roux, *La vie de Patrice Pearse* (Rennes 1932). Translated into English by Desmond Ryan (Dublin 1932)

Desmond Ryan (ed.), *Patrick Pearse, The Story of a Success, being a Record of St. Enda's College, September 1908 to Easter, 1916* (Dublin 1917)

Desmond Ryan, *The Man called Pearse* (Dublin 1919)

Desmond Ryan, *Remembering Sion: A Chronicle of Storm and Quiet* (London 1934)

D. Ryan, *The Rising: The Complete Story of Easter Week* (Dublin 1949)

Desmond Ryan (ed.), *The 1916 Poets* (Dublin 1963)

Dr James Ryan, TD, 'My Easter Week in the G.P.O.', in Sean MacEntee and Dr James Ryan, *Easter Fires: Personal Records of 1916* (Waterford 1943)

Rev. Francis Shaw, 'The Canon of Irish History – A Challenge', *Studies* Vol. LXI, Summer 1972, no. 242

Hagen Schulze, *States, Nations and Nationalism. From the Middle Ages to the Present* (Oxford 1998)

Máire nic Shiubhlaigh, *The Splendid Years* (Dublin 1955)

The Sinn Fein Leaders of 1916 with Numerous Illustrations and Complete Lists of Deportees, Casualties, etc.; with Appendix on New Parliamentary Party, Count Plunkett, Joseph MacGuinness, De Valera, Cosgrave (Dublin 1917)

Elaine Sisson, *Pearse's Patriots: St Enda's and the Cult of Boyhood* (Cork 2004)

A.D. Smith, 'The Formation of Nationalist Movements', in Anthony D. Smith (ed.), *Nationalist Movements* (London and Basingstoke 1976)

Eric Storm, 'Regionalism in History, 1890–1945: The Cultural Approach', *European History Quarterly* 33/2 (2003)

Joseph Sweeney, 'Donegal and the Easter Rising', *Donegal Annual* Vol. VII No. 1, 1966

'They were Schoolboys! The Pearse Brothers at the "Row"', in Christian Brothers Westland Row, *Centenary Record 1864–1964*

Anne-Marie Thiesse, *La Création des Identitiés Nationales. Europe XVIIIe–XXe Siècle* (Paris 1999)

William Irwin Thompson, *The Imagination of an Insurrection: Dublin Easter 1916. A Study of an Ideological Movement* (New York 1967)

Thom's Irish Almanac and Official Directory

Michael Tierney, *Eoin MacNeill: Scholar and Man of Action 1867–1945* (Oxford 1980)

Peter Tosh, *The Pursuit of History. Aims, Methods and New Directions in the Study of Modern History* (Harrow 1999)

Charles Townshend, *Ireland. The Twentieth Century* (London 1998)

Charles Townshend, *Easter 1916. The Irish Rebellion* (London 2005)

Antoinette Walker and Michael Fitzgerald, *Unstoppable Brilliance: Irish Geniuses and Asperger's Syndrome* (Dublin 2006)

Brendan J. Walsh, 'The Progressive Credentials of Patrick Henry Pearse: A Response to David Limond', *History of Education Review* 2006 Vol. 35 No. 2

Brendan J. Walsh, *The Pedagogy of Protest: The Educational Thought and Work of Patrick H. Pearse* (Bern, Oxford 2007)

Louis J. Walsh, *Old Friends: Being Memories of Men and Places* (Dundalk 1934)

Todd Weir, 'Colonial Violence and Socialist Imagination: The Conversions of Ernst Däumig' (Conference Paper)

Eva Roe White, *A Case Study of Ireland's and Galicia's Parallel Path to Nationhood* (Lewinston, NY 2004)

Oliver Zimmer, *Nationalism in Europe, 1890–1940* (Houndmills 2003)

Oliver Zimmer (eds), *Power and the Nation in European History* (Cambridge 2005)

Index

426 Patrick Pearse: The making of a revolutionary